Claude Pepper and Ed Ball

The Florida History and Culture Series

THE FLORIDA HISTORY AND CULTURE SERIES
Edited by Raymond Arsenault and Gary R. Mormino

Al Burt's Florida: Snowbirds, Sand Castles, and Self-Rising Crackers, by Al Burt (1997)

Black Miami in the Twentieth Century, by Marvin Dunn (1997)

Gladesmen: Gator Hunters, Moonshiners, and Skiffers, by Glen Simmons and Laura Ogden (1998)

"Come to My Sunland": Letters of Julia Daniels Moseley from the Florida Frontier, 1882–1886, by Julia Winifred Moseley and Betty Powers Crislip (1998)

The Enduring Seminoles: From Alligator Wrestling to Ecotourism, by Patsy West (1998)

Government in the Sunshine State: Florida Since Statehood, by David R. Colburn and Lance deHaven-Smith (1999)

The Everglades: An Environmental History, by David McCally (1999)

Beechers, Stowes, and Yankee Strangers: The Transformation of Florida, by John T. Foster, Jr., and Sarah Whitmer Foster (1999)

The Tropic of Cracker, by Al Burt (1999)

Balancing Evils Judiciously: The Proslavery Writings of Zephaniah Kingsley, edited and annotated by Daniel W. Stowell (1999)

Hitler's Soldiers in the Sunshine State: German POWs in Florida, by Robert D. Billinger, Jr. (2000)

Cassadaga: The South's Oldest Spiritualist Community, edited by John J. Guthrie, Phillip Charles Lucas, and Gary Monroe (2000)

Claude Pepper and Ed Ball: Politics, Purpose, and Power, by Tracy E. Danese (2000)

Claude Pepper and Ed Ball

Politics, Purpose, and Power

Tracy E. Danese

University Press of Florida

Gainesville · Tallahassee · Tampa · Boca Raton

Pensacola · Orlando · Miami · Jacksonville

05   04   03   02   01   00   6   5   4   3   2   1

Library of Congress Cataloging-in-Publication Data
Danese, Tracy E.
Claude Pepper and Ed Ball: politics, purpose, and power / Tracy E. Danese
p. cm. — (Florida history and culture series)
Includes bibliographical references and index.
ISBN 0-8130-1744-0 (alk. paper)
1. Ball, Edward, 1888–1981. 2. Pepper, Claude, 1900–1989. 3. Florida—Politics and
government—1865–1950. 4. Businessmen—Florida Biography. 5. Pioneers—Florida
Biography. 6. Legislators—United States Biography. 7. United States. Congress.
House Biography. 8. Florida Biography. I. Title. II. Series.
F316.B19D36   2000
975.9'06'092—dc21   99-35314
[B]

All of the photographs are reproduced from the Florida Photographic Collection,
Florida State Archives, R. A. Gray Building, Tallahassee, Florida 32399.

The University Press of Florida is the scholarly publishing agency for the State
University System of Florida, comprising Florida A&M University, Florida Atlantic
University, Florida International University, Florida State University, University of
Central Florida, University of Florida, University of North Florida, University of
South Florida, and University of West Florida.

University Press of Florida
15 Northwest 15th Street
Gainesville, FL 32611
http://www.upf.com

To my wife, Barbara

CONTENTS

ILLUSTRATIONS

SERIES EDITORS' FOREWORD

Claude Pepper and Ed Ball: Politics, Purpose, and Power is the thirteenth volume of a series devoted to the study of Florida History and Culture. During the past half century, the burgeoning population and increased national and international visibility of Florida have sparked a great deal of popular interest in the state's past, present, and future. As the favorite destination of countless tourists and as the new home for millions of retirees and other migrants, modern Florida has become a demographic, political, and cultural bellwether. But, unfortunately, the quantity and quality of the literature on Florida's distinctive heritage and character have not kept pace with the Sunshine State's enhanced status. In an effort to remedy this situation—to provide an accessible and attractive format for the publication of Florida-related books—the University Press of Florida established the Florida History and Culture Series.

As coeditors of the series, we are committed to the creation of an eclectic but carefully crafted set of books that provides the field of Florida studies with a new focus and that encourages Florida researchers and writers to consider the broader implications and context of their work. The series includes standard academic monographs, works of synthesis, memoirs, and anthologies. And, while the series features books of historical interest, we encourage authors researching Florida's environment, politics, literature, and popular or material culture to submit manuscripts for inclusion in the series. We want each book to retain a distinct "personality" and voice, but at the same time we hope to foster a sense of community and collaboration among Florida scholars.

In *Claude Pepper and Ed Ball: Politics, Purpose, and Power*, Tracy E. Danese examines two of Florida's most fascinating and compelling characters. Alternatingly deft and deaf, far-sighted and myopic, Pepper and Ball framed policy and set a vision for Florida between the 1920s and 1980s. In a finely crafted study, the author traces the careers of Florida's two most powerful and influential figures and their tumultuous relationship.

Pepper and Ball both migrated to Florida at the climax of the fabled land boom of the 1920s. Bitterly divided later by philosophical and personal differences, both men were attracted to the Sunshine State for strikingly similar reasons: self-improvement and profit. Pepper, born on a hard-scrabble Alabama farm in 1900 and driven to overcome his poverty, escaped first to the University of Alabama, followed by admission to Harvard Law School and a teaching position at the University of Arkansas Law School. In the summer of 1925, the young professor packed away his books in search of the Florida Dream. Pepper accepted an offer to join a law firm in Perry, Florida, where he also hoped to capitalize on a raging land boom. Following a single term as a member of the Florida House of Representatives, Pepper moved to Tallahassee, where he remarkably emerged as a serious candidate for the U.S. Senate in 1934. Defeated—the corrupt ward bosses of Tampa almost certainly cheated Pepper of victory—the unflappable young man reemerged in 1936 to become Florida's U.S. senator following the death of Park Trammell. The embodiment of youth and New Deal idealism, the unofficial senator from north Florida, Claude Pepper strode the Florida stage. He soon collided with the political and economic ambitions of his nemesis. Ed Ball's emergence as arguably the single most powerful individual in modern Florida history dates from the timely marriage of his sister, shrewd business instincts, and ruthless practices. In 1922, his sister, Jessie, married one of America's wealthiest men, Alfred I. duPont. Distrusting Delaware tax collectors, duPont moved his fortune to Florida, trusting his brother-in-law to manage the Florida portfolio. Rejecting the glitter of south Florida, the irascible and brilliant Ball used the duPont empire to wield clout in the Florida business world and politics.

In a series of titanic clashes, Pepper and Ball battled across the state, climaxing with the senatorial election of 1950. In this well-researched and finely written book, Tracy Danese portrays the Ball-Pepper relationship in vivid and interesting ways. The author is even-handed and judicious, allow-ing the reader to select heroes and villains: Pepper was no saint—he trimmed his ethical sails in dealing with sectional racial issues—and Ball was no unredeeming rogue—he left behind generously endowed charities and parks. Readers will enjoy this modern Florida drama.

Raymond Arsenault and Gary R. Mormino,
Series Editors

PREFACE

This account covers the continuing conflict between two of the most remarkable men who have passed across the stage of Florida politics: Claude Pepper and Ed Ball. Their respective pursuits of ambition and power placed them in the political arena that reached from county courthouses through state government to Washington. Their respective purposes put them in conflict on issues at the level of day-to-day politics. It is intended for those who will find value in an objective assessment of the practical impact of contrasting philosophies at an often ignored level of the political process.

The parameters of American politics have been defined primarily by the exploitation of the vast resources of a land-rich nation. Through most of the nation's history, land has been the principal basis on which wealth was founded, and the political process has been the means for protecting and allocating that wealth. The broad range of concepts known loosely as property rights has been the protective framework for the right to reap the benefits of individual effort. The counterpoint to this notion of individualism has been the collectivization of power through the political process as a mechanism for sharing the nation's wealth.

The system's strength is its remarkable capacity to accommodate the tensions inherent in these two essential elements of the whole. This duality has been a systemic constant even as great issues of war, peace, and social change rise up to crowd it temporarily out of the public perspective. There is, in that dimension, a remarkable substratum of personalized politics. This dimension intrudes only indirectly on the course of larger issues. It is more like part of the infrastructure of all levels of American government, where individual power and purpose ignite in political conflict. It is where conflict becomes personal.

Ball and Pepper personified this dimension of state politics for a significant part of this century. They both arrived in Florida as young men at the height of the Florida Boom. Claude Pepper came seeking his fortune with only a Harvard law degree and a deep-seated ambition to achieve political position and power. Ed Ball came in the company of Alfred I. duPont, who chose Florida as the place where he would focus his talents and vision to build a legacy. When the boom collapsed, followed by the more profound disaster of the Great Depression, these two men found their respective paths to power closely tied to the effects of the compounded economic disaster that befell Florida.

Pepper seized on the promise of Franklin Delano Roosevelt's New Deal as the means to distribute more equitably the bounty of a restructured nation. His successful bid for a U.S. Senate seat following only one two-year term in the Florida House of Representatives was a major accomplishment for one with so little political tenure in the state. It marked him as a major state political figure, and his prominence as a Roosevelt loyalist in the Senate got him national attention.

Ball ascended to total control of the banking and manufacturing enterprises controlled by the duPont Trust in 1935 on Alfred's death. He continued to build the Florida National Bank chain throughout the Great Depression and also implemented the West Florida phase of duPont's grand plan for a manufacturing business founded on Florida's timberland resources. In the early 1940s, he emerged from Alfred's shadow as his own man when he initiated the long fight to acquire control of the bankrupt Florida East Coast Railway Company.

Their paths first crossed in 1929 when they made common cause during Pepper's only term in the Florida House of Representatives on the issue of roads for north Florida. After that, their relationship became progressively strained until their personal animosity and contrasting expectations of the political process became a significant factor in state politics. Their battles were fought across the full span of political and legal forums.

Ed Ball and Claude Pepper each possessed the essential characteristic that allowed him to use politics to seek expression of his purpose through the medium of politics. Ball was the embodiment of rugged individualism in pursuit of economic gain under the protective mantle of property rights. Pepper represented the notion that government had a higher purpose than merely serving as a protective mechanism for economic enterprise. He viewed government as the guarantor of an equitable distribution of the output of the nation's enterprise as a whole. Notwithstanding this stark contrast in outlook, these two men were similar in personal characteristics that set them apart from ordinary people. Each had a driving ambition to acquire and exercise power in the pursuit of individual purpose. Both were highly adept at the art of political manipulation, and both were uncommonly tenacious in pursuit of their goals.

What follows is an account of their long-standing relationship in the Florida political process. It gives a picture of working politics that often remains at the fringe of historical accounts of the grander issues. Still, it is a dimension of politics that lubricates the workings of the whole as it goes about the process of governance.

1

Florida in the Twenties
Prelude to Conflict

When Claude Pepper and Ed Ball arrived in Florida in the mid-1920s, the state was part of a larger national culture in the process of redefining itself. America, unsure where it was headed, was nevertheless rushing onward as if to avoid being overtaken by its shadow. Within that larger metamorphosis, Florida was taken up with its own dynamics of change, trying to cross that verge which somehow separated it from full status in the national family of states. Forces were at work recasting the state's political and economic character, straining at the bonds of isolation which had kept it at the periphery of recognition. Isolated from the axis of the nation's earlier westward expansion by the southern extremity of its peninsular location, there remained something of a frontier character about the southernmost state. It was as if it had been left behind in America's defining westward movement, not to really discover itself until well into the twentieth century.

The modernity of the 1920s intruded abruptly on a Florida habituated to a lethargic remoteness from the mainstream of national life. In the process, there were few of the modulating effects of gradual transition to temper the characteristic perspectives that defined the state. People, intoxicated with the potential of it all, came seeking opportunities to build careers and reap profits in the dynamic process of change. Most were exploiters, concerned chiefly with get-rich-quick schemes in the short run. They were of a mindset that did not concern itself with long-run consequences. Others, fewer in number, came for the long run. These were the builders, the visionaries, the leaders, who came to create an enduring presence—strong individuals who brought with them a diversity of purpose and ideals that produced ongoing tensions as they positioned themselves to advance their own interests. This is an account of two of them and how their pursuits and ambitions sparked bitter political conflict. Both understood politics as a medium for the pursuit of power and expression of purpose. Others also left lasting marks on the state's political history, but the convergence of Claude Pepper and Ed Ball affords a particularly rich view of the world of Florida politics during the middle years of the twentieth century.

A decisive role in the 1918 Allied victory in World War I had left the nation a financial and industrial power of the first order. Yet it was a nation at odds with itself, uncomfortable with its newfound status as a world power. Without apparent purpose, it turned inward, letting its myriad energies run free in crosscurrents of social and economic change. In the midst of this confusion, there were elements of American life that had emerged from the war more robust than ever, and these fueled the engines of change. This was especially true of the economy, which seemed limitless in its capacity for producing wealth. Commerce, industry, and financial markets all raced ahead in tandem, striving to deliver material abundance to those willing to reach for it. Lacking any other sense of direction, the forces of economic production turned consumption itself into purpose. Imbalances in the distribution of the free-flowing bounty did not diminish a perception that approached consensus: America had entered upon lasting prosperity—or so it seemed.

A highly visible segment of the population during the period indulged its restlessness in the pursuit of wealth, riding a wave of prosperity that contained overtones of permanency. In fact, there was nothing permanent about it. It was a cresting wave, one of remarkable endurance to be sure, but destined to last only until its inflated momentum could no longer sustain it. Nor was it all embracing. Farmers, miners, textile workers, and minorities, for the most part, found no place in this prosperity.[1] Overall, wage levels were quite stable, or stagnant, depending on one's perspective, while inflation remained relatively benign, considering the period's almost hypercharged economy.[2] It was all exhilarating. It was the Roaring Twenties, and America was in motion, even if without clear purpose or direction. Against that backdrop, Ed Ball and Claude Pepper each found his way to Florida. In contrast to the image of an America without clear purpose in general, each of these men possessed a strong sense of purpose coupled to a fierce determination and iron-willed tenacity.

A surging stock market was the most visible manifestation of the period, although it was certainly not the only defining force at work. But because its workings were easily observed and comprehended in relationship to the overall economy, at least superficially it afforded a relatively simple and reportable reflection of the nation's material well-being. The stock market symbolized the period by projecting prosperity as the birthright of America. When that notion imploded with the Great Crash of 1929, Wall Street was made the focus of a disheartened nation's bitterness. It became the symbol of the greed and avarice assigned moralistically as the prime cause of the depression that followed.

The Florida that drew Ed Ball and Claude Pepper to it had its own distinctive character, less defined perhaps but still generally consistent with the drive for prosperity that symbolized the larger national scene. Its force was driven by vast expanses of unused and cheap land enveloped by a semitropical climate. To understand the temper of the times and place that drew these two men, it is necessary to juxtapose both the national and the local dimensions of the quest for prosperity in a single context. It is convenient to begin with the national setting.

Following World War I, American industry enjoyed a pronounced wave, albeit brief, of export-driven trade, primarily with European nations rebuilding their industrial and agricultural bases. Within this generalized condition, not all major sectors of the economy shared proportionately in this post-war bounty. Initially agriculture benefited, but as Europe recovered, the demand for agricultural exports declined. American farmers were stranded once again in the recurring dilemma of their own overproduction. Agricultural exports fluctuated dramatically from 1921 to 1924, peaking at higher than post-war levels before starting a downward trend once again.[3] The wave of national prosperity that followed did not, by and large, embrace rural America. The economic expansion was largely an urban phenomenon. Large parts of Florida, particularly north Florida where Ed Ball and Claude Pepper began their careers, were far removed from any general image of prosperity.

In the national picture, a brisk export trade in industrial and consumer goods offset the feared consequences of demobilization of industries geared to war production. That, and vigorous realignment of domestic markets with peacetime production, combined to initiate a short-lived post-war bullish stock market. America had emerged from the war as the world's premier economic power. Its robust industrial base was more resilient than ever, and New York had replaced London as the center of world finance. Yet by late 1919, the country was gripped by a consortium of uncertainties: the Red Scare, prolonged labor strife, rising inflation, nativism and isolationism, and a political malaise resulting from the vacuum of leadership caused by an incapacitated president. (Woodrow Wilson had suffered an incapacitating stroke that left him virtually unable to exercise the powers of the presidency.) Those negative features coalesced to produce a temporary economic downturn. Although inconsistent with the nation's real underlying economic strength, this slump continued until mid-1921, when a slow but steady recovery began.[4] It signaled the start of the "Great Bull Market," a prolonged upward trend of stock prices lasting almost eight years, culminating in the Great Crash of 1929. Some historians start the bull market with the 1924 election of Calvin Coolidge; others place it after the 1926 market correction.[5] What is important here is that it was a continuous upward trend, interspersed with varying degrees of corrections, from mid-1921 until the 1929 crash. It became a symbol of the times. There were elements of truth in and about the symbol, but it was inaccurate as to the whole.

The market of the 1920s is often portrayed as a continuum of irresponsible speculation escalating prices beyond any sensible valuation of underlying assets and earnings. That view is an oversimplification implicit in the moralistic impulse to attach responsibility for the recklessness of the period to the avarice of Wall Street. That storied place certainly bears its share of fault, but its direct impact in creating the national obsession with riches and pleasure was just one of the broad dynamics of change at work within the socioeconomic fabric.

Only a relatively few Americans directly participated in the stock market. Figures derived from brokerage firm testimony before a congressional investigating committee after the crash, and relied on by economist John Kenneth Galbraith, showed 1,371,920 accounts with member firms of the New York Stock Exchange, with approximately another 200,000 from nonmember firms. Allowance for those individuals who maintained accounts with more than one firm would reduce this number. Even so, only about 1.5 million persons from a total population of 120 million (29 to 30 million families) were in the market.[6] Another estimate puts the number at nearer 3 million individual investors, double Galbraith's number.[7] The record keeping of the era precludes a more definitive estimate than the range given, but it is sufficient to illustrate that participation in the stock market was not widespread enough to define the American profile of the period.

The pronounced obsession with riches and pleasure originated from a far more complex composite of causation than Wall Street alone. The introduction of widespread consumer credit and massive advertising amid an onslaught of new products, especially the automobile, produced a monumental binge of consumer spending. The pervasive electrification of industry resulted in a phenomenal increase in productivity to lubricate the flow of consumer goods. Electricity was the leading edge of technology for the period and did much to improve the standard of living dramatically. Emerging communications media—radio and especially the movies—nurtured visions of rich and satisfying lifestyles with deceptive facades of reality. These had a more pervasive effect on the collective outlook of a nation rushing to immerse itself in the embrace of modernism than did the stock market alone. Still, the heady atmosphere of Wall Street is an important element in the mosaic of causation that set Ed Ball on a course of inevitable conflict with Claude Pepper.

The Great Bull Market was not the result of a singular pattern of wholly irrational behavior by investors. For most of the period, the stock market was supported by some measure of conventional investment reasoning. Robert Sobel, a stock market historian, said: "Prices [of stocks] did not rise unreasonably in the twenties, though the advance was indeed dramatic. Rather, they reflected a new, more realistic view of the nation's position and prospects after World War I, and the growth in earnings of common stocks."[8] This view of a rational market up to 1928, even if dramatic in its ascent, was one shared by Galbraith: "Even a man of conservative mind could believe that the prices of common stock were catching up with . . . corporate earnings . . . and the certainty that the administration . . . would take no more than necessary of any earnings in taxes."[9] Of course there is a much more complex construct of causation for the Great Bull Market and the crash that followed, one that includes a hodgepodge of international monetary policy at odds with itself. But such an expanded model is unduly complicated and not germane to the relationship of the stock market to the Florida Boom. The point here is that despite the overlay of recklessness, the behavior of many Americans who left their marks on the period remained rational. Alfred I. duPont, scion of one of America's greatest and oldest industrial families, and Ed Ball, his chief lieutenant and protégé, were two such men. Their actions were rational, and together they left an indelible mark on their adopted state, Florida.

The market's descent to irrational behavior was progressive. The wild advances beginning in the summer of 1928 provided, retrospectively, the first clear signals of the transition. The Florida Boom, an appropriate prelude to what followed on Wall Street, had expired of its own excesses two years earlier. Whatever logic remained in the market's behavior was thereafter subsumed in a frenzy of pure speculation. The Dow-Jones Industrial Index, although periodically undergoing mildly corrective adjustments, remained in a sharply upward trend between 1921 and 1928. It appeared to be so directed for the foreseeable future, if not, as some thought, permanently. From 1922 to 1928, the Standard and Poor's Index of Common Stocks increased from 17.39 to 36.86, the size of the gain increasing each year.

The apparent scientific precision of the various market indexes afforded a beguiling inference of certainty to the heady expectations. Recurring stories of huge profits reaped by ordinary people, as often true as not, gave credence to the notion of a surfeit of riches dispersing itself through multiple layers of society. Although past experience indicated the cyclical inevitability of stock market behavior and booms in general, this experience was pushed aside. In 1928, Standard and Poor's index surged to 59.33, spurred in part by the dramatic increase in margin buying.[10]

The underlying reasons for the market excesses were explored after the collapse when a congressional committee probed the little-known inside world of Wall Street.[11] The committee summoned the elite of Wall Street to testify, along with regulators, such as they were then, and academics. Given the nation's sullen mood, the denizens of the financial world derived little protection from their exalted status of the recent past. Guided by the investigative zeal of committee attorney Ferdinand Pecora, the hearings exposed a complex of practices that, in one way or another, fueled the binge of speculation and ultimate collapse of the market. The disclosure of a variety of questionable institutional practices as well as episodes of personal misconduct—for example, many of the best-known and wealthiest figures on Wall Street did not pay income taxes on their manipulated gains—made it relatively easy to lay the blame for the misery of depression on the institution they represented.

Speculation on margin was another Wall Street practice that contributed to the market's collapse. Brokers loaned their customers money to buy stocks and held the purchased stocks as collateral for the loan. Although legal, sometimes even beneficial, this practice became malignant when it was overextended to individuals whose only means of payment was tied to a continuous rise in the price of the stocks. Not only did it dull customers' awareness of the inherent risks of investing by reducing the requisite cash investment for speculating on stocks, but it also had a distorting effect on the allocation of capital.

As the speculation fed on itself, demand for such loans increased, driving the interest on them higher. These loans were short-term investments, sometimes for only one day. Nonbanking firms rushed to take advantage of the situation by making profitable loans to brokerage houses, thus siphoning funds from the normal capital requirements of corporate operations. Cities Service Company, a petroleum company, made 912 such loans in 1929 for a total of over $285 million; Electric Bond and Share, a large utility holding company, made 1,663 such loans for a total of $867 million. Other well-known companies engaged in this business were Standard Oil Company of New Jersey and Sinclair Oil Company. These short-term investments often earned returns of up to 15 percent, reaching as high as 20 percent in mid-1929.[12] Such returns on short-term and seemingly well collateralized loans were compelling from the perspective of an individual business manager, but they distorted the overall capital allocation process. As was so often the case during the period, these business practices, when viewed individually, were neither sinister nor corrupt. There was no body of law or regulation in effect to temper the surge of lending and borrowing; nor was there an understanding of the collective impact that these activities would have on the economy.

There were other practices that also fueled the ongoing spectacle. Although they were not illegal, it is clear in retrospect that they were bad policy. The rise of investment companies, the forerunner of today's far more circumscribed mutual funds, further blurred the demarcation point between rational and irrational investment concepts. These firms were created to acquire stocks of conventional operating companies. Their portfolio of stocks was their only asset and the price of the investment firm's stock escalated primarily on speculation wholly unrelated to the value and earnings of the companies whose stocks constituted its assets. Even where the underlying corporations had sound earnings and profits, the securities were unduly inflated by the speculation craze, and those in control took maximum advantage of their insider positions. Samuel Insull's gigantic utility empire was such a case.

Electricity was the energy source powering the great rise in industrial productivity, as well as visibly improving the lifestyle of ordinary Americans. Clearly the electric industry was a sound business, and Insull was generally considered one of its pioneering visionaries. Early in the decade, alarmed by the surge in prices of utility stocks, he had publicly warned against the rampant speculation then inflating electric utility stock prices.[13] His warning, perhaps only halfhearted in the first place, went unheeded. Insull proceeded to allow the tide of speculation, indeed manipulated it, to propel the stocks of his various holding and investment companies to ever higher prices. Finally, his empire disintegrated under the strain of excessive leverage.

When faced with what he perceived as a threat to take control of his empire, Insull set out to strengthen his hold with an infusion of additional capital. To raise the collateral value of his holdings, he manipulated his stocks to higher values by an audacious pooling arrangement that came to light only when Congress later conducted an investigation of the utility industry. This investigation, along with the stock market investigation, was the impetus for major New Deal reform legislation. Insull's debt might have been manageable had it not been for the machinations of New York bankers intent on teaching the Chicago-centered upstart where the American world of finance was really controlled. Denying him needed extensions of credit, the bankers forced Insull into receivership. The subsequent failure of the Insull empire became a cause célèbre and a prime example of the intrinsic dangers of the unfettered pyramiding of assets that ran rampant during this period.

Pooling was another of the ambiguous Wall Street insider practices that existed in the gray area of technically legal but unethical business activities. A group of insiders would act in concert to prearrange the buying and selling of a particular stock to cause its price to rise. The success of this scheme depended on outsiders seeing the stock price rising, and buying into it for exactly the purpose that motivated the conspirators: profit on speculation. The conspirators would of course control the timing of their sale of the stock and would then cease their pre-agreed buying support, sending the stock plummeting after they had reaped the windfall induced by the manipulated purchases. Sometimes, the manipulators would go in the reverse direction, sending prices downward. This would set the stage for them to sell short in the targeted stock, reaping profits from the precipitated decrease in the stock's price.[14]

Even the august demeanor and mental dexterity of Charles W. Whitney, president of the New York Stock Exchange, could not obfuscate the fact that such operations, though not strictly illegal, were intended to deceive the buying public. Pooling, while not explicitly proscribed, was in direct contravention of the hallowed purpose of the Exchange, namely, to maintain an "open and free market."[15] The Senate Banking and Currency Committee exposed numerous examples of such manipulation. These revelations were additional catalysts for many of the reforms put in place during the New Deal—reforms that became the foundation of the regulatory mechanisms governing the nation's financial markets today. The stock market is now a much more circumscribed arena for investment transactions than was the case during the Roaring Twenties.

The recklessness of attitude that slowly engulfed Wall Street came to confluence with other currents of social change seeking expression. A steady stream of literature debunked traditional social values and railed against the imposition of new ones.[16] Such iconoclasm implied some measure of intellectual underpinning for the stark materialism of the period. There were always counterforces in the confusing mosaic. The best-selling book of 1925—Bruce Barton's *The Man Nobody Knows,* which depicted Christ as a modern businessman—was a somewhat bizarre example of countervailing attitudes. In reality, it was an attempt to recast Christianity in concert with a business ethic built on the crass materialism of the times. Prohibition was an attempt to curb the appetites of the era. It provoked a pronounced social reaction, as well as a paradox worthy of the era: Billy Sunday, best-known evangelist of the period, on one hand, and Al Capone, most notorious criminal of the period, on the other. The lawlessness denounced by Sunday and epitomized by Capone became a byword for the period. A resurgence of Christian fundamentalism arose in the heartland and even left its mark on the more cosmopolitan centers, but not enough to quench the hedonistic temper of the times.

All in all, the lasting image of the period was one of a reckless materialism. The pursuit of pleasure became the be-all and end-all, and quick and easy riches the means to that end. It was that mind-set that ignited an orgy of speculation in Florida real estate during the early years of the decade. As John Kenneth Galbraith sardonically observed, "The Florida boom was the first indication of the mood of the twenties and the conviction that God intended the American middle class to be rich."[17]

That such a perspective could displace a Protestant heritage of hard work and thrift was presaged in 1919 in that sanctuary of Puritan rectitude, Massachusetts. An Italian immigrant unleashed one of the great swindles of all time predicated solely on the notion that a substantial segment of the population could not resist the urge to get rich easily and quickly. The crux of Charles Ponzi's offering was to trade on fluctuations in foreign currency, certainly not a new concept. His plan was to buy International Postal Union reply coupons and redeem them where the denominated currency sold for more than in the country of origin. He would finance the operation by borrowing money and repaying $15 for every $10 in ninety days. This offered both a return of principal as well as a return on it of over 200 percent a year. For the first trickle of dollars, Ponzi repaid on time, in full, and with interest. This prompted a surge of publicity, and in a few months, his cash flow rose to nearly $1 million a week. Prompt payment of interest and principal continued as scheduled.

It looked as if Ponzi had found the key to unlock the mysteries of trading in foreign currencies. In his brief interlude of apparent success, he acquired a banking house, the Hanover Trust Company, and appointed himself president. With his newly assumed air of respectability, he was cheered by some as the "greatest Italian of all," to which he modestly replied that such distinction belonged to Marconi and Columbus.[18]

Then, an enterprising newspaper reporter ascertained that all the Postal Union reply coupons acquired by Ponzi, and even all those in existence *throughout the world,* were not enough to sustain his momentum.[19] On top of that, Ponzi made one miscalculation after another as to the fluctuations of foreign currencies, and his Old Colony Foreign Exchange Company collapsed. He was tried and convicted of fraud, but not before thousands lost an estimated $10 million. Still, Ponzi had managed a payout by some estimates of $8 million, which led a number of people to believe that he would make good on his offering if the authorities left him alone. It should be noted that in a federal case arising out of the same operations, a jury acquitted him, thus affording a *scintilla* of ambiguity to his status as a fraud.

What Ponzi left as his enduring legacy was a euphemism for get-rich-quick schemes: the Ponzi scheme. In the early years of the 1920s, when the frenzy of land speculation was well under way in Florida and Ponzi was at liberty on an appeal bond, the indomitable Italian "financier" thought he recognized in Florida an opportunity well suited to his talents. He came to Jacksonville as a land developer and announced the laudable goal of repaying his New England investors. To that end, he forswore any share of the profits for himself until a disinterested board of trustees (to be appointed by him) certified that all these investors were repaid. Offering fifty-by-twenty-five-foot lots in tracts of land to be purchased in rural Columbia County, some sixty miles west of Jacksonville, Ponzi gave solemn assurance that they would always be worth the $10 purchase price. Investment units of $10 represented by certificates of indebtedness from his Charpon Investment Trust were offered to investors. The loaned funds would be used to purchase and develop lands, and the proceeds from sales would be used to repay the certificates of indebtedness. Based on an assessment of the Florida real estate market that was patently absurd, even by the standards of the period, he estimated that investments could be turned over six times a year, for an astounding return of "200 percent in sixty days."[20] Five months later, his Florida operation ended with his criminal conviction for failure to properly register the trust operation with the state.[21]

Later, after Ponzi was reported a fugitive, his wife held a press conference as she departed New York City for Italy, seeking the intercession of Benito Mussolini, the Italian dictator, on her husband's behalf. She told the assembled reporters that he had "been misunderstood."[22] His presence was not thereafter noted on the Florida scene, but his spirit lived on in the Ponzi scheme that was to be better known as the Florida Land Boom. Ponzi's headquarters in Jacksonville at 122 West Forsyth Street were within one block of Alfred I. duPont's offices. There all similarity ends. Ponzi represented all the illusionary glitter that adorned the notion of speculation and quick riches. The duPont interests had come to Florida for investment in the long term, not for the quick riches of a Ponzi scheme.

The Florida Land Boom and its consequences were far more complex and far-reaching than Ponzi's original scheme. It was a composite of realities and abstractions that fostered the political climate in which Ed Ball and Claude Pepper commenced their Florida careers. Notwithstanding their starkly different purposes, it was the common arena of politics where these two strong-willed individuals pursued their economic and political objectives—and frequently clashed with each other. To understand that clash, and the philosophical and political differences responsible for it, one must examine the boom years in Florida and their lasting economic and political effects.

The dynamics of Alfred I. duPont's decision to leave Delaware, the maturing of his relationship with Ed Ball, the creation of the Florida National Bank chain, the west Florida investments that became the St. Joe Paper Company, the bankruptcy of the Florida East Coast Railway, and the Ball-Crummer battle over the Florida municipal bond business—all were shaped from events of those years. For Pepper, it was a boom-time land development company that brought him to the small west Florida lumber town of Perry. The underlying rural Populism that the politics of the Great Depression turned to ardent New Deal liberalism made Pepper an unquestioning disciple of Franklin D. Roosevelt. That evangelical relationship created an unbridgeable gap between Pepper and Ball.

While the pursuit of quick riches is the common ingredient of all booms, the Florida Boom was also grounded in the pursuit of luxurious pleasure, a feature not generally associated with such booms as the California and Klondike gold rushes. The balmy Florida winter climate was always the principal selling point for the state's developers. The first promoters were the railroad builders of Florida's Gilded Age, men like William D. Chipley, Henry Plant, and Henry Flagler. It was Flagler's creation, the Florida East Coast Railway, that would later be a focal point in the conflict between U.S. senator Claude Pepper and Ed Ball.

Initially, the railroads provided access to markets for Florida's agricultural produce, the early mainstay of the state's economy. Consistent with the national pattern of railroad building, they had been granted huge tracts of public lands, much like the incentives given in the name of economic development today, as construction inducements. The sale of lands and promotion of settlements were essential to the early development of railroading. At first, transportation of agricultural produce was secondary to the profits from those sales. In Florida, land development was an integral part of the state's economic development. Yet the Florida railroads' most lasting impact was their role in establishing the tourist trade, thereby inextricably linking the state's image to pursuit of pleasure. Railroads transported the wealthy to Florida in the winter months, indulged their pleasures at lavish hotel-resorts, and returned them north when the summer heat rendered the winter playgrounds inhospitable.

Agriculture, the other prong of a two-dimensional economy, provided the principal demand for Florida real estate. There was little semblance of a communication system in the state's vast hinterland away from the railroads' immediate reach that could feasibly support any more people-oriented use of land. That changed dramatically in the years following World War I. Henry Ford's mass-produced automobile was on the verge of reshaping the cultural landscape of America. In Florida, automobiles magnified the potential for access to lands beyond the immediate reach of the railroad lines, forging a linkage between roads, real estate, and building construction in a lasting three-dimensional economic model. That construct was to be a continuing force in the state's development, and a principal dynamic in its political climate for most of the twentieth century.

In the early 1920s, the triad of economic dynamics spawned a more immediate, tumultuous economic phenomenon: the Florida Real Estate Boom. Without Ford's Model-T cars, and the roads on which to operate them, the mass marketing of real estate that was the sine qua non of the boom would not have been possible. The automobile was clearly the linchpin of the state's frenzied development.[23] In 1924, Florida had the largest increase in automobiles of any state, going from 160,000 to 216,000 registered vehicles.[24] Highway construction became the primary function of state government and the medium through which Ed Ball was introduced to Florida politics.[25]

The newfound mobility facilitated the opening of lands previously beyond the pale of development. This in turn nurtured a pervasive system of public improvements to provide roads, parks, bridges, and other amenities required to sustain the burgeoning real estate market. These projects were financed mainly by public debt funded by ad valorem taxes, and in some instances, pledges of anticipated revenues from the facilities to be constructed. During the boom, that form of financing was used freely in developments that indistinguishably merged public and private interests.

After the collapse, Alfred I. duPont saw nothing wrong with that mode of public financing when it suited his purposes. Still, he had abhorred the irresponsibility inherent in its unbridled use during the boom, when city, county, and district officials were often land promoters, bankers, or both. Such officials gleefully entered into what today would be clearly unethical, and most likely criminal, acts in pledging public credit for projects in which they had every expectation of personal profit. After the boom collapsed, and the state's banking system was in near shambles, the local governments could not escape the consequences of their earlier recklessness as readily as the developers and speculators. Although many Florida governmental entities availed themselves of the federal bankruptcy remedies for municipalities enacted as part of the New Deal, the fiscal scars left from the boom took many years to heal.

Such practices were not perceived as outwardly sinister or corrupt. Florida governor John W. Martin saw political control by bankers and promoters over governmental entities as an underlying strength of the state.[26] Few seemed to sense the danger inherent in incorporating the local tax base into the capital structure of multiple projects, all layered on a pyramid of speculation. This had the additional lure of providing tax-free income to the bond buyers and often the promoters themselves. It was not readily apparent to many that a tax base predicated on insanely inflated land values was a prelude to fiscal disaster. With local government effectively coopted by the crazed speculation, the public was virtually without any protective cloak of prudent oversight. Moreover, since the prevailing mind-set of get-rich-quick schemes permeated both private and public realms of action, voices of caution were censured as traitorous or worse. In early 1926, one J. A. Tregoe, speaking in his capacity as the managing executive of the Jacksonville Credit Men's Association, opined publicly that credit practices were verging on the extreme. Two weeks later, his membership collectively demanded his ouster.[27] His comments were seen as a lack of confidence in the economy, an attitude that dampened the prevailing spirit of the times. It was harmful to the chances of success for all.

Fortunately, the state was constitutionally prohibited from entering into debt for nonpublic business purposes, a ban that grew out of railroad defaults in the early days of statehood. Seldom has a constitutional restraint on government spending served its purpose so well. Yet that restraint did not apply to local governments, which proceeded with abandon to amass debt in numerous cities, counties, and special districts. The bloated debt structures left in their wake were a blight on Florida's political and economic landscapes for many years.

Later, those same debt structures were to be a source of profit for that rare breed of adventurer who can recognize the potential for profit in the midst of a financial disaster. In the following decade, when there seemed little prospect for any business enterprises in Florida, two such adventurers—Ed Ball and a northern securities dealer named Roy E. Crummer—sensed opportunity in the situation and took advantage of it. Their ensuing competition sparked one of the intense conflicts that marked Ball's career, one reaching deep into the political labyrinths of Tallahassee and Washington. Pepper was not Ball's principal antagonist in that particular episode, but he played a role in it that provided continuity to the struggle between the two. The fiscal havoc spawned of the Florida Boom and crash defined a common political perspective of the period. A more complete picture of the environment that it produced is important to understanding the temper of the times.

Although it is not clear when or what actually ignited the great frenzy of speculation that was the Florida Land Boom, Miami was clearly the focal point of its origins. In 1896, Henry Flagler had completed his rail line from West Palm Beach to Miami, which was then little more than a place-name on a map. The natural charm of the place was all but obscured by its summer

heat, disease-prone climate, aura of remoteness, and the surrounding swamp-
lands. The fact of rail service became its only positive feature. Like other
great railroad builders, Flagler could submerge such negatives in his own
personal vision of a different Florida. He saw the state as a place where the
pursuit of pleasure by the many would nurture the pursuit of riches by a few
like himself. South Florida, particularly Miami, became a classic example of
how modern development redefined a natural environment. For those engaged in the orgy of development, it was a matter of digging canals, draining
mucklands, and building grand construction projects on the reclaimed land.
The full costs of those changes would be left to future generations to assess,
and to ameliorate where possible.

Although Flagler's vision did not materialize overnight, it proceeded with
persistent progress. In 1885, Dade County's population of 383 hearty individuals lived at a sleepy outpost of civilization. By the turn of the century, the
population had risen to almost 5,000, largely owing to Flagler's railroad.
Five years later, it had more than doubled and was over 12,000. The city of
Miami was incorporated on July 28, 1896, just three months after completion of Flagler's railroad. By 1904, Miami proudly boasted that it had "all
modern conveniences of civilization," including electric lights and a water-
works, sewer system, telephones, and three newspapers.[28] There was nothing in that early growth to presage what was to come when the area's natural
charm combined with the railroad, the automobile, improved drainage
methods, and modern road-building techniques. But by 1919 those conditions had set the stage for the wildest upsurge of real estate values in Florida
history.[29]

The rising real estate market began shortly after the Allied victory in
World War I. By 1920, a trend of accelerating land values was evident as land
transactions in Miami rose steadily from 22,000 in 1920 to 26,000 two years
later. The price acceleration increasingly took on the air of speculation as the
volume increased to 34,500 in 1923 and rose by more than 75 percent to
61,000 in the following year. Then, in 1925, there was a veritable explosion
of transactions, and 174,530 real estate conveyances were recorded.[30] The
city of Miami came to symbolize every excess associated with the intoxicat-
ing effects of the boom. The rest of the state joined in the spectacle but did
not approach the scale of the southeast Florida metamorphosis.

A 1922 feature article in the *New York Times* described the state as the
last frontier, held back from full status in the eyes of its sister states only by
lack of population and an inferiority complex grounded in envy of Califor-

nia. The boom then beginning in the Southeast was a step toward increased population, which in concert with railroads, automobiles, and roads bid fair to overcome the state's inferiority complex. The article also noted the cleavage between the newness in the state's southern reaches and the older southern tradition that prevailed in the north.[31] Native Floridians had mixed feelings about the publicity cascading down on them. They obviously welcomed the newfound wealth but resented the lethargic or slow-witted image of themselves presented by such descriptions as the "sluggish actions of the Florida cracker or conch, the latter word being pronounced conk."[32]

The boom received a tremendous stimulus in 1924 when the state's voters adopted a constitutional prohibition against income and estate taxes. This gesture raised Florida's profile among the upper classes and was viewed by proponents of unfettered capitalism as fitting well with U.S. Treasury Secretary Andrew Mellon's tax-cutting policies and the theme of overall Coolidge prosperity.[33] It played a role in the decision of many wealthy individuals—including Alfred I. duPont—to establish their legal domicile in Florida.

It is impossible to fix the point at which a rising Florida real estate market had transformed itself into self-destructive speculation. Certainly it had reached that stage by 1925, if not sooner. The frenzy had generated a species of transaction forever after associated with the wild speculation of the period: binder transactions. This was selling real estate on "binders," a written promise to convey, but not dignified with the same legal status as a deed. The practice increased the tempo of speculation beyond that measured by the actual conveyances. Binder transactions were a means of expediting land sales when the official recording process, clogged by the volume of transactions, delayed official recordation of the deeds. Not wanting to slow the pace of moneymaking in the frenetic market, the "binder boys" would convey and reconvey on nothing more than a written memo of the transaction, leaving the actual deed supposedly forthcoming on expiration of the binder.[34]

A young Englishman, recently immigrated to America, came to Miami to observe and participate in the boom if the right opportunities arose. He described the impact of the binder process: "In other words, resales were taking place far more rapidly than the law could follow them, and the result, in the case of a block which had been sold, say, six times in as many days—a not infrequent happening—was sheer chaos."[35] Binders operated outside of the recording system, and there was no way of quantifying their impact.

Clearly the practice fostered a far greater turnover of parcels, significantly expanding the volume of transactions taking place and further charging the atmosphere of rampant speculation. The sales were legal on their face and did in fact produce huge and quick profits in numerous instances, frequently before any property actually changed hands. The practice of paying 10 to 25 percent down, with the remainder in two or three payments due in ninety days, enabled relatively small sums to tie up property so that the holder of the binder could then look for a quick turnover of his newly acquired asset.

Notwithstanding the turbulent binder practice, title to property did change hands. There was a legitimate, albeit materially distorted, market structure that produced verifiable and recurring accounts of vast profits made quickly and easily. The large number of such stories, often focused on the famous and wealthy, and appearing in legitimate publications, gave credibility to the phenomenal events taking place. A *New York Times* article in early September of 1925 provided an impressive list of nationally prominent people who had purchased homes and property in a development about twenty miles north of West Palm Beach. It included such luminaries as William Gibbs McAdoo, former secretary of the treasury; Fannie Hurst, a prominent writer of the period; George Ryan, president of the New York City Board of Education; and Governor John Martin of Florida. Two weeks later, promoters of the area announced a movie studio for the same locale.[36] Like most of what was emblazoned across the newspaper pages about the Florida Boom, the studio did not materialize.

The volume of the buying and selling could be gleaned from the massive advertising sections of south Florida newspapers. An issue of the *Miami Daily News* in the summer of 1925 was 504 pages, most of which were real estate ads. In the same year, the *Miami Herald* had more advertising than any other paper had ever achieved. One executive reporting to his out-of-state company on the situation in Miami estimated that some 25,000 real estate salesmen were working out of 2,000 offices there.[37] That number was almost certainly exaggerated, for it was subsequently reported that the number of salesmen licensed by the city of Miami in 1926 was 12,000.[38] At the height of the boom, there were four newspapers in Miami, some associated with nationally prominent names such as former presidential candidate James M. Cox and Cornelius Vanderbilt, one of the progeny of the legendary Commodore Vanderbilt.[39]

The binder practice that marked the Florida Boom was similar in concept to the leveraging that supported the later binge of margin buying that subsequently fueled the wild speculation on Wall Street.[40] Like credit in general, leveraging is no more than a means of marshaling capital for business undertakings. So long as it is based on a realistic assessment of underlying asset value and capacity to produce wealth, it is a proper and valuable component of the free enterprise system. There was no such nexus with underlying value in the buying and selling of land in the Florida Boom. When expectations of appreciation bear no relation to utilitarian asset values, leveraging becomes the energy source for self-destructive speculation. It was a lesson that Ed Ball learned well from his mentor, Alfred I. duPont.

At its height, the rampant speculation was sustained by no more than a tenuous notion that someone would always pay more than the most recent buyer, and that there would always be one more buyer. That so many people could have blithely ignored the fundamental realities of investment logic is one of the mysteries of human behavior. As 1925 wore on, it was clear to any reasonably discerning person that the speculative real estate values in Florida were not supported by any rational assessment of underlying utilitarian value. Alfred I. duPont was one such discerning person. While observing the chaotic scene from the porch of Henry Flagler's Royal Palm Hotel in early January of 1925, duPont told his younger brother-in-law: "Ed, it is the

1. The Royal Palm Hotel in Miami was a favorite haunt of well-to-do visitors who came to south Florida during the height of the Florida Boom. Alfred I. duPont and his new wife, Jessie Ball duPont, were frequent guests in the 1920s before deciding to make their home in Jacksonville. Connell collection.

2. The Hurricane of 1926 contributed to the demise of the Florida Boom. These ships beached on the streets of Miami show what, in Fredrick Lewis Allen's words, "a Soothing Tropic Wind could do when it got a good running start from the West Indies." The Royal Palm Hotel is in background.

3. Southeast Florida was devastated by the 1926 storm. Scenes like this one from Miami marked the beginning of the end of the boom. Real estate sales dwindled to near nothing, tax defaults became endemic, and local governments were saddled with huge debts with no feasible means of payment.

craziest thing I ever saw. These people are on the brink of the precipice right now; and they talk about the good times only getting started. They'll go broke. No other result is possible. The aim is to get something for nothing. It never works—for long."[41] The import of duPont's statement was well suited to the younger man's naturally conservative character.

Throughout his life, Ball evaluated investments on the basis of rational expectations about their utilitarian value. In other words, he judged assets by their capacity to be economically productive in a real sense. That mode of thought was distinctly at odds with the virus of speculation that he and duPont observed all about them from the porch of Flagler's Royal Palm Hotel. There were times, however, when Ball departed from his overall investment philosophy and made decisions that could be called whimsical. His purchase of Wakulla Springs illustrates that side of his nature, although he did intend to make a profit from that acquisition as well as indulge his fondness for Florida's natural beauty.

There was more to the Florida Boom than hectic scenes of buying and selling real estate lots on speculation in Miami. Beneath the frenzy of binder sales and rampant speculation, there were actually remarkable signs of growth. In 1925, at the height of the boom, 425 permits for hotel construction were issued between January and May, and in October it was reported that seventy-six hotels were built.[42] Most of them did not actually open, and among those that did, most lasted only until the collapse. The great period of railroad construction in the nation had ended ten years earlier, but in Florida, railroad building was still in progress, adding a touch of frontier image to the pursuit of pleasure and riches in the East.

Clarence W. Barron, America's premier financial journalist and owner of the *Wall Street Journal* and *Barron's,* was fascinated with everything connected with the state's phenomenal development. He was particularly impressed with the extension of the Seaboard Air Line Railroad from Tampa eastward to West Palm Beach. Before, to go from Tampa to West Palm Beach, one had to travel north to Jacksonville and back down the east coast 285 miles to West Palm Beach. In a series of *Wall Street Journal* articles titled "Florida by the Airline," Barron described his firsthand observations of the region. At the same time, the Seaboard Air Line Railroad was a popular stock on Wall Street, due partly to the perception that it was a part of the emerging airline industry, then a favorite of investors and speculators.[43] Barron's series of articles undoubtedly helped nurture that perception, thereby tightening the connections between Florida's boom-time image and the growing speculation on Wall Street. Barron's eclectic observations grew out of his extensive travels about the state and his great curiosity about all phases of Florida's turbulent development. He was also enamored with the pleasures of spending the winter months in Palm Beach, where he was in his element with the wealthy inhabitants of the nation's newest haunt for millionaires.[44]

At the same time that S. Davies Warfield was pushing his "Air Line" railroad eastward across the state's central reaches, the Florida East Coast Railway, Henry Flagler's creation that had opened the state's east coast, was preparing to double-track its system, financing it with a $25 million bond issue. The phenomenal growth along the east coast boded well for the enterprising railroad, making its bonds a desirable investment. Not until 1931, after the collapse of the boom belatedly took its toll on Flagler's vision for Florida, were those bonds defaulted, putting the Florida East Coast Railway into receivership. The defaulted bond issue later became the vehicle for Ed Ball's twenty-year struggle for control of the railroad. In the process, he came into open confrontation with Claude Pepper, by then the senior U.S. senator from Florida, and the two men developed an implacable hostility toward each other.

The Florida Boom was built on an incredible binge of illusions. As duPont had predicted, it was just a matter of time before it came to an end. At first, those caught up in the spectacle took no notice of the unraveling. Perhaps it would be more accurate to say they ignored it. A selling wave on Wall Street early in 1926, one of the periodic corrections in the ongoing bull market, caused many businessmen to leave Palm Beach early that winter.[45] Their departure illustrated the vague but increasingly discernible relationship of the Florida scene to the increasing tempo of the stock market. By early March, the state's real estate market had noticeably slowed almost to a "standstill," and real estate salesmen filled northbound passenger trains to capacity. It was said they were trying to reach a rumored land boom on Long Island.[46] Meanwhile, the first wave of Florida bank failures occurred.[47]

The symbiotic relationship of bankers, developers, and public officials, distended by the boom's excesses, had fostered widespread insider abuse in significant parts of the state's banking system. The extent of this abuse remained shrouded in secrecy for over fifty years, until historians Raymond M. Vickers and Edward Keuchel forced the opening of public records of bank failures during the period.[48] Those records afforded new insights into the demise of the Florida Boom. Vickers's exhaustive research uncovered a pervasive pattern of insider abuse and official dereliction of duty in the state's banking regulatory process. It fostered relationships like that of the Anthony-Manly combine of Florida and Georgia corresponding banks and the cascading failures precipitated by its demise in 1926. These failures were most likely not the sole cause of the collapse of the pyramid of real estate speculation and overleveraged development projects. Still, they undoubtedly were a severe shock to the state's financial infrastructure, poised as it was at the far edge of fiscal reality.

As if to make sure that the signals sent by the decline in the real estate market and bank failures were sufficiently clear, nature sent a message of its own: in the summer of 1926, Miami was devastated by one of the worst hurricanes in its history. Frederick Lewis Allen produced one of the more memorable and ironic statements about the period when he said the storm "showed what a Soothing Tropic Wind could do when it got a good running start from the West Indies."[49] These were the events that in concert heralded the demise of the Florida Boom.

With each leveraged transaction, the inverted pyramid had become more top-heavy, increasing the certainty of ultimate collapse. By the end of 1926, the inevitable had happened. Only a bare trickle of activity continued in the real estate market, and it was largely a process of liquidation. Most of the money made on speculation had been reinvested in further speculation or paid out in advertising and promotion costs and sales commissions. Many of the state's cities were both overbuilt and overextended.[50] Municipalities did not fully comprehend the dire nature of their situations until the precipitous decline in real estate values deflated their tax bases, impairing their ability to function even at minimum levels of governmental responsibility.

It was not just the "binder boys" or large-scale developers like Addison Mizner who were brought low by the crash. Thousands of ordinary wage earners attracted to the spectacle by the jobs it generated were suddenly faced with no means of earning a living, especially in the southern part of the state where the frenzy had reached its height. In south Florida, where tourism and the real estate market were the main props of the economy, massive unemployment produced immediate privation. The decline in tourism was felt throughout the state, but the industrial bases of cities like Jacksonville and Tampa remained strong enough to mitigate the unemployment in those areas.

Amid the debris, it was difficult to recall that many people had made real profits during the boom, and that some had extricated themselves from the frenzied market before the final collapse. As it turned out, most of the lost fortunes had been the offspring of the very speculation that precipitated the fall. While there were certainly real losses, the wealth consumed by them had existed only on the strength of the speculation craze and had disappeared with it. Although the losses were more like shattered illusions than those of hard-earned wealth, they rippled through the economy with a multiplier effect. The state was left in financial shambles. If there had been such a thing as a composite balance sheet of Florida's business structure, it would have been bleak indeed. At the end, those who had gotten in and out without being last reaped some measure of fortune. They, along with a far greater number of losers, settled down to the realities of living while nursing lingering hopes that the boom would somehow be magically restored with the next winter season. Many simply left the state; some pursued similar, if less flamboyant, dreams in other parts of the country where visions of quick and easy profits were not yet impaled on the horns of reality.[51] One such place was Long Island, where a smaller-scale real estate boom was in progress.

But there was no way out for the local governments that had extended themselves as partners in the boom-time development. Numerous cities, counties, and special districts were enveloped with a shroud of debt that they could not shake off. Perpetuated by the constitutional sanctity of contract provisions on which the bond indentures were based, that debt was to be a troublesome fiscal legacy. The tangled state of affairs affected the business and political climate of Florida for the next fifteen years and was an important element of Ed Ball's business dealings. A look at the extent of the damage done to the fiscal underpinnings of cities and counties will give readers a better grasp of Ball's early political perspective.

When the boom started over seventy years ago, Florida's political machinery had to adjust almost overnight to dramatic growth. As people and development inundated the southern portions of the state, new governmental structures had to be established. The geographic remoteness of the regions where the growth was greatest fostered political perspectives that focused on boom-time conditions. Almost overnight, new cities and special taxing districts sprang up, often in tandem with overreaching and grandiose development projects. Between 1919 and 1925, thirteen new counties, nine of them in south Florida, were created. Fifty-five new cities were created in the same period. In 1925, at the peak of the boom, the legislature incorporated twenty-seven cities, most of them offspring of the boom conditions in south Florida.[52] Precipitous growth was the defining quality of these new governmental units. Cities and counties were in a "vicious competition to build the most elaborate public works" as support for the local development.[53] Developers, bankers, and local officials, acting in concert to attract settlers and investors, often functioned as part of an interlocking network promoting specific developments in which they were interested.[54]

Lacking any mechanism for centralized supervision at the state level, the spree of public debt offerings went on without apparent concern for its cumulative effect on the state's financial structure. No state agency was charged with tabulating the collective impact of the burgeoning debt, much less with exercising any supervisory prudence over the state's political subdivisions in the issuance of it.[55] The extravagant public financing of projects was not confined to south Florida, although the most egregious examples were in those sections where boom conditions were most pronounced. When the day of reckoning arrived in 1929, local governments' public debt in Florida had increased overall from $110 million in 1922 to more than $600 million just seven years later.[56] That was a staggering sum for the time, considering that the *entire* state budget in 1929 was approximately $29.7 million.

The north Florida rural interests that dominated state government were not concerned with the spending habits of "Yankee" newcomers in the south so long as tax revenues continued to flow northward. At the time the two principal sources of state revenues were ad valorem and gasoline taxes. The alarm did not sound in Tallahassee until it was realized that the entire ad valorem tax structure had been burdened to the point of collapse by the spending binge. By 1929, there was a general consensus that Florida was in the throes of impending insolvency. The north Florida rural interests that controlled the machinery of state government were not disposed initially to accept the situation as a responsibility of the state. The pervasive nature of the problem settled on state officials only slowly. In 1927, Governor John W. Martin had told the legislature, "The finances of the State Government never were on a sounder basis."[57] He viewed the banking failures as no more than regulatory problems to be resolved by the legislature and the state's elected comptroller, Ernest Amos. The stark truth of the state's financial situation was finally acknowledged in tandem with the realization that the entire nation was in the throes of a depression. In 1931, as if presented with the demand for final payment on a balloon note, the Florida legislature was forced to reckon with the accumulated costs of the Florida Boom.

The crux of the damage to the state's fiscal integrity was in the radical reduction of the ad valorem tax base which followed in the wake of the collapse. Current real estate taxes had increased in proportion to inflated assessment levels. Payment depended on a continued cash flow into the economy from boom activities. When the collapse occurred and real estate values spiraled downward, there was little incentive to make mortgage payments, much less tax payments, on real estate. The effect was almost immediate. In 1926, 2.3 million acres were seized for nonpayment of taxes. This figure more than doubled to 5.9 million acres two years later and was an unimaginable 11 million acres (almost 30 percent of the state's total) when the 1931 legislature was forced to focus on the problem.[58] As defaults removed property from the rolls, taxes on the diminished remainder had to be increased, in turn causing more defaults. As tax revenues fell, the ability of governmental units to make interest and principal payments on the bonds declined. The first default occurred in 1926 in an obscure drainage district in south Florida, initiating a massive cascade of failures. As national depression settled in, over three-quarters of the state's local governments were in some measure of default on their debts as to either interest or principal, or both.[59] Governmental units were on the horns of dilemma. Some offered to redeem outstanding bonds at face value in lieu of tax payments. Sophisticated property owners could buy defaulted bonds at substantial discounts and receive the face value amount as credit for payment of taxes.[60] While this constituted a reduction in the governmental unit's outstanding indebtedness, it further deflated tax revenues, exacerbating the situation even more.

It was in this atmosphere of crisis that Alfred I. duPont launched his Florida enterprises and introduced Ed Ball into Florida politics. Claude Pepper began his political career in 1928, when he was elected to Florida's House of Representatives from the small lumber town of Perry in rural Taylor County. For these two men, the Florida Boom, its collapse, and the Great Depression established the economic and political parameters within which they each pursued their ambitions. One sought power through politics, and the other was thrust into politics through pursuit of economic power. They had in common a dogged tenacity that combined with their starkly contrasting agendas to ensure constant friction in their relationship. This friction led to an unrelenting hostility interspersed with bitter conflict. Contrary to the myths that grew up around both men, neither controlled the state's political scene. No single person could lay valid claim to that distinction in light of Florida's recognized proclivity for contentious and fractionalized politics. They were but players on Florida's tumultuous political scene at midcentury. Yet they were undeniably major figures in the process. An examination of their characters, purposes, and conflicts reveals much about the political system in which they operated, and how their era shaped our own.

2

Alfred I. duPont and Ed Ball
The Road to Florida via Delaware

In 1935, Epping Forest was a large manorial estate located on the east bank of the St. Johns River approximately five miles south of downtown Jacksonville. It was the Florida home of Alfred I. duPont and his wife, Jessie Ball duPont. Today, the mansion remains outwardly unchanged as a country club for the exclusive residential section that was once the duPont estate. Completed in the winter of 1927, and situated on one of the most picturesque reaches of the river, it was symbolic of Alfred I. duPont's self-imposed severance of his ancestral ties to Delaware. Named for a long past Virginia homestead of Jessie's family, it was an eloquent statement of his commitment to a new family relationship.

As the overseer of his brother-in-law's myriad interests, Ed Ball had been instrumental in procuring the land for Alfred and Jessie's new home. Typical of his penchant for capitalizing on distressed situations, Ball had acquired the property out of the remains of a failed real estate development that had collapsed with the demise of the Florida Boom. During frequent and extended absences of his sister and her husband from Jacksonville, he was responsible for superintending its construction under Alfred's absentee scrutiny.[1]

It was at Epping Forest, shortly after midnight on April 29, 1935, that Alfred I. duPont, one of the most creative and controversial scions of America's oldest industrial dynasty, died at the age of seventy-one.

DuPont's passing set the stage for his protégé and kinsman by marriage to emerge in his own right from the long shadow cast by the famous duPont name. Alfred's multifaceted legacy of business enterprises, then probably the largest business group in Florida, was bound together by the terms of his will into a perpetual charitable trust for the benefit of deprived and crippled children of Delaware. Notwithstanding the perpetual charitable nature of the trust, one controversial provision of the final testamentary disposition gave Jessie the entire income after payment of certain minor specific bequests. His brother-in-law was named one of three trustees but quickly emerged as the dominant force in control of the far-flung and substantial assets left by Alfred. This provision was to fuel political controversy around Ed Ball and his stewardship of the duPont legacy for many years to come. Over nearly the next half century, Ball raised the duPont Trust to the status of a business empire. In the process, he forged his own distinctive place in his adopted state's business and political history.

Alfred I. duPont and Ed Ball, so dissimilar in most respects, complemented each other in characteristics essential to the building of a vast industrial and commercial enterprise out of the debacle that was post-boom Florida. To understand Ed Ball and his career, it is appropriate to start with Alfred I. duPont. His was undoubtedly the defining influence in Ball's life, and the linchpin of their relationship was Jessie Ball, Ed's sister and Alfred's third wife.

Alfred was a direct descendent of Eleuthère Irénée duPont, founder of the family gunpowder business which by mid–twentieth century would be one of the world's great industrial conglomerates. When he was born in 1864, the duPont company was already a major component of the nation's industrial establishment, and an essential provider of the gunpowder that fired Union guns in the ongoing Civil War. Delaware was the principal family domicile and the central point of the duPont business enterprises. The family presence dominated that state's social and political life as if it were a family fiefdom. In that tradition-rich setting, Alfred, the eldest son of the eldest son of the founder, was born into a hereditary prominence.[2]

He attended the Massachusetts Institute of Technology but eschewed a traditional degree-granting course of study, choosing instead an eclectic array of courses ranging from science and technology to music and literature. Alfred was notably gifted in technical and scientific pursuits, as his later successes in improving the making of gunpowder would demonstrate.

The young collegian had a rebellious side to his nature, which found expression when he crossed the class boundaries that defined his social status. He took up amateur boxing and frequented bars and saloons in South Boston, where he freely associated with Boston's immigrant Irish and Italians. There, his ring experience was an entrée to a friendship with the "Great John L" Sullivan, the world-heavyweight boxing champion and favorite of the Irish immigrant working class.[3] He learned more from these encounters than just an appreciation for working-class carousing. Alfred's capacity for reaching beyond the confines of his own privileged class later engendered a special relationship with the workmen in the duPont mills which ripened into an understanding and empathy for working classes in general.

This element of his character would later stand in stark contrast with that of his brother-in-law. Ed Ball could never comfortably effect the demeanor of noblesse oblige that Alfred carried with ease and sincerity. Nor, for that matter, did he try, although he always maintained a courtly manner in his personal and social relationships.

In 1884, deciding his formal education was sufficiently completed, Alfred followed duPont family tradition and became a laborer in the company's Hagley Yard works near Wilmington. There he continued the more practical side of his education, learning the dangerous business of making black powder, then the mainstay of the company's product line. His duties and ten-hour days were the same as other yard workers. The only concession to his family status was a salary of $83 per month, more than double that of other beginning laborers.[4] There was one other major difference between Alfred's status and that of the other workingmen: he was a duPont, and everyone quite naturally took for granted that duPonts would rise in the company structure. His reputation as a black powder expert led the U.S. Navy to send him abroad in 1889 to study European powder-manufacturing techniques. His exploits in dramatically increasing powder production in the Spanish-American War firmly established him as one of the industry's major figures.

His technical accomplishments notwithstanding, Alfred made his principal claim to a lasting place in the annals of the duPont dynasty with his successful effort to prevent the sale of the company to outside interests. In 1902, the death of Eugene duPont, one of the family elders and then the company president, had plunged the corporation into a management crisis. The apparent successor declined the presidency, and one after another, the older family partners turned down the company leadership for various reasons. Unwilling to appoint Alfred to the company's highest position, the other partners considered selling the firm. Alfred made an audacious proposal that he be permitted to buy the company to keep it within the duPont family. With the participation of two of his cousins, T. Coleman duPont and Pierre Samuel duPont, both of whom were better versed in the ways of business than he was, a three-way partnership was put together to take effective ownership and control of the family business. The deal could not have been completed without Coleman and Pierre, but the fact remains that it was Alfred who conceived and launched the plan that preserved the family's legacy in the nation's oldest major industrial enterprise.

While the metamorphosis of the company was under way, Alfred continued to flaunt duPont social convention, enhancing his image of eccentricity within the family. He had undertaken his effort to preserve the family business while embroiled in domestic strife. In 1887, Alfred had married his distant cousin, Bessie Gardner, a practice not uncommon within the far-flung family. This union produced four children but was an unhappy affair almost from its beginning. Alfred's divorce from Bessie in 1905 was a major scandal for the family and a personal tragedy for him. It also precipitated an estrangement from three of his four children that was to last for many years—until a reconciliation was effected by his third wife, Jessie Ball.

Close on the heels of his divorce from Bessie, Alfred went public with his affair with Alicia Bradford, another of his cousins and eleven years his junior. They were married a week after his divorce from Bessie, adding to the family consternation over his treatment of his first wife and their children. This marriage was destined to be only marginally better than his first.

Although Alfred remained the head of production for the growing duPont company, his cousins Coleman and Pierre were the driving forces in its expansion. Gradually, Coleman's interests shifted over time to other pursuits, including politics and boom-time investments in Florida, and Pierre emerged as the primary leader of the corporation. Pierre is generally considered to be the primary builder of the modern duPont industrial organization. The relationship of Alfred and his two cousins deteriorated to the point of complete rupture, and his active role in the affairs of the family business was materially reduced. In 1915, Pierre bought out Coleman, and after a lengthy court battle with Alfred, emerged in complete control of the company. What remained of Alfred's gradually declining role in the firm's management came to an abrupt end. He continued to be a substantial stockholder, and that was the keystone of his personal wealth, but he was no longer active in the management of the family business.

Alfred's long and significant role in shaping the company's destiny was over.[5] His fight with Coleman and Pierre, neither of whom he ever forgave, and his unorthodox domestic life had combined to estrange him from the mainstream of the duPont family and the social life that went with it. Nevertheless, he was still a well-known and formidable personage in his own right.

During this period, the deafness that had plagued him for most of his adult life worsened, depriving him of the pleasures of music and participation in the band that he had formed with company employees. His hearing impediment was also beginning to affect normal conversation, a matter which in years to come would compel him to rely on those he trusted for assistance with his business affairs. Some years later, after his marriage to Jessie Ball, his affliction would be an important element in her urging that he bring her younger brother into their entourage as his "ears" and business confidant. According to her recollection some thirty years after the event, Alfred needed someone who could detect the inflections of voice that often infer honesty or dishonesty in the speaker. He agreed to use Ed in this role, noting that his brother-in-law had other good qualities that would make him a valuable assistant.[6]

Precluded from gainful employment within the company business by Pierre's actions, Alfred sought some endeavor worthy of his name and wealth. In the immediate aftermath of World War I, there were many adventurers looking about for profitable opportunities sure to arise in the vast rebuilding process that would put Europe right again. Most needed capital and a connection to gain admission to the circles of power where they could advance their schemes. Alfred I. duPont suited both particulars nicely. The idea of helping Europe rebuild fitted with Alfred's disposition to blend public purpose with profit. The result was the Nemours Trading Corporation, established in 1919 to consolidate two earlier import-export businesses that he had financed. Alfred left the management in the hands of the promoters who had induced him to back the affair, and it was monumentally mismanaged.[7] By 1920, the post-war recession had taken its toll as duPont stock plummeted when the world's appetite for munitions was temporarily abated. Alfred's net worth fell to somewhere in the neighborhood of $20 million, considerably less than the $400 million attributed to him by the *Los Angeles Examiner* on the occasion of his marriage to Jessie.[8] Still, his image was that of one of the very wealthy, and his name lent credence to the image.

The Nemours Trading Corporation proved to be a continuing drain on his resources. In 1920, he realized that he had to liquidate the operation, even if it meant substantial losses. He adamantly refused to consider bankruptcy, notwithstanding the considerable risk to his diminished fortune that this decision involved. There was something about repudiating honestly incurred debts that flew in the face of integrity for Alfred I. duPont.[9]

At this point, his fortunes became entwined with those of an old Virginia family, that of Captain Thomas Ball of Ball's Neck. Ball was a Confederate veteran and lawyer. The family was neither prominent nor wealthy, but it was to play a major role in defining Alfred I. duPont's final legacy to Florida.

The relationship between Alfred and the Ball family dated from the turn of the century. In 1898, he and two companions had gone on a hunting trip to Ball's Neck, a remote region of Virginia. For accommodations, they took rooms with a local family, the Hardings, who were neighbors and kinsmen to the Ball family. The condition of the two families might best be described as one of genteel impoverishment. In the course of his stay, Alfred became attached to them both. He enjoyed the unpretentiousness of the surroundings, the closeness and warmth of a genuine family relationship, and Captain Ball's embellished stories, especially those of his service with the Army of Northern Virginia under Robert E. Lee. At the time, Jessie Dew Ball was almost fifteen years of age, just three years older than Alfred's oldest daughter. Edward, the youngest Ball sibling, was ten years old. Thereafter, Alfred returned to Ball's Neck on periodic hunting trips. These visits from one of America's most important industrialists were major events for the community of Ball's Neck, and a lasting friendship developed between the Ball family and Alfred.[10]

Eventually, the Ball family relocated to California. Young Edward, along with his sisters, Isabel and Jessie, and his brother, Thomas, all left rural Virginia to find their fortunes in that growing state. Thereafter, occasional correspondence was the principal link in a continuing but distant relationship with Alfred.[11] Thomas was a lawyer, having received a loan from Alfred to complete his law degree at Washington and Lee University. Jessie obtained a teaching position in San Diego. Ed, who had dropped out of school at age thirteen, lived more by his wits in a variety of occupations, most of which focused on selling.

In the midst of the Nemours Trading Company debacle, Alfred had an unexpected and substantial tax liability from the stock dividend resulting from Pierre's taking control of the company. To further complicate his life, his marriage to Alicia, never one of equally reciprocated affection, was deteriorating. Although he had not seen Jessie Ball for fourteen years, their correspondence during this period evinced a growing mutual attraction, especially on Jessie's part. Alfred, undoubtedly influenced by the letters, made plans to take his stepdaughter, with whom he was close, on a trip to the West in the winter of 1920. He included in his plans a reunion with the Ball family, particularly Jessie. Alicia had made her own plans for a winter sojourn in South Carolina with two members of the duPont family with whom she had remained on good terms. When Alfred arrived in San Diego, and before he had seen Jessie, he received news that Alicia had suddenly taken ill and died on January 7 in Charleston.[12] His visit cut short, and without seeing Jessie, he rushed back to the East to attend to the details of his wife's funeral.

One year later, however, Alfred and Jessie were married in Los Angeles, with Ed Ball serving as best man. Alfred had found a ready-made, extended family to fill the void left by his estrangement from his own family, especially from his children. His third marriage provided emotional satisfaction for Alfred. As for the Balls, they were removed forevermore from the "genteel impoverishment" in which he had found them two decades earlier. Beyond that, there can be no doubt that Jessie greatly loved Alfred, a love which was reciprocated and continued undiminished until he died fourteen years later. As noted earler, Jessie was also the instrument by which Ed Ball came to figure prominently in Alfred's life. Ultimately, Ball's name merged with the duPont name in common reference to the "duPont-Ball" interests in Florida.[13] To comprehend how Ed Ball came to be the alter ego of Alfred I. duPont, it is necessary to understand the importance of Jessie Ball in both their lives.

When Alfred married Jessie in 1921, he was at the nadir of his business career. The animosity between him and his cousins who controlled the company isolated him from what he loved most: the family business. Efforts to extricate himself from the financial debacle of the Nemours Trading Corporation were complicated by his refusal to take refuge in bankruptcy. Creditors, convinced that a duPont would ultimately possess the means of full payment, refused to compromise his largest obligations. Meanwhile, the government was pressing for over $1.5 million in back taxes.[14] His 75,534 shares of duPont stock, which had been worth $25 million in April 1920, dropped to $9 million one year later in the general post-war market decline. Despite the realities of his financial situation, duPont never lacked for adventurers who urged on him all sorts of business schemes. Of course, they were all to be financed by him.[15] Without the support of a felicitous family life and almost paranoid about the family "gang" out to do him harm, Alfred was at loose ends. His new wife filled a void in his life, refreshing his perspective and purpose. It was against that background that Jessie advised her husband that he needed someone in whom he, or they, could have explicit faith and confidence. She was describing a person who would be bound to his interests by ties more durable than monetary compensation and opportunism. She was talking about the bonds of family, something that Alfred understood and had keenly missed in the circumstances preceding his marriage to Jessie.[16]

One of Jessie's cousins, Robert Harding, had prevailed on Alfred to finance a revolutionary tomato processing machine. Perfecting such a machine appealed to Alfred's mechanical nature. Without any clear assessment of its commercial feasibility or potential for development, he entered into the venture in 1922. A year later, the machine proved mechanically sound, and Alfred further financed the formation of the Clean Foods Products Company to commercialize it. It was at this point that Jessie urged Alfred to put her brother, Edward, in charge of the food company.

At the time, Ball and two partners were operating the office furniture division of the largest furniture dealer on the West Coast, and according to Ball, he was earning more than $18,000 a year. Ball agreed to take a year's leave of absence from his employers for a yearly salary of $5,000 as a start-up manager for Clean Foods. As it turned out, Ball did not see much of a future in the tomato processing machine. He calculated that only thirty-six of them could process all the tomatoes canned in the United States. Besides the early saturation of the market for the machines, there was another problem. There was no practical way to transport a sufficient number of tomatoes to make each machine efficient without suffering heavy spoilage in transit. Ball advised Alfred to liquidate the operation, and he did so.[17]

While engaged in the process of assessing the tomato venture and with the aid of Jessie, Ed acquired knowledge of Alfred's overall financial situation. There were still some major unliquidated debts remaining from Nemours Trading Corporation. According to his own account given to Marquis James, a duPont biographer, Ball determined to resolve the high interest rate on the remaining bank loan from George F. Baker's New York First National Bank. Baker was a major New York banker, and Ball had never dealt with so much as even a minor New York banker. Alfred probably felt his brother-in-law was overreaching, but with nothing to lose, he agreed to the idea. Going over the heads of bank underlings, Ball arranged a conference with Baker. As the representative of Alfred I. duPont, even an apparent upstart merited some consideration. Undaunted in such company, Ball explained to the financier the glowing prospects for Alfred's tomato processing business and how it was on the verge of great things. In the process, he came away with a renewed loan at 4 percent interest instead of the previous 7 percent.[18] It is not clear whether Ball had already determined to close down the food operation at that juncture. To the harassed Alfred, it was a significant achievement on the part of his young brother-in-law.

Ball next took on the problem of a $1.5-million claim of the White Shoe Company for shoes delivered to Nemours Trading Corporation, but which remained unsold and in storage. After two years of haggling with Alfred's attorneys, the company had refused to budge from its full claim. Once again, according to his own account, Ball reckoned the time propitious for the creditor company to be more reasonable. Perhaps the intrepid agent hinted at bankruptcy, as well as using the quite arguable defenses devised by Alfred's attorneys. After three negotiating sessions, White reduced its claim by more than two-thirds of its face amount, and Alfred eagerly accepted the compromise.[19]

Both of these episodes, which are based on Ball's own accounts, are in the two principal biographies of Alfred and in two short biographies of Ball. Allowing for embellishment, there is probably some truth to them—enough to help convince Alfred that in Ed Ball he had found the strong right arm he needed for his business affairs. Both episodes gained currency well before Jessie's death. If they were blatantly false, it is unlikely she would have tolerated without contradiction their place in her beloved husband's biographies.

While normalizing his business affairs, Alfred relied more and more on Jessie's younger brother. DuPont had the capacity to conceptualize a grand vision consisting of both profit and the public good. Ball, on the other hand, if provided with a vision and resources, could grasp the complex of details necessary to energize both into a dynamic enterprise. He was not completely without vision. He simply kept the vision of the moment in tandem with the realities and circumstances that governed its potential for realization. Ball was a strategist and a superb tactician, qualities complemented by his fearsome tenacity and unyielding combativeness.

In the early years of their marriage, Alfred and Jessie frequently wintered in south Florida, where the real estate boom was reaching its crescendo. It was not in Alfred's nature to engage in speculation, but he was fascinated by the spectacle that he observed. Even though his conservative nature told him that the wildly pyramided land values could not last, he was still attracted by Florida's long-term potential.

Jessie, though, did try her hand in the freewheeling real estate market of the time. She bought two lots on Miami Beach for $33,000 from her own funds, with the vague idea of building a home there. But Jessie was not given to whimsy. Possessed of an appreciation of money born of her straitened childhood circumstances, she was an astute businesswoman who knew her own mind. When it became clear shortly after the purchase that the frenetic pace of Miami was not to their liking, she sold the lots for more than five times their purchase price.[20]

The wildly erratic boom-time atmosphere of south Florida was not attractive to either Jessie or Alfred. They both had witnessed similar but less hectic conditions in California and were not awed by them.[21] More likely, the glitter and artificial nature of it all were an affront to Alfred's old-wealth sense of gentility and his conservative nature.

In addition, Coleman duPont, then a United States senator, was casting about in the ongoing speculation frenzy in south Florida. He had become involved in Addison Mizner's development in Boca Raton, as well as buying into a steamship business in southwest Florida.[22] If the overall atmosphere had not dampened Alfred's enthusiasm for the southern reaches of the state, Coleman's presence would have. Besides, Alfred believed those parts of Florida less affected by the boom-time atmosphere offered more promising long-term prospects. There was an additional factor: Alfred's altruism. The semi-impoverished rural areas of north Florida, especially the panhandle in west Florida, appealed to his sense of doing good in the pursuit of profit.

It was Alfred's preoccupation with tax matters that finally energized his decision to forsake Delaware and start life anew elsewhere. In 1924, the people of Florida had voted to amend the state's constitution to prohibit state income and inheritance taxes. Rapid growth had made the state's financial community acutely aware of the state's capital-starved economic conditions. Bankers seeking to establish a tax haven to attract the wealthy had spearheaded the campaign for passage of the amendment. Such a measure offered much to the state's banking and trust businesses. Florida was hailed as a "Taxpayer's Paradise," a much touted refuge for wealth away from the threat of state levies on income and inheritances.[23]

At the time, Alfred considered Delaware to be controlled by a "gang" of his political enemies, which included cousins Coleman and Pierre. Pierre had left the duPont company to take over the management of an ailing General Motors Corporation, and when he finished that task, he returned to Delaware temporarily unengaged. He took the position of Delaware tax commissioner as a public service, with the avowed purpose of tightening the state's income tax laws in 1925. Proceeds from that tax were earmarked exclusively for Pierre's favorite cause, state education. One duPont family historian says

Alfred had not paid any income tax for the years 1920 through 1926, inferring that such a situation would have been subject to inquiry by Pierre in his role as tax commissioner.[24] The implication is clear that Alfred did not want his enemy, Pierre, in a position to delve into his personal financial affairs.[25] Although there is no evidence to suggest that Pierre improperly used his position, both of Alfred's principal biographers say it sparked his decision to move to Florida.[26]

It is ironic that Alfred's decision should have been influenced by Florida's low-tax climate since he had once championed higher taxes in his native state as part of a reform movement. To put this important decision in perspective, it had far more to do with the deep-seated animosity between himself and his two cousins, Coleman and Pierre, than with any principles of equitable taxation. Still, the Florida constitutional provision must have been most attractive to him, and its preservation became one of his continuing political priorities. Protecting that particular provision of the state constitution became firmly fixed in a larger mind-set of avoiding governmental interference with business and property rights.

Ed Ball inherited this mind-set from duPont. Opposing, avoiding, minimizing, and evading taxes whenever possible became a permanent part of Ball's political agenda. Shortly before Alfred's death, Ball advised him of efforts in the 1935 legislature to repeal the prohibition against income taxes because of the state's continuing financial crisis. Ball then produced Hollywood movie executives to testify before the Florida legislature that they were considering leaving California if that state adopted an income tax.[27] Such tactics were used then, and in the future, to evoke fears of job losses and business decline. Some forty years later, Ball employed similar, but unsuccessful, tactics to prevent the imposition of a corporate income tax by the Florida legislature after a vote of the people had removed the constitutional barrier to it. Ed Ball's continuing resistance to income and inheritance taxes flavored his entire outlook. It was rooted in Alfred I. duPont's decision to leave Delaware to come to Florida, and that decision was what brought Ed Ball to Florida. In later years, Ball's implacable opposition to income taxes and all they stood for contributed to his contempt for Franklin Roosevelt's New Deal and its foremost Florida champion, Claude Pepper.

Pepper came to Florida by a decidedly different route than that traveled by Ball. He came alone, armed only with a degree from Harvard Law School and a job offer in a small country law practice in rural Taylor County.

3

Claude Pepper

Origins of a Politician

In the decades following the Civil War, life in the rural South was defined by two interactive dimensions: an agricultural economy and class stratification. The latter was predicated on economic status and polarized along racial lines. Whites of all classes were bound together by homage to the memory of the Lost Cause and the rule of white supremacy. Although vestiges of antebellum cotton prosperity lingered here and there and a middle class of sorts was taking shape in the cities and towns, most rural southerners existed at or near a subsistence level, with black southerners faring the worst of the lot.

A variety of factors coalesced to perpetuate these conditions. The stagnating effect of a rigid class system was compounded by the divisiveness of an iron-clad code of racial segregation. White and black southerners lived in separate worlds, precluding any attempts by the poor of both races to take combined political or economic action. The one-party political system that emerged after Reconstruction drew its strength from strict obeisance to the rule of white supremacy. The system afforded rural whites a higher social standing in return for a compliant acceptance of their marginal economic status. Even so, there was an incipient awareness that the economic conditions that circumscribed their lives were governed by forces far removed from their day-to-day reality. As this realization became better defined, it spawned a collective antipathy for the financial and monopoly interests (primarily railroads) headquartered in distant northern cities. Railroads and banks, both indispensable to the rural agricultural economy, became the focus of political reform efforts. These sentiments eventually gave rise to an agrarian self-help movement that found its earliest articulate expression in the Farmers Alliance during the Gilded Age.

The Alliance professed to be nonpolitical, even though it was heavily involved in the early efforts to mitigate through regulation the powers of the giant rail trusts. It remained for additional streams of rural discontent to converge before the agrarian movement coalesced under the larger and clearly political banner of Populism. It expanded to embrace not only the cause of farmers who owned their land but also the needs of those lower in the existing order of things: tenant farmers, sharecroppers, and others dependent on the land's yield but without the dignity of ownership status.

Around the same time that rural discontent was coalescing in Populism, there was a separate movement growing from urban economic discord grounded in the natural tensions between labor and capital. In the Northeast and West, miners, textile workers, and industrial workers aligned themselves to confront the forces that sustained the oppressive conditions in which they existed. Like the agrarians, those in the labor movement were acutely aware of class distinctions in American society and opposed the concentration of economic power. Yet the two movements had different objectives that could not be easily reconciled into a unified political force. Monopolies, banks, and monetary policies governing circulation of currency and credit, the lifeblood of the small farmer, were the focal points of agrarian grievances. Wages, the right to unionize, industrial working conditions, job security, and substandard living conditions in the cities were the stuff of labor discontent.

By the early 1900s, the two movements, both born of social and economic discontent, were on the wane. They had lost their momentum to a new dynamic in national politics. A robust America, reaching toward increasing prosperity at home and the lure of empire abroad, was distracted from the needs for domestic reform. The energies of the rural reform and labor movements were not extinguished, but rather caught up in the broader mosaic of the Progressive movement. In turn, the reform dynamics of that movement were overtaken and engulfed by the headlong rush to riches in the Roaring Twenties. Still, in the South, the politics of agrarianism etched an indelible impression into the region's political psyche, leaving a legacy of unrequited discontent rooted in the harsh realities of the existing order of rural life. It was into that political legacy, on the threshold of a new century, that Claude Denson Pepper was born in 1900.

As the era that Henry Luce called the "American Century" came to life, the national political spectrum was expanding to embrace a growing reform agenda.[1] Reflecting the immigrant explosion and the growing impact of industrialization on cities, the emerging movement of Progressivism had a pronounced urban hue about it. Between 1900 and 1920, Progressivism came to the fore in American politics, melding a mix of social and economic issues from the Populist and labor movements into its overarching reform dimension. The tumultuous years and good times of the Roaring Twenties masked the lingering reform movement until the abrupt termination of prosperity in 1929 ushered in the miseries of the Great Depression. Economic disaster beyond anything previously known to Americans soon became the focus of the nation's political agenda, and the noble rubric of a reemergent Progressivism was subsumed in Franklin Delano Roosevelt's New Deal. The scope of the nation's misfortune was so great that it defied incremental improvement. No one, including the newly elected president, knew with certainty what to prescribe for the ailing body politic. Whatever it was to be, however, would have to be far reaching and radical.

As the New Deal unfolded, a young U.S. senator elected from Florida in 1936, but with roots in Alabama's rich legacy of Populism, became totally committed to its full sway of liberal reform. Claude Pepper remained a New Dealer for the next sixty years and, if not the first New Dealer, may be justly said to have been the last.

Support for and opposition to the New Deal set the parameters of domestic politics in America for the middle years of the twentieth century, and well beyond. A strain of class consciousness, always a part of the American political scene, was further embedded into the distinction between liberalism and conservatism in America during this period. Class division did not define American politics in the twentieth century, but it was a recurring source of friction, always near the surface of political reality. As the century passed beyond the midway mark, the political spectrum became much more complicated. Issues of racial equality, gender equality, and environmentalism were pressed into the mosaic of American political thought. These transcended the economic focus that earlier had inflamed the dimension of class division. Against this expanded domestic agenda, America's position in international Cold War politics provided a separate and dangerous flow of activity.

This book focuses on the conflicts between two men—Claude Pepper and Ed Ball—who simultaneously pursued differing objectives through a common political medium. Their continuing conflict was played out against a panorama of state, national, and international issues confronting America at the midpoint of the twentieth century. Such clashes of individual interests, always a subset of the larger political picture, generally remain undifferentiated background noise within the larger scheme of things. Seldom at the fulcrum of decision making on the major issues, they are carried to and fro by the eddies and countercurrents of the political mainstream, only infrequently as part of the history of the period of their passing. To place Pepper and Ball in a common context, it is helpful to understand the dichotomy of their respective purposes in terms of the parameters that circumscribed liberal and conservative politics of their period.

Liberals framed issues in a context of collectivized social justice. Their central purpose was a more equitable distribution of the nation's wealth. Their nemesis was the concentrations of wealth that skewed the balance between the "haves" and the "have-nots" and the individuals who controlled and manipulated that wealth. To achieve their goal, they advocated redistribution of democracy's bounty through the agency of government intervention. The conservative perspective embraced the means of production and creation of wealth by nurturing a symbiotic relationship between the two, hinged on individual effort and creativity. Its philosophical linchpin was a body of rights grounded in property ownership. A productive economy, nourished by free marketplaces and energized by capitalism, was its uplifting mechanism for society as a whole. This perspective was haunted by the specter of individual initiative crushed by the political force of class strife, or worse, class warfare. In the conservative *weltanschauung*, distribution of democracy's bounty was better left to Adam Smith's invisible hand in the marketplace, with aid given by government to the forces of production when necessary.

In addition to the liberal-conservative dichotomy, the political-economic theories of Karl Marx worked their way into the rhetoric of domestic politics in the final decades of the nineteenth century. In the 1920s, as the nation trod gingerly around its newfound status as a world power, questioning and unsure about the responsibilities that went with it, Marxism and socialism came to be seen by most (not all) Americans as distinct threats to the democratic capitalism that shaped their nation. The onset of the Cold War exacerbated the impact of Marxism on American politics and played a crucial part in the phase of the Pepper-Ball relationship that centered on the Florida senate race of 1950.

It was within this environment of conflicting streams of thought that Ed Ball and Claude Pepper used politics for their own purposes. Their paths crossed at the day-to-day, working levels of domestic politics, and their philosophies and experiences—especially their bitter conflicts with each other—are a microcosm of the political scene during the last half of the American Century.

When an emergent Progressive movement banked the fires of Populism shortly before the turn of the century, conditions in the rural South were only marginally better than they had been in the past. Although the promises to better the terms of life through collective action were not fulfilled, they fostered a mind-set in rural southerners that outlived the region's Populist movement. It fostered a realization—sometimes dormant but never completely extinguished—that the faceless concentrations of economic power dictating conditions of life from afar could be balanced only through the machinery of government. Such was the political heritage of Claude Denson Pepper, who was born at the turn of the century in Chambers County, in north-central Alabama. This agrarian legacy melded readily with a far more encompassing philosophy of government thirty-two years later when an aristocratic and charismatic New York governor was sent to Washington to make good on his promise of a New Deal. During the intervening years circumstances, fate, and self-initiative had prepared an Alabama country boy to be a willing instrument in the national metamorphosis born of that promise.

Claude was the oldest surviving child of Joseph Wheeler Pepper and Lena Talbot Pepper. The Peppers were both of southern lineage but without any trappings of wealth or prestige. Their first family home was in Dudleyville, where Claude was born. Later, they moved to Texas, where Joseph hoped to better the family's lot by farming on more fertile land. His efforts proved unsuccessful, and the family returned to Chambers County.

According to Pepper's recollection, it was in Texas that his oratorical talents first came to light. Many years later, Texas congressman Bob Poage told him of a constituent who remembered giving the precocious five-year-old Pepper pennies for his storytelling performances at the local post office.[2]

Claude's memories of childhood are of difficult but generally happy circumstances. The family, though clearly poor, was not completely poverty stricken. Growing up in Chambers County, young Claude probably thought that conditions there were the norm. He did not recognize how poor his family and neighbors actually were until he went off to college, where he observed other, more privileged lifestyles.

His mother, but not his father, displayed evidence of a formal education. Claude later ascribed the equivalent of a "junior college" education to both of them.[3] This was possible in Lena's case, even though it was rare for a woman of her circumstances in rural Alabama to receive a formal post-secondary education. It is doubtful that Joseph Wheeler achieved that level of formal education. In Joseph Guttman's doctoral dissertation on the early years of Pepper's career, on which this account of Pepper's childhood and family life is based, Guttman observes that Lena Pepper's early correspondence showed "complex sentence and paragraph structure, and her spelling and grammar are almost flawless."[4] The correspondence of his father reflected no such refinement and was "simple and crude in usage and structure." Guttman also notes that in 1910, the U.S. Census showed only 13.2 percent of white males above twenty-one years of age in Tallapoosa County (where the Peppers settled on their return from Texas) were literate.[5] Notwithstanding his surroundings, it is clear Claude Pepper's intellect was not suppressed by an illiterate home environment.

4. The birthplace of Claude Pepper in Dudleyville, Alabama.

Regardless of whether they had a formal education, his parents created a warm family environment and encouraged Claude to educate himself into better circumstances. The closeness of the Pepper family, and the love, respect, and care that he received from it—and returned to it—were important elements in his life. His desire for education was always nurtured by his parents, with whom he maintained a close and loving relationship.[6] Later, when Claude achieved success practicing law in Tallahassee, Florida, he moved his parents there and provided for them during the remainder of their lives.

Most accounts attribute the Peppers' move to Camp Hill, Alabama, in 1910 to Joseph and Lena's desire to further their ten-year-old son's educational opportunities. Camp Hill had a grade school through the twelfth grade, which Claude attended, and he later credited his success there to the principal, C. C. Mosley.[7] Claude was associate editor of the school newspaper, a member of the debating team, and senior class president. According to a classmate, Claude and his friend Oscar Chester were the "local intellectuals."[8]

Apparently, Claude also indulged in his share of juvenile mischief during his school days. He set the boys' outhouse on fire, destroying it in the dead of winter. It was a serious matter in a rural school with only minimal accommodations.[9] The gravity of this offense is best understood by those who have suffered the use of an outhouse in the winter and can appreciate the greater tragedy of not having one at all.

Other than the brief Texas episode, Claude's childhood was a product of the small town of Dudleyville and the relatively larger Camp Hill (population 1,500), both typical of rural north Alabama. As Pepper assumed national stature, stories of his childhood naturally became somewhat embellished, but certain aspects of his personality were apparent at an early age: he had a fixation on education, and his outgoing nature was blended with a warmth and freely extended camaraderie that held a natural appeal for people. When combined with his unquestionable oratorical abilities, these qualities became strong political assets. Notwithstanding a pervasive cynicism that now attributes favorable personality traits in politicians to contrived opportunism, it is hard to escape the feeling that in Claude, this side of his character was more sincere than opportunistic. This combination often gave him an aura of persuasiveness even when his positions ran counter to the prevailing views of his audiences.[10] Still, as his focus later became increasingly global and he distanced himself from the inherent conservatism of his Florida constituency, Pepper tended to overestimate the beguiling effects of his personality and oratory.[11]

At the age of fifteen, Claude had his first—and last—experience as an entrepreneur. He encountered an itinerant hat presser, a person who went from town to town pressing and blocking hats. The man, claiming to be a graduate of Columbia University, was a good talker. He impressed Claude, and the teenager decided that the travel and excitement of the hat-pressing business was for him. After outfitting himself, Claude took to the road. The first night, he shared a room with a distressed man who walked the floor all night. The next day, the young entrepreneur learned the man had murdered his wife two nights earlier. It was not a good beginning for the traveling career of the intrepid teenager. After a short time, it was evident that the hat-pressing business did not suit him. He had to pay for a hat that was ruined, almost eliminating his small accumulation of profit. Claude decided it was time to abandon the world of business and returned home. He had never gotten beyond the confines of Alabama.[12] (That same year, 1915, Ed Ball was working as a salesman in California, apparently with somewhat more aptitude for that line of work than Claude Pepper had shown.) Although the young Alabama country boy may not have been cut from an entrepreneurial mold, all the evidence indicates he accepted hard work as a natural ingredient of life.

Political ambition was the most visible trait Claude carried forward from childhood. He recognized this in himself at an early age. Most versions of his biography include the story that he carved his name as "Claude Pepper, U.S. Senator" on a tree. Pepper remembered it as being on the door of the justice of the peace's office; one boyhood friend said it was carved on the door of the outhouse that Claude set afire. Still another version had it carved on a tree.[13] In any event, the inscription was probably carved by Claude somewhere in Camp Hill, and it did indeed symbolize his undying ambition to be in the U.S. Senate. That ambition was eventually realized, and it persisted long after he lost his Senate seat. To grasp the full flavor of that ambition, it should be viewed in the context of the place and time that spawned it.

The Populist legacy that flavored Pepper's early surroundings was the source of his deep and lasting liberalism. He never sacrificed that credo to the expediencies of ambition, although it was sorely strained by his early support of traditional southern racism. Experiences embedded in his memory from early childhood may well have shaped his later political rhetoric with references to class divisiveness.

One such episode involved the "doctors' trust" in nearby Alexander City. When the people of Tallapoosa County needed medical care, they sought it from doctors in that town. Because there were many delinquent accounts, the doctors banded together, agreeing not to treat anyone who was in arrears to another of the trust's members. Notwithstanding an implicit understand-

ing of the need for doctors to be paid, such a collectively enforced depriva-
tion of a necessity of life became something of a cause célèbre and illustrated
the daily vicissitudes of life fashioned by pervasive economic privation.
Later, while at law school, Pepper observed how the Boston medical establishment had stopped a foreign doctor who was a visiting professor at Harvard Medical School from operating a free clinic for the city's needy. In
Claude's view, the doctors had acted from greed. In contrast, he was impressed with the availability of inexpensive cooperative medical care at
Harvard and appreciated the medical treatment he received from army
doctors.[14] Episodes such as these nurtured an awareness of class distinctions
born of the power of one group over another. This awareness undoubtedly
influenced his early commitment to a national health program.

The inequities of single-crop agriculture, with its legacy of the pernicious
crop-lien, made an indelible impression on Claude when he observed them
as a child. Cotton was the money crop, the only acceptable security for the
indispensable credit that sustained the small farmer. As a result, concentration on a single crop almost always produced an oversupply and low prices.
Later, his remembrance of it clearly reflected a populist appreciation of its
effect on his father. As he remembered: "Often, I would ride with my father
on a wagon, carrying three bales of cotton, [to] . . . the town square, on three
corners of which were buyers to offer him what they would. Nobody asked
the farmers how much it cost to grow the crop, nor did anyone care about
the 12 percent interest they had to pay on the money they borrowed."[15] The
tenor of his recollection clearly reflects how his childhood experiences carried forward elements of populist thinking into his mature political philosophy. The indifferent buyers and the bankers who charged 12 percent interest
hid behind an anonymity appropriate to membership in an oppressor class.
(Later, he saw Ed Ball as the personification of this class.) His father's repeated failures at business undoubtedly heightened Pepper's awareness of
the frustrations inherent in the lifestyle of the rural poor.[16] The experiences
and memories from his childhood helped make him an ardent and unyielding New Dealer, who believed that the machinery of government could
impose a minimum of balance for the obvious inequities that existed all
around him.[17]

When Claude finished high school, he wanted to attend the University of
Alabama, the traditional training ground for aspiring politicians in the state,
but he was unable to finance his education. So he settled for a job teaching
school in Dothan. The experience of several manual labor jobs the following

summer heightened his desire to attend the university. He got a loan from the president of the bank in Camp Hill to start his college career. Pepper's memory of E. L. Andrews, the banker who aided him, is much warmer in tone than his recollection of the nameless lenders who did not care about the "12 percent interest [the farmers] had to pay" on the crop loans. With this meager financial base, he left for the university in Tuscaloosa. Shortly after his arrival on campus, he got a job "rolling coal" from 4 to 7 A.M. in the university's boiler room. One of his coworkers was the future Alabama senator John Sparkman.[18]

Pepper thrived in the broader intellectual and social climate at the university. Although he was constrained by his financial circumstances and the need to work, his indomitable optimism and extroverted nature provided him with a full campus life. He became a member of the freshmen class's executive committee, joined several debating societies, and was on the university debating team. Later, he was vice president and then president of the Mid-West Conference of College and University Students. This was Pepper's first adult experience in swaying strangers with his oratorical powers, making him even more determined to enter politics.[19] Although his major field of study was education, his main interests were history, literature, and biography, and he selected courses that catered to those interests. He also took public-speaking courses and was awarded membership in Phi Beta Kappa at graduation.[20] Despite the need to work and his extracurricular activities, Pepper managed to graduate in three years. All in all, his undergraduate record was impressive.

One far-reaching consequence of Pepper's undergraduate days was his brief experience with the U.S. Army. When he arrived on campus in September 1918, the country was in a fully mobilized state of war, with the selective service combing the ranks of the nation's young manhood for the European battlefields. The military did not wish to deplete its supply of junior officers by inducting college students into the enlisted ranks. To avoid the implications of preferential treatment associated with outright exemption, the army simply took over the campuses, drafting all eligible students into the Student Army Training Corps. Claude was inducted in October of his freshman year, and the war ended in November. The Student Army Training Corps was disbanded, but Claude opted to remain in the Reserve Officer Training Corps.

Later, during a summer training encampment, he received a hernia while lifting ammunition boxes. Here fate took a defining hand. Technically, he had suffered a disability while on active duty and was eligible for rehabilitation grants from the government. Claude was elated to learn that his "rehabilitation" entitlement included tuition and expenses at Harvard University Law School. In addition, he received extensive medical care from government doctors.[21] Compared to the medical care in the rural surroundings of his youth—which was both expensive and hard to come by—the army medical care he received made a lasting and favorable impression on him. It could well have made him aware of the possibility of delivering health care on terms other than those dictated exclusively by the medical establishment.

While the University of Alabama had expanded Pepper's horizons, Harvard was even more stimulating for the Alabama country boy. The dean of the law school was the legendary Roscoe Pound. Felix Frankfurter, who achieved fame as a principal member of the Roosevelt "brain trust" and later as an appointee to the Supreme Court, was another of the faculty to achieve distinction. As Pepper later recollected: "Harvard had a profound impact on me. It opened my eyes to a great nation beyond the South; to me it was an entirely new world."[22]

As at the University of Alabama, Claude lived on the brink of privation at Harvard, getting by on the small allowance provided by his army "disability" program and occasional loans. Even so, he threw himself into the law school program with all his usual enthusiasm. He became president of the Beale Law Club, the equivalent of a legal fraternity, and graduated in the top third of his class. He further honed his impressive oratorical skills and was runner-up in the prestigious Ames Moot Court competition. According to his law school diary, the faculty judges had awarded him first place, but Dean Roscoe Pound prevailed on them to reverse themselves and make the award to his opponent.[23] Pepper's law school record was one of determination and accomplishment. It gave promise of a bright future.

After graduation, Claude was invited to be the second member of a two-person faculty at the new University of Arkansas law school. Such was the reputation of Harvard Law School that the new law school dean, the only other faculty member, would consider none other than a Harvard law graduate. Pepper also had prospects with a prestigious Birmingham law firm with large corporate clients, including power companies. He had an encounter with the Alabama governor, then in Boston on state bond business, who advised that such an association would be detrimental to his political aspirations. Claude's populist instincts told him the governor was right, and he accepted the Arkansas law school position.[24]

While at the University of Arkansas, he formed relationships with stu-

dents that combined friendship (there was only a slight age difference between Pepper and students) and professorial concern. In one instance, he
helped a student, Donald Trumbo, to reconcile with his father, who had
disapproved of the youth's marriage. In the process, Claude impressed the
father, who had interests in real estate developments in west-central Florida,
including Taylor County.

In the summer of 1925, the elder Trumbo asked the professor to accom-
pany his son to Chicago to represent him in a corporate reorganization
meeting of the Florida land company in which he owned an interest. Pepper
did so, and while in Chicago, met W. B. Davis, a Florida attorney who
handled the company's business in Taylor County. The Florida Boom was at
its crest, and Davis, apparently anticipating an increased volume of legal
business, asked Pepper to join him in his law practice in Perry. Pepper made
the fateful decision to accept this offer.

According to Joseph Guttman's research, Pepper had been rejected in a
Fayetteville love affair during this period. Always self-conscious about his
homely looks and relationship with women, he may have felt humiliated in
the matter.[25] Now, for the first time, Pepper was earning a reasonable income, and options were opening that could eventually lead to the political
career that he coveted. In light of these circumstances, it might have been
unrequited love that prompted him to cast aside teaching law for the unknown prospects of a small town in Taylor County, Florida. That, and the
high hopes generated by the excitement of the Florida Boom, may have
influenced his decision. Although the boom had hardly touched Taylor
County and the surrounding region, there was an almost magical allure to
the name Florida. Pepper made only a passing reference to love as a factor
in the decision in his memoirs: "Although I fell mildly in love with a daughter
of President Futrell [president of the University of Arkansas], my feelings
were unrequited. And the closest I came to Arkansas politics was to teach a
law student named J. William Fullbright."[26] Whatever the reason, or reasons, for quitting Arkansas for Florida, Pepper never looked back.

By the time he arrived in Florida, his political personality and philosophy
had taken their final form. The rural poverty that he had seen all about him
while growing up, his father's constant struggle to provide for the family, and
his education at the University of Alabama and Harvard had provided an
eclectic mixture of influences.

If political ambition was his dominant motivational characteristic, his
Harvard phase does not seem to fit the traditional southern mold. Why

FLORIDA
COLLECTION

would Pepper choose the distant setting of Harvard over the much more politically oriented University of Alabama law school? At Alabama, he would have been immersed in the same tradition that groomed his old boiler room comrade, John Sparkman, and, at one time or another, such Alabama senators-in-waiting as Lister Hill and Hugo Black. Still, his choice of Harvard was well suited to the expanded political ambitions that he subsequently embraced. There was no question about Harvard's academic prestige. Moreover, Claude's undergraduate experience at a large state university had made him aware of the realities and constrictions inherent in the social stratification that he experienced while a student. He understood the lowly position from which he aspired to political position and recognition, and must have appreciated the value of a famous law school in that quest.

The perception of intellectual and cultural refinement associated with a Harvard law degree would help compensate for his lack of family prominence, wealth, and connections. In addition, he must have recognized that both the substance and trappings of a recognizably broad intellectual base would enhance the effectiveness of his foremost natural talent, his oratorical ability. That dimension alone would have been a powerful attraction to him. The challenge of becoming a Harvard lawyer must have appeared as a decided advantage, especially if one looked beyond the confines of state politics. He would have known that opportunities for prestige and power attached to the Harvard mystique much more readily than to state schools. He may have vaguely comprehended that advantages of friendships developed there had the potential to span horizons beyond state or region.[27]

One such friendship with Harvard origins that ripened into a lifetime political alliance was that with Tommy "The Cork" Corcoran, a powerful member of Roosevelt's New Deal brain trust.[28] In the mid-1930s, Corcoran was one of the Frankfurter protégés prominent in the cadre of young lawyers who drafted most of the reform legislation that was the legal legacy of the New Deal. He was also the principal administration lobbyist, responsible for persuading increasingly reluctant congressmen to endorse Roosevelt's proposed legislation. The president's ill-fated plan to enlarge the Supreme Court and pack it with appointees favorable to his New Deal became a litmus test of loyalty to the administration. Shortly after Pepper's arrival in Washington in 1936 as a newly elected senator, Corcoran worked diligently to persuade the uncertain freshman to support Roosevelt's bill.[29] It marked the beginning of Claude's active participation in shaping the New Deal and an enduring political relationship developed between these two Harvard lawyers based on their shared liberal convictions. When Corcoran subsequently became one of Washington's premier lobbyists and influence brokers, their relationship continued. In the time-honored style of Washington life, Corcoran continued to aid Pepper with campaign contributions from wealthy and powerful clients such as Boston millionaire Lincoln Filene and United Fruit Company president Samuel Zemurry. When labor troubles erupted in Guatemala in the late 1940s, Pepper lent a sympathetic ear to Corcoran's representation of United Fruit's efforts to deal with the situation.[30] Lasting relationships such as these, which reach high into the nation's power structure, are often hallmarks of the prestigious eastern law schools, especially Harvard.

Pepper's decision to study law at Harvard rather than at the University of Alabama was, according to Guttman, one of only two nonpolitical decisions in his life. The other was his decision to move to Florida.[31] As far as Guttman's first claim is concerned, it implies that Pepper's vision did not reach beyond the pale of Alabama politics, so that considerations that drew him away from his native state must have been apolitical.

That was not the case. Pepper's political ambitions were not rooted to a particular constituency or locale. They were a manifestation of desire for political power as an end unto itself, and the cause of liberalism became his overriding purpose for the exercise of that power. In that mind-set, service to a constituency was the price one paid to pursue the larger objective. Pepper's political judgment was always governed more by ideological first principles than by viewpoints emanating from his constituency. Later in his career, he showed an awareness of this decoupling of his philosophical purpose from the concerns of increasing numbers of Floridians. Well before his defeat in 1950, he considered moving to either New York or California, states where he thought his liberalism would be an asset in, instead of an impediment to, his quest for higher office. Alluding to the conservatism of Florida voters, he wrote in his diary, "If I aspire to higher office, is that possible from Florida?"[32] Clearly, his political ambitions were never rigidly constrained by the views of the people of Alabama or his adopted state, Florida. They were grounded first in the cause of liberalism. In his mind, the greater public good flowed from that commitment.

Although Pepper was superb at what is known as "constituent work," it was most often left for his staff to deal with the minutiae of daily detail imposed by the scope of his senatorial duties.[33] His focus remained fixed on the more visionary goals of a liberal, egalitarian society. He recorded in his diary the blandishments that came his way to pay less attention to local issues and assume the liberal leadership of the Senate, and by implication, the nation. In later years, former presidential candidate James M. Cox was one who urged such a course on him. Pepper recorded him as saying, "Now was [my] time to take liberal leadership in the country—not to bother too much about local problems in Florida, but to concentrate on the national" issues.[34] Throughout his senatorial career, it was always a close question whether Claude could mold his electoral persona to the attitudes and views of his constituency. His impressive victories in 1938 and 1944 clearly demonstrated that he could when it did not conflict with his ideological first principles. In 1938, he was safely enveloped in the positive sentiment still existing for the New Deal. In 1944, that sentiment continued, and his early call to arms against Adolf Hitler's Third Reich resonated well with the voting public to maintain his favorable image. Later, when the public no longer embraced liberalism so tightly, Pepper held fast, clinging to his convictions.[35] His focus was always on the collective dimension of the ideal liberal paradigm, which he earnestly desired to create. In time, his purpose in that context overran the collective thinking of the persons for whom he intended it. Whatever were Claude Pepper's faults, lack of steadfastness in his ideological conviction was not one of them.

The intellectual processes at Harvard refined the deep-seated strains of agrarian discontent, the Populist legacy of his rural Alabama childhood, into a vibrant liberalism. Though Harvard was not a monolith of liberal sociopolitical thought, the intellectual ambience of the place nurtured a receptivity to ideological development in its overall molding process.[36] When he went to the Senate a dozen years later, his liberalism came to full bloom. It became his common bond with New Dealers such as Corcoran, Benjamin Cohen, and others of the famed Roosevelt brain trust.

When Claude Pepper arrived in Perry in the summer of 1925, his political credo was in place, awaiting only a process of refinement through public expression in the political marketplace. His sudden departure from Fayetteville delayed the start of that process, but not for long. Within three years, Claude was elected to the state legislature from Taylor County.

The Perry interlude of Pepper's overall career was an important point between desire and fulfillment in the spectrum of his ambitions. Perry was (and is) the county seat of Taylor County, located fifty miles southeast of Tallahassee. In 1925, the town had a population of 2,479. Slightly less than half of the total county population of 13,113 was African-American. His frequent correspondence with his mother portrayed a cheerful and promising town. He advised her that he expected to make $10,000 a year within five years, a handsome sum for a country lawyer.[37] Still, it was an unsophisticated place for one only recently removed from the intellectual environment of Harvard. There were eleven Taylor County students enrolled in the two state colleges. Nine of them were females.[38] Virtually the entire population was dependent, in one fashion or another, on agriculture. That Pepper could impress his new community to the point of sending him to Tallahassee only three years after his arrival speaks well for the refinement of his political instincts as well as his natural gregariousness.

The 1925 Official Road Map of Florida reflected the area's rural isolation. There were surfaced road connections only with Mayo and Madison in the adjoining counties to the east and north. A surfaced road ran south some twenty-five miles but did not extend as far as Cross City, the next comparable town to the south. There was no surfaced road in the direct route westward to Tallahassee. Even so, transportation was marginally better than in the coastal counties south and west of Tallahassee. The automobile represented release from the constraints of such remoteness, and roads were the sine qua non of regional development and a brighter future. The issues involved in planning, financing, and constructing the state highway system were always in or near the mainstream of state politics. Road building was by far the largest item of expenditure in the state budget. It was especially important in local politics, where the isolation of rural living was a constant reminder of the promises inherent in the building of roads.

During the same period, Alfred I. duPont was establishing Jacksonville as the base for his fledgling Florida operations. Ed Ball had moved to that city from Delaware, and as duPont's agent for land purchases, was making himself known in real estate circles across north Florida. With ready cash to buy large tracts of all but inaccessible west Florida acreage, he was a popular figure in Panhandle real estate circles.[39] Not yet generally known as a Floridian, the former furniture salesman was introduced as a businessman of Wilmington, Delaware. Soon the name duPont and his land-buying deputy and their gospel of new roads were all but synonymous with brightened prospects for the barren west Florida region that the boom had mostly passed by.[40] Taylor County was not in the pattern of the duPont land acquisition program, but the Gulf Coast Highway promoted by the duPont organization included Taylor County, as well as its northerly and southerly neighbors. Ball and his colleague W. T. Edwards, another of the duPont entourage from Delaware, worked in the political circles of those counties urging completion of a coastal highway from Tampa to Pensacola. Their efforts were well known in the region and beyond. Firms from as far away as New York solicited duPont for bridge and road construction work.[41]

As a politically aware country lawyer, Pepper knew about the duPont-sponsored Gulf Coast Highway and about his land-purchasing activities farther west in the Panhandle. News of cash purchases on the scale of those made by Ball spread rapidly through the depressed regions of northwest Florida.

Within less than a year of Pepper's arrival in Perry, the boom was over, having largely bypassed most of rural north Florida. The expectations of legal business from land development in Florida failed to materialize, and Pepper settled into the mundane routine of earning a livelihood as a country lawyer in a depressed rural county. He demonstrated exceptional talents in two areas that would be important for his future. His intellect, legal skill, and rhetorical ability combined with his natural affability to make Pepper more than just a good country lawyer. Throughout his career, in and out of public office, he enjoyed a reputation as an excellent trial attorney.[42] Second, in Pepper's first and only term in the Florida legislature, he displayed a natural flair for political combat capable of sustaining the full reach of his ambitions.

Pepper's legal abilities first gained widespread notice in a notorious murder case. A white "moonshiner" had killed two revenue agents, one of whom had been shot in the back while attempting to flee the enraged moonshiner. Gunning down two lawmen did not leave many avenues of justification, and shooting one of them in the back seriously diminished the effectiveness of whatever mitigation remained to the defense. Even so, Davis and Pepper were able to salvage a recommendation for mercy with the initial guilty verdict, thus sparing their client the electric chair. It was an era when swift execution under such circumstances was a near certainty.

Still, when the defendant was offered a plea bargain of life imprisonment on the remaining murder count if he would forgo an appeal of his first conviction, he insisted on both the appeal and a trial on the second count, which involved the back-shooting of the officer trying to flee for his life. Having refused the plea bargain, he was predictably convicted and sentenced to death in the second trial. Pepper, by then the sole defense counsel, managed to thwart execution of the death sentence by cleverly invoking a series of technicalities.

Years later, when Pepper was in the U.S. Senate, this client, still lingering on death row, wrote him. He advised his former lawyer that he was sixty-five years old and inquired if he was eligible for an old-age pension.[43] Perhaps an extreme case of the expectations born of the New Deal, it was nevertheless illustrative of what would in a later generation be known as the entitlement mentality. Only vaguely discernible in the far different context of the depression, the issue of entitlements was to be an important element in Pepper's political success. Of course, there is no indication that Pepper took the inquiry seriously. His recall of the episode was nothing more than a touch of anecdotal irony.

The second exceptional talent that Pepper possessed—his natural flair for political combat—was first clearly seen in his single term in the Florida House of Representatives. This trait might be summed up in a single word: tenacity. It was a trait he shared with Ed Ball.

After only three years, Pepper felt secure enough in his new surroundings to unveil his political ambitions. He ran for the Florida House of Representatives in 1928, defeating a three-term incumbent lawyer. According to his memoirs, Pepper made an issue of his opponent's absence during a vote on a controversial cattle-dipping bill, portraying him as inattentive to his duties. He also told how he asked all his opponents to request their supporters to list him as their number two choice, and in turn he would reciprocate the promise. Second-choice votes were important in the context of Florida's controversial "second-choice" ballot of the period. The fact that he had promised the same thing several times over when it could only be delivered once did not seem to bother him in retrospect.[44]

Pepper's single term in the legislature is generally treated by his biographers as relatively unimportant in the overall picture of his career. They all mention his vote against censure of President Hoover for his wife's invitation to a black congressman's spouse to have tea at the White House. That vote is seen today as a tribute to a young liberal's fight against the evils of southern racism, an indication of the consistency of his political philosophy. Undoubtedly, it reflected a relatively courageous stand on the then-volatile issue of social equality of the races.

In his memoirs, Pepper recounts that 1929 episode, and his unsuccessful effort to exempt senior citizens from the requirement of buying fishing licenses, as indexes of his political philosophy.[45] The latter presaged his role, late in life, as champion of the elderly. He makes no reference to his part in the battle over the Crummer refunding plan, in which he was a strong supporter of the duPont interests marshaled under Ed Ball. That episode will be discussed shortly.

In retrospect, Pepper's vote on the Hoover censure can be seen as a rather sophisticated defense of the office of the presidency against a state legislature's meaningless bleating. Perhaps it was also a hesitant statement of embryonic opposition to the deep-seated racial injustice of the period, but at the time, it did not signal any profound, or even partial, disavowal of the South's traditional white supremacy. Pepper later distanced himself from the inherent conservatism of his constituents, but he knew better than to clearly repudiate white supremacy in the 1930s when he was building a north Florida following. Impaled on the horns of a dilemma that plagued all southern liberals, Pepper was haunted by the racial issue for most of his career.[46]

He believed that his vote in defense of Hoover was the single most important factor in his ensuing defeat for reelection to the Florida house. But there were other factors in play when he sought his second term. His leaning toward a state sales tax, another duPont-Ball favored issue, had more to do with his rejection by the Taylor County voters than did his defense of Mrs. Hoover's invitation to a black congressman's wife for tea at the White House.

Pepper was involved with other legislative issues in 1929, but they are generally overlooked by biographers—and even by Pepper himself in his memoirs. Still, they are much more illustrative of his considerable talents for the actual work of lawmaking. First, he introduced a major proposal in the Florida house for what was then a radical innovation in the state's judicial organization. His bill would have created an intermediate-level court of appeals to relieve the state's supreme court of a rapidly expanding caseload.[47] It was not a bill that would have originated in an outpouring of Taylor County grassroots support, nor was it the product of a unitary desire on his part to improve the state's administration of justice. It was the kind of bill that would have been urged by the state bar association or sought by the state's supreme court. He probably introduced it at the behest of one or the other, or both. Pepper was active in bar association matters during this period of his career and often visited with Justice James B. Whitfield of the supreme court during his time in Tallahassee.[48] Being asked to steer such a proposal through the legislative processes was a credit to his professional and political standing with both bench and bar. Although the bill was ahead of its time in 1929 and failed to pass, there is today an intermediate appellate court structure in the Florida judicial system similar to what Pepper had proposed.

A second issue involving Pepper in his first term as an elected politician is important as a starting point in his future relations with Ed Ball. It also previewed his exceptional oratorical and parliamentary skills in legislative combat. Seven years later, those skills enabled him to make a highly positive impression in his maiden speech before the U.S. Senate.[49] The legislative issue that stirred him to action concerned the seemingly mundane question of gasoline tax allocation between Florida's counties, and the fiscal disaster that had befallen the state with the collapse of the Florida Boom. In fact, it was a highly charged legislative battle, the kind which often influences the course of politics and careers, but which manages to elude the interests of historians and quickly recedes from public consciousness. Pepper's impact was more remarkable in light of his youth and freshman status, and the fact that he was a resident of Florida for less than four years.

In the aftermath of the boom, the state faced the threat of massive bond defaults left over from the freewheeling local government spending on a vast array of public works, especially roads. The cascading defaults of cities, counties, and special districts had converged in a genuine and undeniable fiscal crisis for the state. It fell to Governor Doyle E. Carlton to cajole a contentious legislature into dealing with the perplexing political problem. The principal source of revenue for all government purposes at all levels was ad valorem taxes on real estate. The governor embraced and presented to the legislature a plan developed by Roy E. Crummer, the Kansas securities dealer with whom Ball would be embroiled in controversy for many years.

Crummer's plan called for rehabilitating county and city finances by refunding road and other special purpose bonds through a reallocation of gasoline taxes. That would allow the defaulted bonds to be paid off with proceeds from new bond issues at lower interest rates and supported by the gasoline tax revenues. This would mean less money for building new roads as money was siphoned off to pay for the defaulted bonds. It would also instigate a large volume of bond business in the refunding process, which was Crummer's principal motivation. The proposal generated a regional issue, pitting counties in the throes of excessive indebtedness against those that had not indulged so lavishly in debt-financed spending.[50] It posed the classical "zero-sum" game of diverting limited funds from one use to another, the proverbial bête noire of politicians.

There were no feasible prospects for additional revenues. A state income tax was foreclosed by the constitutional amendment adopted in 1924, which had played an important part in attracting wealthy individuals like Alfred I. duPont to Florida. A sales tax ran head-on into the vehement opposition of powerful merchants' leagues; they portrayed it as a means of relief for large landowners, a stratagem which ignited opposition from the many who saw the sales tax as a class issue. The ad valorem real estate tax base, burdened beyond any possibility of increased tax levies, supported over 84 percent of all state, county, and municipal government spending.[51] There was common agreement that ad valorem taxes could sustain no more of the load for supporting government and should be materially reduced if the state's fiscal system and economy were to be salvaged. That was the only point of agreement that could be reached in the contentious atmosphere engendered by the crisis.

The difficulty lay in the remedy, and that set the priorities of the 1929 Florida legislature. It also fixed the parameters of the first encounter of Ed Ball and Claude Pepper in the world of practical legislative politics. The adversarial posturing that highlighted the session was a classic case of competing special interests vying to embed themselves in the fabric of public policy while excluding others.

A flashpoint in the inter-regional friction was the threat posed to duPont's west Florida land investments by the governor's plan to withdraw road funds otherwise available for that region. It also jeopardized municipal bond holdings of the Florida National Bank chain, then the principal component of the fledgling duPont Florida enterprises. Ball rallied legislative opposition to Carlton's program around the road issue. Roads were a visible and understandable benefit for those counties that would be deprived by reallocation of gas tax monies.

Public schools also worked their way into the controversial proposal since Carlton's plan reached into part of the gas tax revenues earmarked for education. Defending schoolchildren's right to an education was a far more palatable line of defense in 1929 Florida than the well-being of a duPont bank's (or any other bank's) investment portfolio.

The issue placed Ed Ball squarely in opposition to Roy E. Crummer, the Kansas securities dealer hoping to capitalize on the Florida bond refunding market. That phase of Ed Ball's career did not run its course for three decades, during which time it also tangentially influenced his relationship with Pepper. It figured in two congressional investigations, involved ten years of highly complex antitrust litigation resulting in a jury verdict for Ball and the duPont interests,[52] and came to the fore in the 1960s battle to repeal the duPont exemption in the Bank Holding Company Act. Those dimensions will be considered in a later chapter. Here, we are concerned with the 1929 legislative battle over Governor Carlton's gasoline tax proposals and Pepper's role in that battle.

When the legislature convened in April, Governor Carlton presented it with a complicated package of bills designed to restore the state's fiscal integrity. As for road bonds and construction, the governor wanted refunding measures and reallocation of gas tax revenues for that purpose. Both dimensions adversely affected the duPont interests and were strongly opposed by Ed Ball. First, Ball and his colleagues wanted to increase the road-building funds for the Panhandle region, where duPont corporations had acquired thousands of acres of land. This acreage would subsequently be the core of the holdings of St. Joe Paper Company, a principal component of the growing duPont empire. Any diversion of gas tax revenues for refunding would negatively impact road-building objectives in the region. Already, the Alfred I. duPont and Fons Hathaway bridges were completed over portions of Apalachicola Bay, and Crummer's proposal would have severely curtailed or terminated construction on their main feeder roads.[53] The proposal would also have diverted to road bond refunding a portion of gas tax revenues then allocated for school purposes. This feature made an appealing argument for the opposition. As one duPont ally said on the house floor: "If [he] had told his people that he was coming to Tallahassee to vote away their school fund and gasoline money, he would not be among those present."[54]

The plan conflicted with duPont interests in another respect. The Florida National Bank chain held municipal and county bonds as investments. It was the duPont view, hence Ball's, that these represented legitimate debts that would in time be paid in full, providing an attractive return, especially on those purchased at discounted prices. The interest rates on these bonds were at the high levels from the early period of the boom, and any anticipated refunding bonds would be at lower rates. Bondholders with the longer view, such as duPont and Ball, naturally looked askance on the refunding schemes.

Carlton's plan was essentially the product of Roy E. Crummer of the Brown-Crummer Company, a Kansas investment firm.[55] Beginning in 1919, at the start of the Florida Boom, his firm purchased over time at initial offerings some $40 million of Florida local government bonds. In the normal course of the bond business, these were then resold to individual investors. Crummer, a seasoned investments dealer and experienced in the Florida bond business, recognized the potential for profit in both up and down markets. The sheer magnitude of the "down" side of the Florida market offered potential profits beyond normal expectations for someone willing to innovate in the municipal bond market. Crummer was such an individual, and drawing on his extensive experience he developed an intricate redemption and refinancing program for local governments. The first phase of his plan required major revisions in existing Florida law to provide for the diversion of gas tax revenues from current road construction to early redemption of bonds.

Since it was clear that a solution to the state's fiscal crisis would require major legislation of one kind or another, Crummer seized the opportunity of promoting his refunding plan to Governor Carlton as the cure for the state's financial ills. His sense of timing and choice of political tactics were excellent. The plan was viewed more as a salvational measure for the state's fiscal well-being, which it was, than as a mechanism for generating vast profits for Crummer's bond business, which it also was. The governor agreed with Crummer, and the Kansas bond dealer's program became the centerpiece of Carlton's recommendations to the legislature.[56]

The plan had some merit, and strong support from those sections of the state saddled with defaulted bond issues. With defaults becoming more widespread as the fiscal crisis worsened, local government bonds were trading at substantial discounts. On the face of things, it appeared that the local governments could buy up their outstanding bonds at less than par value. Of course, many issues were not in default but did bear higher than current market interest rates, which had fallen substantially due to depression conditions. These, as well as the defaulted issues, could be redeemed by payment from proceeds of refinancing bonds sold at the lower current rates. The diverted gas tax revenues would be the funding source for the refinancing bonds.[57]

The plan flew in the face of those counties that were not overburdened with debt. For them, the continuation of road construction was their hope for a way out of depression conditions through future economic development. They were the core of opposition to Carlton's plan. In their view, they had demonstrated fiscal responsibility by not indulging in overwhelming debt for imprudent projects. It followed that they should not be punished by taking their road funds to bail out less prudent counties and cities, mostly in the south and populated largely by newcomers, most of whom were "Yankees." Just as Crummer's refunding scheme found its place in the governor's proposed solution to the state's financial crisis, Ball's plan to defeat it was developed around the north and west Florida counties' natural opposition to it. The grouping included Taylor County, and that is how Ed Ball and Claude Pepper came to be on the same side in their first legislative encounter.

Pepper was a freshman legislator, while Ball was already a seasoned participant in the north Florida political process. In the 1927 session, Ball had lobbied extensively for the road program and other duPont interests.[58] There is nothing to indicate clearly that they worked closely with each other, but given the circumstances of Pepper's involvement in the opposition to Carlton's program, it is most likely that they did. Even if not, they would certainly have known and approved of each other's positions and roles in the matter. Such battles almost always have a bonding effect on allies in a common cause, even if only temporarily.

The governor's plan, with strong support from the outset, was countered by a smaller but vocal opposition capably orchestrated by Ball. In the first test vote, opponents tried to take the moral high ground by attempting to position the legislature as "disapproving efforts of any municipality . . . or county" to avoid paying its legally incurred debts.[59] The wording before the house was an attempt to stigmatize the governor's proposal as a repudiation of valid obligations, a perspective the proponents anxiously sought to avoid. The debate was heated, but the voice vote overwhelmingly favored the governor's program. So loud were the "yeas," no roll was even called.[60] Even with such a showing of overwhelming support for the plan, Ball and his allies continued to do battle. Crummer's plan was far from assured of passage.

There were several pieces to the whole program, and each piece was a separate bill that had to pass in both chambers. It was a heavy burden for the proponents to carry against a determined opposition, and no effort involving Ed Ball was anything less than determined. The issue was skillfully and forcefully lobbied from both sides. Crummer moved his headquarters from Orlando to Tallahassee to be close to the daily action.[61] While the various elements of the program were debated in the senate, a Crummer executive known only by newspaper accounts as "Mr. Johnson" sat behind the administration's senate floor manager to advise him on details of the legislation. He was accompanied on the floor by the chairman of the State Road Department.[62] Lobbyists were routinely admitted to the floor in both chambers in that era, and the privilege was freely used to influence the flow of debate. It was a tactical advantage sorely missed by lobbyists plying their trade after chamber floor privileges were restricted many years later.

If there was no effort to mask the governor's program as anything other than Crummer's plan, Ball's opposition was equally obvious. One staunch proponent of the program was Senator Pat Whitaker of Tampa. He recalled the fight with Ball years later in a statement to a U.S. Senate subcommittee then investigating the continuing Ball-Crummer conflict: "Every known large commercial interest throughout the state was . . . favorable to the legislation except the interests known as the duPont-Ball faction, which included politicians known to be closely dominated by the duPont-Ball crowd which energetically fought the enactment of the legislation."[63]

Whitaker's objectivity should be tempered in light of his subsequent relationship with Crummer. His statement to the U.S. Senate was made after he had been retained in 1943 to combat Ball's continuing efforts to force Crummer out of the Florida bond market. In that role, Whitaker persuaded the Florida senate (he was no longer a member) to conduct an investigation of Ball's activities. He continued to harbor a strong dislike of Ball and subsequently testified in Crummer's multimillion-dollar antitrust lawsuit against the financier.[64] Even so, the tone of his statement accurately reflected the emotions and perceptions generated by the governor's plan to rescue the state's fiscal standing during Pepper's freshman term. It also marked Ball's emergence as a recognized factor in statewide politics.

In light of the underlying majority in favor of the program, the opposition's tactics were mainly directed at delaying its passage. They consumed much legislative time while being lopsidedly voted down in nearly each instance, all the while providing good copy for the *Tallahassee Daily Democrat*'s capitol correspondent. By the middle of the session's second month, it was obvious that the program had overwhelming support and would ultimately be enacted. It was then that Pepper became noticeably involved. Much debate had centered on the extent of relief that would be afforded to small counties. Pepper questioned the adequacy of figures provided by the Crummer group on this vital point, and his eloquence was noted in the *Daily Democrat*'s account of the debate.[65] The following day, the Taylor County freshman waded farther into the contentious issue. He resorted to a seldom used parliamentary tactic of moving to convene the house as a committee of the whole to furnish a better atmosphere for resolving the differences.[66] Such a move generally connoted a near deadlock on an issue and provided a more suitable parliamentary forum for searching out palatable compromises. In this instance, the majority did not want or need an opportunity to search for compromises; they wanted only the opportunity to get the various elements of the program to a floor vote. Yet Pepper's plea for a calmer and dispassionate inquiry into the problem had an appeal that could not be simply run over roughshod. He had correctly taken the measure of the house's commitment to the fundamentals of fair and reasoned debate. At the least, he had correctly gauged a collective desire not to publicly flaunt fairness and reason. Though such a commitment was not enough to prevail, it gave some relief from the previous lopsided votes and sustained the opposition for further battle.

Pepper's position was supported by a house veteran, D. Stuart Gillis of Walton County, which was on the proposed Gulf Coast Highway route. In opposing a motion to table Pepper's committee-of-the-whole proposal, he said, "I deplore the attitude of the proponents by which they hope to prevent intelligent discussion of these measures."[67] In legislative tactics, a challenge to "intelligent discussion" under such circumstances is most often the last resort of a frustrated minority trying to delay the inevitable. Such was the case as Pepper and Gillis tried to delay their opponents. The majority still held but, surprisingly, by a noticeably diminished margin.

Pepper's forensic talents were noted in the press. The *Daily Democrat*'s coverage was headlined: "Vote on Pepper's Taxation Motion Shakes Majority; Brilliant Plea Is Lost by Lessening Vote." The article continued in praise of Pepper's performance: "Following his masterful address yesterday the eloquent and logical member from Taylor today resumed his attack upon the executive's plan as being unconstitutional and economically unsound."[68] Such praise for a legislator's performance—especially a freshman's—was highly unusual, if not unique.

Pepper was clearly committed to the Ball side and appeared to be part of the inner circle of the opposition. When he offered the opponents' major amendment to stop the administration proposal, Pepper worked in tandem with D. Stuart Gillis, a mainstay of the opposition team, and Representative John E. Mathews, Sr., of Jacksonville, in offering a highly significant substitute amendment. The substitute was an essential part of a parliamentary maneuver calculated to secure the tactical advantage of controlling the amendatory process.[69] Pepper's inclusion in that process indicated an important role, especially for a freshman legislator.

He was also committed to the duPont-Ball road-building program, especially the Gulf Coast Highway segment which meant so much to the rural counties of west Florida, including his own. When the house received news that federal funding would be available to assist completion of the Gulf Coast Highway, an enthused Pepper moved to have the telegram read each day to the full house for the remainder of the session.[70] The release of the news was almost certainly timed by Ball's Washington contacts to persuade the Florida legislature, then in extended session on the governor's program, not to divert funds from the Gulf Coast Highway, a well-recognized duPont project. Proponents of Carlton's program had earlier sought to pressure

Panhandle opponents, as well as punish the duPont-Ball faction, by repealing the authorization for the Gulf Coast Highway.[71] Of course, the proponents of the governor's plan throttled Pepper's proposal. Still, it shows Pepper's enthusiasm for the Ball faction.

The strong majority support for the governor's fiscal program ultimately
prevailed in the extended session, but only after overcoming a well-orches-
trated and determined minority's efforts to influence the legislative process.
It was Ed Ball's first involvement in such a highly contentious and publicized
issue. It would not be his last. Although Senator Pat Whitaker of Tampa later
characterized the opposition as including "politicians known to be closely
dominated by the duPont-Ball crowd," it would be inaccurate to include
Pepper in that category. Although Pepper and Ball started their long political
relationship in mutual effort on a common cause, no available evidence
indicates or refutes that the 1929 session forged a continuing political bond
between them. If and when Ed Ball's papers are made available, that phase
of their relationship may be better ascertained.

For Ball, there were other pressing business matters besides the governor's
road program. The Florida banking establishment was in difficult straits
because of the collapse of the boom and the failure of the Anthony-Manly
bank chain in Florida and Georgia. Working through Ball, duPont quietly
bought up stock in Jacksonville's Florida National Bank and secured a place
for his deputy on its board of directors. In the midst of the gas tax battle, the
Florida banking community was stunned by the announcement of a merger
between the Florida National and Barnett banks, both of Jacksonville.[72] The
new bank would have been the largest in the state, but duPont's holdings in
it would have been materially diluted by the merger. It posed a clear threat
to duPont's embryonic plan to build a banking empire. Ball had to devote
considerable attention to defeating the merger at the same time the Crummer
plan was threatening the duPont interests from another quarter.[73] The trying
days of depression and a wave of Florida bank failures lay ahead, a period
when Ball and duPont would be severely tested in their commitment to
building a viable Florida banking chain. During this period, another duPont
associate and Ball colleague, W. T. Edwards, played a significant role in the
political arena in protecting duPont interests in west Florida. The 1929
session was Pepper's first experience with Ball and Edwards, the principal
political operatives of the growing duPont business conglomerate.

After the session, Pepper returned to Perry and resumed his law practice
and involvement in community activities. He was the town's scoutmaster,

and one of his young charges was Samuel Gilbert Register. Register was the son of the county tax assessor and in his youth spent many hours around the Taylor County Court House. There he developed a good memory for the politics of the time.[74] When Pepper ran for reelection, according to Register, his support for a sales tax during the 1929 session, another Ball political objective, was a major issue in the campaign. Local merchants, always opposed to a sales tax, sought out Alton Wentworth to run against him. Although Pepper attributed his defeat to his vote on the Hoover censure and Wentworth's family's solid reputation in the community, Register said the sales tax was the real issue that defeated him. Whatever the case, no doubt his sales-tax position and Wentworth's solid family ties were contributors to Pepper's loss. To whatever extent his no-vote on the censure worked against him on the racial issue, it was the first time his liberal instincts had been tested in a political setting.

That issue was to haunt him when he ran for the U.S. Senate in 1934. That his position failed to engage with the visceral racist instincts of his constituency was obvious. He did not make such a political mistake again, holding his liberal views on race in check until he was well established in the U.S. Senate. Still, his proclivity for the cosmic approach to the political universe would clash often with the conservative views of his constituency. In 1950, they had clashed once too often, but before then, Pepper had become Florida's first political figure to achieve national prominence and a measure of international stature as well.

Ed Ball, on the other hand, did not aspire to public stature, but by 1950 he had acquired the notoriety and power that come with control of vast economic resources. A certain stature accompanied that, whether aspired to or not, and Ball accepted and used it.

4

DuPont-Ball

Beginnings of a Florida Empire

Alfred I. duPont's first contact with Florida was at the age of ten when he accompanied his mother to north Florida, where she spent part of the winter season for her health. Around 1900, he began to visit Florida with some regularity.[1] By the time he and Jessie were married in 1922, Alfred had witnessed the tremendous changes wrought on Florida's east coast as Henry Flagler extended his railroad and hotel empire southward from St. Augustine to West Palm Beach and Miami.

Flagler's successes had stirred duPont's imagination. But whereas Flagler's motivation was to create a playground for the leisure class, duPont wanted to build on a more lasting economic foundation, one based on production and utilizing the state's untapped labor and natural resources. Flagler had come to Florida to reap a fortune from a narrow consumer economy; duPont came with visions of a producer economy, which was much broader in scope. DuPont envisioned a complete cycle of natural resources husbandry, with finance and manufacturing elements, as well as the social improvement that could be made a consequence of the overall process. In his opinion, the transitory interests of tourists and speculators ran counter to the long-term development of Florida.[2] There is some irony in the fact that Ed Ball would someday merge Flagler's vision of a leisure-based consumer economy for Florida with the duPont legacy of a producer-oriented economic model.

DuPont was not alone in his views of what the state's future should be. His thinking coincided with more sober assessments of the state's long-term welfare from others whose vision transcended the speculative frenzy that was then rampant in south Florida. Herman A. Dann, a St. Petersburg businessman and president of the state's chamber of commerce, was one of those individuals. He told business leaders assembled at a conference at Palm Beach in April of 1926 that the state must build a more permanent foundation than real estate speculation and catering to the leisure class: "Quite without intending . . . we have associated . . . our endeavors with the philosophy of the leisure class. . . . Their philosophy was entirely suited to a vacation period, but it was not . . . [one] which Florida business men could safely adopt as a matter of permanent policy. . . . Our future lies with the workers, the builders, and the investors. . . . The addition of homes, of factories, streets, utilities—all of those facilities which go to make up a modern community."[3]

Though Flagler's unfolding empire was to prove a crucial factor in Florida's economic development, it was clearly too narrow to define an enduring economic base for the state. The broader view expressed by Dann was not critical of Flagler's endeavors, but it did acknowledge that something more than the railroader's vision was necessary for the long-term welfare of the state.

Another prominent voice at the Palm Beach assembly was that of J. C. Penney, philanthropist, developer, and founder of the department store chain that still bears his name. His perspective of Florida's future emphasized the social as well as economic welfare of its citizens. Penney had launched an experimental program in Clay County, Jacksonville's neighbor to the south, to attract small farmers to the state's naturally fertile soil. In his view, the wholesale subdivision of real estate and the speculation it fostered were wrong for the state's long-term prosperity. He told the assembled executives: "Frankly, if we are thinking of permanent values and we would insure the future of the state, I consider it [speculation] unsound and uneconomical. The hope of our present situation is the back country . . . [and] permanent prosperity can not be achieved with the major part of the population in idleness for months of each year."[4]

The tenor of the meeting projected an awareness that Florida required a more solid economic foundation than that associated with the ongoing real estate boom. The unmistakable tone of "boosterism" about the proceedings had been somewhat subdued by disquieting news of troubles in some banks and the abrupt decline in land sales.[5] Even so, the general mood of the assembled businessmen was decidedly optimistic. It was the kind of atmosphere in which men like Alfred I. duPont, Ed Ball, and W. T. Edwards would have been in their element.

The attendance list for the assembly was a roster of the state's business leadership. Although news of duPont's activities was beginning to filter through the state, most businessmen and political leaders were then only vaguely aware of his Florida presence. Some of the Palm Beach attendees would later be involved directly with various dimensions of duPont's Florida enterprises, not necessarily always in tandem with them.

Alfred H. Wagg, for example, who was a well-known businessman and state senator from West Palm Beach, led the effort to enact the Carlton road program in the Florida senate three years later against Ball's determined opposition. J. H. Scales, a businessman and veteran of the state senate from Taylor County, was later a leader in the opposition to Governor Carlton's tax and road legislation. He was allied in that effort with Ball and W. T. Edwards, among others, including the young freshman state representative from Taylor County, Claude Pepper.

Also present at the meeting was Arthur N. Perry, president of Jacksonville's Florida National Bank. Later that year, Ball would commence quietly acquiring stock in that bank on behalf of duPont. Perry's resignation in late 1929 to join the competing Barnett Bank precipitated duPont's direct control of what would eventually become Florida's dominant banking concern.

John H. Perry, owner of a chain of newspapers that included the *Jacksonville Journal,* attended the meeting as well. Initially a strong supporter of Claude Pepper's senatorial career, he was also a close friend and ally of Ed Ball and supporter of the duPont business enterprises.[6] Another attendee, Jacksonville attorney Scott Loftin, was subsequently an interim appointee to the U.S. Senate, and trustee in bankruptcy for the Florida East Coast Railway when Ball initiated his takeover bid for that company.

DuPont and his lieutenants, Ball and Edwards, did not attend the conference. But there is no mistaking the remarkable alignment of many of the views expressed there with duPont's thinking on Florida's future. Obviously, duPont and his surrogates had blended easily in such circles. When they came to Florida, they did not have to bend the business and political leadership of the state to their thinking. They simply joined it, and in time came to dominate it.

There was in duPont's decision to make Florida his new home and base of operations a curious mix of productive urge, pioneering spirit, and altruism. He wanted to make a fresh start for himself and his new family while building something better for the state after the fall from boom-time euphoria that he knew was coming. The latter notion emanated from the duPont family's strong tradition of noblesse oblige. It remained to be determined where in Florida he would make his home and center of operations. He and

Jessie had frequented Miami in the winter seasons at the height of the Florida Boom. The tinsel and glitter, the heedless pursuit of quick profits, the "binder boys," and the frenzied real estate speculation failed to give him any sense of stability or sustainable productivity in that city.

Initially, duPont's attitude toward the state was ambivalent. He appeared undecided whether boom-time Florida was a suitable setting for the abstract vision of social betterment and economic gain then taking shape in his mind. In January 1925, on the porch of Flagler's Royal Palm Hotel in Miami, he had told Ball of his doubts about the speculation craze then engulfing much of Florida.[7] Notwithstanding a lingering uncertainty, duPont concluded that the state had great potential, and he had already established two corporations to begin acquiring Florida land.[8] He remained wary of conditions in October but was nevertheless disinclined to accept the growing number of prophecies of the boom in Florida "bursting" on a permanent basis.[9] As the west Florida land purchases being made by Ball on his behalf progressed, he was slowly making the case in his own mind for the break from the duPont family traditional domicile in Delaware.

It was in late 1926 that Alfred I. duPont made the final decision to quit the place of his birth. His cousin Pierre S. duPont had returned to Delaware in 1925 after successfully reorganizing a troubled General Motors Corporation. With this, his reputation as one of America's premier industrialists and businessmen was even more firmly established. No longer occupied with active management and control of the duPont company, he turned his considerable executive talents to the public arena, accepting appointment as the state's tax commissioner. Alfred feared his detested cousin's newfound authority to pry into his, or, for that matter, any other Delaware citizen's, financial affairs.[10] While this fear may have precipitated Alfred's final decision to relocate, he also knew that to realize his larger vision he needed a younger and more vibrant setting than the small state over which his family had so much control.

As he began to feel relieved of the financial difficulties posed by the demise of the Nemours Trading Corporation, he cast about for other challenges. On November 22, 1926, acting through Ball, he formed another Florida corporation under the name Almours Securities.[11] It became the principal conduit and corporate umbrella for the investments made by Alfred I. duPont in his adopted state. It was also the instrument through which duPont removed his assets from the reach of Delaware's revenue collectors to the more benign tax climate of Florida.

DuPont's land acquisitions had started the year before when Ball made the first of his exploratory trips to the state's Panhandle region. By spring of 1925, Ball had found 13,000 acres on ten miles of Gulf coast for $15 an acre. DuPont accepted his recommendation to purchase the land, and the duPont holdings in west Florida were initiated.[12]

It was in June of that year that Claude Pepper had decided to leave his teaching position at the University of Arkansas Law School and enter law practice in Perry. The circumstances of Pepper's arrival in Perry were decidedly different from those of Ball in Jacksonville. Pepper came to Florida on borrowed money, with a Harvard law degree and a healthy optimism as his only assets. Ball arrived securely ensconced in the full array of tangible and intangible assets inuring to Alfred I. duPont's fortune and fame. His outlook was not optimistic in the same exuberant sense as Pepper's. It was more calculating than instinctive.

As is often the case with perceptions of the wealthy, estimates of Alfred I. duPont's wealth were frequently exaggerated. At the time of his marriage to Jessie, one newspaper account estimated his wealth to be $400 million, an absurd inflation given that it was closer to one-twentieth of that figure. Since this period marks the beginning of Ball's Florida career, and since it started from the wealth of Alfred I. duPont, it is appropriate to consider the extent of that fortune.

On December 31, 1925, duPont's "Comparative Balance Sheet" prepared by a Jacksonville accountant reflected what would today be loosely termed his "net worth"—the sum of $21,604,991.53, very close to the 1922 estimate of $20 million.[13] The use of a Jacksonville accountant so early in his Florida endeavors reflected his determination to make a clean break from his past in Delaware, at least insofar as business matters were concerned. It also helped establish evidence of a permanent abode in Florida, a necessary element in his quest to keep Delaware tax agents from accessing his fortune. Nevertheless, he kept his beloved Nemours estate near Wilmington, and he and Jessie continued to reside there much of the time. The Great Bull Market had substantially improved his position during 1925, especially regarding his E. I. duPont de Nemours and General Motors holdings which were the core of his wealth.

At the end of the following year, his "net worth" had increased to $37,028,049.17, most of the increase being in "stock in other companies," that is, other than Almours Securities. (All figures for 1926 are from duPont's financial report prepared by his Jacksonville accountant.) The principal item of income for that year was dividends from his E. I. duPont de Nemours stock in the amount of $1,682,294.20. He also was buoyed up by the successful conclusion of a long-fought battle with the Internal Revenue Service resulting in a $1,519,276 income tax refund.

Historian and duPont biographer Marquis James estimated his wealth at around $100 million two years later. This increase was largely due to the spectacular rises in his two principal holdings, E. I. duPont de Nemours and General Motors.[14]

Some comparative sense of duPont's wealth is helpful in gauging Ed Ball's start in the affairs of Florida's business and political history. The national average of taxable income in 1926 was $5,249, up from $3,143 two years earlier. The gain reflected the surge of prosperity that marked the period. But this prosperity was not by any means experienced by the population as a whole. In 1929, the first year for which percentage distribution of income levels was reported, 94 percent of families and single adults in America had incomes of less than $5,000.[15] That percentage would have been even higher four years earlier since income generally was rising. For the great majority of Americans, Alfred I. duPont's fortune was vast beyond their comprehension.

By any reckoning, duPont was a very wealthy man when he launched his Florida venture. Not only did his financial report reflect his assets for the year 1925, the year he came to Jacksonville, it also provided an interesting insight into his lifestyle. For the period, his accountant listed $2,076,881 in expenditures, such as "Gifts," $43,206 to charities, over $317,000 for expenses at Nemours, and more than $106,000 for "Yacht Operating." His new yacht, the *Nenemoosha II,* was completed in the summer of 1925.[16] Whatever his concern with uplifting the lives of others, Alfred did not eschew the pleasures of his own class.

Particularly interesting in the 1926 financial report was a $45,044.55 item labeled "Political." The available evidence does not indicate where or how that sum was utilized. It was not used in Delaware since, according to historian and duPont biographer Joseph Wall, Alfred had detached himself from overt involvement in Delaware politics during the election of 1924, when Coleman duPont won election to the U.S. Senate.[17] If the money was used in Florida political circles in 1925, it seems curious that such a large sum would be spent in a nonelection year. Neither Alfred nor Ball could have developed a well-thought-out political agenda for Florida at that early stage. A different format was subsequently adopted for the financial report, and no item labeled "Political" appeared in later reports.

Later, when Ball had become settled in the ways of Florida politics, he advised duPont: "It is my thought that it might be desirable for the Almours

Securities, Inc., to make some contributions to several of these candidates. Of course, we would not show it as political contributions, but as legal fees or under some other heading."[18] The numerous corporate entities that did business under the mantle of Almours Securities nurtured a fiscal ambience that afforded Ball great leeway in his business dealings on behalf of his brother-in-law. His ability to deal in cash in land transactions was a rarity in Florida even before the collapse of the boom, and much more so afterward. That alone would have marked him as a force to be reckoned with, in both business and politics. Ball maximized the array of real and perceived power inherent in his dealings on behalf of duPont. He forged a distinctive political image, a composite of his own personality and the persona of his employer. Following duPont's death, it became more distinctively his own as he emerged from the long shadow cast by his famous brother-in-law.

DuPont's attraction to northeast Florida went back to his childhood visits with his mother. Pleasant memories, especially of the picturesque St. Johns River, combined with more practical factors to influence his decision to make Jacksonville his new home and headquarters for his Florida enterprises. The city was the state's major commercial and banking center. Its location—twenty miles upstream from the Atlantic Ocean—and its marine, rail, and terminal facilities rendered it a major transportation hub. The president of the city's chamber of commerce reported to the 1926 Florida Takes Inventory Congress in Palm Beach that the city enjoyed excellent communications with most of the country. It was within forty-eight hours of over two-thirds of the nation's population. He added that Jacksonville was believed to be the first city of less than 150,000 population to have bank clearings of $1 billion annually.[19] It was also a manufacturing center, with some 437 listed factories turning out goods in 137 U.S. Department of Commerce product classifications.

The effects of the boom were just beginning to be felt as far north as Jacksonville when the collapse came in 1926. Traces of the madness farther south could be detected in Charles Ponzi's abortive scheme to sell residential lots in rural Columbia County from a Jacksonville office. There were other, more tangible signs of the boom's progress northward. The dollar investment in Jacksonville area construction was more than three times higher in 1926 than in 1925, but wild speculation had not yet pervasively undermined the city's economic foundation. As a result, Jacksonville was spared the extremes of the harshly debilitating effects experienced elsewhere in the state following the crash.

The conservative leanings of the city had protected it from the temptations of overextended debt financing. It possessed a reasonably good tax base and was not weighed down with debt for unused and unusable public improvements. There was a soundness to the city that survived the crash. As Joseph Wall put it: "Here was a town where a Yankee could feel at home— the most northern city in spirit anywhere in the Deep South. In Jacksonville men wore proper blue serge suits in the winter, not silky, white pongee outfits that looked like pajamas and felt like nudity. Here the banks were solid stone structures. They looked like banks, not like the Alhambra pleasure palaces that passed for banks in Miami."[20] Jacksonville represented a solid and reliable environment from which duPont could launch his Florida enterprise. For Ball, it served as a congenial base from which he built the duPont legacy into the most powerful business empire in the state over the next half century. That empire was intentionally dismantled by an act of Congress in 1966. Claude Pepper would once again be entangled in the political fate of the duPont legacy under the stewardship of Ed Ball.

From the start in 1925, the embryo of the duPont empire developed in two principal spheres. One was the Jacksonville dimension, consisting essentially of the Florida National Bank chain and later the Florida East Coast Railway, which had its headquarters in St. Augustine. Through them, the reach of the duPont-Ball interests, as they became known after duPont's death, extended southward to central Florida and Miami.

The second dimension was in the western part of the state, that region known generally as the Florida Panhandle. There the duPont emphasis was on land, forest products, and manufacturing—all ultimately grouped under the mantle of the St. Joe Paper Company. It was in the Panhandle that duPont's Florida activities became first noted, then applauded, and later, according to some detractors, assumed the trappings of a near feudal barony.[21] Alternatively, these activities could be viewed as a manifestation of Alfred I. duPont's determination to build for profit and to benefit the people of Florida. The interpretation depends largely on the beholder's view of Ed Ball's stewardship of the duPont legacy to Florida. To assess that stewardship, it is helpful to start with the perspective from which duPont defined his vision for a better Florida, and his own profit. Ball himself was a part of that vision, always professed to share in it, and ultimately, for better or worse, came to be the embodiment of it.

Alfred I. duPont's departure from Delaware was bound up with his sense of estrangement from the duPont family and business. As a consequence, he also felt detached from his ancestral ties with Delaware, more particularly, from the responsibilities to its people which he deemed part of the duPont name and tradition. Without the triad of family, business, and Delaware in his life, he felt a void at odds with his whole sense of self. Through his marriage to Jessie, his affection for Thomas, her older brother who practiced law in California, and the taking of her younger brother as his liege man, he restored a family dimension to his life. His love for Jessie and the familial affection manifested in his correspondence with Thomas and Ed, even on business matters, leave no doubt on that point.

The successful windup of the Nemours Trading Corporation was for Alfred the proving ground of Ed's loyalty and business acumen. That those traits were intertwined with his new family ties was a source of comfort and helped to give him a new sense of purpose. As part of the severance from his past, he also sold his interests in the Delaware Trust Company to a cousin, William duPont, one of the few family members with whom he remained close. The operation of that company had provided him and Ball with their first experience in the world of banking. With the burdens from his past life lifted, duPont could redirect his fortune and creative energies in pursuit of a new vision.

For Alfred, visionary purpose meant more than just the generation of profits. He required a fulfilling of that sense of responsibility he deemed part of his duPont heritage. Florida and its people provided that element of his sense of self. His own summary of the motivation behind the decision, given later in conjunction with litigation, was credibly lacking in altruistic tenor. Still it conveyed his purpose that the Florida enterprises be in pursuit of the public interest as well as for profit: "The collapse. . .of the boom in 1925 and 1926 brought about a situation which threatened to bring disaster to the state as a whole and I concluded that to come into Florida at that time and help out in the reorganization of its finances and productive capacity would be a splendid thing to do and at the same time create an outlet for my energy and offer investment of capital which would ultimately prove remunerative."[22] That this statement made no mention of his quest for a tax haven does not take away from its importance as a factor contributing to his move. His was an outlook for the long term; he told Jessie and Ed that neither he nor they should expect profits from their venture, at least not for many years.[23] And even as death approached, he held to the view that his endeavors in Florida were building for the future, and not for immediate profit.[24] Alfred's two principal biographers, as well as Jessie's, put that light on his motivation.

Other historians of the duPont family do not find such high purpose in Alfred's character, or if they do, it is subordinated to other, less noble traits. They relate his decision to move to Florida as springing from a desire for more wealth and power, which they consider the driving force of the duPont family legacy. In this view, the relationship of wealth to politics is equated generally with corrupt purpose, and by extension to those who prominently bore the duPont name.[25] Such a view misses the splendid complexity of the matter. Certainly the duPonts, including Alfred, had dark shadows in their collective and individual images. That Alfred was motivated by profit is undeniable. Any man who could spend over $100,000 in a single year on operating his yacht could not be oblivious to both the pleasure and necessity of profits. Unlike many born into later generations of inherited wealth, he had a well-grounded appreciation for the capacity to turn a profit as the underpinning of continued wealth. And he understood wealth as a means to pursue objectives linked to but also transcending purely economic purposes.

Wealth, like politics, could be used for purposes of revenge and spite, as well as the pursuit of power and more wealth. That men like the duPonts in general, and Alfred, Pierre, and Coleman in particular, sought to dominate their environments by means of their wealth and power is self-evident. The sum of Ed Ball's life's work indicates that he was well suited to that particular trait of the duPont character. There is no doubt that Alfred and Ball were capable of using—and in fact did use—wealth for purposes of control and dominance. Consider, as evidence, the following sworn statement that they filed with the Internal Revenue Service in 1931: "Just as General Motors controls the Automotive Industry; General Electric company, the world of electrical appliances; Standard Oil, the regulation of the oil market; and the E. I. duPont de Nemours Company, the chemical industry; Almours Securities, Inc., will, within the next decade rehabilitate, develop and virtually control the State of Florida and become the financial bulwark of the South. With such hopes and aspirations, Almours Securities, Inc., was conceived. To such end it is building slowly and surely."[26]

When this language was cited as evidence of monopolistic intent in the 1949 antitrust action filed by Roy E. Crummer, Ball's longtime adversary, Ball attempted to put a different light on it. He said that it represented no more than words of "art" used by lawyers in the narrow context of the 1931 tax issues previously litigated.[27] Such a statement would clearly be evidence in a context of antitrust litigation of intent to exercise monopoly power in a particular economic market. Its presence in the duPont tax case pleadings might be explained by the lawyers in the earlier case not being versed in antitrust law.

It is also possible that duPont himself crafted the language in the statement out of his conviction that he acted with high and noble purpose in his Florida pursuits. He was convinced that his creating Almours Securities was a positive rehabilitative force for a Florida in the throes of economic depression. In that light, and in the context of the earlier case, he deemed accumulations of surplus capital necessary to the continued growth of the corporation, and as such, beyond the reach of the federal tax code's surtax provisions.[28] His juridical declamations on the matter were certainly couched in such language.

In the years that followed, lawyers representing Ball and the duPont interests were much more sensitive to issues bearing on economic domination and control. The issues later raised by Roy Crummer's decade of antitrust litigation never reached the final trial stage on the merits, so there is no judicial finding as to what duPont and Ball meant by the statement in the antitrust context. The words were left to speak for themselves. Certainly, they imply that economic domination of Florida was at least as much a part of duPont-Ball thinking as was the welfare of its people. For duPont, the two were logically linked.

Later, during the Florida East Coast Railway takeover battle, Claude Pepper was convinced that even if domination had not been the purpose of Alfred I. duPont, it was certainly the purpose of Ed Ball after him. A diary entry by Pepper in 1946 read, "The sinister and dangerous character of Ball's domination of the state of Florida becomes more distinct as one sees it more closely."[29] That statement described Pepper's perspective of the duPont legacy in Florida after ten years of Ball's stewardship.

Joining duPont and Ball in the Florida adventure was W. T. Edwards, the husband of one of Jessie's lifelong friends. After assessing the citrus-growing region in 1927 at duPont's request, Edwards reported a fragmented and disorganized industry. It put too much emphasis on volume of output in the near term, with little or no organized concern for the future development and stability of the industry. Such a disjointed structure was not a good fit with duPont's emerging vision for Florida, in which the element of control was crucial.[30] For duPont, and Ball after him, control was a concept that came very close to the economic domination that was proscribed by the antitrust laws. But the fledgling enterprises that constituted the duPont interests in Florida were not yet large enough to run afoul of those laws.

5. Alfred I. duPont. This millionaire scion of one of America's oldest industrial families left his ancestral home in Delaware to settle in Florida following his estrangement from the duPont family hierarchy. He brought with him his new wife, Jessie Ball, and her younger brother, Ed Ball. These two men together built what was for many years Florida's most powerful business combine.

6. Epping Forest, the south Jacksonville riverfront mansion that Alfred I. duPont built in 1927 for himself and Jessie. Ed Ball was the principal overseer of the construction during the many extended absences of his sister and brother-in-law.

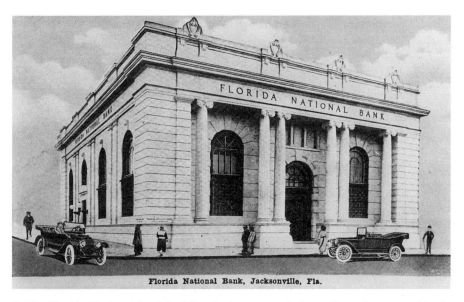

Florida National Bank, Jacksonville, Fla.

7. The Florida National Bank building in downtown Jacksonville as it appeared in the 1920s when Ed Ball launched the acquisition program that made the Florida National Bank chain the largest in Florida.

8. When the Florida Boom ended in 1926, bank failures were commonplace. The worried faces of these Lakeland, Florida, depositors show the devastating impact of a bank run on a community. Ed Ball acquired failed banks around the state, and they became the nucleus on which he built the duPont banking chain into the largest in the state.

While Edwards went about the citrus inquiry, Ball continued acquiring large tracts of west Florida forest lands on duPont's behalf. The use of the region's abundant indigenous pine trees to stock some kind of manufacturing process held a continuing attraction for duPont. There was the possibility that cellulose extracted from the pulp of pine trees could be used in synthetic materials production similar to that at the duPont de Nemours company. When citrus and synthetics failed to satisfy duPont's overall purposes, he eventually turned his attention to some form of paper manufacturing in the Panhandle.[31] During this period, as noted earlier, duPont was also occupied with the Florida National Bank chain in Jacksonville. The entrance of duPont and Ball in the state's banking industry will be discussed later in the chapter. This led to his creation of the St. Joe Paper Company, which remained for fifty years the prime mover of much of the region's economy—a tribute to the strength of duPont's vision and Ed Ball's tenacious pursuit of it.

The Florida Panhandle is a long, narrow stretch of land extending approximately 180 miles from Leon County westward along the Gulf Coast to southern Alabama. Beyond the Panhandle, in the other direction, Jacksonville is approximately 170 miles to the east, near the Atlantic seaboard. At the Panhandle's widest point, the Apalachicola River traverses some ninety miles of mostly second-growth Florida pine forests as it makes its way to the Gulf of Mexico. From there westward, the configuration of the region narrows to approximately thirty miles near Pensacola and the Alabama border. As if to emphasize its distinctive separateness in the scheme of things, most of the region is in a different time zone from the rest of the state.

In the years before the Civil War, cotton and lumber made the Panhandle one of the state's richest regions. As the first-growth timber was exhausted and the market for cotton declined, it slowly settled into the pattern of rural poverty endemic to large portions of the South. In 1925, reforestation was not yet a widely utilized resource management technique, and, as one report put it, "Florida [had] the least to offer of all the pine-bearing states of the South in the attractiveness of its cut-over lands for purposes of agricultural development."[32] There was nothing about the region to attract more than fringe effects of the boom. Nevertheless, Panama City experienced a brief surge in real estate prices in the spring of 1925, sending tremors of anticipation throughout the area.[33] Those expectations faded rapidly when the collapse came the following year, leaving the people as before—mostly dependent on agricultural production from the loamy soil for largely substandard livelihoods.

A notably successful farm of forty acres might yield ten bales of cotton and sufficient produce to carry a farmer through the winter.[34] A net income of slightly more than $2,000 from approximately ten acres under cultivation in Bay County was considered a good result, probably above the norm. In fact, the Florida soil yielded more per acre than did land in most other states.[35] Yet that generalization included the highly productive farm and citrus lands in south Florida. The Panhandle remained underdeveloped and on the verge of rural poverty. Contributing to the economic difficulties was the dearth of interior and arterial roads. As recently as 1923, the Florida Official Road Map showed no paved roads in Franklin, Calhoun, Bay, and Walton counties. In Okaloosa County, there was one road noted as "semihard" from Florida Highway No. 1 (now called U.S. 90) to the Gulf Coast. It was clear that any broad improvement program for the region had to include roads.

Shortly after he arrived in Florida on a permanent basis, duPont's creative attention settled on the Panhandle. He dispatched Ball in 1925 to assess the region's prospects and to look for cheap land. Richard Hewlett's biography of Jessie Ball duPont relied on a series of telegrams in April and early May of 1925 as evidence of duPont's first sizable acquisition in west Florida. The telegrams referred to the previously mentioned 13,000-acre tract on ten miles of Gulf coast purchased at $15 per acre.[36] Probate records of the duPont estate in Jacksonville cited by Marquis James indicate the first substantial acquisition was made early in 1926. Ball purchased over 66,000 acres in Franklin, Bay, and Walton counties, and 800 residential lots in the fishing village of Carrabelle.[37] That there were 800 lots platted within a small fishing village implies that boom-time expectations had reached the northern Gulf Coast, but the crash cut short any hopes for lasting prosperity. With those purchases, the duPont name, and that of Ed Ball, became inextricably linked with the region's fortunes. The core of duPont landholdings, eventually more than 1 million acres, always remained in west Florida, wedded to the production of forest products and the St. Joe Paper Company.

While Ball continued to pursue additional land purchases, duPont considered possible options for utilizing his newly acquired west Florida holdings. His thoughts remained centered on the vision of building a productive community and finding the right setting for such an endeavor. As noted earlier, duPont wanted to demonstrate that social welfare and profit could be successfully harnessed in tandem if initiated and managed in the proper environment. He envisioned a manufacturing operation that would employ large numbers of local workers and raise their standards of living, along with those of an entire community which he would call into being as part of his grand scheme.[38]

At the time, Florida's pulpwood industry was focused primarily on export to out-of-state manufacturing centers. The level of employment provided was at the low end of the economic spectrum, offering little hope of betterment for the people of the region. The use of modern reforestation systems had not yet breathed new life into the cutover and barren scrub woods of west Florida.[39] Some form of industrial production based in the region and utilizing its natural resources and labor was essential, and if paper manufacturing could be introduced to the region, the entire employment structure would be upgraded.

The possibility of harvesting pulpwood suitable for newsprint from second-growth pine forest generated high hopes.[40] Major newspaper companies were interested in Florida's potential for high-quality and inexpensive newsprint production. This potential market remained a leading possibility for the duPont holdings for some time while Alfred mulled over his options.

Ball visited the area in 1935 with his friend, John H. Perry, the Jacksonville newspaper publisher, as well as executives from the *Chicago Tribune* and the *New York Daily News.*[41]

Besides newsprint, there were more proven prospects in container manufacturing. The investment possibilities in that form of production were apparent to others besides duPont and his associates. Southern Kraft Corporation opened the first paper mill in Florida in early 1931 at Panama City and began marine shipments of its product in April of that year.[42] The operation quickly proved the feasibility of paper manufacturing in west Florida, and in the midst of a deepening depression, provided a beacon of economic stability for the rural region. DuPont's decision, several years in the making, was no doubt influenced by Southern Kraft Corporation's success.

Acquiring large tracts of land posed the immediate question of how to earn a return on the investment pending a long-term decision on its ultimate use. It was clear that whatever the long-term decision, it would be aligned around the region's indigenous pine timber. With the nation consuming more than 8 million cords of pulpwood in 1926 (half of it imported), there was clearly a ready domestic market.[43] Edwards entered into a contract in 1931 to supply Southern Kraft Corporation with pulpwood at $5.25 per cord for its new operation in Panama City. To that end, he contracted with a local businessman and pulpwood dealer, G. Pierce Wood of Liberty County, to harvest and deliver the wood on board barges. The contract yielded duPont a profit of $1.35 per acre.[44] That amount could not be realized annually since there had to be a growing period after each harvest. But the west Florida environment was exceptional for growing trees to suitable size for harvesting pulpwood in fifteen to twenty years, compared with approximately seventy years for a northern spruce.[45] Although harvesting pulpwood was a viable operation in the short term, it would not satisfy duPont's ultimate hopes for his enterprise—to enhance and sustain the region's wealth-producing capacity for the long term. Only a manufacturing-based economy could do that.

Still, there were advantages in the pulpwood business besides producing an interim cash flow while continuing to expand an asset base. It was the duPont people's first lesson in the efficient utilization of the principal natural resource within their expanding domain. It also provided access to the region's political power base. The contract with Wood was an example of how politics meshed with business in the duPont-Ball sphere of operations. The pulpwood dealer had been elected to the Florida House of Representatives from Liberty County three years earlier. He was a strong supporter of Ball's efforts in the 1929 legislative session to defeat the Carlton tax plan, which embodied the Crummer bond refunding program. Although Edwards was certainly aware of Wood's political position, it did not outwardly appear to be a factor in the decision to contract with him. Edwards made no mention of Wood's legislative position in his memorandum to Ball and duPont apprising them of the arrangement for harvesting pulpwood. Instead, he cited only Wood's good business reputation and that he owned sufficient equipment, including horses and mules, to do the harvesting. Edwards emphasized that the pulpwood dealer was a thoroughly reliable person who completed what he undertook.[46] That Wood was steeped in the region's politics was something Ball undoubtedly knew from the 1929 legislative battle over the governor's road tax program.

During the following decade, Wood's business expertise in timber matters continued to serve the duPont interests well. He was engaged in 1936 to conduct a detailed study of the total duPont pulpwood holdings preparatory to the formation of the St. Joe Paper Company.[47] He subsequently proved to be a reliable ally in legislative battles and in 1939 served as Speaker of the Florida house. One may conclude that the contractual relationship with Wood was due to his political position, or his pulpwood business expertise, or both. For Ball, it was a synergistic confluence of business ability and political position of the kind to which prudent men were always alert. Beyond that, he did not greatly concern himself.

Land purchasing and information gathering put Ball into contact with other local political figures. These contacts sometimes led to enduring relationships, which often proved important in political, business, and personal matters. One of these was with B. K. Roberts, a young Tallahassee lawyer who was to become prominent in political circles and would eventually be appointed to the Florida Supreme Court by Governor Fuller Warren. Any person with interests to protect in a rural Florida county would seek to maintain friendly relations with the elected sheriff, generally the most powerful figure on the local political scene. Roberts was the nephew of the Wakulla County sheriff, who suggested that his nephew, then near graduation from law school, meet the man who spoke for Alfred I. duPont. Ball liked the young attorney-to-be, not just because he was the sheriff's nephew, but also because he was an intelligent and affable young man. It was the beginning of a lasting relationship between the two.

Initially, Roberts performed small real estate closings for Ball, taking on more important matters over time and becoming a confidant and adviser. He ultimately served as Ball's attorney in the latter's bitter and highly contentious divorce proceedings many years later.[48] Roberts also became good friends with one of his contemporaries in the legal profession, Claude Pepper, then practicing law in nearby Perry. They were both active in bar association matters, and Roberts helped Pepper in his early senate campaigns.[49]

Such relationships were part of a larger, interlocking network that was the infrastructure of the Florida political scene, a scene for which Ball was well suited. They were important elements of Ball's maturing political prowess, along with the mystique and money of the duPont fortune. For inhabitants of the Panhandle, Ball represented a growing and impressive array of fortune and power.

When G. Pierce Wood conducted his assessment of duPont pulpwood holdings in west Florida in 1936, they came to 381,811 acres, with an average land value of $3.91 per acre. The value of forest products came to another $5.25 per acre, making the pulpwood lands owned by Almours Securities and its subsidiaries worth $3,487,044.[50] This was the major part of the west Florida land holdings that later came under Ball's control following duPont's death. Shortly after Southern Kraft Corporation had successfully launched its operations in Panama City in 1931, W. T. Edwards began organizing other Gulf Coast communities to promote themselves as sites for additional paper mills. In his report to duPont on these efforts, he wrote: "In trying to carry out this work I feel that I am carrying out your idea of helping to upbuild [sic] Florida and put her back on her feet as quickly as possible."[51] That statement by Edwards supports the view that duPont's purpose reached beyond economic gain and power to the betterment of those ordinary people on whose labor his enterprises depended.

While Edwards was so engaged, Ball was building a viable banking group in the midst of worsening economic conditions, including a continuing wave of bank failures around the state. It was not an auspicious time for such an undertaking. To understand Ball's role in building the Florida National Bank chain into the state's dominant financial power, it is helpful to understand the economic climate in which it was accomplished.

In the spring of 1926, the New York Times reported real estate sales in south Florida to be at a "standstill" with speculators and salesmen packing northbound trains on rumors of better markets on Long Island.[52] Yet there seemed to be no widespread comprehension of what was beginning to unfold. In April, reports given at the Chamber of Commerce's Palm Beach conference indicated a wariness regarding the real estate market, but no distinct consciousness of the eventual magnitude of the impending collapse. The president of the Exchange National Bank of Tampa, J. A. Griffin, reported that the Florida banking establishment was extraordinarily sound, holding more resources on a per capita basis than any other southern state.[53]

Less than three months later, two Palm Beach banks failed, both pulled down by the collapse of Addison Mizner's grandiose plans for a luxury community at Boca Raton in Palm Beach County. Like so many other dreams spawned of the Florida Boom, Mizner's had been precariously balanced at the pinnacle of the speculation frenzy. Within a few weeks, fissures appeared in the Anthony-Manly chain of affiliated banks in Florida and Georgia. Unrelated to the Palm Beach County situation, the Manley banks in Georgia were on the verge of default due to the gross mismanagement of W. R. Manley, architect of the group and its principal executive. A lawsuit filed against Manley alleging massive fraud combined with the shock of the Palm Beach failures to precipitate a cascading wave of bank closings. These caused the Georgia group as well as the Florida banks affiliated with it to come unraveled. By the end of 1926, over 150 banks in Florida and Georgia had closed their doors, many never to reopen. The Anthony chain had controlled 9 of 13 banks in Palm Beach County, and J. R. Anthony was considered the most powerful banker in Florida.[54]

Although the torrent of failures abated somewhat, and some banks reopened, the 1926 closings initiated a period of spasmodic waves of failures lasting well into the national depression. The Florida failures were linked to collapse of the boom and were aggravated by grossly negligent, and frequently criminal, management conduct. In *Panic in Paradise,* lawyer-historian Raymond Vickers details numerous episodes of insider and "policy" loans, clearly undercollateralized and frequently not secured at all. In several instances, such loans exceeded the entire invested capital of particular banks.[55] The series of bank failures peaked again in July 1929 when the Citizens Bank of Tampa failed. DuPont and Ball capitalized on the deteriorating situation by buying up failed and distressed banks. They did so in a fashion clearly advantageous to themselves, but their acquisitions were also generally favorable to stranded depositors of the failed banks.

DuPont initiated his acquisitions of Jacksonville bank stocks in a highly demoralized banking climate, especially for many depositors who saw lifetime savings evaporate with the closing of the local bank. As with his vision of a producer economy in west Florida, duPont saw the building of a strong banking group, one in which conservative loan policies protected depositors' funds, as a rehabilitating force for the state.[56] DuPont's initial efforts in Jacksonville quickly focused on the Florida National Bank, the smallest and weakest of the city's three major financial establishments. Working quietly through Ball, and using the Almours Securities Corporation as the acquiring mechanism, duPont quietly amassed a sizable block of Florida National's common stock.

Almours owned sufficient stock by 1927 to warrant a seat on the board for the duPont interests. It was filled by Ed Ball.[57] From this vantage point, he was privy to the inside workings of the bank and became conversant with the overall conditions within the state's banking community. He was able to glean much information on the industry not available to the general public regarding the insider abuses and mismanagement that accompanied many of the closings. More important, Ball was in an insider position from which to fight the bank's management when it proposed a merger with its chief competitor, the Barnett Bank. As noted earlier, such a move would have materially diluted duPont's growing control of Florida National.

Arthur N. Perry, president of Florida National, had positioned the bank in a number of boom-time loans of dubious quality, and the merger was intended, at least in part, as a cure for the bank's weakening condition. Ball did not become fully aware of the reach of Perry's poor loan policy until well after duPont assumed control of the bank.[58] Outwardly, the merger was benignly portrayed as part of a national trend toward consolidation in the banking industry. It was approved by both boards of directors and announced publicly by banner headlines in the *Florida Times-Union* in April 1929.[59] Because the merger posed a threat to duPont's plans, he and Ball decided to prevent it. Ball told Perry of their intention to apprise other stockholders of duPont's view that the merger would be detrimental to Florida National stockholders and reflect poorly on the bank's reputation as a secure institution. Apparently, the size of duPont's holdings coupled with the perceived impact of the duPont name on other stockholders was sufficient to dissuade merger proponents from going ahead with the plan.[60]

Less than three months later, the failure of the Citizens Bank and Trust Company in Tampa precipitated another string of closings, once again plunging the state's banking establishment into chaos.[61] The panic spread to St. Augustine, and signs of it began to appear in Jacksonville. Although Ball held no formal executive position in the bank, he personally monitored the ominous atmosphere settling over the tellers' floor of the bank. When he had seen enough to indicate a "run" in the making, he determined to take steps to ensure the bank's ability to respond to depositors' withdrawals. What happened next gave rise to the legend of how Ball risked a major part of the duPont fortune to contain what otherwise would have been a fatal "run" on the bank's assets. It is a legend founded on fact.

Perry, still president of the bank, was ill, and Ball suggested that he leave the bank for the day for a needed rest. Then Ball took some $20 million worth of market-valued securities from the Almours holdings and expressed them to New York as ready collateral for an emergency loan. DuPont, in Europe at the time, cabled his approval of the action in the now well known words: "You're on ground. Use own judgment but pull our bank through."[62] Even though the leading local newspaper refused to publish his announcement of available cash reserves for fear it would reflect badly on the city's other banks, Ball managed to spread the news by word of mouth that duPont money was in place to back deposits. Still, depositors showed up at the bank the next morning to see for themselves. As tellers honored withdrawals, they told each customer, as casually as possible, that duPont had placed $15 million of his own funds at the bank's disposal. This news quieted the situation, and the feared run was averted.[63] Today, after three generations of federal deposit insurance, Americans have little appreciation of the pervasive panic that could engulf an entire community at the perception of a bank nearing default. But it was part of the temper of the times.

The news of actual failures elsewhere in the state heightened the existing tension. In poorly run banks, extended beyond their liquidity by undercapitalization and poor loan portfolios, the management could do little to avert runs induced by rumor and panic among depositors. Once started, the withdrawals continued until a bank was forced to close its doors. Few banks of the period could withstand a sustained run without reserves generally beyond reach of the endangered institution. Ball had clearly risked a substantial portion of his boss's fortune to provide liquidity to the Florida National Bank in dangerous times, and duPont fully understood what that had meant. As he later told Ball at the height of another series of "runs" around the state, "We are certainly giving the people of Florida the finest and cleanest banking system they have ever enjoyed, and they should understand this and act accordingly.[64]

The handling of the Florida National crisis of 1929, more than any other event, symbolized duPont and Ball's shared commitment to a sound banking institution. Ed Ball may have had serious failings in many respects, but panic under extreme pressure cannot be counted among them. And it was Alfred I. duPont's strong sense of social responsibility that allowed his personal money to be placed at risk—an action that, above all others, redeemed the situation. After Florida National weathered this crisis, it was clear to discerning observers that Ed Ball was the de facto executive in charge. His was the guiding hand as the bank increasingly assumed a duPont identity, even though Perry remained in titular command.

5

Banks, Pulpwood, and Depression

Ed Ball's direct intervention in Florida National's management during the crisis had left Perry doubtful about his own position as president of the bank. In early 1930, he abruptly resigned to become vice chairman of Barnett Bank.[1] News of Perry's resignation came as something of an unpleasant surprise to duPont. In the troubled times resulting from the spasmodic bank failures around the state, the sudden resignation of the widely respected bank president cast doubt on Florida National's reputation for stability. Ball advised duPont that in the prevailing circumstances, the duPont name was necessary in active management to reassure the public of the bank's sound condition. To that end, Alfred assumed the presidency of the Florida National Bank in February of 1930, further solidifying Ball's role as the de facto managing executive.[2] The way was then open for full-scale development of a financial realm in the growing duPont-Ball empire. It was hardly a propitious time to embark on such an endeavor; economic conditions were darkened by events far more calamitous than the Florida banking crisis.

Four months earlier, in October of 1929, the nation had been shocked out of its euphoria by the abrupt collapse of the stock market. There followed a precipitous decline in the overall level of the nation's business activity. It had occurred with a sudden ferocity and pervasiveness unlike any of the previous market crashes. Within a few weeks, it was evident that the situation was far more than a mere "market correction." The manufacturing and agricultural sectors of the nation's economy had been eroding for some time, and through 1929, bank failures occurred across the country at alarming rates.[3]

As the stock market crash pushed a tottering national economy over the edge, Florida, already in the grip of economic strangulation, fell even deeper into the yawning abyss that was the Great Depression. There may have been some perverse consolation for Floridians that the state was no longer alone in its economic misery, but that was small comfort at best.

The bank acquisition process started by duPont and Ball in Jacksonville had commenced before the stock market crash. The Lakeland National Bank had failed, and federal officials, trying to ensure a continued banking presence in that community, offered a charter to the high bidder for its assets. Proceeds from such sales were applied to depositors' claims against the failed institution. DuPont, acting through Ball, outbid his Jacksonville competitor, the Atlantic National Bank, for the Lakeland bank's office building and other remaining assets. In the process, Almours Securities acquired its first banking operation outside Jacksonville. In September, the first of a new chain of Florida National banks opened in Lakeland. The stock market crashed less than sixty days later.

As depression conditions pushed more of the state's banks toward failure, opportunities were presented for individuals with capital and the temerity to risk it in the highly uncertain economic climate of Florida. DuPont was such an individual. Acting primarily on the counsel of Ball, he selectively seized on certain of those opportunities. Before the end of the year, the small central Florida town of Bartow had seen both its banks close. Ball advised duPont to move into the void left by the double failure, and the Bartow Florida National Bank opened at the end of the year. In quick succession, the duPont-Ball combine moved to acquire charters in Orlando, Daytona, St. Petersburg, and Miami.[4]

The pattern was similar in each case. Bank regulators trying to salvage troubled banks, or preserve what could be saved for the benefit of depositors, sought solvent entities to take over failed institutions' remaining assets. If the locale and situation looked promising to Ball in the long view, duPont's Florida National stepped in to buy up what remained of the insolvent bank. Through such arrangements, regulators maximized funds for stranded depositors and maintained necessary banking services in the affected communities. Investors with ready capital backed by nerves of steel were essential to the process. They also profited handsomely from it in the long run. Men like duPont and Ball were comfortable in pursuit of the long term even when faced with great obstacles in the short term.

Ball's efforts to build the Florida National Bank chain met with strong political opposition from some quarters of the industry. In the spring of 1930, the Citizens Bank and Trust of Tampa, which had failed in July 1929, was embroiled in a highly contentious liquidation process.[5] Ball entered into

an agreement with the federal liquidator to purchase the failed bank's building and other assets with the expectation of opening a Florida National
branch in Tampa. Although the sale would have benefited the stranded
depositors of the defaulted institution, it met strong opposition from local
banking circles, precipitating a major political confrontation between Ball
and the established political power of Hillsborough County. Peter O. Knight,
founder of Tampa Electric Company, a prominent businessman and a
powerful political figure, was a director, investor, and officer in the Exchange National Bank of Tampa, one of Tampa's surviving banks. The
businessman-banker-politician was a close friend of U.S. Senator Duncan U.
Fletcher, then Florida's senior senator.[6] Knight launched a lobbying campaign to deny Ball the charter and preclude a duPont entry into the Tampa
market.

Knight's first effort was to dissuade the U.S. comptroller of the currency,
J. W. Pole, from granting an application, even though Ball had not yet
actually filed for a charter. Knight knew of Ball's negotiations with the
liquidator and clearly considered competition from the duPont banks a
serious threat. He moved quickly to thwart the Jacksonville banking group's
penetration into the Hillsborough County market. In a letter to Pole he cited
the dramatic decrease in deposits in Florida banks, and those of the Tampa
Bay area in particular, and he insisted that further competition would seriously jeopardize those banks still open in the region. He pointed out that the
agitation for the new charter came not from the public at large but from the
liquidator, whose only concern was to sell the failed Citizens Bank and Trust
building. In an unabashed plea for government protection from competition, Knight came directly and emotionally to the point: "The local banks
having gone through hell during the past years are entitled to the protection
of the government, and they [should] be permitted to strengthen themselves
instead of being weakened."[7]

He did not let the matter rest there. At the state level, Knight made his case
against Ball to a receptive Governor Doyle Carlton on purely political
grounds. He wrote in a letter: "I think Mr. Ball is quite ambitious to control
the situation politically in this state, especially to obtain control, if possible,
of the next legislature. And I think the establishment of a bank here by him
. . . is more for political purposes than anything else."[8] Ball's strong opposition to Carlton's 1929 bond refunding program was still an irritant to the
governor, and it was common knowledge in political circles that Ball intended to continue the fight in the 1931 legislature. In another letter to

Carlton, marked "Confidential," Knight told him how dangerous Ball was to the state because of his public statements regarding the precarious situation of many banks. In blunt language, the Tampa banker told the governor: "I assume you have heard of the activity of Mr. Ball, duPont's son-in-law [sic], in connection with banking circles in this state. His activities in that connection are such as that in my opinion he is the greatest menace now to this state that we have in it."[9]

Carlton replied to Knight: "I agree with you on the duPont Activities in this state and was no doubt the first to raise the danger signal. Early last year I put Mr. Ball on notice that I would not be governed by him."[10] Carlton would undoubtedly have been receptive to Knight's suggestions to dampen Ball's legislative influence. Knight's letters make clear that Ball's reputation for sharp politics as well as shrewd business dealings had made him a man to be reckoned with in the state's political and business circles.

That he was making enemies in high places did not temper Ball's tenacious pursuit of duPont objectives, but he did suffer setbacks. Contrary to later myths of invincibility, Ball did not always prevail in the political arena. His losing efforts in 1929 and 1931 to stop Carlton's bond refunding program, his unsuccessful (until 1949) support of a state sales tax to relieve real estate taxes, and a resounding defeat on a banking bill in 1953 all bear witness to that fact.[11] Ball could not overcome Knight's opposition to a Tampa charter, and Florida National did not enter the Tampa market.

A somewhat different version of this episode by biographer Marquis James cast duPont in the role of benevolent businessman-statesman, refraining from unleashing ruinous competition on the Tampa area for the greater community good. James's account has it that the federal comptroller of the currency informed Ball that entry of Florida National into the Tampa market would impair the viability of the other two Tampa banks, one of which was Knight's. When duPont was advised of this, he told Ball to withdraw their application, saying he would not be a party to endangering the banks that had survived the 1929 Tampa panic.[12]

It is more likely that Ball knew he could not overcome the political opposition put in place by Knight, and he and duPont simply put the best face possible on their setback. In denying the charter, Comptroller Pole had taken exactly the position advanced by Knight. There was a certain plausibility to the case of ruinous competition made by the Tampa banker, but it is most unlikely that concern for the other Tampa banks would have governed the decision of Ball, or duPont for that matter. Interestingly, before Claude

Pepper and Ball became implacable foes, Pepper and Knight were political enemies as a result of the Tampa businessman's strong support for Park Trammell in the 1934 senatorial election.[13]

While Ball was constructing the Florida National Bank chain, duPont kept abreast of his efforts through almost daily correspondence with his brother-in-law. The tenor of the letters shows that duPont retained final authority but was trusting more and more to Ball's judgment. The process of acquiring banks while the nation was rapidly sinking into depression required a highly refined and intuitive business acumen braced by steel nerves. It was during this period that Ball's versatility and resolve as a businessman began to define the image that became legend in later years. Still, it should be remembered that there was more to it all than Ball's uncommon abilities. The duPont name afforded a measure of confidence that attracted depositors made wary by bank closings in their communities. It was a reassuring factor around the state. Ball reported through the troubled summer of 1930 that either deposits increased or withdrawals stabilized when people realized that the legendary duPont name was behind the bank.[14]

The month of June was especially difficult, with Ball dealing with events on a day-to-day basis. As 1930 wore on, the nation was plunging deeper into depression with little understanding of what was happening or how to stem the downward spiral of economic conditions. Florida bankers, like their counterparts in other parts of the troubled nation, dreaded a "run" of depositors that could drain a bank of its available reserves, forcing it to close its doors. Runs were fueled as much by rumor as reality, so that prophecies of disaster were frequently self-fulfilling. In early summer, Ball feared major statewide bank closings that he judged would put more than $30 million in depositors' funds at risk. He was not fearful for the fiscal stability of the Florida National banks because of his and duPont's operating philosophy of maintaining a high margin of liquidity. Still, he knew that runs on other banks could induce panic in Florida National depositors that even those high margins could not sustain. He reported this intelligence to DuPont, saying that what he saw looming over the horizon would be no "light breeze" but rather a "tornado." He again made arrangements for temporary loans from New York banks secured by duPont company stock to provide liquidity if the "excitement should happen to reach Jacksonville."[15] duPont gave prompt approval to his arrangements, a further indication of his growing confidence in Ball.[16] Five days later, Ball advised duPont that a major bank in St. Petersburg had failed, as well as four more in Miami. Even though he anticipated more closings within the next few days, he was cautiously optimistic that the runs would not reach as far as Jacksonville.[17] His judgment was correct.

Ball was quick to seize the opportunity presented by the St. Petersburg failure. He quickly applied for a charter there and was advised less than a week later of its approval. In the same letter in which he reported on the St. Petersburg charter, he told duPont: "Also as you know, the Florida National Bank [in Jacksonville] is becoming more liquid every month and by the end of this year should be in almost as good condition as the Lakeland and Bartow Banks, who can pay off all of their depositors and still have money left in the till."[18]

Liquidity was the key element in the management philosophy that governed the new bank chain. It reflected the inherently conservative nature of both duPont and Ball, as well as duPont's view that a bank was primarily a steward of its depositors' money. It existed to make money for its stockholders only secondarily.[19] The linchpin of this management philosophy was the loan policy quickly established by Ball and sanctioned by duPont. Collateral was required for all loans, even those to officers and directors.[20] Ball's attention to this policy was reflected in his instructions that payments were to be deducted from paychecks of bank officers who were delinquent in their loans, a departure from the previously lax attitude in such matters. He based the amounts of the payments on his own assessment of what those officers could afford without impairing their responsibilities to their families. In one case, he determined that a particular officer had only himself and his wife to care for and could afford a stipulated withholding each month.[21] Perhaps in this attitude toward the bank officers, one can find the roots of the fierce loyalty to Ball that was commonplace in so many—but by no means all—of his employees. In it one can also find evidence of his strong urge to exercise personal control down through multiple layers of management.

The confidentiality of bank records make the extent to which "policy" considerations occasioned departures from the conservative dimension of the Florida National's loan policy a matter of conjecture. Ball told the president of a bank with whom he was negotiating a merger "to discontinue the making of new loans, particularly so-called policy loans which, in my opinion, usually are not backed with proper collateral."[22] Policy loans were those made without strict adherence to collateral requirements to individuals who could be helpful to the lender in other matters, a not unusual practice in Florida banks during the period. Even though the practice offended Ball's inherently conservative business sense, his correspondence with duPont indicates that he utilized so-called policy loans where expedient to foster political and business relationships favorable to duPont interests. The ability to make loans on terms favorable to the borrower is a powerful leveraging mechanism, one used frequently to nurture self-serving political relationships. Of course, such benevolence did not extend to borrowers at large, and any questionable loan tended to put depositors at some measure of increased risk. It was, and most likely still is, a dilemma inherent in the inevitable relationship between economic and political power.

Besides the acquisition of banks, Ball was deeply involved with duPont in the management of the securities portfolio held by Almours Securities, including trading and, occasionally, speculating in the stock market. Almours was the holding instrument for duPont's entire investment in Florida and was the foundation on which everything else was supported, including Ball's acquisition of new banks.[23] Almours was also a source of income to duPont and Ball, and at times, the ability to control its disbursements was important in maintaining the secure image of the banks' balance sheets. On some occasions, Ball delayed Almours's dividend checks to maintain optimum balances in required banking reports filed with federal regulators.[24] The practice illustrates Ball's proclivity for operating at the edge of the law when it suited his purposes, and maintaining the image of a strong balance sheet was such a purpose. It was indicative of the fixation of both dupont and Ball on the image of liquidity for the bank chain they were linking together in the Florida National group. Some critics maintained that the loan policy denied needed capital in the communities served by duPont's banks. Perhaps so, but no Florida National bank failed, and no Florida National depositors lost money in those tumultuous years. That was as much a part of the legacy of Ed Ball as it was of Alfred I. duPont.

There does not seem to have been a formal corporate structure in the early duPont organization. Ball did not hold the outward trappings of authority, but he had a firm grasp on the reality of power. Being duPont's brother-in-law certainly enhanced his position of power. It is clear from the correspondence between Ball and duPont that Ball answered directly to duPont, and so did W. T. Edwards. Still, the implied scope of Ball's authority, and the deferential tone of some of Edwards's letters and memos to him in the late 1920s, indicated that Ball was emerging at that early stage as a firm second in command to duPont. During duPont's frequent absences from Florida, his brother-in-law was clearly in charge. Ball's natural inclination for exercising the manipulative power of money led him to focus on the financial dimension of the duPont enterprises.[25] After 1927, the political details of road building and day-to-day management of timber operations in the Panhandle were largely left to Edwards. Yet Ball maintained the dominant role in political affairs for the organization. He emerged as duPont's chief adviser on political matters, and Edwards increasingly appeared to act under his direction.

Even before duPont settled on the final vision for his west Florida enterprise, he knew that whatever it might be, any large-scale improvement there depended on curing the region's lack of roads. In Florida, while all roads may not have led to politics, they certainly started there. He understood that to bring major change to the order of things in the Panhandle would require a committed participation in the rough-and-ready workings of state and local politics. While duPont himself was ill suited, both by inclination and social position, for such a role, it was one for which his tenacious and combative brother-in-law was a near perfect fit. Ball instinctively understood the manipulative powers of the duPont name and fortune in the political arena, and he was, by nature, not disposed to using any more of either than that minimally necessary to achieve his assigned purposes.

DuPont saw the road shortage in the Panhandle as the major obstacle to the progressive development of the region, including his own plans which were still in the formative stages. He recognized that any suitable solution would be, by any score, a highly political undertaking. The existing state road plan was oriented toward the tourist trade centered on the east and southwest coasts. The reason was clear. Tourism was estimated to account for more than 40 percent of the state's income, and the automobile was a major factor in it.[26] Those regions were the principal areas of growth. The plan, though administered by a state road board appointed by the governor, was still the creature of the legislature, always subject to changing political currents.

DuPont's plan was simple. He wanted to shift more of the state's road-building resources to the upper west coast, where his landholdings were steadily increasing. Shifting funds from planned east coast roads to the remote Panhandle was a formidable political task. To that end, he set Ball and Edwards to organizing a collective effort to promote a coastal highway from Tampa to Pensacola. In Alfred's expansive vision, that highway would someday link up with Florida's east coast, providing a continuous coastal highway for the entire state. For the present, however, he focused only on the upper west coast.

Acting through his two lieutenants, Ball and Edwards, duPont created the Gulf Coast Highway Association. It had a broad membership of local political and business leadership, mostly from counties in northwest Florida with much to gain from such a project. To integrate that purpose with the region's overall economy, the coastal highway was seen as the catalyst for a system of feeder roads, all to be part of the fledgling state highway system. Such a network posed distinct benefits for lands previously locked in rural isolation, including those of the growing duPont holdings in the Panhandle counties.

DuPont was the president of the Gulf Coast Highway Association, and Edwards served as executive vice president. Ball, listed on the letterhead as honorary vice president, was never far from the center of the association's activities. Barron G. Collier, a nationally known southwest Florida developer, was another honorary vice president. His name afforded the organization a wider geographic base, giving it an aura of support from the southwest part of the state. Edwards was the organization's principal operative. He described his role as doing the "the hoof and mouth work" of the group.[27] Using the resources and prestige of the duPont name, he and Ball created a smoothly efficient political machine dedicated to road construction in northwest Florida. It well served those duPont interests that happily coincided with road building, and others not so directly associated. It was under the mantle of that organization that Ball found entry to the labyrinthine world of Florida politics.

In addition to highway construction, the duPont interests were affected by banking and taxes. The series of bank failures that had facilitated Ball's bank acquisitions also produced a flurry of reform proposals in the state legislature. In the initial stages of constructing the Florida National Bank chain, Ball was inevitably drawn into such issues. As a large landowner, the duPont organization was also concerned with the numerous matters relating to relief for the overburdened ad valorem tax rolls. This gave rise to Ball's continuing efforts to enact a sales tax, efforts which failed repeatedly until the state's budget deficit in 1949 left a reluctant legislature and Governor Fuller Warren with no alternative. Ball also strived to maintain the constitutional prohibition against state income and estate taxes that had helped attract duPont to Florida.[28]

The conduct of large and complex business ventures inevitably entails influencing the course of governmental action, nurturing policies favorable to one's interests and preventing unfavorable ones. Such is the essence of lobbying. When conducted to advance business interests, it generally carried (and still does) a pejorative connotation. Ed Ball, never one to worry about public opinion in the abstract, did not allow that to deter him. To the contrary, he seemed to relish it—especially when winning. Yet Ball was quite adept at utilizing public opinion when it suited his purposes. He used public opinion to his advantage in furthering the interests of the Gulf Coast Highway Association and later, as we shall see, in his fight for control of the Florida East Coast Railway.

Lobbying was (and is) a continuing component of the Florida legislative process. Before the advent of annual sessions with the constitution of 1968, the practice of legislative persuasion reached a frenzy of activity every two years in an intense sixty-day legislative session. The session was the most visible part of the process, but there were also subtler, less visible dimensions to it. Any diligent person pursuing interests in the political arena knew that success depended on having a core of reliable relationships around which a larger commonality of viewpoints could coalesce on important issues. Ball was by nature such a diligent person. Developing and maintaining those relationships was a year-round matter, an element woven into the fabric of business operations the same as any other element of prudent management. As already discussed, the $45,000 "Political" expenditure in duPont's 1926 financial report indicated his appreciation of the process. Ball was even more finely attuned to it.

Ball's initial political experience came through duPont's highly visible involvement in Delaware politics. While the latter was an intensely private person, he was also a duPont of Delaware, quite capable of exerting himself on matters he considered important to his own interests. He generally raised such issues to matters of principle, at least in his own eyes, and fought them openly and in a straightforward manner. Even when he set about the sorry spectacle of removing his son's given name by a bill in the Delaware legislature, he convinced himself that he was right. In that instance, he failed miserably since even he could not bring a majority of the Delaware legislators to deprive a young duPont of the birthright in his given name.[29] By contrast, Ball was not prone to concerning himself overly with rationalizing political issues as matters of principle. When he did, his field of vision was primarily defined by his sense of property rights.

DuPont eschewed overt involvement in politics after he came to Florida, contenting himself mostly with pronouncements on policy issues he deemed important to his goals. He left direct action to others, principally Ball, on matters affecting duPont interests. Even with such apparent aloofness, it quickly became apparent that when Alfred I. duPont issued statements, his lieutenants moved quickly to give substance to his words. Notwithstanding duPont's obvious affection for Ball, the younger man did not presume to be duPont's equal. His brother-in-law was, after all, *the* duPont in the organization. It was his fortune, his name, and he signed the checks. There was no doubt on that score on the part of Ball or anyone else of consequence.

Although Ball had to work his way into the state's political process as an outsider, the duPont name and the fortune perceived to be at his disposal certainly made things easier for him. Using both to full advantage, he quickly assumed the role of a force to be reckoned with in Florida politics. In time, it was as much reality as image. Along with Edwards, he pursued the duPont political interests from the "Highwayman's Hideout," a large, stately house close to the Capitol in Tallahassee. There, during the once-every-two-year legislative sessions, they catered to legislators and other influential politicians. The name of their haunt conveyed the primary interest of its congenial hosts, but conversations there undoubtedly embraced the full range of Florida politics and their impact on the rapidly expanding duPont interests in the state.

Around 1939, Ball and Edwards moved their base of operations from the Highwayman's Hideout to the fifth floor of the Floridian Hotel on Monroe Street, within easy walking distance of the Capitol.[30] Most of the legislators took lodging at that hotel during the sessions, as did many lobbyists. In the evenings, the proximity of common living quarters, rocking chairs on a long front porch facing Monroe Street, and well-stocked hospitality suites nurtured an atmosphere of conviviality. It was an atmosphere in which whiskey, poker playing, and other relaxations blended easily with political discussion, enriching and clarifying the merits or demerits of proposed legislation. Such was the grist from which understandings on legislation were milled.

Every county commission, city council, chamber of commerce, large landowner, and developer in the state had concerns about the location and building of roads. Each statutory designation of preference in the state's road system was, in effect, an allocation of state funds among competing regions. Each required a legislative enactment, and the competition was intense. Roads were concrete measures by which a legislator could be reckoned a success or failure in bringing benefits to his home district. For those in legislative leadership positions, the ability to parcel out roads to allies in the legislative process was the currency with which a power base could be maintained and enhanced. It involved state monies for maintaining existing roads as well as building new ones. Local interests sought to have them designated as part of the state highway system to reap a share of the gas tax revenues earmarked for road maintenance. Even while locked in the bond refunding battle of 1929, the legislature still passed thirty-nine separate pieces of legislation designating road preferences.[31] This was not unusual for the times, and it illustrates the pervasiveness of road-building politics during a legislative session. It was a zero-sum game; the amount of tax revenues available for roads was always less than the demand. When one interest won, another lost. Ball, Edwards, and other practitioners of the lobbyist's craft dealt with each other and the legislature on those terms. The intensely competitive environment fostered by it was one for which Ball's combative temperament was well suited. All this was wrapped in the rhetoric of fairness, equity, and high-sounding public policy to raise local or regional interests to a perception of compelling state need. Beneath it all, there was only one issue: who had the votes, and who got the roads?

Ball's first immersion in the Florida legislative process was during the 1927 session. His emphasis on roads was already well established. The Gulf Coast Highway Association was functioning, with Ball and Edwards promoting road building in the Panhandle at every opportunity.[32] About the same time, as discussed earlier, Ball was also unobtrusively buying stock on behalf of duPont in Jacksonville banks, particularly the Florida National Bank. Although banking issues were also of great concern to the duPont organization, the primary concern was clearly roads at this stage of the duPont organization's development.[33]

In the larger picture, the full impact of the boom's collapse was not yet clearly impressed on the state's political consciousness. Headlines in the *New York Times* early in 1927 had warned, "Florida Is Facing Serious Reaction; Conditions Vary, but All Sections of the State Feel the Aftermath of the Boom."[34] Nevertheless, Governor John W. Martin told the 1927 legislature, "The finances of the State Government never were on a sounder basis."[35] That was true, as far as it went. State government was not in debt, being proscribed from issuing debt by the state constitution. The fiscal disaster brewing in the counties and cities as a result of the bonding spree during the boom was only slowly becoming understood. It would not emerge as a full-scale state crisis until the 1929 legislative battle over the Crummer refunding program.

Meanwhile, in 1927, the Great Bull Market on Wall Street continued to roar forward, and Florida lawmakers operated in the blissful pretense that matters would be set right without politically risky action on their part. The legislative process proceeded as usual, and the classifying of new and future roads continued, oblivious to the fiscal deluge about to descend.

Ball's initial exposure to the Florida legislative process was not altogether to his liking. His reports to duPont were often couched in terms of disdain for legislators and the legislative process. Like other lobbyists from around the state in pursuit of highway funds, he had several bills pertaining to specific road projects to steer to passage. The allocation of finite resources pitted one competing interest against another in the zero-sum game of budgeting. In order to advance one's own program, it was necessary to defeat or diminish another. Ball found himself confronted with this dimension of the process when Miami interests opposed his efforts in order to further their own. Legislators from different regions aided both sides. Faced with stalemate on a particular measure, the leader of the Miami group sought Ball out in Jacksonville to search for a compromised way out of their mutual opposition and stalemate. Maneuvers such as this were most likely at the expense of some third party also competing for a share of the political largesse, but deemed less powerful and hence not privy to the proposal. Ball reported the matter to duPont, adding that he might agree with the Miami proposal: "This afternoon I am leaving for Tallahassee, and if he will pull off his henchmen and let our Bills go through first, I am inclined to agree to his proposition."[36] Ball's concern for whose bills went first illustrates the mistrust inherent in such dealings.

Lobbyists routinely bemoan the level of intelligence and competence of legislators and other lobbyists, particularly those who oppose them. Things were no different in 1927, and Ball was no exception. His complaining along those lines brought a sympathetic response from duPont midway through the second month of the session: "I surely sumpathize [sic] with you in your efforts to try and make a silk purse out of a bunch of sows' ears, regardless of the fact that sows are usually supposed to be ladies. In other words, your efforts with the Legislature seem, as is usually the case, to be more or less unappreciated, but I must congratulate you on your bulldog persistence, which, after all, is the foundation upon which all success is based."[37]

Two days later, Ball reported to duPont: "As I wired you last night, we have at last gotten things lined up in the Florida Legislature, and yesterday and the day before we succeeded in putting through most of our road and bridge bills," and only "one bridge bill and two road bills" remained to be passed.[38] It was an impressive debut for a lobbyist, even for one with the duPont name and power at his disposal. In the same letter, Ball hinted to duPont of his inclination to distance himself from the process in the future: "Lobbying is a new experience to me and while we have gotten practically everything that we wanted and went after, I do not think I will tackle the job of lobbying again during this lifetime."[39]

Although difficult to discern with certainty, it appears that Ball did step back somewhat, leaving pursuit of legislators in the capitol's hallways to Edwards. Thereafter, Ball's involvement generally took the form of holding forth at the Highwayman's Hideout during sessions, always readily accessible to the action in the legislative hallways, but in rather more comfortable and commanding circumstances than those afforded by the capitol rotunda. There was never any doubt on one point: Ball set the strategic direction of duPont political affairs.

After duPont's death, Ball's distance from the capitol's hallways added a certain mystique to his image as the real power of the duPont organization. Ball clearly held the reins of power, notwithstanding his public protestations that he was just one of the trustees. By the 1940s, a pattern had emerged. Edwards and Henry Dew, another longtime duPont associate and distant relative of Ed and Jessie, assumed the mantle of duPont lobbyists with a continuing presence in Tallahassee; Ball would come to Tallahassee several times during a legislative session.

Ball traveled on the Gulf Wind, the afternoon passenger train from Jacksonville to Tallahassee. He, the other duPont people traveling with him, and any legislators who might be on the same train would often have drinks together.[40] Well known to the train personnel who catered to him, he conducted almost courtly proceedings during the three-hour trip, perhaps venturing some well-chosen words, over drinks, to legislative traveling companions on some pending issue. After arriving at Tallahassee, Ball and selected guests might have dinner at one of Tallahassee's political haunts, such as the Silver Slipper Restaurant. There, in the intimacy of a small private dining room, the party could enjoy drinks from a private whiskey stock (Leon County was officially "dry" in those days) followed by large steaks or a plate of fried fresh Gulf seafood. In the midst of the good-humored conversation and bantering, a word or two of explanation to a legislative guest on an upcoming amendment to a banking or tax bill would always be in order.

In later years, he would entertain at Southwood, a stately plantation south of Tallahassee acquired by the St. Joe Paper Company in 1958. Part of that property with the home on it was purchased from and leased back to a federal judge who had presided for a period in the Crummer antitrust case against Ball and the duPont Trust. The propriety of that transaction was questioned closely in 1965 by Congresswoman Leonor Sullivan of Missouri during a House committee hearing on amendments to the Bank Holding Company Act at the instigation of J. A. Maloney, editor of the Apalachicola newspaper and one of Ball's more devout enemies.[41] One amendment would have stripped away the exemption that allowed the duPont Trust to function as a business conglomerate combining banking and industrial operations under a single ownership, a distinct advantage accruing almost uniquely to the duPont Trust. Evidence before the committee related that on February 13, 1957, U.S. District Judge Dozier DeVane had directed a verdict of dismissal in favor of Ball and other duPont defendants in the Crummer antitrust suit. The following October, the Southwood Farm manager for St. Joe Paper Company contracted to buy Judge DeVane's property, which was then leased back to the judge and his wife for a rental of $50 per month. The congresswoman made much ado of the fact that the purchase price was considerably more than the $30,000 assessed value. The clear implication was that an inflated price was paid to the judge in recognition of his earlier ruling on the antitrust case. Other congressmen came to Ball's defense, one urging that it would be unfair to question DeVane's integrity since he was now dead and unable to reply to the charges against him. In this context, it should also be noted that in those years, Florida real estate assessments for tax purposes were notoriously deflated. Actual market price was invariably far greater than assessed value. Sullivan's line of questioning was then terminated.[42] In all likelihood, she sensed that, in the male-dominated atmosphere of the time, further pursuit of the matter would be construed as an unwarranted assault on the honor of a dead judge. Whatever her reason, it worked to Ball's advantage.

In the 1940s and 1950s, although Ball had less direct involvement in state political matters, he expanded his presence in the nation's capital as the principal spokesman for the Florida duPont interests. By then, they were becoming generally known as the duPont-Ball interests. He maintained a suite at the Carlton Hotel for his and other duPont executives' use while in Washington.[43] Initially, his primary concerns at the national level were taxation and general banking issues. Later, the quest for control of the Florida East Coast Railway and the battle over the Bank Holding Company Act of 1955, with its provision exempting the duPont Trust from its divestiture mandate (mentioned above), were of major importance to Ball and the duPont Trust. When the battle for control of the railroad commenced, Ball was required to be in Washington for prolonged periods. Not only did he have to combat the Atlantic Coast Line Railroad, but, by then, he had the formidable opposition of Claude Pepper, Florida's senior senator at the time. The young Taylor County representative who had been his ally in the 1929 session of the Florida legislature was to become a determined opponent to the growing concentration of economic power represented by Ball. The FEC railroad takeover and the Bank Holding Company Act issue were milestones in Ball's career and were involved in his continuing conflict with Pepper. More detailed treatment of each follows. They are mentioned here to illustrate the diversity and complexity of the continuing matters in which Ball over time involved himself as the controlling voice of the duPont empire.

In the early 1930s, as Ball and Edwards were giving substance to the duPont organization's political prowess, Alfred was wrestling with how best to give form to his vision. He had brought with him to Florida only the vaguest outlines of the manner in which he would use his wealth in his adopted state. His final plan emerged over time. During this period, Ball's efforts were largely focused on building the banking dimension of the fledgling empire. Still, he was involved to a great extent in all the activities affecting duPont investments, including those in west Florida. Ball was not the kind of person to let any part of the expanding duPont interests slip beyond his immediate control. His involvement in both the duPont business enterprises and the personal affairs of duPont expanded Ball's circle of associates and allies first in Jacksonville and then wherever the duPont interests reached throughout the state.

The full range of his activities was not strictly confined to the business or political spheres. Like most businessmen, Ball participated in charitable activities. There were synergistic reactions inherent in such endeavors that facilitated and enriched political relationships. His colleague W. T. Edwards spent considerable time and effort for many years promoting state care for tuberculosis patients as head of the state tuberculosis board. Eventually, the state hospital for treatment of that disease was named after him.[44] In 1938, Ball and Edwards worked together with Claude Pepper on arrangements for a Roosevelt birthday party to promote care for crippled children, a special interest which Ball inherited from duPont. That endeavor not only benefited crippled children but also nurtured a congenial relationship with the principal Roosevelt supporter in Florida.[45] This was still in the cordial period of the Ball-Pepper relationship.

Political considerations permeated all of Ball's endeavors to some extent.

Even where business concerns were his dominant purpose, his management decisions always allowed for political ramifications. This included both considerations sharply defined at the moment as well as future ones only vaguely discernible at the time of decision but with potential for the long term. It was in the realm of the long run that Ball conducted the affairs of the duPont empire. Other executives associated with the growing duPont conglomerate worked in concert with Ball's predilections along these lines. Outsiders sometimes approached them suggesting arrangements considered politically advantageous to duPont interests. For example, one would-be arranger sought to put Ball next to a newspaper publisher who controlled a growing chain of rural weekly newspapers. He informed a Florida National executive whom he knew: "The thought struck me that it might be well to get these two men together. The newspaper man needs some financial assistance, and your friend needs political influence."[46]

In most instances, Ball's approach to combining politics and business was more direct than working on charitable projects favored by politicians. It spanned a wide spectrum from helping secure appointments for persons deemed supportive of his interests to helping obtain government contracts for friends and family.

One prominent Jacksonville attorney, who was a principal duPont lawyer from the beginning, sought duPont's help through Ball in securing a federal judgeship. Both Ball's cynicism and his pragmatism regarding politics in general are evident in correspondence on the matter. Concerning the supplicant's qualifications, he told duPont: "[The supplicant] is fitted by nature for a Judicial position, as I believe he is lazier than the average; also, he appreciates the honor . . . of this position and believes it will enhance his already excellent social position in the community. In addition to these qualifications, he and his wife are probably worth some $2,000,000.00 to $4,000,000.00 and . . . are in a better position to support the honors of a Federal judgeship.[47] More important to Ball than the financial and social qualifications was the following: "I am satisfied that on any questions in any way affecting your interest, that he would have a friendly disposition, which seems to be absent with so many Courts where a person of some financial standing is concerned."[48]

That Ball expressed such thoughts is not surprising; in politics people are inclined to aid those who are not inimical to their interests. That he put it in writing with such candor illustrates his conviction that pursuit and protection of one's interests through political influence were legitimate activities.

It may also indicate that he did not expect anyone to be reading his private letters to duPont in the future. Unfortunately, such intrusions are essential to the practice of history. As it turned out, the lawyer did not get the appointment after the White House learned that he had publicly supported Al Smith in the 1928 election.[49]

Ball was in his element when it came to manipulating political influence in the cause of business or, sometimes, family. This is seen in an episode involving Alfred's son, Alfred Victor. In 1928, the elder duPont publicly supported Herbert Hoover, perhaps more as a reaction to his cousin Pierre's support of Al Smith than out of deeply felt political conviction.[50] While on an extended trip to Europe, he cabled his support, declaring "National Prosperity" to be the main issue of the campaign and proclaiming Hoover the most suitable to preserve it.[51] Ball was set to the task of organizing "Democrats for Hoover Clubs" around the state.

The 1928 presidential campaign was marked by religious bigotry because of Al Smith's Catholicism. This was particularly true in the traditionally Democratic South. In Florida, Sidney Catts, Florida's most prominent anti-Catholic politician, teamed with the Ku Klux Klan to focus attention on Smith's religion. Following duPont's instructions, Ball steered clear of direct anti-Catholicism, emphasizing instead the "wet-dry" issue, saying Prohibition would be safe under Hoover.[52] Even so, association with the anti-Catholic bigotry of Catts and the Klan tainted him. It was a feature of the campaign that Ball's later critics unduly attributed to him after bigotry became a more commonly condemned social and political vice.[53]

Still, Ball emerged with surrogate standing for duPont in state Republican circles. Although those circles were not very crowded in Florida's solidly Democratic political climate at the time, they were very important for purposes of federal patronage during Republican administrations in Washington. As it turned out, the Hoover administration was the last of those for a long time, but Ball made the most of it while he could.

When a new federal building was authorized for Jacksonville, a local architectural firm sought Ball's assistance in securing the contract, a question of Republican patronage in a town where prominent Republicans were scarce. In a brief return memo, Ball, displaying his propensity for couching matters in a legally binding manner, responded as follows: "Your letter of November 18th received, and on behalf of Messrs. Massena and duPont I agree to co-operate every way possible with you in securing the architectural work on the Federal Building to be constructed in Jacksonville, with the understanding that whether the contract is awarded either in the name of your firm singly, or in the names of the two firms jointly, the architectural fees are to be divided `fifty-fifty' between you and Messrs. Massena and duPont."[54] The architectural firm seeking his help was the same one that had designed and supervised construction of duPont's Epping Forest mansion. The previous relationship did not deter Ball's effort to garner half the fee for Massena and duPont, the firm in which duPont's son was a named partner.[55] Two weeks later, Ball reported to duPont that he was working on the matter and had secured the Duval County and state Republican organizations' endorsements of the architects.[56]

In the practical work of building favorable political relationships, duPont routinely deferred to Ball's judgment but generally reserved final approval for himself. When the local director of the Internal Revenue Service in Jacksonville solicited a contribution for the Republican Party, Ball agreed, but had to seek duPont's approval even though it was only for $250, a relatively small amount. DuPont returned Ball's memo with his initialed approval.[57] Today, such a request from an official of the Internal Revenue Service would be akin to bribery and a political scandal of the first magnitude. DuPont and Ball referred to decisions in this sphere as "policy" matters. As already noted, they used the same terminology in their discussions about giving undercollateralized bank loans to helpful, influential individuals.

During the time Ball was establishing the Florida National Bank of St. Petersburg, a group of local developers wanted assistance from duPont in salvaging a bankrupt country club and housing development. He asked Ball for advice: "Do you know anything about this organization? I presume they want money, which, as you know, I would prefer not giving them. If it is a matter of policy to assist them, that is another proposition." Ball did not know of the developers and could see no advantage in aiding them. He promptly responded: "There is no reason that I know of why it would be good policy to be a member of this club, particularly, as you say you would prefer not to give them money, which is the only thing they are looking for."[58]

When Senator Daniel Hastings of Delaware, appointed to the U.S. Senate on the death of duPont's cousin Coleman, requested an interview with duPont to discuss a loan, the latter was alert to the possibilities stemming from a congenial relationship with him. It was a "policy" matter, and he instructed Ball to inquire of their Washington tax attorney "whether such influence as he [Hastings] might bring to bear on the authorities would possibly have any direct bearing, ultimately, on our interests."[59] Two days later, duPont advised Ball that Hastings had "reduced his request to $15,000, and I assume he would take less. . . . The question involved is purely one of policy, and I should like to have your views on the subject."[60] The correspondence does not show the loan was made but strongly suggests that it was up to Ball's discretion to do so. As with Ball's views on the question of aiding the lawyer seeking the federal judgeship, "policy" questions were always a matter of assessing the potential for advancing duPont interests.

A chain of banks doing business statewide was a powerful mechanism in the context of implementing so-called policy decisions. Lawyer-historian Raymond Vickers notes in *Panic in Paradise* that bankers have always used loans as instruments of political influence. He discusses the well-known activities of Nicholas Biddle and the Second Bank of the United States in its battle with President Andrew Jackson over the issue of central banking to fix a historical precedent for the practice. He also gives examples of the practice among Florida bankers and uses the traditional secrecy of banking records to support his rather sweeping conclusion.[61]

Short of barring all political figures from borrowing money, the influence inherent in the ability to make so-called policy loans is inevitable. Against the strong inferences in the episode with Hastings, there is the fact that duPont and Ball instigated a strict loan policy for the Florida National banks to require adequate collateral for loans, and refused signature loans altogether, a practice which the bank itself says extended well into the 1970s.[62] Yet the very nature of "policy" questions is that they stand apart from what might be called normal operational considerations, being subject to paramount considerations of political expediency. It is impossible to assess the purposes behind departures from standing loan policy, the extent to which they were routine, and if so, whether they were for corrupt purposes. Still, it is clear that Ball utilized the full range of business resources within the duPont empire in implementing "policy" decisions.

The ability to make or withhold loans, hire attorneys across a vast spectrum of business activities throughout the state, make covert political contributions by way of legal fees, provide employment to friends and family, buy and sell property for cash—all these, and more, were the raw ingredients of Ed Ball's political power. They are inevitable attributes of concentrations of economic power, and there is no evidence to suggest that he eschewed the use of them. Still, no one ever linked Ball with the probable cause needed to charge him with a specific criminal act or course of conduct, although many tried. As any lawyer knows, failure to prove illegality does not necessarily negate the fact of it. If one puts aside legality as a judgmental standard, and pursues instead a judgment of Ball based on ethical and moral considerations, the matter becomes even more difficult. In that realm, it is subject to considerations more philosophical than historical in nature and is better left to the ethicist or moral philosopher.

While Ball was building a network of political relationships, Claude Pepper was doing the same. He had been elected to the U.S. Senate, and in 1941, G. Pierce Wood, the Liberty County pulpwood dealer and former Speaker of the Florida House of Representatives, became his executive secretary and personal confidant.[63] Pepper's appointment of Wood, known in political circles as a Ball ally, indicates that Pepper and the duPont organization, which meant Ball, were on good terms.

There is other evidence to support that view. The New Deal was still the focal point of national domestic politics, and Pepper was identified closely with the Roosevelt administration. In the waning days of the 1940 presidential election, when the Democratic coffers were nearly exhausted (as was usual then and now), Pepper had solicited funds for Roosevelt's New York campaign office from selected Florida businessmen. He recorded in his diary that Ball pledged $1,000 and was one of the four who responded.[64] Ball's disdain for the New Deal was well known, but he did not allow it, at least at that early date, to interfere with his pragmatic approach to politics.

While the expansion of the banking dimension of his growing empire was proceeding under Ball, duPont was still focused on newsprint as the principal product of his incipient west Florida venture. He followed with great interest the work of Dr. Charles Herty, a pioneer in the field of making newsprint from southern pine. The idea of being first in a new industry appealed to duPont, and with Southern Kraft's success in container paper, he quickly oriented Edwards toward building a mill for newsprint production. Edwards started buying up properties in Port St. Joe, a nearly deserted fishing village on St. Joseph's Bay in Gulf County. His acquisitions included the local telephone company and the Apalachicola Northern Railroad, the only rail link to the pulpwood harvests in the counties to the north. More important, Edwards established a presence with the Southern Newspaper Association, the major potential customer for southern newsprint if it could be economically produced. Herty's work had convinced duPont it could be, and Edwards produced a pro forma showing a profitable result with newsprint as the product of a new mill operation.[65]

The whole scheme was abruptly reoriented when Ball confronted duPont and Edwards with his own figures indicating the potential for a much larger profit margin in Kraft paper. To this, he added the uncertainty in the yet-to-be-proven Herty process for making newsprint. DuPont dropped the newsprint plan that Edwards had worked so hard to bring about, and adopted instead Ball's proposal to manufacture Kraft paper.[66]

Historian Joseph Wall makes the case that this episode disheartened Edwards, who was suffering from an array of illnesses at the time. That there had been a competition between the two men was adumbrated occasionally in correspondence between them and duPont, although never stated directly. Edwards was the husband of one of Jessie's closest friends and enjoyed near family status on that score, as well as for his faithful and competent service. While this episode clearly marked the emergence of Ball as second only to duPont in the organization, his control had been building almost from the beginning. The manner in which he positioned himself in the conduct of political affairs was evidence of his progressive ascent to power. Edwards continued with the organization and, according to Jessie's biographer, enjoyed her protection in later years when Ball attempted to discharge him.[67] Less than a year after the decision to proceed with the container paper venture in west Florida, Alfred I. duPont was dead, and Ed Ball became the sole voice of an expanding duPont empire.

6

A Florida Senator and the New Deal

After being defeated in his bid for reelection to the Florida legislature, Perry seemed a much smaller place to Claude Pepper. Depression conditions stifled the meager economic activity that had survived the collapse of the boom, and the town's bank failed, taking with it what little savings the young lawyer had amassed. His law partner, "Judge" W. B. Davis, advancing in years, was anxious to retire. There was little prospect of Pepper's expanding his law practice, and even less for his political fortunes in Taylor County.

Tallahassee, the political center of the state, offered greater opportunities to a person of Pepper's professional and political capabilities. He had tasted of its relatively heady atmosphere during his single legislative term and found it to his liking. His work with the state bar association had established him in capital legal circles, especially with individuals like Curtis L. Waller and B. K. Roberts. Waller, an older lawyer who had befriended him before his election to the legislature, provided free room and board in his home when Pepper served in the 1929 session. When Waller offered him a partnership in his Tallahassee practice late in 1930, the former legislator eagerly accepted the position.[1]

When Pepper moved to Tallahassee, the nation was entering its first full year of depression. As conditions worsened, officials and the machinery of government that they operated seemed immobilized, unable to fully grasp the magnitude of human hardship then settling over the country. The resources of state and local governments and private relief organizations were quickly exhausted, with only meager impact on the expanding human misery settling over the nation. In Washington, the Hoover administration seemed to rest its faith in the power of the invisible hand of the marketplace to right things in due course. It was a faith not shared by the growing number of Americans who saw their lives and their family's welfare crumble away.

It was not that government officials were indifferent to the nation's problems, but rather that they were befuddled by them, unable to come to terms with the fact that government was the only mechanism that could act on the scale necessary to counter the situation. When such steps as the creation of the Reconstruction Finance Corporation were finally taken, they came too late to resuscitate a near prostrate economy. Breezes of discontent were becoming stiff winds of change over the political landscape. Pepper's political instincts, honed by the strong strains of Populism from his rural Alabama youth, were sensitized to the impending transformation of the political landscape.

While a member of the state Democratic Executive Committee in 1928, he had received a letter from the governor-elect of New York, Franklin Delano Roosevelt. It was shortly after Herbert Hoover's defeat of Al Smith, and Roosevelt was then assessing his own prospects for the Democratic presidential nomination four years hence. His election as governor of New York, close though it was in the midst of the Hoover landslide, marked him as one of the few Democratic leaders with the potential to reverse the flagging Democratic Party's fortunes.[2] Seeking to establish his own image of party leadership, one independent of his ties with Al Smith, the patrician governor-elect had corresponded with over 500 Democratic party loyalists, one of whom was Pepper.[3] He solicited their views on the future course of the party, and Pepper, responding with his customary enthusiasm, waxed eloquent in his espousal of liberalism as the centerpiece of party philosophy. The then newly elected state representative from Taylor County focused his advice on making the party "genuinely . . . the liberal party of the nation," with Roosevelt at its helm.[4] Within two years of that exchange, the New York governor was viewed by many as the prime contender for the Democratic nomination. The *Tallahassee Democrat* editorialized, "In feeling around for the most available and best equipped candidate to head the Democratic national ticket in 1932, there seems to be an almost universal demand for Franklin Roosevelt, now governor of New York."[5] Later, Pepper would build on the brief correspondence of 1928 to claim, "I had been a New Dealer before there was a New Deal."[6] There was a good measure of truth in that assertion.

It seemed a long road from defeat in rural Taylor County to a seat in the U.S. Senate, but for Pepper, single-minded as he was, it was no more than the course of ambition. It proved to be a much shorter road than he could have possibly imagined when he left Perry. In Tallahassee Pepper continued the process of building a political base that he had started during his brief legislative career. The key to that process was his undeniable affability harnessed to a superior speaking ability, his principal political stock-in-trade. Throughout his career, he relied heavily on his oratorical talent, and for the most part, it served him well. In 1944, he would come from behind to defeat four opponents in the first primary, a feat attributed to his superior speaking abilities. As an unfriendly writer later pointed out, "Friends and foe agree: Pepper won in 1944 on sheer jawbone."[7] Contemporaries, including those who opposed his politics, Spessard Holland and George Smathers, for example, agreed on his unique oratorical talents.[8] When he announced his candidacy for the U.S. Senate in 1934, the *Tallahassee Democrat* noted in its account of the event: "Pepper is one of the state's most effective speakers, a quality which placed him in the service of the Democratic party in many public meetings during the last presidential campaign, and has caused him to be one of the most sought after speakers at numerous gatherings since that time."[9]

His oratorical flair and prodigious memory for names and detail combined easily with his effusive personality. He also had an innate intellectual curiosity and was well educated—having benefited from the rigors of a Harvard legal education. When all this was tempered with his homespun Alabama heritage and self-deprecating sense of humor, it became an impressive combination in the political marketplace. Without trying to mask completely the finely honed intellect that lay just beneath his humble origins, Pepper managed to appear neither haughty nor overbearing to his largely rural north Florida supporters. His remarkable debut in statewide politics four years later, without any intervening political offices, was clear evidence that he used his talents well in developing an effective political personality. Pepper quickly became known in his new community for his legal ability, unstinting loyalty to the Democratic Party, and, of course, his oratorical prowess.

The Taylor County murder case that had first brought his legal talent to public attention continued to be a prominent news item in north Florida as it made its way through the appellate court process. Although other lawyers had become associated with the convicted murderer's cause, Pepper continued in the forefront of the news coverage it generated. His attack on the death penalty was an imaginative and cleverly concocted technicality. He argued that there was no properly designated executioner under state law, and lacking such, the death penalty could not be carried out. It was a novel argument, to say the least, raising sufficient question to cause the death penalty to be held in abeyance while it was resolved. Pepper exhausted his client's remedies in the state appellate system and carried the matter to the federal courts.[10] Although he ultimately lost the case, the resulting notoriety was beneficial to his legal career as well as his political aspirations. The client was not executed but remained in prison the rest of his life.

One lawyer, in subsequently assessing Pepper's election prospects against incumbent U.S. senator Park Trammell, wrote of his legal reputation: "The members of our office are satisfied that Mr. Pepper is considered one of the ablest lawyers in the State by the members of the Pinellas County Bar. We feel the members of the legal profession over the state consider him with the same high esteem."[11]

As Pepper's small band of Tallahassee supporters canvassed their acquaintances statewide on his behalf, comments such as the above frequently came from lawyers and nonlawyers alike. Such opinions of him often derived not so much from personal knowledge but rather from his rapidly spreading reputation. Unlike today, when reputations are bought and paid for with professional image builders using sophisticated "spin" techniques, in the 1930s Pepper built his reputation through his own efforts and those of his friends. While perception undoubtedly played a role in the process, it was an era when reality still had a significant role in shaping perception, instead of the other way around.

Not long after reestablishing himself in Tallahassee, Pepper was invited to be a principal speaker at a major statewide Democratic Party rally held in Mariana, a neighboring town west of Tallahassee. It was a distinct honor for a defeated one-term Florida house member who had been a resident of the state for barely five years. The affair was intended to bolster the party's resolve following the state's first-ever defection in 1928 to the Republicans since Reconstruction. His speech was reported as having held the crowd "enthralled," as he declared "Democracy [Democratic Party] offers the greatest hope to mankind." The speech was printed in full in the *Tallahassee Daily Democrat.*[12]

Pepper's reputation as a speaker and Democratic Party loyalist soon spread beyond Tallahassee, and he was asked by the party's state Executive Committee to speak on behalf of its candidates around the state.[13] He was a member of local civic clubs and was especially sought after as a luncheon or dinner speaker. His speech-making style was one of unabashed patriotism combined with a flair for American history, always a good suit for a southern politician. When he addressed the Tallahassee Kiwanis Club in 1931 taking a Thanksgiving theme, he covered the full spectrum of American history, lacing it with old-fashioned patriotic overtones. He traced the nation's greatness from Plymouth Rock through the World War, ending with the thought that the nation "not only had much to be thankful for, but also much that the rest of the world could emulate."[14] It was patriotic oratory at its southern best, and the new, young lawyer in town was a master of the art. Even more important, his style and flair generated abundant newspaper coverage. It was a powerful tool for an aspiring politician before the mindlessness of television sound-bites replaced personal contact as the medium of choice for political discourse.

Within three years, Pepper had built a solid base of friends and professional colleagues in Tallahassee. There was little doubt that he was popular and well liked in professional, political, and social circles. His bar association activities and speaking engagements extended beyond Tallahassee, enabling him to establish an embryonic statewide network.

All this was done in the political atmosphere engendered by the Great Depression, which by 1933 was the dominant feature of life in America. President Hoover, always fearful of intrusive government, was unwilling to commit to any significant expansion of federal powers to relieve the situation. Still, he was not oblivious to the plight of the rising number of unemployed. He appointed Walter S. Gifford, president of American Telephone and Telegraph Company, to coordinate local relief efforts, even though he continued to consider such efforts essentially private or local in nature. Although unable to conceptualize governmental action in the context of individual need, he could grasp its application in the institutional sense. His belated and wary acceptance of the Reconstruction Finance Corporation as a means of aiding the increasing number of failing corporations indicated that his mind ran to institutional approaches, not human ones. Pepper's instincts, on the other hand, pointed unerringly to the human dimension. The misery of unemployed individuals with hungry families remained compartmentalized in Hoover's mind as part of the realm of private affairs, a realm in which government had no business intruding. While urging businesses to aid in local relief efforts, the president continued to insist that in the American system of government, Washington had but a minimal role to play in the worsening situation. Meanwhile, the increasing scale of hardship brought on by economic collapse overwhelmed private, state, and local government agencies that had traditionally dealt with relief of human misfortune.

Massive unemployment personalized the trauma of institutional failure. Not everyone went hungry, but huge numbers did, especially in the larger urban centers. There, one could witness the spectacles of breadlines and the dispossessed living in shanty towns known as "Hoovervilles." It was sufficient to awaken others to the possibility that they might be next. On farms, agricultural prices plunged, prompting a farm "Holiday," a form of protest in which farmers refused to deliver their produce to market in an effort to force up prices. There were other confused and desperate forms of collective self-help as the realities of depression permeated rural America.[15] The visible trappings of hard times were ominously present, in one form or another, across the country. It bred a sense of helplessness in the unemployed and dispossessed, a bewilderment as to what had befallen them and how it had happened. It was a watershed in American political life. In the consternation of it all, there emerged a festering certainty on one point: A disaster had occurred and it transcended the American faith in the redemptive powers of individual effort. There was a perception percolating through the collective misery that only the national government was capable of concerted action on the scale necessary to put the nation back on course.

Yet Hoover seemed to hold firm in his belief that intervention by the government in the private affairs of its citizens was a worse threat to national survival than the existing situation.[16] He could not bring himself to realize that the human misery produced by massive unemployment overwhelmed the private affairs of individuals and became, itself, an institutional feature of national life. If left unchecked, it was but a prelude to a radical alteration in the role of government—perhaps, some thought, even revolution.

Claude Pepper intuitively sensed the incoming tide of change and made plans to rise with it in pursuit of his political ambitions. He also had a driving urge to help those he saw afflicted by the system. It is difficult to determine which of these two traits was dominant for both were interwoven into the fabric of his being. Franklin Delano Roosevelt was anything but a populist, but his patrician background notwithstanding, he intuitively understood that the national misery had to be confronted at the human level as well as in the nation's institutional structure. He was swept into office in 1932 by a landslide of human need speaking through the polls.

Pepper confided to some of his closest friends in 1933 that he was seriously considering running against Florida's junior senator, Park Trammell, a former Florida governor and seventeen-year veteran of the U.S. Senate. It was an audacious suggestion coming from a thirty-three-year-old lawyer who had lived in the state only eight years and been defeated for reelection to the state legislature after a single term. As he later recalled in his memoirs: "They didn't laugh. . . . And we all knew my credentials were slender. But fresh breezes were blowing in America, and a fellow who caught the right one might be able to ride it all the way to Washington."[17] His immediate circle of friends approved, and agreed to help him. They reached out to an expanding circle of acquaintances throughout the state and soon began to gather adherents to Pepper's cause.[18] His assessment of the rising temper for change and his sense of timing were both accurate.

The man on whom Pepper and his friends set their sights was an accomplished professional politician but also one locked into old ways. Trammell was not imaginative enough to sense the imperative of change growing in the body politic. He was a lawyer and had held public office continuously since serving as mayor of Lakeland in 1902. He had served in the legislature, state cabinet, and as governor before his election to the U.S. Senate in 1917. Despite his longevity in public office and his experience, Trammell's outlook was limited and his record unimpressive. He did not fathom the pervasiveness of the unrest and misery that had set in or the presentiments of fundamental change brewing. He was voted the senator "least inclined to work" by the Washington press corps and was openly ridiculed for using his Senate office as a bedroom and kitchen to save on expenses.[19] One Winter Haven lawyer responding to an inquiry on behalf of Pepper referred to Trammell's "blistering inefficiency." Even so, the same lawyer emphasized the great advantage of incumbency in the Congress, which had, by then, started enacting President Roosevelt's New Deal. He thought that since the "doors of the Treasury Vaults" had been opened for the "Forgotten Man," most incumbents, including Trammell, would be reelected.[20]

Pepper's perspective was different. He thought the already enacted elements of the New Deal were but a harbinger of more profound change to come, changes which he saw as the embodiment of his vision of liberalism. His instincts told him that incumbents unable to grasp that trend were vulnerable to newer and younger leadership. When the campaign got under way, Trammell's record of inaction was the main focus of Pepper's attack.

John H. Perry, the Jacksonville newspaper publisher and friend of Ed Ball, wrote Pepper that Trammell should be "indicted and convicted for his inaction."[21] Perry remained a close Pepper supporter for many years but broke with him in the early 1940s over his unsuccessful efforts to secure administration approval of the cross-Florida canal, a project highly favored in Duval

County.[22] Perry was close to Ball, who was also a canal supporter, and both of them opposed Pepper in his 1950 bid for a third term.[23] By then, Ball had far more reason to oppose Pepper than simply the canal. Those developments will be examined in subsequent chapters.

The situation was different in 1934. Evidence indicates that Ball and the duPont organization supported the Pepper candidacy. Ball later said as much when he admitted to a writer that in the early days he "helped the buzzard get elected."[24] In any event, it is clear they did not oppose him. It is unlikely Ball and Perry would have been on opposite sides in the 1934 Senate race in light of their similar political views on the development of Florida and the needs of the nation. Friends and political allies almost from the start of Ball's Florida career, they remained so for many years. Duval County, home to both Perry and Ball, was a focal point of Pepper support in 1934 and voted more than two to one for him in the first primary. Ball most likely remembered Pepper's role in the fight against the Carlton road program, referred to then in political circles as the Crummer bond program. That would have been reason enough for Ball to support him, but there was another. Pepper had supported the sales tax while in the legislature, a measure strongly favored by Ball.[25] The sales tax, although not enacted until 1949, was a perennial issue in state politics at the time, and the Crummer bond refunding program also remained a controversial issue even though already enacted into law.

John E. Mathews, Sr., a prominent Duval County legislator, made his opposition to the Crummer bond program a prime reason why he should be returned to the statehouse. Pepper's opposition to it would have won favor in Duval County, which generally considered itself penalized by the shifting of road funds under the Crummer plan.

As noted, Ball strongly opposed that program for two reasons: Crummer's refunding program posed a serious impediment to the duPont road-building plans for west Florida and also threatened the long-term appreciation potential for the Florida National Bank's holdings of municipal bonds. Jacob C. "Jake" Belin, president of St. Joe Paper Company and Ball confederate for close to half a century, had not yet joined the duPont organization in 1934. Still, his impression, based on many years of close association with Ball, is that the Jacksonville financier viewed Pepper's 1934 candidacy favorably.[26] It is tempting to assume that Ball would naturally favor a professional politician like Trammell over Pepper. But that was unlikely in light of Peter O. Knight's support of the incumbent. The Tampa banker and businessman's strident opposition to Ball's efforts to obtain a bank charter in Tampa and their continued competition rendered collaboration in the same political camp unlikely.

In addition to Trammell and Pepper, there were three candidates in the 1934 first-primary election: Hortense K. Wells, James F. Sikes, and Charles A. Mitchell. A crowded primary boded ill for Trammell since challengers tended to focus their attacks on the incumbent. But from the start, Pepper's youth and vigor attracted surprising statewide support, and the race quickly narrowed to a battle between him and Trammell.

The focus on Pepper and Trammell was evident from campaign ads of Sikes attacking both Trammell and Pepper. Trammell was cast as an ineffective public servant, on the "public payroll for more than a quarter of a century," and who, in seventeen years in the Senate, had only passed four unimportant pieces of legislation. Ironically, Pepper was alleged to have supported the "Brown-Crummer bill" for foreclosure of tax certificates, an effort to tie him to the controversial Crummer bond refunding program, a charge he effectively refuted. He was also said to be "recognized in legislative circles as [the] most active and highly paid professional lobbyist for special interests in Florida."[27]

Trammell also hammered at Pepper for his lobbying activities with vague references to his representation of "special interests" groups. The longtime incumbent, who had given tepid support to Roosevelt's New Deal measures, resented Pepper's persistent professions of support for the New Deal. At one point, increasingly irritated by the inferences that he was no friend of the very popular president, Trammell said, "If you listen to Claude Pepper you would wonder how Franklin D. Roosevelt got along in Washington without him."[28]

It was a theme that Pepper seized on and never relinquished, always professing support for FDR and the New Deal. Pepper continued to attack the incumbent's lethargic record and competence. In one instance, he focused on Trammell's failure to vote on a piece of alcoholic beverage legislation because he confused a "roll call vote" signal for a "quorum call." Pepper used the innocuous incident to question the ability of a senator who, after almost three terms, could be confused by such fundamental elements of senatorial life.[29]

The candidates had no major differences on substantive issues; all favored Roosevelt's New Deal as a means of curing the nation's economic malaise.[30] Yet Pepper made the most of that popular common denominator even though Trammell had actually voted for most of the New Deal programs. It was Pepper's rhetorical ability that enabled him to articulate more clearly than Trammell his empathy with the public's acceptance of Roosevelt's efforts to pull the masses from the depths of depression. Playing to the popularity of Roosevelt's program, Pepper made it seem that he alone was vital to the president's plans to revive the nation.

When the first-primary balloting was completed, Pepper trailed Trammell by less than 4,000 votes out of more than 172,000 cast. It was a very impressive showing for the little-known but articulate and brash young lawyer from Tallahassee, one who had been a Floridian for less than ten years.

As a harbinger of things to come, there were voting irregularities in Hillsborough County, a traditional attribute of Tampa politics. Fistfights broke out at one West Tampa precinct between rival factions attempting to interfere with individuals trying to exercise their franchise. The sheriff, prominent in the county's machine-controlled politics, responded by arresting two city policemen and two former prosecutors said to be intimidating voters. In keeping with the norm of that city's elections, the *Tampa Morning Tribune* reported that "election day fighting was nominal," although the matter was seen as more serious by newspapers around the state.[31] The *Morning Tribune*, a staunch opponent of the political machine that made such a mockery of the Hillsborough County electoral process, later became a strong Pepper supporter.

The recognition of Pepper as a decisive threat to Trammell in the second primary did not diminish the task of the challenger. Incumbency was a powerful political tool, and Trammell had taken advantage of his entrenched position to build a wide base of support over the years. In addition, he was supported by powerful political elements in the Tampa Bay area, and the full force of the Hillsborough County "machine vote" was brought to bear on his behalf. Supporters in the region apprised Pepper of that fact. A colleague from the 1929 legislature advised Pepper's campaign manager that Peter O. Knight, the powerful businessman who had earlier prevented Ed Ball from obtaining a bank charter in Tampa, was actively supporting Trammell in the second primary. The news came from an employee of the local electric utility who told a Pepper supporter that he would have to support Trammell because of Knight's position. Knight was head of the Tampa Electric Company, a major employer and a key component of the city's business structure. Another report from the Tampa Bay area indicated that the "local situation" was acute, and "so much bitterness . . . from the first primary . . . indicates there will be more gasoline poured on the fire."[32] It was an accurate assessment of what was to come in the runoff election.

The second primary was in the same mold as the first, but without the diluting effects of the three eliminated candidates. The campaign charges included some new dimensions. Trammell accused Pepper of being the beneficiary of a $100,000 "slush fund" put up by unspecified "special interests," and reminded voters that the Tallahassee lawyer had been a "lobbyist for the special interests while he was in the legislature."[33] Pepper charged Trammell with using "federal employees all on the government payroll" to go about the state "spreading malicious and scandalous rumors" about him.[34] It is unlikely that such a slush fund existed, although it was reported that Pepper spent more money in the first primary than the other candidates.[35] Charges that Trammell used federal employees in his campaign probably contained elements of truth. He had been in office for a long time, and many federal employees in Florida owed their jobs to him. That they would support him was no surprise, and it was not considered a serious allegation under prevailing political mores. This was simply one of the benefits of incumbency, benefits which Pepper would one day seize for himself. Soon after his election two years later, Pepper asked Tom Corcoran, the administration lobbyist seeking support for the president's unpopular "Court-packing" proposal, to provide him a list of people employed by the U.S. Department of Agriculture in Florida.[36] The new senator was to waste no time in ingratiating himself with Florida's federal employees.

Immediately following the first primary, Pepper received favorable reports from his cadre of supporters throughout the state. Even allowing for the partisan nature of the reports, it was clear that his strong showing won him major political status in the state.[37] Convinced more than ever of the seriousness of Pepper's threat, Trammell stepped up his attack. He repeated and embellished the charges that his opponent was the beneficiary of a "slush fund" provided by special interests seeking to remove Trammell from the Senate.[38] The *Tampa Morning Tribune* found these charges almost ludicrous, opining that no special interest like the "Power Trust" or the "Munitions Trust" would waste money on removing an opponent as ineffectual as Trammell from office.[39]

Pepper traveled the state extensively, using a sound-truck to carry his distinctive voice and message to neighborhoods normally beyond the reach of campaign rhetoric. The novel campaign device was first used in Florida by David Sholtz in his 1932 gubernatorial campaign.[40] It was an excellent medium for Pepper's distinctive voice and speaking ability. Today, like the torchlight parades of an earlier period, sound-trucks are historic relics of past campaigns.

In the second primary, the *Tampa Morning Tribune* became an even stronger supporter of Pepper. This was due as much to the paper's opposition to the machine politics that controlled the Ybor City and West Tampa votes as it was to the challenger's appeal. Pepper was invited by a Tampa newspaper editor to schedule the windup of his campaign there and observe for himself the corrupt polling practices prevailing in certain areas of the city. Pepper accepted the offer and witnessed firsthand the theft of the election.[41]

The final vote was 103,028 votes for Trammell and 98,978 for Pepper. Trammell had survived by the slim margin of 4,050 votes out of a total of 202,006 votes cast statewide. His margin of victory was clearly in the manipulated vote in several Ybor City and West Tampa precincts. In eleven predominantly Latin precincts, Trammell received 6,511 votes to Pepper's 360 total, giving him a margin in those precincts alone that was greater than his statewide margin of victory. The *Tampa Morning Tribune* analysis of those polling places showed some voting as high as 446 to 1 for Trammell and one casting 715 votes for Trammel and just 75 votes for Pepper. The persistent singularity of views on candidates was nothing less than amazing in those precincts, as it had been in previous elections. Just as those voters could previously claim to have elected local officials, the Tampa paper concluded that "the voters of Ybor City and West Tampa may now lay claim to having elected a United States Senator."[42]

Pepper had personally observed the wholesale voting frauds on his election-day tour of polling places. He described what he saw in a written statement marked "Not for Publication" pending his decision on whether to lodge a formal protest.[43] The practices that he had observed were generally known in state political circles as regular features of Hillsborough County politics. The system was commonly referred to as the "hot vote," meaning that it could be delivered by the machine.

The essence of the scheme was use of "repeaters," groups of persons, generally of Latin extraction, hired and brought into successive precincts to vote in lieu of registered voters there. It hinged on intimidation to dissuade valid voters from exercising their right to vote. This was accomplished by machine-controlled deputy sheriffs and clerks being posted at the precincts to oversee the electoral process. In the parlance of the system, it was known as controlling "the table," referring to the table at which the voting lists were kept for verification of registration and payment of the poll tax. The deputies were heavily armed, some with shotguns, and even machine guns according to Pepper's account. Their function was not only to intimidate legal voters from attempting to vote, but also to create diversions to obfuscate the arrival and voting of "repeaters," who sometimes voted several times in one precinct. They would concoct disturbances or fights to draw attention away from the goings-on at "the table." If a registered voter insisted on his right to vote, he was told he had already voted, and if he persisted, deputies would arrest him for creating a disturbance or, in an ironic twist, for being a "repeater."[44]

On election day, Pepper was accompanied to one of the more notorious precincts by a municipal judge who wanted the candidate to see for himself the methods of intimidation used. He suggested that Pepper talk to a particular man standing almost a block away from the polling place. When the deputies saw the man talking with Pepper, they quickly approached and charged him with creating a disturbance. He was arrested, leaving Pepper standing alone and bewildered at the blatant perversion of the electoral process.

One independently documented episode from the first primary illustrated the fraudulent voting practices observed by Pepper in the second primary. A woman voter, ironically a Trammell supporter, witnessed the flagrant use of "repeaters" at several precincts. Repulsed by what she observed, she reported her observations in a sworn affidavit. According to this affidavit, several carloads of Spanish-speaking men arrived at the same time, and going inside together, they crowded aside the "line of American voters" and voted in the places of registered voters whose names were provided them by the workers at "the table." One individual whom she identified by name, also known as "Macho" around the polling places, arrived on three different occasions at one polling place with carloads of "repeaters." When he saw that she was taking notes on what was occurring, he forcefully took the notebook from her, dislocating her collarbone in the process.[45] It was a matter of some risk for people to interfere with the fraud in process. Another woman who attempted to photograph "repeaters" in action was also subjected to harsh physical treatment, and her camera was broken.

When it suited the purpose of those in control of the machine, legal processes could be manipulated or thwarted. The sheriff of Hillsborough County was one of those in control. One citizen, well known for his outspoken opposition to the machine, was arrested the night before the first primary and held under $5,000 bond, an extreme amount for the minor offense involved. The sheriff refused to release him even when prominent Tampa citizens made bond for him. When they obtained a writ of habeas corpus, the sheriff and his deputies simply refused to obey it, even when the judge telephoned them and ordered the release. This and numerous other blatant episodes of fraud and intimidation were carefully documented by a committee of the county Democratic Executive Committee and published in the form of advertisements in the newspaper.[46]

The "machine" at the root of this state of affairs was not under the direct control of Trammell or any other specific candidate. Pat Whitaker, the state senator from Hillsborough County who fought Ball's opposition to the Crummer bond refunding program and was subsequently hired by Crummer in his continuing battle with Ball, was also defeated in the second primary by the same "machine" vote.[47] The individual most frequently associated with control of Tampa politics was Peter O. Knight, who, as noted before, had earlier prevented Ball from obtaining a bank charter in that city. He was the president and founder of Tampa Electric Company, an officer in the Ybor City Land and Investment Company, a director of the Tampa Gas Company, and his banking interests included a directorship in the Columbia Bank of Ybor City. His diverse business interests and wealth afforded him a widespread sphere of political influence. His law practice was politically oriented and statewide in scope, although his principal sphere of political power was in Hillsborough County and the Tampa Bay area. It included representation of clients before numerous governmental bodies, reaching at times to cities as far away as Jacksonville.[48] In the "morgue file" biographical sketch of him maintained by the Associated Press at the time, it was noted that "his endorsement for office was more often than not the equivalent of election."[49]

Pepper conceded victory to Trammell without lodging a formal protest of the Hillsborough vote. His decision not to formally protest the election outcome may have been influenced by the knowledge that in certain rural counties, where he had been strongly supported, there had also been voting irregularities. Because of the depression conditions, many persons were allowed to vote without having paid the requisite poll tax. Possibly, those votes would have been thrown out also, tainting Pepper with scandal much like that which he would have been protesting.[50] His decision not to protest was to serve him well in the not distant future.

Soon after the election, Pepper attempted to call on Knight. Having experienced the Tampa political power broker's might at first hand, he most likely wanted to use the visit to establish good future relations between them. Pepper seemed to think that he could always win people over to his side by personal persuasion, and often he was right. The defeated candidate missed seeing Knight in person but later received a letter from him. Knight must have been impressed with Pepper's political potential and expressed admiration for his "magnificent campaign . . . and the wonderful manner in which you have accepted your defeat."[51] In the letter, Knight explained his longtime relationship with Trammell, and how he had managed Trammell's earlier successful gubernatorial campaign even though opposed by such prominent area political figures as Pat Whitaker and Howell Lykes, a member of one of Florida's most prominent business families with extensive cattle and shipping interests. Knight went on to discuss the outcome of the senatorial election in near pontifical tones: "I could have told you six months ago what this county would do; and nothing could have changed that. The votes cast for Mr. Mitchell in the first primary were only complimentary. They were in fact, Trammell votes."[52] This was a frank, even if boastful, statement of Knight's political prowess and the legerdemain by which he sustained it.

Pepper did not thereafter make much effort to ingratiate himself with the Tampa power broker. His attitude toward him was much like his later attitude toward Ball. When the Florida House of Representatives passed a bill in 1939 regulating electric utilities, Pepper thought it "just retribution for the public plundering he [Knight] had carried on for more than a quarter of a century." He added, "I had insisted on it being done."[53] Nevertheless, the legislation did not pass the state senate, and Knight's Tampa Electric Company and the state's other electric utilities remained outside the ambit of state regulation for another dozen years.

The letter from Knight to Pepper confirmed what Pepper's 1929 legislative colleague W. J. Bivens had reported after the first primary: Knight had made a pact with Charles A. Mitchell to support him in the first primary if he would prevail on his Tampa Bay friends to swing to Trammell in the second. Mitchell and his supporters agreed to the proposition.[54]

What neither Pepper nor Knight could know at the time was that the Tampa "hot vote" episode had set the stage for an astounding turnabout two years later: Pepper's unopposed election to the U.S. Senate.

In 1936, there occurred the highly unusual event of both Florida U.S. senators unexpectedly dying within six weeks of each other. Trammell died in early May, followed the next month by the state's senior senator, Duncan

U. Fletcher. Pepper's close defeat only two years earlier made him a strong choice for the first vacant seat. His reputation as a party loyalist had been bolstered by the manner in which he conducted himself in declining to contest the Hillsborough County voting irregularities. The widespread fraud there had become known around the state's political circles and to the public in general. It was generally accepted that the election had been stolen from the personable, young lawyer through Tampa's "hot vote." As a result, Pepper gained stature in Democratic circles for ostensibly placing party solidarity above personal advancement.[55] Pepper's enhanced standing within the party cadres did not prevent other prominent figures, including former governor Doyle E. Carlton, from also coveting the vacated Trammell seat. Undaunted by the caliber of the potential opposition, Pepper promptly announced his candidacy. News of his announcement appeared side by side with the account of Trammell's funeral in one Tallahassee newspaper.[56] In politics, decorum yielded easily to the political exigencies of being early on in the hustings.

After Senator Fletcher's death, Pepper quickly determined that he would have a greater chance for success if he went after Fletcher's vacant seat instead of Trammell's. At the time, there was a tacit understanding in Florida's political world—amounting to something of a Democratic Party tradition—that one of Florida's two senators would be from north Florida and the other from south Florida. Due to the state's size and regional diversity, this was of some importance in maintaining a harmonious balance in the Democratic Party in the era of single-party politics. Trammell had been the "southern" senator, while Fletcher, from Duval County, was viewed as the "northern" senator. Pepper, a north Floridian, had flown in the face of that tradition by running against Trammell in his 1932 race. He now surveyed the crowded field for Trammell's seat as the representative of south Florida and came to a belated appreciation for the tradition of dividing the state's senatorial representation between its two regions. His intention to seek Fletcher's vacant "northern" seat was not only more in keeping with party tradition, it offered him better prospects for victory.

The shift suited his purposes well since his main strength was in the northern counties, including Duval. It was a shrewd move, capitalizing on the tradition that he had flaunted two years earlier, as well as his good standing in party circles and favorable image with the public in general. As a result, Pepper received the Democratic nomination for the open U.S. Senate seat without opposition, a rare feat in Florida's contentious single-party politics.

His election to the two years remaining on Duncan U. Fletcher's unexpired term was assured. An editorial prophecy of the *Orlando Sentinel* following the 1934 election had come to pass. It had said: "Someday, in some election, the people of Florida are going to give Pepper another break—or a new deal. That is the general feeling. It is now Saint Pepper."[57]

This election marked the fulfillment of a lifelong ambition of Pepper's and the commencement of a career that would encompass most of the next half century. To add to his personal satisfaction, shortly after the election Pepper married Mildred Webster, a woman he had met five years earlier while in the Florida House of Representatives. Like his liberalism, the marriage was a lasting, albeit sometimes stormy, feature of the remainder of his life.[58]

Pepper and Charles O. Andrews, elected to fill Park Trammell's unexpired term, were both sworn in to the U.S. Senate on November 4, 1936. It was an anomalous situation—both senators from the same state being sworn in at the same time. There was no precedent under Senate rules in such circumstances for designating one of them as the state's senior senator, a matter of some importance in the senatorial scheme of things. Pepper voluntarily deferred to his new colleague, and Andrews became the state's senior senator. Pepper's self-effacing demeanor in what could have been a contentious situation drew approval from his senior colleagues. It was a refreshing attitude in a climate where inflated egos and ambitions often converged to cause unwanted complications for those in control. The Senate leadership undoubtedly noticed the new, fiercely loyal member of the Democratic team.

When Claude Pepper took his seat in the Senate, the Roosevelt era was approaching its fifth year, with the nation slowly recovering from the unprecedented depression that had called the New Deal into being. Although the president still enjoyed major congressional support, there were growing signs of restlessness over the expansion of executive power and the radical changes wrought in the nation's system of government. Business and industry continued and increased their resistance to the regulatory regimes imposed on their affairs and the deficit financing that became the norm under Roosevelt. From the left, a cacophony of extreme proposals was raised by the likes of such radical reformers as Louisiana's Huey Long, Dr. Francis Everett Townsend, and Father Charles E. Coughlin. They pressed for more radical redistribution of the nation's wealth than did Roosevelt in his vision of a New Deal. This far-left element posed a real challenge to the president's leadership of the liberal dimension of national political thought.[59] Yet the most serious threat to the New Deal and to Roosevelt's leadership came from within the constitutional tripartite structure of government.

The U.S. Supreme Court displayed a clear hostility to the thrust of federal programs into realms of American life previously considered sacrosanct from government intrusion. It had invalidated major elements of the New Deal, effectively curtailing further efforts at reforming and restructuring the American economy. After brooding over the situation for some time, Roosevelt used his overwhelming victory in 1936 to challenge the Court in a direct confrontation. His solution was to restructure the Court with enough of his own appointees to ensure a receptive attitude toward his initiatives. Although the legislation was clearly within the prerogative of the president to propose and the Congress to pass, Roosevelt's transparent purpose—to subordinate to his will a branch of government coequal to the executive—was easily discernible. A growing array of opponents, including some normally loyal to his programs, thought he proceeded with complete disregard for the hallowed principle of equality and balance between the three branches of government. That balance was sacred ground to constitutionalists, and as it turned out, Roosevelt's well-known uncanny political sense failed him in a major way.

The plan was formally presented to Congress on February 5, 1937, early in Pepper's first term. The initial reactions to it were guarded because its full import was not immediately grasped by the collective consciousness of the Congress and the public. That reception turned rapidly to vehement opposition as the proposal's far-reaching implications became better understood. It quickly became known as Roosevelt's Court-packing scheme, providing a decidedly pejorative connotation to the whole thing.[60] It marked a watershed in the political climate that had fostered the New Deal, signaling the end of near absolute presidential power over a compliant Congress.

It was against that backdrop that Pepper launched his Senate career, and he quickly became known for his unfailing support of Roosevelt and his programs.

Pepper's commitment to Roosevelt and the New Deal was put to the test in the battle that ensued over FDR's Court-packing plan. His instincts as a lawyer told him that the president's proposal was a clear threat to the concept of an independent judiciary, a constitutional principle deeply embedded in American legal and political doctrine. He did not "like the smell of the whole thing," opining that whatever his decision, it would be a "bad one in any event."[61] When the plan was unveiled, Pepper declined public comment until he could give the "matter careful study." The unquestioning commitment to the New Deal, which later became his hallmark, was not yet so firmly in place.

Harvard lawyer Tommy Corcoran approached Pepper to persuade him to support the president. It was the beginning of a lasting friendship between these two young men who found common alliance in Rooseveltian liberalism. Pepper must have expressed his dislike of the plan because Corcoran attempted to shift the onus for it from Roosevelt to the attorney general, Homer Cummings, saying the latter "had some kind of hold" on the president because of past political favors." That was disingenuous, to say the least, since Cummings had acted on direct orders of the president in drafting the legislation. Corcoran was trying to make the scheme more palatable to a dubious new senator, one who had already stamped himself as a Roosevelt devotee, by distancing the president from the plan's more objectionable parts.[62]

In the political tumult that followed the unveiling of the plan, Pepper's indecision prompted Corcoran to arrange a direct meeting between the freshman senator and the president. This was the first real personal encounter Pepper had with his idol, and it was an eye-opening affair for the newly elected and third-youngest member of the Senate. He was promised help in the 1938 election and was given to believe that the Army Corps of Engineers would take favorable action on the Florida cross-state canal, which Pepper (along with Ball, Perry, and other north Florida businessmen) supported. Pepper hesitantly agreed to support the proposal but was greatly relieved later when Roosevelt backed off the plan after the hopelessness of its enactment became clear for all to see, including Roosevelt.[63] While the festering Court-packing battle worked its way to a conclusion, there were other matters with which the new senator had to contend.

Even though it was generally accepted that a new senator should be seen and not heard, Pepper was eager to test his oratorical prowess in the hallowed chambers of the nation's most deliberative legislative body. The "maiden speech" was then considered one of the rites of passage for new senators. Usually boring and dealing with uncontroversial subjects, these speeches were patiently tolerated by veteran senators as something to be endured in the normal course of institutional tradition. After observing a discreet period of silence, Pepper chose for the occasion a pending appropriations bill for the administration's relief program.

The bill was a harbinger of declining congressional support for the president's New Deal. With economic conditions generally perceived as improving somewhat, concern over a balanced budget had reasserted itself. The relief appropriation was mired in controversy over the question of funding.

To reduce total federal outlay, proposals had been made to raise the states' matching requirements for Works Progress Administration grants. On opposing sides in the clash were the anti–New Deal Democrats and those fully committed to the Roosevelt program. The Democratic majority leader, Joseph Robinson of Arkansas, had proposed a compromise measure to find a way out of the impasse that had developed. The situation presented an opportunity for the Florida newcomer to declare unequivocally his commitment to the New Deal and President Roosevelt.

Pepper spoke for over forty minutes against those of the "old guard" who put fiscal concerns ahead of human needs. He took his colleagues to task for "deserting their president" and not extending the "social frontiers" as promised in the Democratic platform.[64] The speech was well received, and in his memoirs, Pepper wrote that he was accorded the unusual distinction of a standing ovation by his Senate colleagues.[65] Newspaper columnist Drew Pearson was effusive in his coverage of Pepper's efforts: "The speech was one of the greatest of its kind ever heard in the chamber. First speeches by newcomers are usually very dull and cautious affairs. Pepper's address shattered this precedent. It was extraordinary in brilliance of delivery and stunning effect. . . . Five minutes [after Pepper started] all eyes were riveted on him and the senate was as still as the tomb."[66]

With this speech, Pepper not only established his oratorical prowess but also set the standards by which he would judge issues and individuals for most of his career—their compatibility with Franklin Roosevelt and the New Deal. For him, the New Deal and the cause of liberalism were the real "constructive work" for which he had come to the Senate, while other concerns foisted on him by constituents were often viewed as impediments to it. His devotion to Roosevelt and the New Deal was absolute.[67] In time, it became his point of departure from the more conservative thinking of his Florida constituency, including most of the state's business community.

For Ed Ball, the New Deal was nothing less than anathema, but he did not let that interfere with his efforts to maintain cordial relations with Florida's new senator. After Alfred I. duPont's death in 1935, Ball had assumed undisputed control of his vast business interests as executor of his estate and as the dominant trustee of the duPont Trust, which was its offspring. The myriad of New Deal reform legislation issuing out of Washington reached deep into the diverse enterprises entrusted to his care. He viewed the growing body of restrictive laws and regulations as wholly unwarranted infringements on the natural rights of private property and his proprietary prerogatives arising out of those rights. Even though Pepper was unequivocally committed to those measures, Ball nevertheless had to seek his help in protecting the duPont Trust's interests. Pepper was a rising star in Washington, rapidly becoming a prominent figure in Senate and administration circles. Harold Ickes, Roosevelt's trusted and long-serving secretary of the interior, noted in early 1938 that the "President thinks he [Pepper] is one of the best men to come out of the South in a long time and this seems to be the general impression."[68] Thus Pepper was a valuable ally for someone seeking relief from the specifics of economic reform legislation and its accompanying torrent of regulations. Notwithstanding the obvious philosophical chasm separating Ball and Pepper, their relationship was correct, even cordial. For Ball, that was good business; for Pepper, it was good politics—that is, up to a point.

The Jacksonville businessman-banker developed an amicable relationship with Pepper and his wife, and frequently socialized with them. Another businessman who struck up a relationship about this time and promised to contribute to Pepper's upcoming 1938 campaign was a Boston Irishman named Joseph Kennedy.[69] In a different setting, as discussed in the previous chapter, Ball and his colleague W. T. Edwards worked with Pepper in late 1938 planning a Roosevelt birthday dinner for the benefit of crippled children.[70] Interestingly, when Ball died almost a half century later, he left the bulk of his own considerable estate, said to be in excess of $100 million, in trust for the benefit of crippled children.[71]

Ball traveled frequently to Washington, calling on Pepper, as well as other members of the House and Senate, on matters affecting his diverse interests. Sometimes, perhaps with other Florida businessmen of similar interests, he would entertain Pepper over dinner and libations. The first mention of Ball in the Senate phase of Pepper's personal diary is the entry for February 13, 1938. Pepper describes having dinner with Ball and some other unnamed Florida bankers at the Mayflower Hotel in Washington. They complained to him that the combination of government borrowing and excessive taxation was absorbing capital needed to resuscitate business—by then, a familiar refrain to Pepper and other New Deal senators. They spent most of the evening together. Over after-dinner drinks, Pepper listened to more of their arguments that income taxes were too high.[72] The evening had a convivial air about it, and the diary entry does not disclose whether it had any impact on Pepper's views.

The young New Dealer may have listened with apparent sympathy to such complaints, but he never agreed with views opposed to levels of taxation he deemed necessary to fund "constructive work" on social programs. Indeed, there is little or no evidence in Pepper's diary, memoirs, or papers to indicate that he was ever concerned about the levels of taxes, save once. In 1955, after returning to the private practice of law, he found himself in the 50 percent income tax bracket. He confided to his diary that "income tax is really shocking as I have to pay over half my income to Uncle Sam."[73] Yet, as an elected official, Pepper's proclivity for social welfare programs found its corollary in his willing acquiescence to high levels of taxation. Throughout his career, he seldom showed any concern with the fiscal consequences or tax burdens associated with his "constructive work."[74] His wholehearted endorsement of Dr. Francis E. Townsend's plan for a guaranteed $200-a-month pension for everyone over the age of sixty-five was a case in point. Pepper's embrace of it was not diminished by the clear fact that it would have bankrupted the federal government.

Meetings such as the one with Ball and the other bankers were (and are) routine in the lives of senators and congressmen, and those whose business it was to influence them. Two weeks after his meeting with the Florida bankers, Pepper was called on by railway union lobbyists. His total commitment to the New Deal and the pro-labor legislation that it fostered made meetings of this sort much more to his liking. The union men were there to seek reaffirmation of his position on the wage and hours bill, and to assure him of their union's full support in his upcoming reelection effort.[75]

Those assurances were given in 1938 while Pepper was engaged in his first reelection bid for a full term. At the time, an important element of New Deal pro-labor legislation, the wage and hours bill was being held up by opposition from southern Democrats afraid that the measure would eliminate the wage differential, which was important in enticing industry to the region. Pepper, advised by his supporters to avoid or oppose the measure, openly and emphatically endorsed it. His first-primary victory over two other opponents was notable because of his strong support of the New Deal, including especially the wage and hours bill. It dispelled the notion rising from some quarters that Roosevelt and his recovery program were losing their political edge. Quite to the contrary, Pepper's victory, and that of Lister Hill in Alabama, were seen as solid endorsements for the New Deal from the South, a region thought to be drifting away from the president.[76] In Washington, House members initially wary of the wage and hours legislation were emboldened by the Florida election result to sign a discharge petition releasing the bill from the committee where it was stalled. The bill was the only major piece of New Deal legislation enacted in 1938, and Pepper's reelection victory was a major factor in its passage. All this further enhanced Pepper's standing with the administration. He was now clearly a favorite with the president.[77]

Pepper had been appointed to the Foreign Relations Committee at the outset of his Senate career. It was a prestigious assignment for a freshman, an indication that he quickly found his footing in the intricate labyrinth of internal Senate politics. It was politically advantageous because of the widespread news coverage given to its members in dealing with the impressive subject matter of international affairs. It provided a platform on which members could appear in statesmanlike postures on matters of international concern with less of the political risks inherent in taking positions on domestic issues.

Throughout the 1930s, the nation was distinctly isolationist in outlook. It was an extension of the disillusionment following World War I, a feeling which intensified with the nation's preoccupation with the depression. This

9. Claude Pepper was a masterful campaigner and orator. Here he is addressing a small crowd in a rural Tampa area grocery store during his successful bid in 1938 for a full term.

10. Pepper was a Democratic Party loyalist throughout his career and often participated in campaigns for other Democrats. In 1964, after his return to the Congress as a representative from Miami, he joined with fellow Miami congressman Dante Fascell to campaign for vice presidential candidate Hubert Humphrey, then running on the Democratic ticket with President Lyndon B. Johnson.

attitude was generally reflected by the Foreign Relations Committee. In Pepper's case, service on this committee led to the vortex of the most complex and heated fusion of foreign policy and domestic politics in the twentieth century: the Cold War and its offspring, McCarthyism. That topic will be dealt with later in the context of Pepper's post-war politics. Here, we will look briefly at how he went against the tide of the prevailing isolationism as a prelude to his post–World War II foreign policy involvement.

Following his 1938 first-primary victory, Pepper and his wife, Mildred, went to Europe to attend the Interparliamentary Conference at the Hague. It was a relatively innocuous junket of the type typically indulged in by members of the Foreign Relations Committee. For Pepper, however, it was to have far-reaching consequences. His friend Joseph Kennedy of Boston, father of the future president, John F. Kennedy, was ambassador to Great Britain, and arranged for Pepper and Mildred to be invited to a party attended by the king and queen. Pepper met with the president of Ireland, Eamon De Valera, and went on a grouse hunt at the English estate of Bernard Baruch. All in all, it was a heady experience for a young man who had never been abroad before.[78] Intrigued and alarmed by the rise of Nazism in Germany, he added that country to his itinerary.

While in Germany, he chanced to see Adolf Hitler, the Nazi dictator, in person and up close. It was not an actual meeting, but Pepper was able to observe him having dinner at a nearby table in the restaurant where he and Mildred were dining. Later, when urging early support for England and France against Germany, he would allude to the evil and immorality he saw etched in the führer's face during this episode. As 1939 wore on, with war spreading in Europe and Asia, Pepper was genuinely convinced that the United States could not avoid becoming involved. He felt that the sooner it joined the war effort, the better the outcome would be.[79] When the United States was jolted from its myopic isolationism by the attack on Pearl Harbor, Pepper's earlier warnings clothed him with a statesmanlike mantle of foresight. (Less than ten years later, he would draw on a personal meeting with another dictator, Joseph Stalin, to again run counter to prevailing sentiment in foreign policy. Unlike his prescience in 1939, his subsequent post-war intuition proved to be his undoing.)

In 1940, Pepper eagerly supported Roosevelt's tradition-shattering bid for a third term. He campaigned and raised money for him. When the Democratic coffers were nearly exhausted in the latter stages of the campaign, Pepper was one of the New Deal loyalists asked to solicit contributions. Businessmen who normally would have little use for the New Deal still found it advantageous to stay in the good graces of senators who could help them ameliorate its impact on their interests. When Pepper solicited Florida businessmen for contributions, he included Ball, who responded with a contribution of $1,000, a sizable amount at that time.[80] The Jacksonville financier was never known for lavish contributions in his own right but preferred to take the credit for inducing others to give. This instance of his direct giving indicates that Pepper and Ball continued to be on good terms notwithstanding the latter's growing contempt for the New Deal.

During this period, Pepper continued to move leftward in political outlook, even beyond that necessary to be consistent with his support of the New Deal. In foreign and domestic matters, this was the beginning of a widening gap between him and the mainstream views of his Florida constituents. His expanding circle of political and social friends in Washington was reflective of his rising status, the combined result of his favored position with the administration and his membership on the Foreign Relations Committee. Because he was a member of that committee, doors were opened to him in Washington's international community. Social engagements on an intimate scale with ambassadors and other Washington personages were not uncommon. There he participated in discussions of world events, all of which portended U.S. involvement in the war then raging in Europe.[81] He had a warm friendship with the Soviet ambassador, Maxim Litvinov, which included taking piano lessons from Madam Litvinov.[82] Pepper enjoyed his piano lessons, another manifestation of his eclectic nature. His relationship with Dr. Francis E. Townsend, whose endorsement of him was an important help in the 1938 campaign, continued, and by 1942, Townsend was telling him that people all over the country considered him "a future president."[83]

Pepper continued to work on issues brought to him by constituents, but increasingly, he saw this as interference with his main purpose: the cause of liberalism. The cross-state barge canal, a favorite of north Florida business interests, was one such long-running issue. Canal supporters were especially demanding, and after one session with them, he wrote, "I have been and am damned tired of the canal."[84] Roosevelt had promised help on the canal as an inducement to bring Pepper around on the Court-packing issue, and the senator persevered in the effort despite his irritation over the demands of the canal supporters. In the waning months of peace, he got a commitment from the president to include the canal appropriation with the St. Lawrence Seaway project, only to lose it later in the press of war funding.[85]

Pepper, always close to personal financial difficulty, maintained a limited private law practice and had some investment interests in business concerns. He was retained in a case involving the Ringling estate (the circus family), serving as co-counsel with Jacksonville attorney A. Y. Milam. Often, such legal work was merely a sham for the payment of fees to elected officials without any expectation of real legal service. In Pepper's case, his legal ability was real, and his professional part in the case was substantial. He actively participated in the litigation, and, hopeful of success, he expected to receive a good fee. He confided to his diary regarding the case and its possible consequences for him, "Let us hope I can have the chance for economic independence—the struggle for the liberal cause will be a lot easier."[86] Later, Milam performed extensive legal work for Ed Ball, including handling part of his divorce case. In 1950, he was also prominent in the Jacksonville business community's effort to defeat Pepper.

As Pepper was developing a Washington prominence, the war effort became the all-consuming purpose for the entire government. Although the social programs fostered by the New Deal were subordinated to that effort, they were only postponed, never forsaken. Pepper continued to be on a friendly basis with Ball and other duPont executives, helping with a port project in Port St. Joe, site of the St. Joe Paper Company, and collaborating with Ball in attempting to locate a wartime shipyard in that town.[87]

In early 1944, Ball was severely injured in a dual-train collision and was hospitalized in North Carolina. Pepper wrote a friendly letter commiserating with him about the accident. Ball responded by saying the letter "did much to cheer me up." Notwithstanding the amicable tone, the recuperating businessman could not let the opportunity pass to chide Pepper on the New Deal. He added, "The only thing that I know that is tougher than a train wreck has been surviving in business through the depression and the regulations and regimentations of the New Deal; so, having survived both so far, I really feel that I have a right to be optimistic."[88]

It was in the early 1940s that Ball undertook what can best be termed the definitive step in shaping the Florida business empire started by Alfred I. duPont, one which ultimately stamped it with his own identity and personality. He launched what was to be a twenty-year battle for control of the bankrupt Florida East Coast Railway system. More than anything else, it was Pepper's strident opposition to that effort which created and perpetuated a lasting hostility between the two men. But first, there were two unlikely events in 1944 that contributed to the fissure in their relationship: the closing of an army hospital in Palm Beach and the presidential veto of a tax bill. These two episodes culminated in Ball's opposition to Pepper's 1944 campaign for a second full term. The friendly response to Pepper's "get well" letter in January 1944 was the last genuinely amicable exchange between the two men.

7

Patterns of Conflict
1944

The Florida senatorial election of 1950 stands out as the most memorable episode in the long chain of events in the continuing relationship of Claude Pepper and Ed Ball. It has been termed, generally by those inclined to Pepper's side of the story, the "dirtiest" political campaign in Florida's political history. In that version, a clique of special interests led by a reactionary Ed Ball put up a candidate more to their liking, George A. Smathers, to defeat Florida's popular and liberal senior senator. Their success was owed to a malicious distortion of the senator's liberalism built on the twin evils of racism and McCarthyism. That construct has been more recently tempered by the view that Pepper's defeat was caused primarily by his own political posturing to achieve leadership status in the extreme left wing of the Democratic Party and his strident apologetics for the USSR's Cold War policies.[1]

The truth of the matter lies somewhere in a composite of those two views, coupled with undercurrents of causation reaching back six years. A series of events beginning in early 1944 energized a metamorphosis in Pepper and Ball's relationship. Until then their differences had been issue driven, not having reached the levels of personal animosity that would subsequently characterize their feelings for each other. These events go mostly unnoticed in accounts focused on more momentous episodes of political history. Yet they are the stuff of practical politics, and it was, after all, practical politics that bound these two men together in a mosaic of political purpose and causation.

World War II had reached a clear turning point by 1944, and ultimate Allied victory seemed assured. War production had reinvigorated American business and industry from the malaise of depression, raising even higher expectations for the postwar period. Florida had shared in the prosperity brought about by the wartime economy, with Pepper helping many Florida businesses make their way through the tangle of wartime regulations to profit from lucrative war contracts. Yet beneath the prosperity and overarching national unity behind the war effort, there were fissures of political discord reaching from the federal level into state political settings. Business interests continued to chaff under the New Deal regulatory structure. With prosperity returning, the reform framework set in place earlier seemed increasingly irrelevant and counterproductive to an economy running at maximum production. In addition, pervasive wartime production controls and high levels of taxation exacerbated the discontent. For Pepper, expressions of such discontent were but examples of greedy war profiteering, which he decried in terms not far removed from the rhetoric of class warfare. He was equally strident in his views of labor leaders when they deviated from what he deemed proper support for Roosevelt. For Pepper, the president personified both the war effort and the cause of liberalism.[2] Anything short of unswerving support for Roosevelt's policies was, in his eyes, near treason.

In mid-1943, Roosevelt sent to the Congress a revenue bill seeking $11 billion in new tax revenues to fund the war effort. The demand for goods and materials of every type for the war was fueling the nation's economic engine to a frenzied pace. As industrial output quickened and victory appeared assured, high levels of taxation, profit controls, and mandated contract renegotiation provisions became increasingly obnoxious to businessmen. They were a constant source of friction between corporate America and the Democratic administration. War production and the prosperity that followed in its wake replaced economic reform as parameters of domestic legislation. The private sector was deemed an essential partner in the process, its voice better received in the Capitol lobbies than had been the case in the depression atmosphere just a few years earlier. With peace coming into view and profits soaring, business was no longer reticent in urging its views on a Congress showing increasing disinclination to follow the Roosevelt administration agenda. There were voices to the contrary. Some argued that business was overplaying its hand with the war not yet over, and the need for national sacrifice still apparent to the ordinary American. Still, that did not deter an increasingly strident posture on the part of business spokesmen as they lobbied for lower taxes and fewer controls.[3]

It was against this backdrop that President Roosevelt initiated the request in late 1943 for increased revenues to fund the war effort. The war was far from over. The invasion of Europe had yet to start; Nazi forces occupied most of Europe and large portions of the Soviet Union. In the Pacific, Japan still held most of the territories it had seized early in the war. Clearly, the United States had a long distance yet to travel on the road to victory, and with the outpouring of military effort necessary for victory came the continuing need for an outpouring of the nation's resources. Taxation was the visible manifestation of this dimension of war, and recurring tax measures by 1943 had become all but routine in the wartime regimen of the nation's capital. Roosevelt's measure carried over to the following year and became known as the 1944 revenue bill.

In peacetime, revenue bills are traditional targets of opportunity for special interests seeking relief from real and perceived grievances. Amendments are placed on such measures pertaining to matters wholly unrelated to revenues, matters which, if standing alone, would never be enacted, but which are insulated from executive veto by the need for the revenues. The patriotic fervor of national unity in the war effort had imposed some measure of self-restraint on the normally antagonistic attitudes of business toward government controls and taxes. As the war outlook improved, those restraints were relaxed, and business became more assertive in seeking to influence the legislative process. That turn of events meshed with the rising restlessness of a Congress that considered itself too long under the heel of the man in the White House. In that setting, the revenue measure introduced in 1943 was transformed into a myriad of relief measures by special interest lobbyists who found sympathetic understanding from a Congress anxious to reaffirm its equality with the executive branch.[4] The proposed new revenues were cut back to a meager $2 billion, of which only half was actually to come from new or increased taxes. As the measure made its way through the committee process, it was festooned with amendments, making it a major relief measure for business and industry. The Florida duPont interests, along with numerous other business groups, had a stake in several provisions of the complicated versions of the bill that emerged from the tax-writing committees of both House and Senate.

The bill's most controversial nonrevenue component relaxed the "renegotiation" provisions of existing procurement laws. At the outset of the war, Congress had imposed an administrative review process on the profits generated by war contractors. It became euphemistically known as "renegotiation." The review panel, administered by midlevel bureaucrats from each procuring agency of the government, had power to "renegotiate" contracts, requiring after-the-fact rebates from companies whose profits were found to be excessive. It was a tedious and time-consuming process, without any readily comprehensible procedural or substantive provisions for the businessman to follow. In such conditions, there was little or no predictability as to what profits the review boards would find proper in the after-the-fact proceedings. Even so, under the frenzied circumstances of total war conditions, it was a crude but effective counter to price gouging by unscrupulous businessmen, at the same time being a distinct hindrance to the conduct of honest business practices. To the average citizen, the sums involved were enormous.

Consolidated Vultee, primarily an aircraft manufacturer, illustrates the situation. It had set aside more than $80 million for renegotiation rebates in anticipation of the outcome of reviews of its profits on certain contracts. Its case illustrates the economic and operational paradoxes that flavored the public perception of the issue. Its profits had more than doubled, going from about $7 million to more than $19 million in one year. Its earning per share had nearly tripled, going from $4.86 per share to $13.77 in the same period.[5] There was little likelihood that this profit would not be perceived by the public as excessive, even with the tremendous increase in output that the company had managed in aircraft production. The situation made easy prey for demagoguery, allowing little room for rational discussion of whether the profit margins were justified. The sheer scope of the numbers rendered them unfathomable to the general public, leaving profiteering and greed most readily assimilated in the ordinary person's perception of the situation.

Public uncertainty rapidly turned to skepticism when fueled by examples of clearly excessive demands by businessmen. In one well-publicized case, a corporate spokesman wanted only a "5% profit on gross war business, after taxes."[6] That would have given him profits of $5 million in 1944, more than fifty times the total worth of his company at the beginning of the war. Such examples pointedly implied that the offending businessmen had not increased their capital investments by anything near the same multiple, leaving the clear impression of excessive profiteering as a result of the war effort. In the twenty months preceding enactment of the 1944 revenue measure, there had been 13,000 actual contract renegotiations, saving over $5.3 billion in rebates and reduced prices.

The administration opposed the provisions attached to the revenue bill that would have allowed judicial review of renegotiated price proceedings and exempted "standard goods" from the process. This latter provision was important to the makers of thousands of generic peacetime products incorporated into the manufacturing processes of war goods. It would have substantially narrowed the scope of the renegotiation process, which, at that time, reached virtually the entire spectrum of goods that went into the war effort. When asked what remained subject to renegotiation under the amendment, one congressman replied, "If you can't shoot it, it is exempt."[7] The administration viewed it as a blatant case of political overkill.

Packing boxes and containers used for the packing of military products, such as those made by St. Joe Paper Company and other container manufacturers, came under the proposed exemption. Charles H. Murchison, a Harvard classmate of Pepper's and best man at his wedding, was hired by a consortium of paper companies, including St. Joe Paper Company, to lobby for an exemption for containers. No doubt, it was hoped that he would have a friendly reception from Pepper, a member of the Senate Finance Committee.[8] Pepper helped to rewrite the renegotiation provisions of the bill in a compromise that left intact much of what Ball and other Florida businessmen wanted.[9] The choice of Murchison had been a good one. There were other reasons Ball strongly favored the bill.

Buried deep in the funding measure as it finally made its way to the Senate floor was a provision materially affecting the tax consequences of Ball's proposed takeover of the Florida East Coast Railway. It had to do with the deductibility of interest accrued, but not actually paid, on defaulted bonds. The bonds of the Florida East Coast had been in default for the years 1939 through 1941, and the bankrupt railroad had claimed interest accrued but not paid on them as deductions against taxable income for the periods involved. The Internal Revenue Service had subsequently questioned these deductions, which if disallowed, would have created substantial tax liabilities. These liabilities would have carried over to the new owners of the Florida East Coast when it emerged from bankruptcy. At the time, Ball's St. Joe Paper Company was considered the most likely new equity owner of the railroad.[10] In section 121 of the Revenue Act as passed, the IRS view of the interest deductions was materially altered in favor of whoever would be the new owners. Taxable gain realized on property transferred in certain bankruptcy proceedings, including section 77b proceedings under the Bankruptcy Act, was made not recognizable for tax purposes.[11] The Florida East Coast bankruptcy proceeding was under that section of the Bankruptcy Act. It was a provision of material importance to Ball in his long-running battle to take over the Florida East Coast Railway.

In another section of the revenue bill's final version, there were favorable taxation provisions for the sale of timber, treating gain from such transactions as capital gains instead of ordinary income. For companies with large timber holdings such as St. Joe Paper Company, it promised substantial tax savings. Just as Claude Pepper never met a tax he did not like, Ed Ball never met one he liked—except, that is, the Florida sales tax.

Virtually every executive agency having fiscal responsibilities in the procurement process was opposed to the measure as it finally came out of the Senate Finance Committee. Most of the opposition had to do with the renegotiation provision. The bill had been intensely lobbied, and there was something in it for everyone besides the meager additional revenue finally allowed for funding the war effort.

By early 1944, there were clear indications that the myriad of relief provisions in the bill had made it unpalatable to the administration. There was talk of a veto, the first ever of a revenue measure.[12] If the president determined to go that far, it would signal another showdown between the executive and legislative branches in an election year. With Roosevelt pressing the outer limits of political reality by seeking a fourth term, it was generally believed that he would not go out of his way to alienate the Congress. It was not the kind of issue that the media could comprehensibly relate to the public. Although Roosevelt's pronouncements on the renegotiation provisions did ignite some public indignation, the issue was mostly a Washington insider affair. It created great tension within Washington's interlocking circles of power. This was especially true when those circles of power were restlessly circumscribed by what was probably the strongest aggregation of executive power in the nation's history. As the bill made its way to final passage, and tension between the Congress and administration began to mount, Pepper was in Florida, campaigning for reelection. The bill passed both House and Senate by substantial majorities and went to the president for his approval—or veto.

It should be emphasized here that ever since the Court-packing battle seven years earlier, Congress had chaffed under what might best be described as the unrelenting leadership of an exceptionally strong president. The balance between the legislative and executive powers, always precarious in the nation's loosely structured constitutional framework, was again under strain. The press of wartime, like the depression conditions of the preceding decade, clearly favored the executive in the perennial power struggle between the two branches of government.

Alben W. Barkley of Kentucky was the Senate majority leader, chosen by his Democratic colleagues at the urging of Roosevelt by a one-vote margin seven years earlier. Not an overly forceful person, he had served the administration faithfully, being sometimes called the president's "stooge" or "Whitehouse errand boy."[13] As the Senate seethed under the executive yoke, Barkley endured the humiliating existence of a majority leader unable to defend its independence from the encroachments of a strong-willed chief executive. When the Revenue Act finally passed in early February of 1944, Barkley and the House Democratic leadership met with Roosevelt and Vice President Wallace in the ailing president's bedroom to discuss the measure. Roosevelt announced almost casually that he was going to veto it. Knowing of the strong support for the measure in both houses, the Democratic leaders urged him to let it become law without his signature, saying the revenue—though a small amount of money—was necessary. They defended the other provisions of the bill as being justified in some instances on their merits, and in others, by the realities of the political situation. They warned the president that a veto would stir up an already irate Congress, one increasingly restless and not likely to bow readily to Roosevelt's wishes.[14] The Senate leaders explained to him that there was not enough at stake in the overall scheme of things to risk an open breach within his own party. The strong-willed president disagreed.

In late February, Roosevelt sent to Capitol Hill a scathing veto message, one which seemed clearly calculated to impugn the collective integrity of both chambers. Alluding to the inadequacy of the revenues provided in the bill, he called it "a small piece of crust" instead of the loaf of bread he had asked for to prosecute the war. He said he might have been content with that if it had not "contained so many extraneous and inedible materials."[15] He then coined a phrase that has since become a staple in liberal polemics on tax policy: "In this respect, it is not a tax bill but a tax relief bill providing relief not for the needy but for the greedy."[16] He also called specific attention to the provisions giving relief to holders of securities of bankrupt corporations as well as the timber sales provisions, both having impacts on duPont interests in Florida.

The resulting effect was exactly as the Democratic leadership had warned FDR in their bedroom conference at the White House. Congress was in a furor, intent on making a point of its independence and integrity. Political writer and novelist Allen Drury, then a Capitol Hill reporter and daily observer of the unfolding drama, described the situation: "The rift this time has gone too deep for any but the most temporary healing. The words chosen [by Roosevelt] were too deliberate, the basis for the action too flimsy and illogical, the thing too obviously a deliberate blow at Capitol Hill for anyone to either forgive or forget."[17] It was clearly a power struggle of grand proportions between the executive and legislative branches. It proved to be the nadir of Roosevelt's relations with a Congress increasingly disenchanted with his near legendary power. Pepper, even though one of only thirteen senators who supported the president, later concurred in that assessment of the situation, but without regretting his support of Roosevelt at the time.[18]

The House overrode the veto by a vote of 299 to 95, far more than the constitutional requisite. The next day, Barkley took to the Senate floor to make a reasoned and, at times, impassioned response, calling for an override of the presidential veto. It was a matter of high drama, the Senate leader of Roosevelt's own party opposing him and asking that his veto be overridden. It was the most direct challenge to Roosevelt's leadership of his entire presidency, more so even than the Court-packing battle, and it came from within his own party. To make his point more emphatic, Barkley announced he would resign his leadership position so as to remove any feelings of personal obligation to the president for helping him be chosen as majority leader in the first place. Arrangements had already been made within the Senate's ruling circles for him to be immediately reelected to the Democratic majority leadership position, further emphasizing the widening breech between the president and his own party. Senators of both parties rallied around Barkley. In this confrontation with the chief executive, the majority leader stood as the symbol of the institutional integrity of the Senate. That gave the senators a better basis for overriding the veto than trying to defend the myriad of special interest provisions nestled within the body of the tax bill.

Campaigning in Florida, Pepper kept in close contact with the rising temper of the situation. Predictably, he sided with Roosevelt, although not immediately sure he would vote to sustain the veto. Referring to Barkley in a diary entry of the period, he said, "Bumbling Barkley has bumbled again."[19] The next day, almost with tones of pettiness, Pepper wrote, "FDR did not regard him [Barkley] as a strong enough leader to be fully trusted. He is not a natural leader, sometimes lacks industry."[20] Contrary to that assessment, Barkley was widely viewed as a tried and faithful administration loyalist, one who subordinated his own political standing and well-being to White House directives. This is a good example of Pepper's tendency to judge a situation wholly on the basis of his unswerving fidelity to Roosevelt and what he deemed to be the liberal cause. It illustrated how his ideological blind spot and almost slavish loyalty to the president clouded his assessment of the collective attitudes of his colleagues and, increasingly, the public as well.

After reflecting on the matter, Pepper decided to return to Washington and defend the president's veto.[21] His staff, sensing the inflammatory impact of Roosevelt's strident language in the veto message, advised against it. They told Pepper it was hopeless, adding that his primary campaign in Florida afforded a good excuse to be absent from the Senate when the vote was taken. He was flying directly in the face of overwhelming Senate sentiment against the president. It was clearly a futile gesture, one which sounded good in principle, but which could only damage him further with Florida business interests as well as with his Senate colleagues.

The night before he left for Washington, Pepper was invited to the home of Herbert Wolfe, a prominent road contractor and political figure from St. Augustine. The road contractors endorsed the bill's renegotiation provisions, and Wolfe was their spokesman. He pressed Pepper on how he was going to vote on the veto, but Pepper would not tell him. Later, Pepper thought Ball had tried to use Wolfe to ascertain his position.[22] In fact, the road contractor had his own reasons for wanting the veto overridden, and believed that Pepper agreed with him and other Florida businessmen on the issue. Pepper's vote to sustain the veto was seen by Wolfe, and many other Florida businessmen, as a breech of faith.[23] Six years later, George Smathers was invited to Wolfe's St. Augustine home to meet with Ed Ball and discuss running against Pepper.[24] That meeting and its consequences will be discussed in a subsequent chapter. It is mentioned here to show that Pepper's 1944 vote angered most Florida businessmen, not just Ed Ball. To them, it appeared a hopeless and unnecessary gesture on the part of Pepper, one with no apparent reason other than to serve as a symbolic slap in the face of business. It could also be said to have been a measure of his loyalty to the leader of his party, the president.

Senate feeling was so overwhelming against the president that when the matter came before the Senate, only Pepper spoke in defense of the veto. When he rose, there were impatient cries of "Vote! Vote!" by senate colleagues wishing to push on with the matter. Insisting on his senatorial right to speak, he continued, couching his comments in terms of winning the war and preserving the Democratic Party. He quoted at length from the letter he had received from Roosevelt in 1928 when he was but a mere house member in the Florida legislature, recounting how he had then espoused liberalism as the cornerstone of the party. Avoiding serious discussion of the vetoed legislation, he embarked on a paean to Roosevelt. He said the president would be "a star that will shine in the history books and the hearts of mankind, that will be as luminous and as fixed as the North Star."[25] He noted his part in rewriting the compromised renegotiation provisions but considered it more important to support the president. He translated the issue from one of taxation to the future of the Democratic Party as the focus of liberal leadership for the nation, referring to the "many downcast and oppressed peoples" championed by Roosevelt.[26]

As usual, Pepper's oratory was brilliant, but his judgment in this instance was strikingly at odds with the overwhelming majority of his Senate colleagues. His praise for Roosevelt was not only irrelevant but distinctly unwelcome. His insistence on speaking did not sit well with a chamber impatient to assert itself against the very president Pepper sought to deify. His reference to the 1928 letter from Roosevelt prompted a facetious inquiry from another senator as to how Florida had voted in that election. When Pepper replied Hoover had carried the state, his dramatic impact was lost amid the laughter in the chamber occasioned by the incongruity of his response. Otherwise, Drury thought he might have changed some votes, but certainly not enough to alter the outcome.[27] Twelve Democrats and a lone Republican, William R. Langer of Idaho, voted to sustain the veto.[28]

The events surrounding Pepper's defense of the Roosevelt veto took place early in the 1944 primary campaign season, before any major opponent had taken the field against him. Although his shrill polemics on liberalism were becoming increasingly unpopular in state political circles, his strong support of a president still popular with the public, and his foresight in 1939 in urging the defeat of German and Japanese aggression against prevalent isolationist sentiment, left him still in good standing with the voters.[29] Shortly after his defense of the veto on the Senate floor, the man who would give him the greatest trouble in the primary announced his candidacy. Pepper believed strongly that this candidate was backed by Ed Ball, and there is evidence that he was correct.[30] There was yet another episode triggered by Pepper that riled Ball, one which the financier took personally and was not apt to forget or forgive.

In early January 1944, Pepper and his wife were guests of a wealthy supporter in Palm Beach. While there, Pepper visited the posh Breakers Hotel, a luxury resort then sequestered into government service as the Ream Army Hospital. The hotel was owned by the Florida East Coast Hotel Corporation, a subsidiary of the Florida East Coast Railway Company. Someone in attendance during Pepper's visit told him that the convalescing soldiers were not allowed by the hotel owners to stray more than "two feet" off the walkways around the golf course. Pepper was quick to sense the potential for political drama in what could be taken as mistreatment of veterans—wounded veterans at that. He immediately sided with the wounded veterans, advising his military hosts "that the golf course [should] be taken over" for their benefit.[31] The incongruity of convalescent veterans playing golf did not hinder his quick pronouncement in favor of the wounded soldiers against the privileged class symbolized by the Breakers Hotel (and including Ed Ball).

At the time, the army general responsible for maintenance of military hospitals was considering closing the hotel-turned-hospital and returning it to its owner, the Florida East Coast Hotel Corporation. That company and the Florida East Coast Railway were both owned by the same entity but were separate corporations. The Florida East Coast Railway was in its thirteenth year of bankruptcy, and Ed Ball was then engaged in his long-running effort to take over the bankrupt corporation.

Sometime after Pepper's visit, a group of convalescing patients from Ream Army Hospital visited his Washington office asking for his intervention to prevent the closing of the installation. W. Robert Fokes, then an aide to Pepper, remembered the visit but could not recall how the wounded soldiers got from Palm Beach to Washington. The soldiers were clearly ambulatory, and Fokes recalled that they were enjoying their time at the posh Breakers Hotel while recuperating from their war wounds. Whether this incident ignited Pepper's determination to keep the hotel in army service, or whether he was already determined to take on Ed Ball over whatever pretext conveniently presented itself, is not clear. In any event, the Breakers hospital episode gave him what he needed to attack Ball.[32]

In early April, near the height of the primary campaign season, the army announced its intention to close the hospital for financial reasons. Patients would be transferred to other facilities, and the Breakers returned to its owners. The next day, Pepper fired off a telegram to President Roosevelt asking him to stop the transfer and, in keeping with the political purpose of his move, released the text of the message to the press. He told Roosevelt, "There is deep feeling that the action . . . has been influenced either by the present management of the corporation which owns the hotel, or by a mistaken policy of economy by the War Department."[33] He added, "The corporation is headed by Edward G. Ball of Jacksonville, brother of Mrs. Alfred I. duPont, and in charge of the duPont interests in Florida."[34] Pepper un-

doubtedly intended to charge the issue with overtones of the selfish wealthy—
the duPonts—running roughshod over the poorer classes—in this instance,
the wounded veterans. In that vein, avowedly liberal as well as mainline
publications reported the issue, portraying it as one of wounded veterans
being displaced to suit the pleasures of the idle rich.[35]

According to Raymond Mason of Jacksonville, Ball's later business associate, close friend, and biographer, "Nothing ever got Mr. Ball's blood boil-
ing quicker than this erroneous statement, for in fact neither Ball nor the
duPonts had any connection with the hotel either prior to or at the time of
the incident."[36] Technically, that was correct. Ball did not control the railroad, and the hotel subsidiary was not at issue in the bankruptcy. Yet by
1944, he had emerged as the majority owner of the defaulted Florida East
Coast Railway bonds and was clearly the leading contender for control of
the bankrupt corporation. Still, his claim to the railroad was being vigorously contested by the Atlantic Coast Line Railroad, and his position was
still uncertain. It would be another eight months before his majority ownership of the defaulted bonds was even recognized by the Interstate Commerce Commission as the prelude to equity control.[37] Ball considered Pepper's statement a deliberate lie, and a gratuitous one at that. The irate
financier dispatched Jacksonville attorney A. Y. Milam, frequently retained
by Ball in duPont legal affairs and Pepper's co-counsel in the Ringling case,
to Washington to inform Pepper of his mistake and demand a retraction.

Fokes remembered the Milam visit. Pepper would not see the emissary
and left the formality of receiving Ball's message to his aide. Later, Fokes told
Pepper what Milam had said about Ball's lack of management control over
the hotel, and Pepper issued a guarded retraction. The retraction was not
suitable to Ball, and there the matter remained.[38] Earlier that year, Milam,
a former speaker of the Florida House of Representatives, had considered
but then rejected running against Pepper.[39] Perhaps Ball picked Milam to see
Pepper because he presumed the senator would be receptive to his former
cocounsel on that score. Six years later, Milam was to be deeply involved in
the effort to defeat Pepper. According to J. C. "Jake" Belin, Ball neither
forgot nor forgave those who opposed or affronted him, and Mason con-
firms that in his account of this episode.

Pepper may well have assumed that Ball controlled the hotel because of
his emergence as the dominant figure in the Florida East Coast takeover
battle, a matter that had been prominent in the news for two years. From the
comments he heard in his January visit to the hospital about prohibiting

soldiers from walking on the grass, Pepper would have been quick to attribute such orders to Ball, whom he correctly presumed to be supporting his opposition. Given Ball's contentious and legalistic disposition, the episode provided a personal affront to add to his growing list of reasons to oppose Florida's junior senator. Pepper's overriding liberalism as displayed in his futile defense of the Revenue Act veto would have sooner than later driven a wedge between the two men. The Breakers episode only hastened the inevitable.

Eleven years later, and after Pepper's 1950 defeat, the two antagonists met by chance in the state banking commissioner's office in the Capitol Building in Tallahassee. Pepper awkwardly suggested to the banker-businessman, then at the apex of his power: "Ed, we are growing old. We should stop fighting." People did not commonly use Ball's first name in addressing him, and that may not have sat well with the crusty financier. Conversely, former senators did not generally address their contemporaries, either friendly or otherwise, in other than a familiar manner. In any event, Ball would have none of Pepper's conciliatory tone and replied, with clear reference to the Breakers episode, "You threw a brick at me without cause and I threw one at you."[40] With like petulance, Pepper responded, "You threw a brick at me in '44 without cause first." According to Pepper, the two exited the office in which the encounter took place "Alphonsing and Gastoning at the door as to who should lead."[41] There was some more conversation in the hallway between them on a matter affecting one of Pepper's clients, laced with a strained effort at humor by Pepper. Pepper left the encounter with his low opinion of Ball once again confirmed. He wrote in his diary, "[Ball] is the same small and vindictive man towards anyone who opposes him as always. . . . The old [sic] fun he knows is making money, boasting and drinking (besides exercising power)."[42] Pepper's polemical defense of Roosevelt's veto of the tax bill, a measure favored by Ball and businessmen throughout the nation, and the Breakers affair had destroyed with finality what little understanding and tolerance for each other might have remained in their relationship.

Shortly after Pepper's performance on the Revenue Act veto, Duval's County Judge Ollie Edmunds joined a field of three other little-known candidates seeking to unseat the state's senior senator. It was rumored that Ball had enticed him into the race, and Pepper was advised by friends that Ball was definitely raising money to defeat him. One Jacksonville supporter told him that Ball and C. G. "Cliff" McGeehee, another prominent Jacksonville businessman and political figure, had agreed to raise $60,000 for Edmunds, an enormous sum for the time.[43] Edmunds, who, as a county judge, had presided over the probate of the duPont estate, was well acquainted with the powerful financier. Ball was frequently before him on matters involving the complex provisions of duPont's will and establishment of the duPont Trust. Later, when Edmunds became head of Stetson University, that institution became a favored beneficiary of Jessie Ball duPont's charitable giving.

There is little direct evidence that Ball was the proximate cause of Edmunds's candidacy, and that is the view of one student of Pepper's political career.[44] Still, Edmunds's announcement of his candidacy shortly after Pepper's histrionic defense of Roosevelt's veto lends some credence to the supposition that Ball was involved with Edmunds's decision. Ball added substance to this supposition in later years when he as much as said that he advised Edmunds during the campaign.[45] Pepper charged in a Miami speech that a fund of over $150,000 had been raised to defeat him by those "who hate President Roosevelt and [Pepper] for their defense of this country against selfish domestic interests and foreign aggressors."[46]

It was but a small step to name Ball and the duPont Trust as those "selfish interests." The charges were made two weeks before Pepper issued the press release naming Ball as the cause of mistreatment of wounded veterans at the Ream Army Hospital in Palm Beach. Pepper did not hesitate to imply that opponents of Roosevelt, and, by extension, himself, were nothing short of collaborators with the enemy, as seen in his reference to their hatred of Roosevelt for his defense of the country. During the presidential campaign of 1944, he linked the law firm of John Foster Dulles, a prominent Republican and Thomas E. Dewey supporter, to Hitler with the same carefree abandon. He referred to Dewey as an isolationist, tantamount at the time to accusing him of being a Nazi supporter.[47] His reckless use of such charges in 1944 was but an ironic harbinger of similar tactics to be used against him six years later. For those who did not agree with his liberal views and policies, no measure of opprobrium was out of order. Pepper's ego was such that he readily associated himself and his idol, Roosevelt, with the purest of the good, and their opponents with the forces of darkness and evil. It was an attitude that played well so long as the general public still believed strongly in Roosevelt and the war effort. Pepper correctly sensed the continued strength of that belief in 1944.

Pepper won his second first-primary victory, but not by the 100,000-vote margin of his 1938 triumph. His margin had shrunk to an uncomfortable 10,000 votes.

Even though generally held in contempt by most of the Florida business community, Pepper continued to enjoy some support from that sector. He used a private corporate airplane in the campaign, a significant contribution at the time in a state as large as Florida, and one that could remain undetected under the lax campaign-reporting laws of the period.[48] He was also close to the management of Pan American Airlines, the Miami-based American international air carrier. The company wanted to maintain its hold as the exclusive American carrier for foreign air travel from the United States, but Pepper was troubled by its monopoly status.[49] Nevertheless, he recognized that he owed Pan Am a political debt for its support and helped maintain the company's monopoly status. He felt that he could rebuild on that base of business support in the future.

All in all, Pepper viewed his prospects for reelection as favorable. He had been elected to the U.S. Senate once without opposition (1936), and with two first-primary victories (1938 and 1944). He had withstood attacks aimed at his liberal racial views, even though he felt compelled to reaffirm his commitment to segregation after the Supreme Court outlawed the Democratic white primary in Texas.[50] The racial climate of 1944 was charged with determination by southern whites to preserve a segregated social structure. Pepper's drive for national recognition as a liberal leader had run counter to the innate racism of his Florida constituency. It had been a bothersome thing during the campaign, but he had survived it with a reaffirmation of segregation.[51]

Pepper's role in Roosevelt's fourth victory and his own impressive reelection sent him back to Washington more self-assured in his liberal views, confident of his own imperviousness to attacks from opponents of himself, Roosevelt, or the New Deal. He was now at the pinnacle of his Senate career.

With Pepper returned to Washington, Ed Ball had much to occupy himself besides ruminating on the outcome of Florida's senatorial election. He was approaching what seemed to be the end of his quest for control of the Florida East Coast Railway. He was also deeply immersed in forcing his old adversary, Roy E. Crummer, out of the Florida municipal bond business. In addition, he was embroiled in a bitterly contested divorce. In early 1945, the Interstate Commerce Commission determined that the St. Joe Paper Company, acting through Ball, had acquired over 51 percent of the entire issue of the bankrupt railroad's defaulted bonds. It meant that the duPont Trust would have "control of the reorganized company" when the district court bankruptcy proceedings in Jacksonville were completed.[52] The commission had rejected a hastily contrived effort by one of the opposing bondholder groups to bring in the giant Atlantic Coast Line Railroad to foil Ball's take-over bid. The commission's language heralded ultimate duPont victory—more accurately, ultimate Ball victory. He had tenaciously persevered, de-spite adverse rulings and opposition from powerful competing business interests, in aggregating a majority interest in the crucial defaulted bond issue. Still, the matter was not yet fully resolved. The Atlantic Coast Line had the right to appeal, a right which the giant railroad intended to leverage to the maximum with the help of third-term U.S. senator Claude Pepper. A new dimension to the long and open phase of the Pepper-Ball hostility, already set in motion by the Revenue Act veto, the Breakers episode, and the 1944 Edmunds candidacy, was about to be set in motion. In this instance, Pepper was the moving force.

In January of 1945, Pepper and McD. Champion "Champ" Davis, presi-dent of the Atlantic Coast Line Railroad, were corresponding on a first-name basis about the matter. Pepper had initiated contact with Davis shortly after his successful 1944 reelection campaign. Afterward, Pepper wrote a short note to the railroad executive thanking him for the services of the Coast Line's Washington lobbyist in acquiring space on trains for him and his friends when accommodations were difficult to obtain.[53] Pepper formally entered the proceedings in April when he filed with the commission a "Mem-orandum" attacking Ball's fitness to control the railroad on an array of grounds, including the somewhat quaint allegation that Ball "has not been averse to attempting to influence public policy."[54] (The protracted fight over control of the Florida East Coast Railway is the subject of the next chapter.) Pepper's intervention in the case commenced after the 1944 primary elec-tion, when his power was enhanced by his third triumph and he enjoyed a favored relationship with the Roosevelt administration. He now felt secure enough to throw down the gauntlet to his Jacksonville adversary.

Events in a much larger dimension soon intervened to influence the course of the Ball-Pepper conflict. President Roosevelt's death in April of 1945 transformed the Democratic Party's leadership structure. Harry Truman was not the type of man that Pepper envisioned as a proper successor to the already legendary Roosevelt. He considered the high-pitched Missourian akin to a mere machine politician, unworthy to carry forth the liberal tradi-tions of a president "as luminous and as fixed as the North Star."[55] Pepper's diary entries for this period foreshadow his hardening leftist orientation in foreign affairs. He expressed satisfaction that Winston Churchill, Britain's wartime prime minister, was defeated by the Labor Party, declaring that

Britain would now have a government "that would truly serve the people," and that "the Labor victory will give hope to liberals everywhere."[56] It was in this period that Pepper attached himself firmly to Henry A. Wallace, the man he had supported over Truman for the vice presidential nomination at the 1944 Democratic convention. Wallace had emerged in the immediate postwar years as the acknowledged leader of the radical left wing of the Democratic Party.

There now occurred a major milestone in the shaping of Pepper's political destiny. He arranged an extensive trip abroad, including a long stay in the Soviet Union. Even though he was a senior member of the Foreign Relations Committee, that committee would not authorize his trip, so he arranged to go as a member of the Small Business Committee. The stated reason was to study foreign trade possibilities for American small business operations.[57] However, it was his position on the Foreign Relations Committee that attracted attention and defined the importance of his status while visiting the Soviet Union.

During this early postwar period, Pepper was still working on behalf of Pan American Airlines trying to arrange a better allocation of European flights for that carrier. He also noted in his diary that the Pan Am private corporate airplane was at his disposal for travel by him and his staff. As a prelude to his foreign trip, he visited with President Truman to clear his European trip, a routine courtesy between members of Congress and the president in matters of foreign affairs. While with Truman, he asked for help with Pan Am's route allocation problems.[58] It was clear that Pepper had not completely alienated himself from the embracing support of business. Notwithstanding the strong business opposition he had experienced in his reelection campaign, he still harbored some reason to believe that his previous support could be rebuilt. Other events would overshadow the question of his standing with the Florida business community. The foreign trip on which he embarked in August 1945 was to set the stage for the future course of his senatorial career.

Pepper left the United States on August 15, on the famous Cunard liner the HRMS *Queen Elizabeth,* bound for Great Britain. The war in Europe had ended four months earlier, and Japan announced its unconditional surrender on the day of his departure. Pepper was venturing into the world of foreign affairs as a senior member of the Senate Foreign Relations Committee at the inception of the postwar era, the period which ushered in the Cold War. While in Britain, he met with various political figures, including Winston Churchill, whose defeat earlier had stunned Western politicians, and Ernest Bevin, foreign minister in the new Labor government. In keeping with his deepening liberalism, he did not care for Churchill, saying "he has no warmth, a typical Tory," while the Labor Party prime minister was "a great and good man who came up the hard way."[59] Pepper's liberal partisanship was always the basis of his evaluations of people, no matter the circumstances. Such a judgmental proclivity, when balanced and modulated by the realities of the situation, is an important, even essential, dimension of partisan politics. With Pepper, it was carried to extremes. As a result, his grasp of people and broader political realities was often distorted by the philosophical filtration mechanism that nearly always governed his judgmental processes.

After leaving Great Britain, he spent several weeks in Europe surveying the destruction wrought by six years of warfare. There he observed the complex problems in reconstructing functioning governments in nations previously occupied or obliterated by the Nazis. The outlines of what would be nearly a half century of conflict between East and West were being adumbrated from the ashes of the conflagration unleashed by Hitler.

From Europe, he proceeded to the most important and fateful phase of his trip—the Soviet Union and a personal meeting with Joseph Stalin. His single encounter with the Soviet dictator did much to shape his foreign policy views and pronouncements. As it turned out, Pepper was not the only member of the U.S. Congress visiting the Soviet Union at that time. His visit with Stalin, which was arranged by the American Embassy, came right after a similar visit by the chairman and three members of the House Foreign Affairs Committee. When Pepper's meeting was subsequently used to castigate him as being soft on communism, he protested that the House members were not given that label. He failed to take into account that their recorded reactions to Stalin differed greatly from his own.

The mutual suspicions between the Soviet Union and its Western allies had surfaced throughout the war, and they became much more intense in the months following final victory. The Soviet Union showed little sign of honoring its pledges to permit the establishment of self-determination in the Eastern European nations it had occupied, and to demobilize its huge army. Even so, its relationship with the United States had not fully deteriorated in mid-1945 to the Cold War's state of semibelligerence. It was not wholly unrealistic at the time for Pepper to have some hope that the distrust between the West and the Soviet Union could be dispelled by mutual trust and understanding. Yet the overt optimism about future relations between the two nations that he bought away from his meeting was viewed as blind naïveté in the perspective of later years. Pepper's foreign policy views, as they ultimately emerged, were essential elements in his defeat by George Smathers. They are more appropriately discussed in the context of the 1950 campaign. Here, they are intended only to juxtapose Pepper's Moscow trip to his initial actions regarding his battle with Ball over the Florida East Coast Railway.

8

A Railroad War and Its Aftermath

The completion of the Florida East Coast Railway to Key West in 1912 by the legendary Florida developer and railroad builder Henry Flagler was considered one of the era's great engineering feats.[1] Its construction through an island chain, over long spans of ocean on huge trestles, was a remarkable accomplishment, a tribute to its creator's vision and perseverance, as well as the remarkable construction skills of his engineers. Once a train-ferry service to Havana was initiated, his system offered the only contiguous rail connections along Florida's east coast and into Cuba. Linked to the Caribbean from its position on the state's prosperous east coast, Flagler's railroad was a major component of Florida's economy and growth.

When the Florida Boom ignited the state's economy as a prelude to the Roaring Twenties, Flagler's railroad rode atop the ensuing wave of prosperity. In 1924, as the boom was cresting, the line earned a handsome $11.46 per share on an increase in gross revenues of 25 percent over the previous year.[2] Even with the relatively high dividends of the period, that was an impressive performance, and prospects seemed even brighter for the coming year. Counting on continued traffic growth, management had embarked on an ambitious expansion program aimed at upgrading the system, including double-tracking the line between Jacksonville and Miami. The program was funded by a new $150-million bond issue marketed under the auspices of the legendary J. P. Morgan and Company. Proceeds were to be used to pay for the planned improvements and to help refund the existing $12 million in outstanding First Mortgage Bonds. Under prevailing conditions, it was a sound undertaking. During the preceding eight years, the company's income available for fixed charges (an index of the line's financial condition) was a healthy 3.63 times the existing debt requirements. The management was proud that it had reduced the ratio of operating expenses to operating revenues from 82.6 to 66 percent in just under three years. All in all, the Florida East Coast (FEC) was a living realization of its founder's vision. Insofar as diligent inquiry could reveal in 1924, the newly offered bonds—known as First and Refunding Bonds—gave every appearance of being an attractive and safe investment.

The first of these bonds were issued in 1925, the year that Claude Pepper arrived in Taylor County and Ed Ball commenced his Florida career in Jacksonville. Like so much else that lingered after the shattered illusions of the Florida Boom, these instruments of debt played a crucial role in defining the setting in which the intractable hostility between the two men ran its course. The bonds became the core of prolonged and complex legal proceedings to establish control of the Florida East Coast Railway, a battle that saw Claude Pepper do everything he could to diminish Ed Ball's power over Florida's economy and politics.

As Florida's economic collapse was subsumed in the larger calamity of national depression, the Flagler railroad's financial condition rapidly eroded in tandem with the state's economy. The dwindling freight and passenger revenues could not keep pace with the expansion program and meet the debt service requirements of both the first and second mortgage bonds. The first default occurred with the railroad's failure to meet the September 1930 interest payment for the 1924 First and Refunding Bonds. A second default came six months later. At that time, the railroad was owned by the testamentary trust (Bingham Trust) of the late Mary Lily Kenan Flagler Bingham, the remarried widow and heir of Henry Flagler. The trust advanced $2.2 million to cure the first two defaults. Yet when two more occurred in September of 1931 and early 1932, it declined to advance the necessary funds, leaving the struggling railroad on its own. The throes of depression were taking their toll on the Florida economy. This left receivership as the only alternative for the hard-pressed management.[3] William R. Kenan, Jr., the company's president, entered a stipulated arrangement with Standard Oil Corporation of Kentucky, one of the company's creditors, to petition for a receivership in the federal district court at Jacksonville.

The petition by Standard Oil, the FEC's answer to it, and the order establishing the protected debtor status for the insolvent railroad were all entered on the same day. The past ties of Henry Flagler with the combine that had been John D. Rockefeller's Standard Oil Trust probably facilitated the petition. Regardless, the oil company's legal position was no more than that of an unsecured creditor (a relatively minor one in the overall scheme of things).

Other than lending its name to the proceeding's commencement, the mighty Standard Oil played no further role of significance in the matter. Kenan and Scott W. Loftin, later the interim appointee to the Senate seat of Park Trammell on his death, were designated receivers. They managed the railroad under the district court's supervision for the next ten years in receivership. After the receivership was converted to a formal bankruptcy in 1941, Loftin continued as trustee in bankruptcy, but Kenan was replaced by former Florida governor John W. Martin. Loftin was the principal trustee during the battle over control that followed, but his role was primarily custodial.

As the FEC went into the protective embrace of receivership, Ed Ball was locked in political battle with Governor Doyle E. Carlton and Roy E. Crummer. Their controversy was over the question of if and how local governments should refund the massive debt left over from the boom-time spending binge. That was the beginning of Ball's fierce competition with the Kansas bond dealer in Florida's tumultuous municipal bond refunding arena. At the same time, the Jacksonville financier was adding more acreage to duPont's growing west Florida landholdings and expanding the chain of Florida National banks under deepening depression circumstances. Claude Pepper had moved from Perry to Tallahassee, where he was resurrecting his political and professional bases for another foray into politics. There was no reason for either of them to have more than a passing concern with the railroad receivership proceedings in Jacksonville.

The proceeding initiated by Standard Oil was not hostile to the Florida East Coast Railway. It was intended to afford the distressed company a legal shelter from creditors while court-appointed receivers attempted to put its financial house in order. Finally, after failing to effect an internal reorganization acceptable to the creditors, the receivers petitioned in January 1941 to place the railroad in bankruptcy. This allowed the federal district court wider jurisdiction in resolving the contentious litigation that had developed over control of the bankrupt railroad. It was an exceptionally complex legal proceeding to begin with, one that became even more so when politicized by Pepper's appearance as a formal party. The politics of the matter are the central concern of this account, but that dimension was inextricably woven around the legal battle for control of the bankrupt railroad. For readers to fully grasp why and how Pepper opposed Ball's effort to seize control of the FEC, an explanation of the proceeding's legal nature is in order.

The purpose of receivership or bankruptcy proceedings is twofold. First, the court is charged with protecting the debtor from the cascading effects of multiple creditors seeking to collect on defaulted obligations. The objective is to allow the harassed debtor corporation a respite during which measures for fiscal rehabilitation can be explored and put in place. Second, the court is charged with overseeing the management of the company to conserve its assets for the primary benefit of the creditors, and the stockholders secondarily. This is done by appointment of receivers or trustees in bankruptcy, who serve as officers of the court with a fiduciary duty to both creditors and stockholders. Creditors with debts secured by liens attached to specified property have the highest priority (after certain other claims, such as wages) on the debtor's assets. Bondholders generally fall into that category. Common stockholders, that is, the equity owners, have the lowest claim. In the normal course of business events, ownership carries with it the potential for the greatest returns, as well as the greatest losses. That principle carries over into receivership proceedings. All the common stock of the FEC was held by the Bingham Trust when the petition for receivership was filed.[4] The $12 million in First Mortgage Bonds issued in 1909 was the senior debt, secured by a first lien on all the railroad's properties, except for certain equipment trusts not relevant to this inquiry. The First Mortgage Bonds were never in default. The outstanding junior debt was the 5 percent First and Refunding Bonds dated September 1, 1924, of which $45 million of the $150 million authorized had been issued.[5]

An additional factor complicated the FEC reorganization proceedings. Because the debtor was a railroad, somewhat akin to a public utility in legal contemplation, the resolution of its status was also subject to the jurisdiction of the Interstate Commerce Commission (ICC) under the provisions of the applicable federal bankruptcy law. That agency's primary responsibility in the matter was to determine the disposition of the company in the context of providing efficient rail transportation to the shipping public. Secondarily, it was to fulfill its primary charge in a manner that protected the rights of creditors. The dual responsibility was intended to promote the "public interest."[6] In this bifurcated jurisdictional arrangement, the question of control was primarily in the ICC's hands, subject to the final approval of the district court to ensure equitable treatment of creditors.

Beyond the district court, there was appellate jurisdiction in the circuit court of appeals. Discretionary appellate review rested finally in the U.S. Supreme Court. In the ensuing course of highly contentious litigation, the FEC proceeding passed through every level of jurisdiction several times over a period of twenty-seven years.

The 1924 First and Refunding Bonds, widely held by various institutions and individuals, became the crucial element in determining control. The asset value of the railroad was sufficient to pay off the First Mortgage Bonds but fell short of paying off the second secured issue, the First and Refunding Bonds of 1924. The central issue on which control of the railroad turned was the collective claim of the holders of the later bonds on the debtor's assets. The First Mortgage Bonds were assumed to be secure, and after the road's revenues increased dramatically in the early years of World War II, their payment was an accepted certainty.[7] But even with the increased revenues, the assets were still not sufficient to satisfy completely the claims of the second set of bondholders. It became evident that there would be nothing left over for the holders of the line's common stock. Their stake in the railroad was declared valueless, and the First and Refunding bondholders were recognized by the commission as the de facto equity owners. They were entitled to all assets remaining after payment of the First Mortgage Bonds.[8]

Normally, bondholders are represented by institutional trustees or committees charged with the fiduciary duty of protecting their interests in the debtor's assets. In this instance, the Bankers Trust Company of New York, acting as trustee under the First and Refunding Bond Indenture, promptly filed a separate suit to foreclose the second mortgage bonds.[9] The intention was to fix the mortgage holders' equitable claim on the railroad properties described in the bond indenture as security for the loans represented by the bonds. This set the stage for the claim of bondholders, or their successors in interest, to whatever remained of the railroad's assets after the senior mortgage bondholders were paid. In time, the Ball faction became the successor in interest to a majority of the junior bondholders in terms of par value of those bonds (the amount of debt stated on the face of each bond).

As economic conditions improved in the late 1930s, sophisticated investors could sense potential long-run value in the railroad that held a virtual monopoly on rail transportation on Florida's east coast. Signs of interest in control of a reorganized FEC began to appear. A majority of the outstanding First and Refunding Bonds were deposited with a committee under the auspices of J. P. Morgan and Company, the original underwriter of the bonds. Several large institutional holders were represented on the committee. A well-known Miami businessman, S. A. Lynch, controlled a substantial minority of the bonds represented by the committee, which came to be known variously as the "5% Committee" or the "Depositors Committee."[10] The committee's plan submitted to the ICC involved a recapitalization and internal reorganization that, if approved, would have left the road substantially indebted under a new first mortgage bond indenture. It involved issuing new bonds to refund a portion of the existing debt, with the difference made up by some form of equity securities. The road's earnings at that point had not yet reflected the dramatic rise in revenues that came with the increased transportation demand due to the war effort. As a result, several large institutional First and Refunding bondholders felt the new debt was beyond the railroad's means for repayment. They rejected the proposal, which was then disapproved by the ICC.

At this stage, the ICC placed great emphasis on the rights of the bondholders to be repaid from the debtor's assets. The financial dimensions of reorganization, with all the ramifications of equitable treatment for the secured creditors, were clearly the dominant factor in the collective consideration of that agency. The duPont group and Ball were not significant factors in the initial reorganization proposal.

Throughout the proceedings the parties were, for the most part, large and sophisticated financial institutions. Later, Ball would be portrayed as taking advantage of small bondholders by buying at discounts from supposedly hard-pressed investors seeking to salvage some meager part of their investments. It earned him the pejorative sobriquet of speculator and exploiter as the matter degenerated from a legal proceeding to a political donnybrook.[11] Even though he bought at substantial discounts, there was nothing unusual about that. It was (and is) commonplace in the case of securities of bankrupt corporations. Stocks and bonds of companies in financial distress always trade at discounts predicated on the basis of risk involved and likelihood of survival. It is a high-risk form of investment or speculation, depending on an investor's economic purpose. If successful, it lends itself to retroactive characterization as either predatory speculation or shrewd investment, depending on one's predisposition toward the winner. Ball's quest for control was in the category of investment but also reflected his penchant for acquiring and exercising economic power. In the political invective that ensued, he was variously portrayed in populist terms as an exploiter and speculator.

There was nothing mysterious in what the Jacksonville financier was doing, even though Ball was notorious for his secretive business practices. The market prices of FEC bonds—but not the prices paid by Ball—were easily tracked in the daily quotes of publicly held bonds. He refused to disclose the actual prices paid to bondholders as he amassed a majority interest in the First and Refunding Bonds. His position in this regard was sustained throughout the proceedings by court and ICC rulings. It was repeatedly held that the written instruments of debt were legally worth par value, that is, $1,000 per bond as a claim on the bankrupt's assets. The actual price paid by successive purchasers of the bonds did not diminish the amount of the debt each represented as due the holders.[12] Companies like J. P. Morgan and Company, Equitable Life Assurance, New York Life Insurance, and the Prudential Company were more than able to protect their interests in such dealings. Individual investors outside the duPont group also bought at discounted prices with the intention to hold the bonds as long-term investments on advice of competent securities dealers.[13]

In the early 1940s, the investment prospects for railroad bonds were generally improving, due in some measure to favorable tax treatment afforded bonds over the common stock of bankrupt railroads. This was most likely a reflection of the tax provisions of the vetoed 1943 measure (discussed in chapter 7), which Ball, as well as business interests throughout the nation, had favored. The act had passed without a recorded dissenting vote in the Senate, but Pepper voted to sustain a presidential veto of it.[14] After the fight for control of the FEC became general knowledge, purchases of its depressed bonds were sometimes inspired by the duPont management's solid reputation in Florida.[15] The impact of the legendary name in business matters remained a potent factor even as Ball developed a reputation for sound business judgment in his own right. When he made his initial large-scale offer to buy First and Refunding Bonds from the deposit committee headed by J. P. Morgan and Company, they were at 16½, and most of the bondholders represented on the committee accepted.[16] That figure was published as part of his public offer, but the always secretive Ball still refused to divulge the actual or average price paid for his holdings in the FEC bonds during the proceedings. An average price would have disclosed the book value of the investment on which Ball's claim to control was predicated. While not legally relevant, it would have provided a powerful political argument for those who sought to disparage his claim of "ownership" by characterizing him as an opportunistic speculator. When Ball decided to seek control of the FEC, he was competing primarily with highly sophisticated institutions and financiers, men every bit his equal in resources, business acumen, and political audacity. This remained true when his principal adversaries became McD. Champion "Champ" Davis, president of the Atlantic Coast Line Railroad, and his companion in litigation, Claude Pepper, senior U.S. senator from the state of Florida.

After considering the matter for over a year, Ball started buying small lots of First and Refunding Bonds sometime in the latter part of 1940.[17] Alfred I. duPont had been dead for several years, and this marked Ball's first major initiative to expand the duPont interests beyond those that his mentor had contemplated in his lifetime. Ball began purchasing these bonds before the ICC stated definitively that the First and Refunding bondholders were effectively the equity owners of the corporation, and before the FEC operations started to reflect a cash surplus. Apparently, the financier had not yet decided to attempt to seek control of the organization but was looking at the matter as an investment, much as he viewed the depressed Florida municipal bonds during the same period. If that was his initial view, it changed shortly afterward.

When the United States was pulled into World War II, the fortunes of the FEC, already improving with the general economic conditions, took a pronounced turn for the better. The German submarine menace off Florida's east coast and gasoline shortages left rail shipment as the principal commercial transportation option. In Florida, the war brought large-scale military activity and construction, creating a surge in transportation demand. The FEC began to show increasing profits, leading rapidly to a substantial cash surplus. An astute businessman, one imbued with faith in the long-run economic potential of Florida, could extrapolate those circumstances to envision post-war economic expansion. Ball was such a businessman. Control of the railroad as an operating entity became a more attractive proposition than merely owning secured bonds representing claims against its properties. That was evident to Ed Ball, whose belief in Florida's long-term potential had led him to purchase municipal bonds at substantial discounts at the height of the Great Depression. Ball had absorbed Alfred I. duPont's faith and continued that investment pattern after his death, albeit with little, if any, of the leavening effect of his mentor's altruism. In that vein, he assayed the intrinsic worth of the bankrupt Florida East Coast Railway and decided to pursue control and dominion over it as an operating railroad. It held, in his shrewd assessment, potential for great economic leverage in what he foresaw as a post-war boom in Florida. As it turned out, his judgment was correct.

During this time, other things occupied Ball's attention. He continued adding municipal and county bonds to the investment portfolios of the banks in the Florida National system.[18] These bonds had also been severely depressed by the chaotic financial conditions prevailing in Florida's local governments during the previous decade. Still, like the FEC bonds, they were showing signs of slowly recovering from the depths to which they had sunk at the outset of the Great Depression.[19] Ball came into direct competition with Roy E. Crummer, his old adversary from the 1929 and 1931 state legislative battles over bond refunding and gas taxes. The large-scale debt restructuring, which followed passage of Governor Carlton's 1931 bond refunding scheme, had created a brisk and lucrative business in municipal and county bond refinancings. It also continued to be a volatile political issue. A former banker, businessman, and state legislator from Pasco County, one of the focal places of controversy in the Crummer program, testified about debt restructuring before a U.S. Senate investigating committee. He estimated that Crummer and the duPont-Ball interests together accounted for about 95 percent of the total state refunding business, and that Crummer had about two-thirds of it.[20] There is no way of knowing with certainty if the market was so divided, but those estimates are most likely a good approximation of the situation. It was essentially a two-sided contest, with the duPont group initially holding the smaller part. In the end, Crummer held virtually nothing, and the duPont banks were the dominant force in the municipal bond refunding market.

Municipal and county bond business was conducted in a highly competitive and politicized arena mostly at the level of local governmental units. In 1930, when the state was compelled to become involved in this business to prevent complete financial failure of overextended counties and municipalities, the reach of political involvement was expanded accordingly. Ball and Crummer were not only astute and tough businessmen, but also highly adept at political manipulation and infighting. Their competition ultimately led to a political imbroglio that reached from county courthouses and city halls all over Florida to the highest reaches of state government, and into high levels of Washington political power.[21] Later, Ball's role in the Florida road bond refunding competition would be cited by the ICC as one of several grounds for concluding that his control of the FEC would be incompatible with the "public interest."[22]

Claude Pepper was entangled in that episode also, although his involvement took a rather circuitous course. Sometime in mid-1941, he helped Roger O. Main and H. S. Wheeler, an Orlando securities dealer in municipal bonds, set up an appointment with the U.S. Postal Inspection Service to initiate an investigation of Crummer's bond refunding business.[23] Pepper was initially disposed to the Ball side, but without any of his customary zeal for the causes he embraced. Ball subsequently maintained under oath that he never spoke with Pepper or anyone else—including Main—about precipitating the investigation. Still, in light of Main's senior executive position with the duPont organization, it would have been logical for Pepper to assume that Main was speaking for Ball.

The Postal Inspection Service was later joined by the Securities and Exchange Commission in the investigation instigated by Main, and eventually Crummer was indicted in Kansas for mail fraud arising from his Florida bond refunding operations. Crummer then used his own political weight to persuade Florida's other senator, Charles O. Andrews of Orlando, to launch a counterinvestigation. By then, the events of 1944 had soured Pepper's and Ball's relationship, and Pepper joined Andrews in calling for a Senate investigation to target Ball's use of political power to ruin Crummer's business in Florida. Eventually, that investigation led to a prosecution by the U.S. Justice Department, which was dropped under suspicious circumstances set in motion by Crummer's attorneys. Bribery allegations implicating Crummer with high Justice Department officials surfaced in a separate investigation by the House Judiciary Committee. These revelations forced President Truman to fire one of the Justice Department attorneys involved.[24] While Ball was fighting Pepper over control of the FEC, he was also engaged in defending himself before the Senate committee convened as a result of the joint action of Pepper and Andrews. It was chaired by Nevada senator Patrick McCarran and was completely unrelated to the FEC battle. The Senate probe and the Justice Department investigation by the House Judiciary Committee are mentioned here to show the pervasive and overlapping scope of entanglement between the two men.

In January 1941, shortly after the FEC receivers placed the troubled railroad in formal bankruptcy, a committee representing some members of both classes of secured creditors filed a reorganization plan with the ICC. It represented "not less than" 5 percent of the First and Refunding Bonds and "not less than" 10 percent of the First Mortgage bonds. When Ball saw the committee's plan, he immediately recognized that its implementation would materially diminish the value of his holdings. He initiated his own action to acquire the debtor's capital stock as a lever for wresting control of the bankrupt railroad from the entanglements of bankruptcy. Unsuccessful in this initial effort, he then claimed standing to intervene as a creditor on the basis of his small holding ($10,000) of First Mortgage Bonds and his larger ($100,000) holding in First and Refunding Bonds. These relatively small holdings had clearly been acquired for the purpose of achieving standing in the legal fight for control of the railroad. While the claim was sufficient to afford the requisite standing, it also cast Ball as an adventurer and interloper, using his minor creditor's status to leverage his cause far beyond protection of his small, albeit valid, claims. Later, the Atlantic Coast Line used a much smaller claim, unsecured and legally inferior to Ball's First and Refunding Bonds, as the fulcrum on which to leverage its claim to ownership.[25] At this stage, Ball's position and strategy were essentially those of a creditor seeking protection of his secured status. He had not yet fixed on what would become his principal strategy to claim full ownership.

The first duPont reorganization plan was filed with the ICC on March 4, 1941, and resembled that filed earlier by the bondholders' committee, with two important exceptions.[26] The committee plan did not provide for any duPont representation on the reorganization board. Ball's plan called for two "duPont" members on a five-person board. It remained vague as to how controlling interest would ultimately be vested in the duPont group.[27] The ICC virtually ignored the duPont position and adopted the committee's proposal with only minor alterations. Ball's petition for a modification of the commission's order recognizing duPont status on the board was denied, and the plan went to the district court in Jacksonville for approval.

As the various bondholder groups maneuvered for position, the ICC had recognized, at least implicitly, that the First and Refunding bondholders would have the superior claim to equity ownership in whatever remained of the railroad after payment of the senior bondholders. Ball's next gambit stemmed from the ICC pronouncement that "the first and refunding mortgage bondholders are entitled to the entire equity in the property remaining after satisfaction of prior indebtedness."[28] Judging that pronouncement to state the ruling principle of law that would ultimately prevail, Ball based his future strategy on it. He set about recasting his standing by acquiring a majority in par value of the First and Refunding Bonds. There was nothing at this point to presage the final setting in which he would do battle for the railroad. His battle was with Wall Street interests that were contending for protection of their status as creditors, not as eventual owners and operators of the railroad.

World War II had started, and Senator Claude Pepper, basking in new-found stature for his prescient calls for support of England and France against Nazi Germany, was occupied with supporting President Roosevelt's war plans. He was involved on a more mundane level with breaking the virtual monopoly of the U.S. Sugar Corporation on sugar production in the fertile Everglades region.[29] He had not yet broken with the duPont interests led by Ball. Pepper's strong antipathy to monopolistic power did not arise overnight in the context of his fight over the FEC railroad. It was a continuing part of his political persona, implanted there by the populist traditions from which he came. Yet, as a practical politician, he could temper his philosophy to suit the exigencies of political circumstances. In the case of his supporter Pan American Airlines, he was bothered somewhat by its monopoly status on foreign air travel from the United States, but nevertheless collaborated in helping maintain it.[30] The Atlantic Coast Line Railroad had not yet entered the fray.

Pepper's stature with the Roosevelt administration was on the rise in 1942, and as a member of the powerful Senate Foreign Relations Committee, he enjoyed a strong political position. When S. A. Lynch of Miami, who later was to bring the Atlantic Coast Line into the FEC fray against Ed Ball, was considered for a diplomatic post, Undersecretary of State Sumner Welles called Pepper for his opinion on the appointment. At the time, Pepper did not evince any deep interest in Lynch in his diary entry noting the episode, and he made no further mention of the appointment.[31] He was two years away from standing for reelection, ample time if necessary to mend any political fences that might need tending. When Roger Main, president of the Florida National Bank in Jacksonville and one of Ball's principal lieutenants, wished to arrange an appointment with postal inspectors regarding supposed mail fraud in Crummer's bond refunding scheme, he arranged it through Pepper's office. Pepper met frequently with duPont executives, including Ball, regarding various and sundry governmental actions affecting the vast business activities of the duPont Trust.[32] The fateful events of 1944, which were to have such an impact on his relationship with Ball, had not yet started to unfold.

During late summer of 1942, Ball undertook a multifaceted round of negotiations to increase his holdings in the FEC's defaulted First and Refunding Bonds. Lynch, the Miami securities dealer and owner of a substantial amount of those bonds, joined ranks with him. At the same time, Ball talked with Arthur M. Anderson of J. P. Morgan and Company about buying up the bonds held by the deposit committee. The talks culminated with the already mentioned offer tendered by Ball at a price of 16½, that is, $165.50 per $1,000 bond. Ball limited the offer to those bonds on deposit with the committee. In this way, he effectively neutralized a major element of the opposition to his plans. He had removed what had been a major obstacle at the ICC to his position and used no more cash than the bare minimum necessary to achieve majority equity status.

Ball purchased approximately $8 million face value of the bonds held by the committee, all of which were owned by major financial institutions.[33] While the talks with Anderson were going on, Ball also approached the Atlantic Coast Line management to solicit its active collaboration, but failing that, he sought its passive acquiescence in his endeavor to acquire the FEC. According to Ball, he had an agreement with Lyman Delano, chairman of the board of the Atlantic Coast Line, consenting to his proposed control of the Florida East Coast Railway. The agreement necessarily had to include George C. Cutler, chairman of the Safe Deposit and Trust Company of Baltimore, the holder in trust of controlling stock in the Coast Line Company, parent corporation of the Atlantic Coast Line.[34] Since he voted the stock, his role was crucial. That Ball had his agreement is demonstrated by Cutler's subsequent testimony before the ICC in favor of the duPont plan.[35] Lynch, then allied with the Ball faction, was an active participant in the discussions.

The next stage of the proceeding was for the district court to approve the ICC order, which had virtually ignored the duPont claim. But before that court reviewed the matter, Ball garnered a majority interest in face value of the First and Refunding Bonds as a result of his negotiations. With the presumed support of the Atlantic Coast Line, and the ICC language regarding the preferred status of the First and Refunding bondholders, he was confident no major obstacles remained in his path. Ball had, through some very shrewd maneuvering, placed the duPont group in the favored position defined by the ICC in its first order. He controlled a majority of the par value of the First and Refunding Bonds, a position which the ICC had equated to equity ownership of the railroad. This state of affairs had come about between the issuance of the ICC order and its review by the district court. From there, Ball would fight the battle for full ownership and control.

When the matter came before the district court, the impact of the increased revenues caused by stepped-up wartime transportation demand was evident in the company's suddenly swollen cash reserve. It was more than enough to pay off the First Mortgage bondholders.[36] This drastically altered the situation in which the various parties were posturing for position. The FEC was clearly worth something more than speculative value. It was now distinctly possible for the railroad to emerge debt-free from its fiscal travails if an appropriate plan for recapitalization was adopted. Ball recognized that fact and maintained the position thereafter that the FEC should reemerge in a debt-free condition. In contrast, other plans being proposed at the time would have resulted in the railroad emerging heavily indebted.

Ball's position was particularly suitable to his status as majority holder of the junior debt. He could accept equity securities in a reorganized company for his majority share in its junior debt, thereby eliminating the need for new debt in any proposed recapitalization scheme.

Ball insisted that a debt-free proposition was more consistent with the "public interest" in a viable and efficient railroad operation than debt in any recapitalization proposal.[37] Yet public interest should not be taken as his pole star in arriving at that position. For him, it was more a conclusion than a cause. Ball's thinking always resided in the financial sphere of the case, and in his perspective, the public interest followed from a satisfactory resolution in that dimension. The public's interest was best protected by a debt-free railroad, which followed as a matter of course from the establishment of his control through majority ownership of the First and Refunding Bonds. The increased revenues and Ball's newfound status as majority bondholder in the First and Refunding issue caused the district court to return the case to the ICC for a third major round of hearings.[38]

For reasons not clear from the available evidence, Lynch parted company with Ball sometime late in this phase of the proceeding. Ball's interest was clearly emerging in the realm of a profitably operating railroad, while Lynch seemed interested in acquiring equity ownership and selling it for an immediate profit. After Lynch enticed the Atlantic Coast Line's new president, McD. Champion Davis, to recant the earlier agreement between Lyman Delano—the Coast Line's now deceased president—and Ball, the so-called Lynch-ACL plan was announced.

The interest of the Atlantic Coast Line in acquiring control of the FEC was apparently prompted by the Lynch overtures. The dramatically increased operating revenues for the smaller Florida road no doubt influenced that decision. Perhaps like Ball, Davis sensed the prospects for Florida in a thriving post-war economy. If so, he was slower than Ball, who had already started acquiring the First and Refunding Bonds. By now, the state's vaunted tourist trade was again on the rise notwithstanding wartime conditions, up more then 20 percent over the previous year. Most of the travelers came by train.[39] There were other sound business reasons to support Davis's belated move. The parent Coast Line system, headquartered in Connecticut, was an enormous transportation company serving much of the Atlantic seaboard between Richmond and Jacksonville, and into central Florida. It was connected in an interlocking system of corporate ownerships, including the Louisville and Nashville system, making it a dominant feature not only on the east coast but also throughout much of the Southeast.

Although the FEC was a minuscule operation compared to the mighty Coast Line system, its near monopoly on Florida's east coast rail service made it an important link in the emerging strategic perspective of the larger company.[40] This appreciation of the FEC evolved in the mind of McD. Champion Davis, the president of the Atlantic Coast Line after the death of Lyman Delano. Ball had thought he had an agreement with Delano approving duPont control of the FEC.

As ACL corporate thinking moved toward acquiring the FEC in early 1944, Pepper was winning another first-primary victory over the strong opposition of a substantial segment of the Florida business community. When Pepper returned to Washington secure in his enhanced Washington standing, he was certain that Ed Ball had been the principal cause of his reelection problems.[41] Although there would have been business opposition to Pepper without Ball's involvement, Pepper was correct in his perception of Ball's leadership role in the effort to defeat him. He lost no time before acting on that perception.

When McD. Champion Davis announced in Jacksonville in early November of 1944 the joint effort with the Lynch faction to take over the FEC, Pepper was also traveling in northeast Florida, again tending political fences, but this time from the vantage point of recent victory. He sought out Davis for a private meeting and inquired about the details of the proposal just announced by the ACL president. According to Davis, Pepper was in full accord with his outline to gain control of the FEC, and declared his immediate support.[42] If the thought had not already occurred to Davis, the astute railroad executive quickly gathered from his meeting with the senator that the latter's involvement could work to his advantage. Pepper was a prominent Florida political figure with national stature, and a favorite of the Roosevelt administration. His impact would not be lost on a federal agency whose board members were appointed by the president, subject to confirmation by the Senate, and dependent on the Congress for their budget.

And so Davis and Pepper started their close and effective collaboration. Davis wanted the FEC to merge it with his much larger Atlantic Coast Line and thereby increase that company's presence in the Florida rail transportation market. Pepper was less concerned with the intricacies of rail transportation needs in Florida than he was in thwarting Ball's quest for greater economic power. To his way of thinking after Ball's effort to defeat him in the 1944 election, stopping the Jacksonville financier's bid for the railroad was in the public interest in and of itself. The newfound interest of the ACL president in acquiring the FEC fitted nicely with that of Florida's junior senator, forging a symbiotic union between them from the political opportunism of the moment.

With the full support of the Atlantic Coast Line, S. A. Lynch, previously associated with the Ball faction, formally petitioned for late intervention in the proceedings in November of 1944. The Miami financier sought to present what was ostensibly his own plan for reorganization, but it was clearly marked with the manipulative hand of Davis. Under this plan—the Lynch-ACL plan—Lynch and his associates would acquire controlling equity in the FEC, which would then be sold to the Atlantic Coast Line. The non-Lynch holders of First and Refunding bonds, including the duPont group, would receive less than the par value of their holdings, primarily in new debt securities of the reorganized railroad.[43] Leave was granted for the late filing, but after hearing the details of the proposal, the ICC rejected it.

Not only was the Lynch-ACL plan totally unacceptable to Ball, but he considered the actions of his former ally and the Atlantic Coast Line to be serious betrayals of trust.[44] It added a personal dimension to the prolonged legal battle that followed. Nevertheless, Ball's position was greatly strengthened by the subsequent ICC ruling. It held that on payment of the senior debt, "the first and refunding mortgage bondholders are entitled to all the assets of the debtor. There should be distributed to them *all new securities to be issued upon consummation of the plan* [emphasis added]."[45] Thus, in early 1945, given his ownership of the majority of the First and Refunding Bonds, it appeared that Ball had succeeded in achieving a majority of the equity ownership and control of the railroad. Yet the fight for control was only just beginning, and far more challenging problems for Ball were yet to come.

In the years of legal and political combat that followed, the ICC's 1945 language became the legal and, to Ball's way of thinking, the moral linchpin for his prolonged fight for the Florida East Coast Railway.[46] It is important to understand how Ball translated his bond holdings into an unyielding claim to equity ownership. It was that claim which Pepper and Davis sought to obliterate under the rubric of public interest. The face value of the outstanding First and Refunding Bonds was $45 million. As of January 1, 1946, $30 million of defaulted interest had accrued, making $75 million the total amount of indebtedness secured by the junior mortgage.[47] With the First Mortgage Bonds paid off with the increased wartime revenues, the accrued principal and interest of the second bond issue would become the senior claim against all the corporation's remaining assets. At that point, the duPont interests, using St. Joe Paper Company as the holding mechanism, owned 53 percent of the bonds.

The $75 million claim was secured by a first lien that was ultimately enforceable by compulsory sale of the assets. The bondholders could bid up to that amount without incurring any real cash outflow, while an outsider would have to pay at least that in actual cash. This, of course, neither the ACL nor anyone else was willing to do. Absent such a bid, the majority bondholder's claim on the assets was, in practical terms, equivalent to equity ownership. That was the basis of Ball's recurring insistence after the 1945 ICC order that he owned the railroad. He told a Tampa securities dealer, "If he [Pepper] attempts to confiscate the property of Florida citizens for the benefit of outsiders, without knowing the facts . . . it shows that his position is taken only on the basis of personal spite."[48] That remark expressed Ball's view of his own standing, and on that basis, he was willing to do battle for as long as it might take. His subsequent adversaries, the Atlantic Coast Line and Claude Pepper, would hammer Ball's legal concept on the anvil of "public interest" until it was hardly recognizable. Ball's theory of ownership was grounded in fundamental principles of property rights, a concept that in Pepper's thinking was subordinated to his own views of the collective public interest. The matter was set to take on the distinctly political overtones of the age-old battle to balance property rights of the individual against the collective interests of the body politic.

Generally, elected officials are hesitant to openly take sides when essentially private business interests are contested in public forums between parties of equal stature. This is especially true with an issue that lies within the jurisdiction of a regulatory body established to remove the subject matter of an issue from the political arena. The Interstate Commerce Commission is such a body. It was designed to apply a consistent set of legal principles to resolution of issues arising under a congressionally established national transportation policy. Such forums are presumed to be beyond the reach of political interference, and generally that presumption is valid. Working in tandem with the foregoing principle is an axiom of political life: politicians like to avoid controversy, especially where the political merits of involvement are made uncertain by technical and legal complexities. The safer course is to let the matter run its course in the prescribed jurisdiction. If and when political figures do intervene, it is most often with little more than a public statement expressing confidence that the law will run a just course to a fair result for the favored party. That was essentially the extent of participation by Senator Andrews and the two Florida house members, J. Hardin Peterson and Joseph E. Hendricks, who initially joined with Pepper.[49] Unlike his Florida colleagues, Pepper chose not to follow the safer course. He plunged into the ICC proceeding in person, publicly stationing himself squarely in opposition to Ed Ball's determination to control the Florida East Coast Railway.

When he entered the FEC proceedings, Pepper did so with all the means at his command. His entry both altered the nature and upset the balance of the proceedings. He bought to the battle not only the formidable weight of his political position but also a superior legal mind with which to wield it. His true motivation in entering the prolonged battle will always be open to conjecture. Like his decision to espouse a conciliatory postwar policy toward the USSR, his action leaves unanswered the underlying question: Why? His claim to be protecting the public interest against the rapacious monopolistic designs of Ed Ball appeared almost fatuous against the more obvious motive of political retribution for Ball's part in the 1944 election. Certainly he was greatly influenced by the normal emotions of revenge. At the same time, he could not tolerate in either his self-image or his public image such baseness of motive. In the judgment of this writer, he had no trouble subsuming the revenge motive into his own already well defined populist sentiments against concentrations of economic and political power.[50] Having done so, he assumed his customary stance of righteousness.

After the events of 1944, Pepper had little reason to attempt resurrecting what had been, at best, only a tenuously amiable relationship with Ball and the duPont interests. Given the futility of any political reconciliation, his opposition to Ball and the moneyed class he epitomized melded nicely with the pronounced populist strains of his liberal image. As one supporter, a Kentucky editor in the John Perry newspaper chain, told him, "[Even if Ball wins] he will be the best windmill against which you can tilt your lance during the next election."[51] The corollary of that advice was not as apparent to Pepper; Ball could also "tilt a lance" in the coming election, scheduled for 1950. In late 1944, that contest seemed far off to a newly reelected U.S.

senator, and Pepper assumed the role of "knight errant" in pursuit of the political dragon that was Ed Ball.

When the January 1945 ICC order came down, it appeared to foreclose any reorganization plan other than one vesting full control in the duPont group. Ball had victory within his grasp. The immediate legal problem confronting the ACL was to find some grounds to induce the ICC to reopen a case already long overdue for conclusion. The FEC had been in receivership and bankruptcy for more than fourteen years, and the current phase of the litigation had been in progress for almost four of those years. The ICC had stated in two different orders that the First and Refunding bondholders were the appropriate successors to the equity ownership of the corporation. Legal arguments to the contrary, grounded in arcane details of recapitalization and creditors' rights, had been exhausted.

At this juncture, the ACL lawyers fixed on the issue of "public interest," referred to in section 77 of the bankruptcy law as defining the parameters of agency decisions under that act. The attorneys determined to hinge their renewed efforts on that loosely expressed criterion as the basis for denying Ed Ball the Florida East Coast Railway. In light of the ICC's already known predilection for the First and Refunding bondholders, it was a formidable legal challenge; to meet it, Pepper's presence was essential. This legal strategy meant that Ed Ball would be the issue, and his character and stewardship of the far-reaching duPont business interest would be on trial. Although complex financial details and consideration of creditors' rights continued to figure in the ensuing ICC actions, there was no mistaking the distinctly politicized nature of the case after Pepper and his ACL ally combined their mutual effort in the political arena. It was an arena well known to them, one in which each was adept at operating, as was their adversary, Ed Ball.

"Champ" Davis, as the ACL president was called, considered Pepper vital to exerting the necessary pressure to have the case reopened. After visiting with individual commission members following the January 1945 order, he wrote Pepper: "It is going to take considerable pressure to have the case reopened and the facts considered, but I now think there is a possibility and, while I hate to jam the matter up to you, I think you are the key to that situation."[52]

Pepper threw himself into the effort with the all the zeal he customarily reserved for the causes of liberalism. For him, the fight with Ball had assumed that dimension. In true lawyerlike fashion, he set about familiarizing himself with briefs and transcripts of the previous proceedings. He was assisted by the ACL legal staff and had numerous meetings with them to discuss and formulate strategy. He frequently met with Davis, often in the railroad executive's private railcar.[53] During the next several months, Pepper and the ACL president developed a close working relationship, one from which Pepper received the full measure of perquisites due his position as a senator and ally in the common endeavor. As Pepper became more entwined with the ACL's effort to gain control of the bankrupt railroad, his role was correspondingly appreciated by his corporate ally. The ACL Washington lobbyist was attentive to his needs, as well as those of his friends and staff, and Pepper acknowledged the solicitous attention he received.[54]

Nothing indicates that Pepper was illegally influenced to take a course he would not otherwise have taken. Whatever the merits or demerits of Pepper's intervention in the FEC case, it was his deliberate decision, made for his own reasons and not those of the Atlantic Coast Line management. There was nothing about Champ Davis or his railroad that would accord them any different standing in Pepper's eyes than Ed Ball, except, of course, that they had not publicly opposed his reelection. As Martin Anderson of the *Orlando Sentinel* observed, "With Pepper it was a case of the lesser of two evils."[55] Still, Pepper enjoyed the corporate embrace, gratefully accepting Davis's proffered amenities over the extended period of their collaboration. He and his staff also accepted similar treatment from other corporate constituents.[56]

Pepper understood what Davis meant by the use of pressure to bring about a reopening of the case. He was quick to look to his friends in organized labor for help in presenting an image of public support for his position. He dealt with the national union representatives in Washington, where he was recognized as a staunch New Dealer and friend of labor. After a personal conference with the Railway Labor Executives Association, an umbrella organization for twenty rail unions, he advised Davis that the group "took action to intervene in the East Coast Case and will join and work with us in any way possible."[57]

It was a far different matter with the officials of the unions representing employees of the FEC in Florida. They vehemently opposed the ACL takeover and Pepper's support of it. Although Pepper tried to tell them that a victorious Ball would not be amenable to labor's needs, the Florida unions remained solidly committed to the duPont effort.[58] Later, when the reorganized FEC under Ball defied the same unions in the longest rail strike in American history, the Florida union leaders deeply regretted their course of action.

Pepper also established direct contact with members of the ICC regarding the case. He and Davis readily engaged in ex parte contacts with several commissioners about the reopening of the proceeding.[59] In the Washington environment of the time, Pepper's partisan role invoked no ethical questions. Such practices were not critically noticed, as would be the case today. Still, the imposing presence of a powerful U.S. senator explaining the ACL position to members of a federal quasi-judicial agency was a distinct advantage in exercising a litigant's right. When one commissioner expressed some doubt that he would sit on the ICC panel hearing the oral arguments to reopen the case, Pepper urged him "to please sit on the panel" when he presented the ACL case.[60] That commissioner, for reasons extraneous to Pepper's intercession, did not sit on the panel, but not because Pepper did not try to persuade him. There was nothing superficial about his efforts. Pepper's actions left no doubt that he was fully and openly committed to stopping Ball's drive to take over the Florida East Coast Railway, and would use the full spectrum of his formal and informal powers to accomplish that goal.

While Davis was planning the strategy to reopen the FEC proceeding in late 1944, his senatorial collaborator had other matters that required his attention. Pepper's close friend and leader in the far-left wing of the Democratic Party, Henry A. Wallace, was nominated by an ailing Roosevelt to be secretary of commerce. There was an effort to defeat his confirmation, but the dwindling cadre of liberal administration supporters in the Senate rallied to his cause, and he was ultimately confirmed.[61] That fight with the more conservative elements of the Senate heightened the public awareness of Pepper's drift farther to the left. In the context of the FEC battle, this further highlighted his leftist philosophy, and by extension, his antibusiness proclivity.

In early 1945, the war was heading rapidly to a victorious conclusion for the Allies. With the collapse of both Germany and Japan imminent, attention was beginning to shift to domestic politics and post-war economic policy. The impending breakup of the victorious Allies was only vaguely discernible, and there was little public comprehension of the trend of events that would shortly breach that alliance beyond repair. When the Cold War became the dominating fact of domestic politics, Pepper's battle with Ball became part of an orientation that pushed the senator to the extreme left of American liberalism.

Pepper's attack on Ball and the duPont interests was couched in strident populist and labor rhetoric, with strong overtones of class division. It was perceived by many as evidence of a deep antipathy for private enterprise, only a short step in the public's eye from proof of outright communist sympathies. Initially, nothing in Pepper's decision to oppose Ball in the FEC matter gave rise to that perception. It emerged over time as he associated himself more and more with the far left, especially in his positions on the Soviet Union. Never one to tone down his political views, he was also outspoken on behalf of leftist causes. His strident advocacy for conciliatory relations with the Soviets created a public perception of undue affinity for the Cold War enemy. Pepper's proclivities for couching issues in the rhetoric of class division served to strengthen that perception.

In early 1945, petitions to reopen the case on a variety of grounds were filed by several parties, including the Lynch faction. They sought essentially the same reorganization, with slight modifications, that had been rejected in the January 1945 order. It was quickly supported by the ACL, and on April 13, Pepper filed his formal petition to enter the case as a private citizen acting on "behalf of the public."[62] His intentions were generally well known even before then, and he was seen as a major force in what, at that stage, was still viewed as a battle between Lynch and Ball for the railroad.[63] After the proceedings were reopened, the ACL filed its own plan, under which it proposed to absorb the FEC outright, effectively ending the independent existence of Henry Flagler's creation. After this turn of events, Lynch was no longer a major player in the matter. The battle lines were drawn for the remainder of the fight, with Ball and the duPont interests on one side, and Champ Davis's ACL and Claude Pepper on the other.

In oral arguments to the ICC for reopening the proceeding, Pepper freely borrowed from the ACL positions on the technical and financial dimensions of the case. But his main focus was clearly the public interest issue, and Coast Line lawyers let him set the tone for that crucial part of their case. Pepper's legal skills and oratorical eloquence made him a powerful force. In a long and carefully prepared statement of his reasons for opposing Ball, he first elaborated how the larger and experienced ACL was better suited to assume operation of the FEC system. Having paid lip service to the case's technical and financial aspects, he went straight to his principal issue: Ed Ball.

The financier-businessman was the focal point on which Pepper remained fixed throughout his involvement. In his view, allowing the duPont interests—particularly Ball—to control rail transportation on Florida's east coast posed a danger to the public. He put Ball's character in the vortex of the reconfigured proceeding, saying, "I have raised the question as to whether it is in the public interest . . . [to have the FEC controlled] . . . by one estate, especially when it is common knowledge that estate is operated principally by one man, Mr. Edward Ball." He went on to say, "It seems to me that it is a growing concern to the public as to the reaching out of the duPont estate into the economic control of the state."[64] It was clear that Pepper's concern with the public interest was cast in terms of his view of Ball's personal unfitness, and only incidentally with a properly run railroad operation on the Florida east coast.

Over the long course of the struggle, Pepper's negative opinion of Ball and its roots in the 1944 election were not lost on the public.[65] Even though his opposition to Ball was clearly consistent with his populist aversion to concentrations of economic and political power, the circumstances of his appearance, closely following Ball's well-known opposition to his reelection, pointed to revenge as his operative motivation. This overshadowed whatever real concerns he had with the philosophical and practical ramifications of Ed Ball's increasing economic and political power. He misjudged the public's appreciation of his abstract views on wealth and power versus a more mundane understanding of jobs and local control versus outside interests. Bound in tradition to the Old South but with an urbanized character struggling to emerge at mid–twentieth century, Florida was subconsciously holding to its old identity and heritage. Ball's position resonated with that dimension of the Florida political psyche. The Florida East Coast Railway was a part of that heritage, as was, to some extent, the duPont name and the business empire growing around it.[66] The Connecticut-based Coast Line Company owned by testamentary trusts having their headquarters in Baltimore was not.[67] Claude Pepper had positioned himself with outsiders in his apparent bid for revenge against one of Florida's own. It was the only period of Ball's long career where he enjoyed a modicum of public support, perhaps even popularity. As Pepper threw himself into the FEC battle, he continued to be involved with other, larger issues emerging on the international scene.

On August 15, 1945, the day Japan's unconditional surrender ushered in the post-war era, Pepper began his extended fact-finding trip to a war-ravaged Europe and Soviet Union. Ostensibly undertaken to explore trade prospects for American small businesses, it became the factual framework from which he claimed expertise to speak on Soviet-American relations. Later, it was to have adverse repercussions on his political career.[68] His subsequent foreign policy views, which he based on that experience, initiated a public perception that cast Pepper in the role of apologist for Joseph

Stalin and the Soviet Union. If he was seeking revenge against Ball in 1945, his trip to Russia unwittingly assisted in laying the foundation for Ball's revenge five years later. Although he was absent from the FEC proceedings during a crucial period, Pepper's formal appearance and active participation had already achieved the desired impact on the ICC. The January 1945 unanimous decision in Ball's favor was set aside, and the matter was recast by the ICC, with the central issue being the public interest and Ed Ball's incompatibility with it. Claude Pepper was the essential force in turning what had been all but final victory for Ed Ball into a new and highly uncertain battle. It was one with parameters set more in the political arena than in the arcane realm of railroad finance and operating efficiencies. Many years later, after Pepper congratulated him on his victory in the FEC matter, Ball, with unusual graciousness, attributed the crucial reopening of the case to Pepper's "influence" with the ICC and his "so eloquently argued" presentations at the hearings.[69]

Proceedings before regulatory bodies focused on abstract questions of public interest take on a different hue than those where economic, engineering, or financial issues are dominant. The flow of evidence, expanded beyond normal restraints of probative relevance, is judged more by its volume than any fact-determining qualities. When Pepper refocused the ICC on the public interest as the dominant issue, the atmosphere of the proceedings changed accordingly. It shifted from strictly legal parameters to the realm of public relations and political considerations. Both sides in the dispute had the resources to continue the fight under the changed circumstances.

In the reconfigured setting, Pepper's senatorial position afforded him a high pulpit from which to denounce Ball's unsuitability to operate a railroad consistent with the public interest. Ball and the duPont interests were not without resources and means appropriate to the changed circumstances. The Florida National banks located on the Atlantic seaboard were used to influence their customers in favor of keeping the Florida East Coast a Florida-operated and independent railroad. Ball and his Florida National executives made use of the mutual support network that existed between business, civic and political leaders, and bankers. He took full advantage of the natural fear of employees and FEC union leaders of a large and unknown "outside" corporation. The FEC's main repair facility was the Bowden Shops between St. Augustine and Jacksonville. It was a major employer in the region, and there was widespread fear that it would be shut down if the ACL was successful. Brochures conjuring up that vision were prepared by union leaders opposed to the ACL takeover. In some communities, they were distributed by bank executives, adding more credibility to the allegations of economic disruption. The unions were intense in their opposition. One such union pamphlet referred to the ACL's statements as a "mantle of deception" looking by "devious means or otherwise to strip it [the FEC] of the identity by which it has been known since September, 1895, and to place employes [sic] . . . in the category of the unemployed."[70] The Miami chamber of commerce entered a formal protest against the ACL proposal, as did the Jacksonville chamber six months later.[71] One of Pepper's friends, an editor in the Perry newspaper chain, called Ball's performance a public relations "masterpiece."[72] It was a masterful performance by the Jacksonville financier.

The ACL countered by using its considerable influence to attract support to its side. Most of its witnesses were shippers from the west and central parts of the state where the ACL already served, but there was also a statewide sampling of shipper views in the array of ACL witnesses. They testified that the ACL gave good service and would do the same for the east coast.

Those witnesses produced by Ball were mostly from the crucial east coast, and they testified that the economic well-being of the east coast depended largely on the FEC continuing to be a Florida-owned and -operated railroad. Their views on the shipping needs of the area were considered more to the point by the hearing examiner assigned to hear the case and make recommended findings of fact for the ICC.[73]

During this stage of the hearings, Pepper was absent on his trip to Europe and the Soviet Union. While Pepper was gone, the ACL lawyers kept his office abreast of the proceedings, all the time urging on the senator a more active role before the ICC.[74] When he returned, Pepper resumed direct participation. In a memorandum filed in February 1946, he restated and further elaborated his objections to Ball's control. Concentrating on Ball's personal power as head of the duPont Trust, with all its various business enterprises, he again noted that Ball had "not been adverse [sic] to attempting to influence public policy" in Florida.[75] He proceeded to give new, larger figures representing the worth of the duPont holdings as evidence that such power in Ball's solitary control should not be expanded by giving him the Florida East Coast Railway.

To portray Ball's personal involvement in what he deemed arbitrary use of the trust's vast powers, Pepper recounted a rental policy imposed by Ball on tenants in the then-new duPont building in downtown Miami. The building's ground floor was one of the most desirable locations in the city, and Ball required tenants to bank with the Florida National Bank located in the same building.[76] That example, repeated frequently and magnified throughout the proceedings, was used to show Ball's exploitative and despotic "ruthlessness."[77]

The ACL attorneys also accused Ball, with support from Pepper, of manipulating public opinion and improperly inducing the Southern Railroad to intervene in opposition to the ACL plan.[78] In the strident advocacy of Pepper and the ACL lawyers, such actions by Ball were seen as further evidence of his "ruthlessness."

There was no mistaking the highly personal and derogatory nature of Pepper's disparagement of Ball's character. Some factual basis for what he said could be gleaned, at least inferentially, from the evidentiary record, but Pepper couched his conclusions in highly pejorative and speculative terms more for political than probative effect. Even though his insinuations were within the purview of fair comment in the charged adversarial setting of the proceeding, they nevertheless drove the wedge of personal hostility even deeper between the two men. In Ball's view, Pepper's verbal tactics deliberately distorted the facts for the singular purpose of wrongfully depriving him of his property rights. For a man of Ball's temperament and inclinations, nothing could be more damning of a person. It was something he would not forget.

Pepper and the ACL attorneys were able to refocus the ICC's perspective so that the broader consideration of the public interest subsumed the equitable rights of the First and Refunding bondholders. In April 1947, even though the hearing examiner who listened to all the evidence recommended that Ball be given control of the railroad, the ICC reversed its previously unanimous decision in Ball's favor on a split vote. Four commissioners explicitly dissented from this ruling. The majority determined that vesting control in Ball and the duPont Trust was inimical to the public interest as argued by Pepper and the ACL attorneys, and held that the debtor railroad should be absorbed by the larger ACL system.[79] The ICC's order accepted virtually every allegation made against Ball and his management of the duPont enterprises, even though the hearing examiner, having personally observed the demeanor of the witnesses and having heard their testimony, had determined to the contrary.

Pepper called it "a just and hard won decision," noting that "[it] will arrest but not stop Ball's empire grabbing in Florida."[80] When Pepper released a report on his part in the FEC decision to radio stations around the state, the city-owned station in Jacksonville, WJAX, refused to air it. The station manager told Pepper that he was afraid of "duPont political retribution" against him and the city-owned station.[81]

The matter next had to go back to the district court in Jacksonville for approval. There the ICC order was reversed with a judicial declaration that the rights of the creditors had been unduly impaired. Ball was back in a commanding position, but the fight was not over. The case was once again sent back to the ICC by the district court.

Pepper renewed his efforts. He requested that Secretary of Defense James Forrestal ask President Truman to add the weight of the White House to the effort to stop Ball. He also asked Democratic House Leader Sam Rayburn to intervene in the matter.[82] By that time, however, Pepper's standing with the administration and its congressional supporters had diminished to almost nothing as a result of his strident pro-Soviet views. When he sought Truman's help directly, the president told him he would look into the matter, but it is unlikely that White House interest went any further.[83] Had Franklin Roosevelt been alive, the outcome would almost certainly have been different.

There now started a prolonged period in which the district court repeatedly overruled the ICC's orders, remanding the matter for further consideration by that body, only to have it reaffirm three times the previous decisions in favor of the ACL plan for merger. The ACL appealed to the circuit court of appeals in Atlanta and then to the U.S. Supreme Court to reverse the district court's ruling, only to fail at each appellate level.[84] While it appeared that the ICC was intent on awarding the railroad to the Atlantic Coast Line, it seemed that the courts were equally determined that the rights of the bondholders—personified by Ball—should prevail. The court of appeals noted that the ICC's vision was "foreshortened by a too intense regard of, and preoccupation with, the question of which should control the debtor, St. Joe or the Coast Line." The court further explained that the ICC reached its conclusion "at a sacrifice of the private interests . . . to give effect to the supposed dominant public interest that Coast Line should have the properties."[85] There was little doubt that Pepper had effected a material change in attitude at the ICC, but it was equally certain that the courts continued to see the matter as essentially one of property rights. In that hand, Ball held the high cards with his majority interest in the First and Refunding bonds, and their aura of equity ownership.

While the matter was working its way through the appellate courts, Pepper was caught up in the major political battle of his career: his 1950 reelection campaign. (See chapter 9 for a comprehensive discussion of that campaign.) The campaign marked the end of Pepper's active participation in the FEC case. His role had been the principal factor in reopening the case after the January 1945 decision awarding the FEC to Ball and the duPont Trust, and in positioning ACL for control of the company. In doing so, he had angered a large sector of voters, especially the FEC union leadership and a major segment of the Florida business community. Although he had irritated the business community on a variety of issues, the FEC fight came to be an unequivocal symbol of his antibusiness disposition. In addition, the Florida rail unions would not forget his opposition to their efforts to protect their jobs. Pepper could not shake that consequence of his drive to deny Ball control of the railroad, and it came back to haunt him in the 1950 election.[86]

After Pepper's defeat at the polls, the ACL continued its pursuit of the FEC, and Ball just as tenaciously fought it every step of the way. In 1951, the ICC issued two lengthy opinions reaffirming its decisions to vest control in the ACL; Ball appealed each, and won.[87] By 1958, the protracted litigation, without Pepper's flamboyant participation, had dimmed in the public consciousness. Finally, in 1958, after still another lengthy round of hearings, the hearing examiner recommended that the ICC revert to its position of thirteen years earlier and award equity control of the bankrupt railroad to the First and Refunding Bondholders. That was the point at which Pepper had entered the fray. A weary ICC, now freed from the senator's fiery exhortations to save the people of Florida from economic despotism, again reversed itself, finding that new light on old circumstances dictated that the public interest would be best served by vesting control of the FEC in the duPont Trust—more particularly in Ed Ball.[88] A short time later, the Jacksonville district court approved the decision, and Herbert E. Wolfe of St. Augustine and J. Turner Butler of Jacksonville were named with Ball as reorganization managers.

The Herbert E. Wolfe named with Ball to the reorganization board was the same person who in 1944 had invited Pepper to his home to inquire how he intended to vote on President Roosevelt's veto of the Revenue Act of 1944. Later, Congressmen George Smathers visited with Wolfe in his St. Augustine home, where he renewed his acquaintance with Ed Ball and talked about the upcoming 1950 Florida race for the U.S. Senate.

Ball emerged firmly and finally in control of the Florida East Coast Railway through the duPont Trust's ownership of the St. Joe Paper Company, the nominal holder of the First and Refunding bonds. This quest for control, more than any other event in his long career, illustrates his unswerving tenacity in pursuit of what he deemed the best interests of the duPont Trust and its property rights, and his own attendant power. The railroad continued to be part of the duPont Florida empire until Ball's death, and remains so today.

9

The Election of 1950

Most people see the 1950 U.S. Senate race in Florida as the definitive expression of the conflict between Ed Ball and Claude Pepper. There is something ironic in that perception since the battle for control of the FEC was much more of a direct encounter between the two men than was the Senate race. Yet the railroad battle lacked the popular focus and journalistic attention lavished on the race for the Senate. The Cold War overtones, Pepper's national stature, the personal drama of his opponent George Smathers (backed by the reactionary Ball) turning on his older mentor and benefactor, and the mystique of duPont power all coalesced into a national political event. As a result, the election has assumed near legendary proportions as one of the most bitter and ugly campaigns in Florida political history. That view works well in an abbreviated account but overlooks many of the circumstances, issues, and people that circumscribed the event.

Given the backdrop of McCarthyism, it is tempting to think of the election solely in that context: Ball, the reactionary businessman, manipulates the hysteria of McCarthyism to defeat his liberal enemy, Claude Pepper. Unfortunately, such an approach falls short on two counts. It does not allow sufficient consideration of the complex issues debated in the campaign, and it overemphasizes the role of Ball. If viewed in a perspective limited to Pepper and Ball as the operative elements of the narrative, there is a lack of completeness about it. The "liberal versus reactionary" model distorts by feigned simplicity a perspective that must be more complex if it is to fit with a comprehensive understanding of the politics of the period. Additional dimensions must be integrated into the paradigm. This expanded context does not diminish the importance of McCarthyism and Ball's fixation on defeating Pepper as major factors in the election. Those forces worked in tandem with others, and all played a part in shaping the outcome.

First there was Pepper's continuing involvement with the far-left element in domestic politics. To this he coupled a persistent apologetic tone to his pleas for understanding and accepting Soviet foreign policy. Pepper's increasingly leftist orientation cast him naturally in an antibusiness posture, antagonizing most of the state's business community. In addition, his proposal for a national health program set the medical profession squarely against him.[1] In the face of mounting criticism, Pepper continued to believe that he could pursue with impunity a national political agenda increasingly divergent from Florida's emerging postwar conservatism. His insistence on running counter to the Truman administration's foreign policy initiatives also put him at odds with the most powerful political figure in the country: the president of the United States.

Another force that Pepper had to contend with was his opponent, George Armistead Smathers, every bit Pepper's equal in pursuit of ambition but with an ear closer to the political ground. Smathers has been frequently portrayed in popular and journalistic accounts as little more than an implement of Ed Ball's ruthless determination to destroy Pepper.[2] In fact, he was an independent and forceful political figure pursuing his own agenda. As it happened, that agenda more correctly fitted the temper of the time than Pepper's prototype of unabashed New Deal liberalism coupled to a conciliatory approach to the threat of Soviet ambitions. Smathers's rhetoric on the question of Pepper's loyalty may have been overcharged, but the general thrust of his questioning of Pepper's attitudes toward the Soviet Union was certainly relevant to a senate campaign in 1950. To properly warrant the label of McCarthyism, the storm of accusations launched by Smathers would have had to have been without foundation in fact. Such was not the case. Pepper's well-documented record of Soviet apologetics provided the requisite factual basis on which to exonerate Smathers from charges of McCarthyism. That Smathers's timing and purpose synergistically coincided with Ball's desire to defeat Pepper was not necessarily of their own doing, but it was eagerly seized upon by both.

Still another force in the 1950 senate race was the emerging reality of the Cold War. Hardly five years had passed since the great Allied victory in World War II, and already the world was being transformed again into a dangerous place for democracy. For most Americans, it was made that way by the aggressively expansionistic designs of Soviet Communism. In April of 1948, the Soviets had used military force to blockade the Western Allied forces in occupied Berlin. The response had been the Berlin airlift, primarily an American effort, which supplied American, British, and French occupation forces and over 2 million German civilians in the isolated city until September 1949, when the blockade was lifted. During that time the North Atlantic Treaty Organization was formed between the United States and its European allies, unequivocally committing American military might as the first line of defense against Soviet aggression in Western Europe. In the Far East, the Chinese Communist leader, Mao Tse-tung, had resumed his prewar insurgency against the Chinese Nationalist regime of Chiang Kai-shek and forced him to abandon the Chinese mainland for Formosa. Mao had imposed a communist regime on the world's most populous country, leaving Americans confused and frustrated as to how it had occurred. Although the reality was otherwise, at the time the global situation looked to most Americans as if the worldwide march of communism was being directed unilaterally by the Soviet Union through its ruler, Joseph Stalin. Armed tension between America with its Western allies and the forces of communism now encircled the globe. The Cold War was very much a fact of everyday life for the American public. Its impact on the domestic political scene was greatly exacerbated by the unprincipled ambitions of a junior U.S. senator from Wisconsin.

In February 1950, the new phenomenon of McCarthyism burst upon the American scene when Senator Joseph R. McCarthy, in an otherwise insignificant speech to a minor political gathering in Wheeling, West Virginia, accused the secretary of state of knowingly harboring over 200 communists in the State Department. When he raised his cry against the internal threat of communists buried deep in the U.S. government awaiting Soviet orders to overthrow it, the domestic political scene was transformed. Even though McCarthy was subsequently exposed as a liar and charlatan, the widespread fear of betrayal by communist forces from within quickly embedded itself in the American political psyche. We now know that it severely distorted the politics of the time as to the extent of Soviet capabilities, but that knowledge does not invalidate the threats of Soviet foreign policy objectives at the time. Today, the cry of McCarthyism is often intended as an oblique denial of the dangers posed by the postwar rupture of East-West relations. To assume that stance is to warp the politics and emotions that flowed from a sober realization of those dangers in 1950. It implies that those raising the question of a communist threat to the United States during those years were of the same fraudulent bent as McCarthy, knowingly deceiving the public into believing that a threat existed when none in fact did. That view is no less valid than was McCarthy's assertion of the grave dangers of the threat to U.S. security from within. Even if Senator McCarthy had never made his speech in Wheeling, the positions taken by Claude Pepper on American foreign policy vis-à-vis the threats of Soviet aggression would have been valid issues in his 1950 reelection campaign.

Pepper's famed oratory and powers of persuasion could not bridge the gap between where his national ambition pointed and where the middle ground of Florida politics beckoned. Ed Ball and George Smathers were at that gap to take full advantage of the disjunction between Pepper's vision of the future and the political realities of the present. Sixteen years earlier, Pepper had taken advantage of a somewhat similar detachment from political reality when he portrayed Park Trammell as unable to deal with the changing times brought on by the depression. But there were also major differences between the two campaigns—the dynamics of the 1950 campaign were much more complex than those of the earlier campaign, for example—and any comparison between the two should be tempered by that realization. Still, Pepper in 1950 was no stranger to stretching to the point of distortion allegories aimed at political opponents. His frequent pejorative references to those of differing viewpoints as "isolationists" or "betrayers of the people" are examples of this point. His use of such expressions in the prevailing context of the times intentionally implied a moral and political turpitude far more sinister than that conveyed by the terms themselves.

Like the depression before it, the Cold War precipitated a tumultuous sea change in domestic politics. But unlike the bitter disillusionment that turned America inward following the Treaty of Versailles after World War I, the dangerous instability caused by the East-West breach after World War II produced the opposite reaction. The nation faced outward, albeit reluctantly and hesitantly, positioning itself as the principal barrier in the path of presumed Soviet aggression. As noted earlier, Pepper, almost disdainfully, appeared oblivious to the realities and dangers emerging from the reconfigured postwar world. He increasingly moved toward the radical left as he spoke out strongly for a conciliatory approach to the worsening relations between the Soviet Union and its former allies. His views in this regard did not resonate well with what was evolving as the prevailing American attitude toward the Soviets and their leader, Joseph Stalin. The collective memory of Munich's appeasement and its triggering effect on Hitler's final apocalyptic vision was etched in the public's consciousness. It nurtured a determination not to repeat that mistake so soon again.

There was a striking irony in Pepper's position. He had stood almost alone in 1940 against the isolationism that blinded the nation to the aggressive designs of Nazi Germany and Imperial Japan. He was one of only a few public figures with the courage to urge early U.S. action to stop the march of totalitarian aggression. When the fullness of those threats was finally recognized, he was hailed for his courage in facing the earlier overwhelming isolationist sentiment to the contrary. Yet only six years later, in a dangerous postwar world, he seemed intent on disregarding the lessons of appeasement learned at Munich. He once again moved against a rising tide of public sentiment. This time, however, he urged a policy of restraint and forbearance in the face of a more complex perception of aggression. The public opinion that had been conditioned to accept the Soviet Union as an ally in the defeat of Hitler repositioned itself in light of Stalin's belligerent postwar stance. The tragic consequences of the efforts to appease Hitler were too fresh for similar overtones toward Stalin to gain more than a politically tenuous foothold at the fringe of public opinion. The mainstream of liberal thought accepted the realities of the East-West confrontation, and the bipartisan foreign policy of containment was, on the whole, a common ground of bipartisan agreement.

Still, Pepper persevered in his course well after American mainstream liberalism had recognized the threat in Soviet intentions. Perhaps he thought he could resurrect his image as a lone voice for a course of action that was unpopular now, but which would later be proven correct. Such an image would certainly enhance his stature as a postwar leader in foreign policy and strengthen his claim to national leadership.

For most Americans, the danger from Stalin's Communist behemoth was adumbrated by events that followed close on the heels of Allied victory. The Soviet refusal to demobilize and remove millions of soldiers from Eastern Europe in the face of what seemed to be clear treaty obligations translated to proof of aggressive intentions, as far as American public opinion was concerned. Moscow's domination of the puppet governments established in Eastern European countries under the rifles of the so-called liberating forces of the Red Army was a clear harbinger of Soviet intentions. Legions of Russian troops posted in Eastern European countries from the Baltic to the Black Sea appeared poised to overrun Western Europe at the first opportunity. At the same time, international communism, the handmaiden of Soviet intentions, reasserted its primary goal of world revolution. The more benign dogmatism adopted by Stalin to facilitate the wartime alliance with the West was abandoned. There was little doubt that the return to the more strident revolutionary stance was orchestrated from Moscow, and the American Communist Party obediently fell into line.[3]

The stage was set for the emergence of real and imagined internal threats in tandem with the greater external one posed by Soviet communism. Not until the opening of the Russian Communist Party archives after the Soviet collapse forty years later would the direction of Moscow in the affairs of the American Communist Party be confirmed.[4] Even so, this was widely assumed to be true in the years following the war. The contemporary testimony of former American Communists such as Elizabeth Bentley, Whitaker Chambers, and Louis Budenz unfolded before the American people a sinister internal presence of Soviet communism. Confrontation between U.S. and Soviet troops all along what Winston Churchill wrote into history as the Iron Curtain added to rising international tensions. In retrospect, the gravity of the internal threat was somewhat less than it appeared at the time. Still, to an anxious citizenry, it was rationally perceived as a real danger to the nation's security. Somewhat less rationally, but with some supporting evidence, the threat was thought to be abetted by traitors from within. It took only a small dash of demagoguery to stir a rational measure of concern into a caldron of irrational emotions and fear.

Against this state of affairs, men like Pepper and Henry A. Wallace, his close ideological ally and friend, raised their voices on behalf of American understanding and forbearance toward the Soviet government. Soviet actions that most Americans viewed as clear evidence of a policy of aggressive expansion were seen by these men as an understandable quest for security. This group condemned Anglo-American policy aimed at restraining the Soviets, saying it denied them the hard-fought arrangements for national security to which they were entitled by the common victory over Germany. Their collective voice was heard as one of moderation, opposed to confrontation over issues seen as negotiable by reasonable persons. Confrontation, in their view, was almost a sure path to another war.

Pepper was recognized and hailed in some quarters for his strident advocacy of this view.[5] Of course, he was reported at length and with glowing praise in the far-left press, including especially the house organ of the American Communist Party, the *Daily Worker*.[6] His views were also publicized prominently in the mainstream press, ensuring his general and widespread recognition as a leading Russophile. As evidence of Russian intransigence mounted, what Pepper considered the voice of moderation increasingly appeared badly misguided, even to the point of reckless disregard for the nation's security. To some, it appeared deliberately calculated to serve Soviet interests. His private audience with Joseph Stalin, on whom he afterward lavished praise and admiration, exacerbated that position in the eyes of the public.

Pepper, as already described, had undertaken his extended fact-finding trip to Europe and Russia in the waning days of the war. After traveling extensively in Europe, he arrived in Moscow in mid-September 1945. Holding a senior position on the Senate Foreign Relations Committee, he warranted serious consideration from the host governments of the nations he visited. He undoubtedly hoped to enhance his stature by positioning himself at the center of postwar foreign policy deliberations. It was probable that he would ascend through the seniority system to the chairmanship of that important committee. Yet in what might have been an indication of diminished stature with the Senate leadership, the committee would not officially sanction his trip. It is not clear how the journey was arranged. As previously noted, he recorded in his diary that he traveled as a "subcommittee" of the Senate Small Business Committee to assess potential foreign trade opportunities. Some later accounts reported that he traveled at "his own expense."[7] Regardless, the visit with Joseph Stalin had little or no real impact either on foreign trade or on the conduct of international relations, other than to render more difficult the task of those American officials responsible for foreign policy.[8] It was not until five years later, in the turmoil of Florida politics, that Pepper's foray into one-man diplomacy left a lasting mark on his career, and then it was not at all what he had intended.

A consideration of one generally overlooked dimension of Pepper's Russian trip will help readers gain a better understanding of how the trip had negative consequences for his political career. It points to the amazing disjunction between Pepper's comprehension of what the Cold War was all about and the emerging bipartisan understanding of it that became the basis for postwar U.S. foreign policy. That disjunction quickly became the defining feature in his public image and finally was the principal factor in his 1950 defeat. Later, when he lamented the unfairness of being singled out for harsh criticism as a result of the visit, he could not seem to grasp the stark differences between his course of action and that taken by his four House counterparts who collectively made a similar visit to Stalin. No consideration of the 1950 Florida Senate election is complete without an appreciation of that divergence of viewpoints between Pepper and others who assessed the situation from similar vantage points.

To dwell on Pepper as a victim of McCarthyism without exploring the prevailing environment is to miss the larger point of it all. It begs the question of whether he was the innocent victim of McCarthyism, or whether his own politics called down the wrath of the voters with McCarthyism but an expression of that operative reality. It ignores his own pursuit of political opportunity and ideology to the point of glaring nonconformity with the mainstream of his constituency. In politics, that can be sometimes interpreted as honesty of conviction. If not perceived in that light, it is generally fatal to a political career. Such was Pepper's fate.

The delegation of congressmen in Moscow at the same time as Pepper officially represented the House Foreign Affairs Committee and visited with Stalin immediately before their Senate counterpart. That party included the chairman of the House Foreign Affairs Committee, William M. Colmer of Mississippi. Both visits were arranged by the American Embassy and were set up separately, probably in deference to each chamber's sensitivity to its status of bicameral equality. At the time, the U.S. ambassador, W. Averell Harriman, was absent from Moscow, and George F. Kennan was chargé d'affaires. He accompanied each party and acted as interpreter. Six months later, Kennan wrote the so-called Long Telegram initiating the process by which the concept of containment became the linchpin of U.S. Cold War foreign policy. Pepper quickly positioned himself as a vocal opponent of that policy.

The conclusions drawn by the four House members from their visit stood in stark contrast to those of Pepper. Their viewpoints and the assessments of Kennan in the "Long Telegram" illustrate how far Pepper strayed from the evolving mainstream of informed opinion on the Soviets. He was obstinately set in what increasingly appeared from emerging evidence to be a blind disregard of the threat posed by the Communists. Subsequent events hardened that perception.

Colmer's synthesis of his group's meeting with Stalin was a sobering appreciation of probable Soviet aggressive intentions. It urged a firm policy, confrontational if necessary, to stay further Soviet encroachment in Europe and the Middle East. While recognizing the great sacrifice made by the Russian people in defeating the Nazis, the House report did not anticipate any substantial demobilization or decrease in Soviet armaments production. It noted the role of the NKVD, as the Soviet secret police was then known, in keeping strict control over the Russian people, and Stalin's unchallenged position as absolute dictator. The unanimous conclusion of the four congressmen was that the United States should maintain a policy of firmness with the Soviets while trying to find common grounds on which to negotiate from a position of strength. They did not dilute that view with any hope that conciliation might bring the Soviet government to a position of reasonableness, specifically disavowing the policy of appeasement toward the Russians begun during the war.[9]

As would be expected, Kennan's "Long Telegram" was a much more in-depth assessment of Soviet character and purpose. Kennan was a career diplomat widely recognized for his intellectual qualifications as an expert on Russian affairs. His analysis established the foundation for the bipartisan American foreign policy that endured throughout the Cold War. Kennan's view of Soviet intentions had evolved over his tenure in the Soviet Union as an American diplomat. It was nearly fully developed—although not widely articulated—at the time of Pepper's visit.[10] In essence, Kennan said in the "Long Telegram" that the Soviets saw the world divided into two hostile camps, capitalist and communist, and, in their view, there could be no real peaceful coexistence between them. He attributed their mind-set not to any rational assessment of the outside world but to the Soviet leaders' need to justify their autocratic rule by the existence of external threats.[11] Kennan, like the four congressmen, and with far more penetrating reasoning, urged a policy of holding the Soviets to the present limits of their empire. His ideas became embodied in the term "containment," which was the cornerstone of U.S. foreign policy for the next forty years.

Unlike Pepper, who optimistically expected that conciliatory treatment would induce reasonable international conduct by the Soviets, Averell Harriman, Roosevelt's wartime ambassador to the Soviet Union and one of the Democratic Party's leading foreign policy experts, saw only the gravest danger in such a course. During the period when the United Nations was being established, he told the press: "We must recognize that our objectives and the Kremlin's objectives are irreconcilable. The Kremlin wants to promote Communist dictatorships controlled from Moscow, whereas we want, as far as possible, to see a world of governments responsive to the will of the people."[12] Pepper's position seemed to a growing number of people to render him squarely opposed to such reasoning. To them, he appeared unable to grasp the obvious.

Kennan reported to the State Department that Stalin told the House group and Pepper essentially the same things.[13] The stark contrast between the viewpoints that emerged vividly illustrates how Pepper's ideological fixation set the parameters of his judgmental process. Pepper was not a communist, and probably not even a radical. Yet his evaluation of what he saw and heard while in Moscow was rigidly circumscribed by an overriding commitment to the cause of liberalism and all its icons. The Soviet promise of complete equality and elimination of class divisions found a niche in the idealistic imagination of some elements of the American left, the segment of the political spectrum where Pepper felt most at home. He did not falter in his commitment to democracy, believing earnestly that a workable version of it could emerge from Marxism if a tolerant coexistence between the United States and Soviet Union could be brought about. Pepper's proclivity for judging issues and individuals exclusively, and often hastily, on the basis of their fit with his concept of liberalism was evident; his political rhetoric was always polarized along those lines. In the final analysis, his judgments were not compatible with mainstream American political sentiment. He persistently and loudly proclaimed his views, even as his twin refrains of good intentions and understanding toward the Soviets were subsumed by the contrary realities of the Cold War.

Pepper's first public report of his visit was a radio broadcast from Moscow following his audience with Stalin. His innate exuberance in matters in which he felt strongly served him poorly in this instance. He spoke in superlative terms about the greatness of the Russian people, their culture, and the Soviet leadership. He emphasized the "great debt to Generalissimo Stalin, the Red Army and the people of the Soviet Union for their magnificent part in turning back . . . the evil Nazis . . . , and their blows against the Japanese." In light of the almost nonexistent Soviet involvement in the war with Japan, these comments appeared detached from reality. He was effusive in his gratitude for what "this great Generalissimo, this mighty army and this heroic people have done toward the destruction of tyranny and the restoration of freedom and independence in the world."[14] Without question, the Soviet people had fought a most difficult and heroic war against the Germans, but these words subsequently echoed with an especial irony as the permanence of Russian hegemony in Eastern Europe stifled any notion of freedom and independence for that region of the world.

Pepper continued in the same vein in a *New York Times* article he wrote about his trip. Describing the emotions evoked in him by his audience with Stalin, he recounted being "privileged to talk with the single most powerful man in the world, the man who is going to determine in a large way what kind of world ours is to be."[15] In any realistic assessment of those words, the essential truth of them is apparent. Coming from Pepper, however, they seemed like cowering acceptance of Stalin's despotic power. Pepper told the Soviet dictator "that he was very much admired in the United States and often, in the most cordial manner, is referred to as Uncle Joe."[16] Later, these words seemed particularly ill suited for the frightening reality that was Joseph Stalin. Preserved on the front page of the *New York Times,* this phrase made him appear inane or naive, if not actually dangerous. Pepper's effusive manner of expressing his feelings toward the Russian ruler was incongruous with the perception of the Soviet dictator that rapidly took root in the American public consciousness.

The well-traveled senator affirmed his views immediately on his return. He started off the first year of the postwar era with an address to over 790 people who had paid to hear him talk under the auspices of the Soviet American Committee, a clearly pro-Russian organization.

A few days later, he was getting heady encouragement to carry forward the banner of liberalism from former Democratic presidential candidate James M. Cox, who had campaigned in 1920 with Franklin Roosevelt as his running mate. This party elder statesman told him "now was the time for [Pepper] to take liberal leadership in the country—not to bother too much about local problems in Florida, but to concentrate on the national" political picture.[17]

Words of encouragement like those of Cox found a receptive hearing from the man who considered himself a worthy successor to Franklin Roosevelt. Although Cox was no Soviet sympathizer, Pepper construed such encouragement as validation for his tolerant and forbearing posture toward the Soviet Union. It confirmed for him that the path he had chosen was the correct one, both for the good of the country as well as for the fulfillment of his own political destiny. For him, those two dimensions converged into a singularity of purpose. His tactical objective was to persuade the Florida electorate to keep him in office to fulfill that destiny. As it turned out, his vision of destiny obscured the short-term imperative of convincing the voters that he deserved reelection. Not only did he misjudge the public's reaction to the Soviet threat, he also misjudged the man whom fate raised up to succeed the legendary Roosevelt.

Pepper privately held Harry Truman in low regard from the day he assumed the presidency, but did allow some begrudging respect for Truman's tough handling of war contractors and industrialists for profiteering on military contracts.[18] In Pepper's eyes, the man who had received the 1944 vice presidential nomination instead of his friend, Henry Wallace, was incapable of filling the void left by Roosevelt's death. He commented on the new administration with a disparaging note in his diary: "The political crowd is now in the saddle and they are beginning to run hard."[19] His diary entries reveal a growing disdain—almost contempt—for the Missouri machine politician who now occupied the White House.

The new president was not from the same mold as Roosevelt. After thirteen momentous years at the center of national and world attention, the New York patrician had assumed an aura of legendary proportions. His character and style were deeply impressed on the operative mechanisms of government. Harry Truman made no pretense at trying to fit the Roosevelt pattern.

After an evening at the Stork Club in New York City with Justice Hugo Black, Henry Wallace, Henry Morgenthau, and other liberal luminaries of the Roosevelt era, Pepper noted in his diary that Truman's name had not been mentioned once. To Pepper, the omission illustrated that the new president was not important enough to even warrant a place in the table conversations of those who were the true heirs to the New Deal legacy.

That same evening, Pepper had been a featured speaker with Wallace at a large New York meeting of the National Citizens Political Action Committee, a left-wing organization with a mixture of leading noncommunist liberals, communist sympathizers, and avowed communists. Always conscious of public approval as a barometer of acceptance of his positions, he observed in his diary that he had received the "longest applause at introduction, second only to Wallace." For all of his very considerable political intuition, he could not, at this stage of his career, differentiate between a Madison Square Garden crowd of radical leftists and the bedrock of his Florida constituency.

The compass needle of his ambition was pushing Pepper to higher aspirations. He considered himself a leader in the liberal movement, not only in the Senate but also in the nation. He confided a generalized course of action to his diary: "I am going ahead with my plan of working largely in the fields of foreign policy and humanitarian legislation."[20] There is no doubt Florida's senior senator saw himself with a political destiny beyond the mundane confines of merely representing Florida in the U.S. Senate. After all, his role model, the person whose successor he now began to perceive in either himself or Henry Wallace, shone "in the hearts of mankind . . . as luminous and as fixed as the North Star."[21] As he compared himself to his former senate colleague who now occupied the White House, his ambition, fueled by visions of a world made peaceful and harmonious through his efforts, began to creep ahead of his political judgment.

Pepper was told by friends and supporters of his increasing divergence from the mainstream of his constituency, particularly in north Florida, his traditional base of political support.[22] With his unbounded self-confidence—some would say an unbounded ego—he persisted on the course he saw as directed at his higher goals. He underestimated the extent of that divergence, always confident he could effectively explain it away if and when compelled by political necessity. His lack of apprehension about the appellation "liberal" was not altogether unreasonable at the time. He was well aware that his adopted state, like Alabama, had Populism planted deep in the political psyche. His populist-oriented New Deal liberalism was not the anathema in rural Florida that it later became. It coexisted in something of an ambivalent equilibrium but always subject to being pushed aside by the more robust conservatism of the region, especially when aroused on the issue of race. Later, communism would have the same effect when, as was often the case, it was linked to the race issue.

In 1950, the term *conservative* still had about it the faintly pejorative connotation left from its association with the Hoover administration and the depression.[23] Outside the context of race, liberalism could be at least tolerated in Florida and viewed as a positive good in some quarters. Still, the brand of liberalism that Florida's senior U.S. senator openly embraced and aspired to lead went beyond the pale of acceptable eccentricity.

It was during this period that Pepper raised the question to himself and political intimates of whether his Florida constituency was compatible with his mounting ambitions. As discussed earlier, he gave some thought to moving to New York or California, where he thought his liberalism would be better received. That idea persisted even after his defeat. Later, he allowed to his diary that it was rather "wacky" to consider becoming a New York senator with an Alabama accent.[24] It is worth noting that one Washington reporter observed in 1947 that his "fine oratorical voice has about lost its Deep South [accent]."[25]

When urged by supporters to be more "middle of the road," Pepper responded that he could not be, adding almost condescendingly that "it would be alright in the long run."[26] On another occasion, supporters told him that his stand on labor legislation was very unpopular. He replied, "It will subside, or I'll fight it out at the proper time." Friends in rural north Florida's Gadsden County warned Pepper that his "liberal" views on race were beginning to harm him in that area.²⁷ His desire to be a liberal leader of national stature required him to walk a fine line between the racism expected by his white southern constituency and the inexorable movement toward racial equality required in the larger context. He seemed oblivious to the clear inconsistencies in such a dual course.

After Pepper made a speech in a black church in Los Angeles, he received a letter informing him that accounts of the speech inferred he endorsed social equality between the races. He heatedly denied any such belief. He hearkened to the memory of his two grandfathers—killed in action as Confederate soldiers—to prove his views were no "different from [his correspondent's] or any other southerner's about racial equality."²⁸ Yet when businessmen in Jacksonville expressed unease with some of his domestic and foreign policy positions, he recorded in his diary: "Jax [sic] most reactionary city in the state. All they want one to do is betray the people."²⁹ It was much the same story in Tallahassee, where he told a group of displeased city officials that he was considering moving his residence from that city.³⁰ Although Pepper noted that he soothed their ruffled feelings, it is likely they remembered the cause of their discontent more vividly than his soothing words.

Pepper's oratorical talent made him capable of articulate invective in castigating those who disagreed with his conciliatory tone toward the Soviet Union. In yet another speech before the National Citizens Political Action Committee, he said of those who urged a hard line against the Soviets: "There are still selfish and unscrupulous men who place their desires for personal power and profit above the welfare of the Nation and the world, blind and stupid men who are worked upon by the unscrupulous, who are their tools, their helots, obeying their divisive, cynical, and disruptive orders to wreck world peace at all costs. Chief among the weapons of these sinister forces today is the weapon of anti Sovietism. Not a morning passes but that I read in the newspaper some new and conscienceless attack upon our great ally that, be it remembered, which for nearly two years singlehandedly held the line against the engulfing hordes of the Nazi juggernaut."³¹ For the reflective listener, the incongruity of ignoring Great Britain's 1940 stand against Nazi might while Stalin marched in tandem with Hitler in the conquest of Poland was a glaring distortion of recent historical reality. For the pro-Soviet audience, it fitted the rationale of a reality retrofitted to coincide with current political purpose.

At the time, the Truman administration was struggling to shape a bipartisan foreign policy with which to present a united front to the Soviets.

Pepper's language was clearly aimed at those efforts and the men who were fashioning the embryonic policy of containment. It was particularly grating to men like Secretary of State James Byrnes and Senator Arthur Vandenberg, the leading Senate Republican on foreign affairs, and on whom the administration depended for bipartisan support.[32] A united stance on foreign policy was vital to the conduct of the nation's foreign affairs. Pepper, a senior member of the Foreign Relations Committee, had sufficient stature to render his persistently contradictory tone toward the administration a distinct hindrance to the appearance of unity. This was clearly his intent, and it was reported to that effect to the public.

Pepper achieved a high level of notoriety for his foreign policy positions. As if to emphasize his ideological symbiosis with the Soviet Union, he frequently condemned British-American solidarity and attacked British imperialism.[33] At times, he had to skirt the edge of logic to show his ideological solidarity with the Labor government that had replaced Churchill's Tory Party in power.[34] He maintained that the United States was propping up the antiquated imperialism of Great Britain, all the while ignoring the glaring incongruity of his tolerance for the emergence of a modern Soviet empire. His positions attracted national attention, most of which was negative. He was condemned in terms every bit as vitriolic as those he used on opponents.

In August 1946, he was negatively portrayed in the *Saturday Evening Post* article "Pink Pepper." It delved into his liberalism—strongly inferring that it smacked of class warfare—attacked him for being self-centered, too egotistical to cooperate in the clear national interest, and for securing unduly favorable treatment for supporters in disposal of war-surplus materials, a highly lucrative enterprise at the time. It summed up in bold type: "Champion of Soviet Russia and the Common Man, Claude Pepper Is Known Both as a Great Liberal and 'The Most Dangerous Man in the Senate since Huey Long.' Is He Eying 1948?"[35]

Pepper persisted in running counter to the administration's foreign policy initiatives, eventually opposing the Truman Doctrine, crucial elements of the Marshall Plan, and the whole concept of containment. He spoke against Truman's peacetime draft bill for over six hours on the Senate floor.[36] Because he actually voted in favor of passing some of these measures, he could later claim to have supported them. Yet his real efforts were aimed at amending them to the point of nullifying their intended purposes. He consistently maintained that U.S. foreign policy was aimed at undermining the United Nations, saying that peace should be achieved through that body and not through direct confrontation between individual superpowers.[37] Pepper's posturing in the face of a rising consensus on the dangers of Soviet intentions began to isolate him from the evolving bipartisan mainstream of foreign policy. By the time Pepper opposed military aid to Greece and Turkey in 1947, he was no longer being taken as seriously as he once had been.

His antics in opposing Truman's nomination at the 1948 Democratic convention dashed what little prospect remained for conciliation with the new administration. His unsuccessful efforts to nominate Wallace, his subsequent attempt to entice General Dwight D. Eisenhower into the race, and, failing that, his announcement that he was willing to accept the nomination to keep it from Truman—all amounted to little more than a comic spectacle. His subsequent campaigning for the party ticket was judged ineffectual and did nothing to reinstate him in the president's good graces.[38] Harry Truman's memory was probably not as long as Ed Ball's, but it was long enough to reach to Pepper's next election.

Political observers in Florida noted that Pepper's national activities, especially his foreign policy and pro-labor positions, were politically damaging to him at home. He was no longer the nearly unbeatable protégé of Franklin Roosevelt; others could realistically covet his seat.[39]

While Pepper labored to establish himself as a leader of the nation's far left, he was also prominently involved in reversing Ed Ball's apparent victory in the fight for the Florida East Coast Railway. If Pepper had not intervened in the railroad battle, it is unlikely that his pro-Soviet politics would have assumed significant proportions in his and Ball's relationship. Ball would not have let something that abstract, to his way of thinking, govern political decisions, which, for him, were first and foremost business decisions. In any event, the fiery businessman had other, more compelling grounds for devoutly wishing Pepper's political demise than the senator's foreign policy views.

In addition to the railroad fight, there were the Breakers episode, Pepper's Revenue Act veto override, and Ball's long-simmering contempt for the New Deal. For Ball, Pepper's cardinal sin was his disdain for the sanctity of property rights, especially those of Ball and the duPont empire committed to his care. This was made clear in the view repeatedly expressed by Ball that Pepper was trying to confiscate his "property" in the Florida East Coast Railway.[40] Although Pepper's pro-Soviet orientation in foreign affairs and his doctrinaire liberalism did not actuate Ball's opposition, they did provide an ideological dimension and patriotic overtone to fuel his intense dislike of the senator.

In the years leading up to 1950, Ed Ball's power in the Florida political arena had steadily increased as his span of influence in the state's business affairs expanded. Because such power, by its nature, is difficult to measure with any precision, the historian is compelled to rely on perception and inference. In politics, as in the performing arts, perception and reality are hardly distinguishable. In the late 1940s, Ball began to be regularly noted by the political press. Early in 1947, Allen Morris featured Ball in his well-read "Cracker Politics," the state's first syndicated political column. Morris called him the "wizard of the duPont-Florida National empire" in a short account of an appearance before a congressional committee in which he downplayed his own political prowess.[41] As a result of his fight with Claude Pepper over the Florida East Coast Railway, his name had become much better known through the 1940s in the state's business and political press. It was widely assumed—and for the most part, accurately—that he possessed the means of power and the will to use it.

His influence reached into the highest levels of state politics, and he was well known in Washington. Jacob "Jake" Belin, the longtime St. Joe Paper executive and Ball confidant, remembered an episode that illustrated his long reach into the labyrinthine halls of political power; although this episode occurred in 1962, Ball's access to the political power brokers was just as good during the 1950 election campaign. Belin was asked by Ball to meet some "hunting guests" who would be arriving on a military aircraft at nearby Tyndall Air Force base. Without further knowledge of whom he would be meeting, Belin and the base commander were greatly surprised to see three of the four military joint chiefs of staff in civilian clothes and Senator A. Willis Robertson of Virginia disembark from one of the government's luxury aircraft.[42]

Robertson was chairman of the Senate Committee on Banking and Currency, the committee of jurisdiction over the provision of the Bank Holding Company Act, which exempted the duPont Trust from operation of the act. That provision permitted the common ownership of bank holding companies and nonbanking enterprises, such as the Florida East Coast and the St. Joe Paper Company, by charitable trusts. It was essential to the combination of the diverse enterprises of the duPont Trust into the concentration of economic might that was the source of Ball's power. At the time, Ball was concerned with the possibility of the repeal of that provision as a result of the strike against the Florida East Coast Railway. While the high-ranking military officers were of marginal importance to Ball, they were very important to Robertson. The formidable military presence in Virginia was a valuable component in that state's economy. A good relationship with the nation's top military officers helped maintain that presence and was always a continuing priority with a Virginia senator.

The outing was of mutual benefit to all parties. Everyone enjoyed the hunting trip, and Ball had done a favor for his Virginia friend, who happened to be chairman of the Senate Banking and Currency Committee. Later, when the matter of repealing the charitable trust exemption got to the Senate floor, however, Senator Robertson, then locked in a difficult reelection campaign, sided with the railroad unions against Ball.

The almost continual battle with Roy E. Crummer over the state's bond refunding business was also a reflection of the multifaceted reach of Ball's myriad interests. It should be noted that while Ball wielded considerable political influence in the Crummer matter, he was countered by comparable influence on the part of his adversary. There is ample evidence indicating Crummer's bond refunding practices were highly irregular, and more than one court found them fraudulent. It should be noted that in other cases, they were declared legal.[43] Crummer himself was indicted for securities fraud as a result of the investigation instigated by a Ball executive, but the charges were dropped under questionable circumstances. The tangled web of investigations, lawsuits, and political intrigue reached ultimately to Washington. The only certainty was that it was a grand-scale exercise of political influence by both Ball and Crummer, his opponent of the moment. The Kansas securities dealer had been close to Governor Doyle Carlton, and through him, found the crucial support for enacting the bond refunding program in 1929 that established his Florida dominance in that field.

Ten years later, Ball was a close friend and supporter of Spessard Holland, who won the 1940 gubernatorial race. In that contest, Holland's opponent, Francis Whitehair, a well-known lawyer and politician from Volusia County, made frequent reference to Holland as a tool of Ed Ball and the duPont interests.[44] Later, Whitehair was a principal attorney for Crummer in his long-lasting antitrust suit against Ball. His cocounsel was Robert Pleus, a staunch supporter of Pepper in the 1950 election. Intertwined relationships such as those were the marrow of Florida politics.

When Holland initiated direct state oversight of county road and bridge bond refunding, Ball's Florida National Bank chain was the major purchaser of those securities. As a result, Crummer was displaced as the dominant securities dealer in the lucrative refunding market.[45] Ball, whose tenacity matched his thoroughness, then launched a campaign to drive Crummer from the state altogether. He lodged a complaint with the state's securities exchange commission, an arm of Florida's unique elected cabinet system, and succeeded in having his competitor's state securities dealer's license revoked. Some of Ball's correspondence produced by Crummer's lawyers later showed that Florida officials had a friendly, compliant attitude toward Ball and his objectives.[46] At about the same time, as discussed previously, a Florida National Bank executive, Roger O. Main, and another Florida bond dealer initiated a separate investigation of Crummer by the U.S. Postal Inspection Service and the federal Securities and Exchange Commission.

Those moves prompted a counterinvestigation of Ball by a Senate investigating committee chaired by Senator Patrick McCarran of Nevada. While that investigation was formally initiated by a resolution cosponsored by both Pepper and the other senator representing Florida, Charles O. Andrews, there is some evidence that Crummer importuned McCarran to undertake the investigation. Against that there is McCarran's statement on the floor of the Senate that Senator Andrews's persistent requests that he (McCarran) chair the subcommittee were the prime reason for his role.[47] Andrews, from Orlando where Crummer's Florida operations were headquartered, was ailing at the time and died before McCarran's report was made to the full Senate. In any event, it is clear that Crummer wielded ample political power and was a strong force in his own right.[48] That investigation and the Crummer federal antitrust suit provide detailed and highly complex evidentiary trails of Ball's political power and his use of it.[49] During the same period, Holland was elected to the Senate seat of the deceased Andrews, and his friendship with Ball continued through the remainder of his career.

The McCarran report was delivered to the full Senate in July of 1947, but it was not an official report of the entire subcommittee. No other member of that committee shared the chairman's views of what the record of their investigation showed, nor did they report their own views. As a result, McCarran's report is the only synopsis of the lengthy evidentiary record. The gist of it was that Ball and his lieutenants were able to influence the U.S. Securities and Exchange Commission and the Postal Inspection Service to wrongfully prosecute Crummer, and that this official intimidation forced Crummer to cease doing business in Florida. McCarran summed up Ball's power as being such "that the economic life of the State and well-being of its people may be affected more by [his] . . . power than by the power of the government of the state itself."[50] Holland, it will be recalled, had been summoned by McCarran's subcommittee and questioned about his relationship with Ball. After election to the Senate, he was better received and more persuasive in his explanation of the bond program that had favored Ball's banks than he had been before the subcommittee earlier as a mere ex-governor.[51]

There can be little doubt, as the McCarran Report shows, that by 1950 Ed Ball was a formidable force in Florida politics. While he did not exercise virtual control of the state, as some detractors and admirers alike contended, his wrath, once ignited, was not to be taken lightly by those who crossed him. In 1950, Ball's whole sense of political purpose was focused on Pepper. As recalled by Belin, Ball was singularly fixed with a "bitter determination" to defeat the state's senior senator.[52] Then again, so were many other Florida businessmen, as were most of the state's doctors and those union men who had vehemently opposed his role in the FEC case. Arching over this formidable array of opposition loomed the specter of Pepper's pro-Soviet attitude in the increasingly hostile climate of the Cold War.

In late summer of 1949, it was clear that Pepper would draw opposition, although no specific candidate had risen to the formidable challenge. Associated Industries of Florida, then the principal political arm of the state's business community, had always attacked his liberalism, especially his continued adamant support for the Townsend plan, which had proposed comprehensive pension benefits for all citizens far beyond the Social Security benefits enacted during the New Deal. That organization stepped up its attacks on his pro-Soviet stance as the 1950 campaign season approached. Articles from the *Daily Worker* lauding Pepper were widely disseminated by Associated Industries to make the point of his pro-Soviet leanings.[53] The business community was actively seeking a candidate to oppose him. Two well-known Jacksonville businessmen, Jim Merrill and C. G. McGehee, were known to be canvassing the state for someone to run against him. McGehee was the president of Associated Industries and had been linked with Ball in the 1944 effort to defeat Pepper.

The anti-Pepper campaign was reported to Spessard Holland's administrative assistant for the senator's benefit by one of his law partners in Orlando.[54] Holland was not directly involved in that effort, but he was most likely sympathetic with it. In any event, like any practicing politician, he kept himself abreast of developing events in his state.

In light of the widespread dislike of Pepper in the business community, it is unlikely that it devolved on Ball alone to organize the opposition to him.

Undoubtedly the Jacksonville financier was aware of the effort and almost certainly supported it from the outset. It may have been that he was the driving force, but the evidence available for this analysis does not make that point one way or the other. The movement to oppose Pepper was not the effort of a single man, even though Ball may have been a galvanizing force. There were others beside the Jacksonville financier, especially a young ex-Marine, Miami's second-term congressman, who had reason to wish Pepper's defeat. There was no particular malice on his part toward Pepper; he simply coveted Pepper's senate seat. After being mustered out of the service early with Pepper's help, Smathers had wasted no time in launching his own political career. He ran for Congress and upset a four-term incumbent in 1946 with an uphill campaign, then was reelected without opposition two years later. The tall, athletic, and good-looking marine combat veteran was almost a "storybook" political figure.

Like Pepper, he had a driving political ambition, but he had enjoyed a more comfortable upbringing than had Pepper. His father was a practicing attorney in Miami, having left a federal judgeship in New Jersey due to poor health. There was a political tradition in his family. His uncle served one term as U.S. senator from New Jersey, and his father was appointed to the federal bench by President Woodrow Wilson. Young Smathers, like Pepper, was a natural leader. He was elected student-body president without opposition at the University of Florida, a rare feat in the highly competitive campus politics of that institution. He was also a star on the basketball and track teams. In 1938, he was Pepper's campus campaign manager and maintained a friendship, albeit with widening differences as to political philosophies, with the senator until the 1950 campaign. After acquiring his law degree, he was appointed assistant U.S. attorney in Miami through Pepper's patronage.[55] He first received favorable public recognition for his successful prosecution of a "white slavery" ring. In 1942, he volunteered for the marines and saw eighteen months of service in the Pacific theater. His tour included some combat experience, from which he emerged as a major.[56] By early 1945, Smathers had been reassigned to nonessential legal duties with the navy. He sensed the imminent conclusion of the war, and, feeling that he had done his fair share, he was anxious to return to civilian status to commence his political career. Like thousands of veterans who had served, he felt that what remained to be done could fairly be left to those with less service. His eighteen months in the Pacific seemed adequate to satisfy his patriotic obligations.[57] Smathers's war service, perhaps less extensive than that of some veterans, was still respectable by any reckoning and was sufficient for political credibility. He sought Pepper's help in obtaining a discharge from the Marines. His efforts to secure an early release under the circumstances were not unusual for a combat veteran, especially one with political connections. He made full use of those connections.

In a series of letters to Pepper and his staff, Smathers sought their help in expediting his early discharge. Pepper assisted him, as would be expected given their relationship at the time. In several letters, Smathers expressed political views compatible with Pepper's well-known liberalism. (These letters were published during the 1950 campaign by Pepper to show how Smathers had betrayed his friendship by running against him.)[58] By 1949, much had changed in the relationship between the young congressman and his senatorial mentor. The daunting realization that the United States stood at the brink of a war far more dangerous than the one just finished was the predominant fact of American political life. Smathers's ambition burned every bit as intensely as did Pepper's, but unlike the senior senator, he was completely in accord with the U.S. policy of resolutely containing Soviet expansion. A clear difference in political philosophy on this crucial point distinguished the two men. Although this difference has subsequently been portrayed by some of Smathers's detractors as mere political expediency, it was the defining issue of the 1950 campaign, notwithstanding Pepper's retreat from the extremes that had marked his earlier postwar views. Pepper had established a record on that score, and when the time came, Smathers intended to hold him to it. It should be noted that the Korean War commenced after the election in late June of 1950, and Pepper then strongly supported the U.S. leadership role among the United Nations forces sent to repel the North Korean Communist invasion of South Korea. But by then, he had lost.

In 1949, Smathers was well established politically, having been reelected without opposition the previous year—the same year in which Pepper had attempted to deny Truman the Democratic nomination. As it became conventional political wisdom throughout the state that Pepper would draw opposition, it also appeared increasingly possible that whoever took up the challenge had a reasonable chance of success. Still, it was equally obvious that Claude Pepper, notwithstanding his pro-Soviet views, was still a highly competent politician who had a way with the voters. His defeat was by no means a given outcome. Smathers's name began to be widely mentioned in political circles as a likely candidate.[59] The event that triggered his actual candidacy was a request from President Harry Truman.

As recounted by Smathers, he was summoned to the White House in the late summer of 1949 to see Truman. The two-term congressman knew that it was rare, although not altogether unique, for a junior House member to receive such a summons. As a young congressman, he had developed a limited rapport with the president. Truman's favorite relaxation spot was the naval base at Key West in Smathers's congressional district. As a courtesy to the local Democratic House member, the president invited Smathers to visit with him during his sojourns there. Through these casual meetings, Smathers was known to the president, who now served in his own right after his upset victory in 1948 over New York governor Thomas E. Dewey. When he received the call, Smathers assumed Truman wanted his support on some proposal or another deemed important by the administration. Arriving at the Oval Office, Smathers was greatly surprised when, after some inconsequential discussion, Truman told him he wanted him to run against Pepper. Smathers vividly recalled the salty Missourian saying, "I want you to beat that son-of-a-bitch Claude Pepper."[60]

At the time, Smathers was not seriously considering entering the race, and he was surprised by the president's near commanding tone. Although he had ambitions for higher office, either the governor's mansion or a Senate seat, his immediate reaction was that taking on such a formidable opponent as Pepper was premature and overly ambitious for a second-term congressman. Smathers thought Truman's insistence was most likely due to Pepper's insulting attacks on him in the attempt to wrest the 1948 Democratic nomination from him, first in favor of Henry Wallace and, when that failed, in favor of General Dwight D. Eisenhower.[61] Of course, Smathers was also very much aware of Pepper's attacks on administration foreign policy. While the congressman was surprised, it would be something of an overstatement to say he was shocked.

In later years, Pepper maintained that there was no truth to the story that the president asked Smathers to run against him. To support this contention, he pointed to the fact that he had campaigned for Truman in 1948, and the president had held no grudges for his support of Wallace and Eisenhower over him for the 1948 Democratic nomination.[62] That thesis does not comport with the rough-and-ready style of politics Truman learned in the Pendergast machine in his native Missouri. Recent research by one Smathers scholar shows that Truman's appointment book reflected a meeting on August 10, 1949, with Smathers in the White House Oval Office. An annotation in the original indicates Truman told the young congressman to "go down to Florida" and "make a survey and report" back to him on the political scene.[63] Undoubtedly, such encouragement from the president was a strong factor in Smathers's decision to run for the Senate. He then set about the quest in earnest, no longer bothered by any question of premature timing. This interpretation of what precipitated Smathers's candidacy is convincing. It is most likely that Truman—and not Ed Ball—was the deciding factor in inducing a young George Smathers to run against the state's senior senator. At that time, Smathers did not know Ball well, having had only minimal contact with him during his relatively short tenure as a Miami congressman. He had met the Jacksonville financier before his first campaign for Congress when Smathers and another lawyer tried to interest him in investing in an effort to acquire the first television license in Florida. Smathers remembered Ball "banging the table for emphasis" as he told the young entrepreneur-lawyers that "we don't spend money on these damned foolish ideas."[64] After that, the two men had little contact until Smathers was assessing his chances against Pepper. The president of the Florida National Bank in Miami invited Smathers to lunch with Ball. The about-to-be-candidate was more impressed with Leonard Usina, the bank president, than he was with the "little fellow who didn't have much to say."[65] Nothing decisive concerning Ball's support in the approaching election came from that meeting. Their next contact was a short time later.

Herbert E. Wolfe, the St. Augustine road contractor who had tried to ascertain Pepper's vote on the 1944 Revenue Act veto override, was just as determined to see Pepper defeated as Ball was. Road building was a highly politicized business in Florida, and Wolfe had a statewide network of political contacts as a result of his prominence in that field. He agreed to be Smathers's chief fund-raiser. To that end, he brought the candidate together with prominent businessmen who were potential contributors. As Smathers remembered it, Wolfe was a major and valued customer of the Florida National banks, and he and Ball were friends. Later, Wolfe was named to the reorganization board of the Florida East Coast Railway when Ball finally acquired control of it. Wolfe arranged a meeting between Ball and the candidate at his St. Augustine home. There, Ball showed more interest in Smathers's candidacy than he had demonstrated for his television proposition in their encounter in Miami some years earlier.

Anxious to defeat Pepper, he fixed on the affable young Miami congressman as the means to that end, and Ball became a Smathers supporter at that meeting. In Smathers's assessment, Wolfe played a much more important role in financing his campaign than did Ball.[66] That is not to minimize Ball's role, but rather to put it in perspective. The Jacksonville banker-business-man was not as interested in electing Smathers as he was in defeating Pepper. For the candidate, such supporters are valuable, but their focus is necessarily more on degrading the subject of their displeasure than on taking steps to advance the candidate's campaign. While the former tactic is certainly a factor in getting votes, the latter is essential to an effective campaign. This is a subtle distinction, but an important one to the candidate seeking to extol his own merits rather than his opponent's demerits. As it turned out, Smathers did both, but he is remembered mostly for his successful exploitation of Pepper's views on Joseph Stalin and the Soviet Union.

Ball introduced his candidate of choice around the duPont statewide network. Smathers came several times to Ball's office in Jacksonville and was often invited to the afternoon ritual of drinks in Ball's austere personal quarters in a Jacksonville hotel suite. He remembered the convivial atmosphere engendered by libations and the hallmark toast of Ed Ball: "Confusion to the enemy." At their first such meeting, the congressman was introduced to various duPont executives and other Ball associates, and questioned on his organization in west Florida. Ball gave him names of persons who would be helpful in his campaign. Present at that meeting and subsequent gatherings were Jacob Belin and other duPont people who would figure in the coming campaign.[67] They joined with others not affiliated with the duPont interests to play important roles in the smoothly efficient statewide campaign organization put together by Smathers.

Much has been written about Ball's political activities, including the Smathers campaign. Unfortunately, such writings depend mostly on indirect or inferential information. Some of it comes from Ball himself. Yet most often when speaking openly on the subject, he would self-effacingly deny any significant impact on the political process, all the while knowingly conveying the opposite meaning. His denials of political power bespoke much of its actual existence and potency, which was his intention in the first place.[68] The lack of direct evidence is not surprising. Observable details in a political campaign merge indistinguishably into a larger perception of the event itself, leaving little real evidence of their passing. Still, the perceptions of Ball's activities in the 1950 campaign derive some measure of substance from the diversity of their sources, which include Ball himself, as well as Pepper's account given in his memoirs.

One version of Ball's involvement in the 1950 campaign is presented by Robert Sherrill in his *Gothic Politics in the Deep South.* Sherrill's perspective of southern politics shows a clear contempt for the southern conservative politician. His approach is fixed on character assassination of the same kind as that charged in his book to Smathers in the 1950 race. Allowing for that, his account of an interview with Daniel T. Crisp, a Jacksonville advertising man and political consultant, warrants attention regarding the role of Ball in the campaign. Crisp told Sherrill that he had been in the pay of Ball and unnamed others since the 1944 campaign against Pepper with the sole purpose of generating opposition to Pepper. According to Crisp, it was a multifaceted effort involving real and "paper" organizations dedicated to the defeat of liberal candidates, especially Pepper. He said Ball was not such a big contributor personally, but that his real value was his ability to induce others to contribute, citing Ball's obtaining money from businessmen around the country, like the oil tycoon H. L. Hunt of Texas. Crisp allowed that he had ample funds for his effort, most of it raised by Ball.[69] The overall strident polemics of Sherrill's book as well as its journalistic sensationalism warrants a note of caution in relying too heavily on it. Yet the directly quoted words of Crisp fit what is known of Ball's modus operandi in politics.

Jacob Belin's independent recollection is generally in accord with Crisp's account of Ball's value primarily as a collector of funds rather than a contributor. Belin remembered that Ball knew Crisp, although he was not sure of any details about their relationship. More to the point, he plainly described Ball's political methods: "You would call it today dirty politics."[70] He recalled in a generalized way how Ball used various of the companies under his control to assist in the campaigns of his favored candidates, as well as his considerable influence with newspaper men, some of the most important of whom were his personal friends and shared his deep-seated conservative political beliefs.[71]

With due circumspection for Sherrill's obvious purpose to disparage Smathers, and taking his account of the Crisp interview with the inferences fairly gleaned from Jacob Belin's description of Ball's political methods, it is likely that Crisp did Ball's bidding in the 1950 campaign. It is also equally probable that Smathers was not directly responsible for the substance of the most scurrilous parts of the campaign. To this writer, he was persuasive in denying that Crisp was working under the auspices of his campaign.[72] Pepper himself seemed to agree with that assessment, but he held Smathers responsible for not disavowing it.[73] Smathers's statewide headquarters and Crisp's offices were both in Jacksonville, making it possible, if not likely, that some liaison existed between the two. Even so, it should be remembered that in 1950, television had not yet obviated the necessity of numerous personal appearances throughout the state by candidates. It is likely that Smathers would have been mostly occupied with keeping a rigorous travel schedule and raising money, leaving little time for direct involvement in campaign literature production. Still, as Pepper maintained, he did not disavow it and willingly reaped the political benefits of it.

As the year opened, Smathers's imminent announcement of his candidacy was all but an accepted fact. Pepper was not oblivious to the reality of his situation and was shoring up his traditional sources of support. One group that never wavered in its support for him was the state's Jewish community. His strong stand for a Jewish state in Palestine and his ardent liberalism were well suited to the fundamental views of that constituency. In late 1949, the *Jewish Floridian* observed that the duPont interests were willing to spend "millions" to defeat Pepper for his role in the railroad battle. Pepper's friendship with Lou Wolfson, a prominent Jacksonville Jewish businessman, was mentioned in the article.[74] Pepper had been anticipating opposition and began to assume it would be Smathers.[75]

In early January 1950, Smathers launched his campaign from the central Florida city of Orlando. It was one of the largest political extravaganzas ever seen in Florida. Hundreds of autos loaded with Smathers supporters were reported heading to Orlando in caravans from other sections of the state.[76] The Orlando coliseum was packed with cheering supporters of the Miami congressman, and the affair received extensive and favorable press coverage throughout the state.

Unrelated news stories were indicative of the environment in which the campaign was launched and subsequently fought to a conclusion. On January 12, the front page of the *Tampa Morning Tribune* featured the first invitation to the state's black voters to participate in the Democratic primary since Reconstruction. That tended to fuel the racial overtones that would be characteristic of the campaign. The day before, there had been a debate in the U.S. Senate on the extent of proper welfare measures, and in its report the *Morning Tribune* featured Pepper prominently as defending "welfare proposals."[77] A week before, the public became alarmed by reports that the "Reds Are Reported Massing Ships for Invading Formosa," and the *Miami Herald* editorialized on the need to continue the occupation of Japan to defend it from the Communist threat.[78] Only the day before Smather's Orlando announcement, an editorial in the *Herald* had reminded its readers that Pepper, despite his disavowals, was "trying to outdo Henry A. Wallace as the special pleader for Stalin" and was an "ardent advocate of the theories of the hand-out state."[79] Given this political climate, it would have been impossible for a U.S. Senate campaign in 1950 not to have focused on Pepper's apologetics for Stalinist foreign policy.

Smathers's opening speech in Orlando evoked the full array of fears and emotions spawned by such a climate. The stream of issues covered in his talk was in the forefront of public awareness, not just in Florida but across the nation. Smathers should not be condemned for addressing them, even if his frequently strident and accusatory rhetoric was excessive. Pepper's past record was clear for all to see, notwithstanding his having taken some belated steps to tone it down in the preceding year. It was in that vein that Smathers's campaign came to be condemned by many as McCarthyism at its worst. But in 1950, Smathers's rhetoric was not judged by the electorate as unfair or dirty politics. The outcome of the race validates that assessment. That fact speaks to the temper of the time. It may also speak to the public's low capacity for discernment of propriety in politics. In any event, the campaign quickly assumed intensely personal overtones due to the past relationship of the two men. Pepper adroitly played on the image of the younger man turning on his mentor and benefactor for the greedy purposes of the evil monopolists personified by the duPonts. The series of letters from Smathers to Pepper in which the younger man sought early release from the marines was used to that end. Pepper also remembered the advice he had received from his newspaper friend and tilted his "lance" at Ed Ball.[80]

While Smathers made Stalin Pepper's bête noire of the moment, Pepper used the duPont name, and by extension that of Ed Ball, for the same purpose. Smathers was referred to as the "duPont lawyer," or some variation on that theme, at every opportunity. When he took Smathers to task for voting against a minimum wage bill, Pepper said "the people are still waiting for the duPont Lawyer opposing me to tell them how a worker can support himself . . . on wages of less than $16 a week."[81] When he referred to Smathers's plea for his help to get out of the marines, it was that "duPont lawyer opposing me" who made the request.[82] When Pepper charged that radio commentator Fulton Lewis had unjustly maligned him over some transgression, it was the "Fulton Lewis who I am sure is in the pay of the duPonts."[83] Speaking in the north Florida town of Lake City, he said Smathers was running against him because "the duPont crowd got hold of him in 1949 and offered him a vast campaign fund to make his race against me and the people."[84]

And so, on it went relentlessly, sometimes to the point of near-comic dimensions. When national columnist Drew Pearson, a Pepper supporter, took issue with the *Saturday Evening Post*'s article "Pink Pepper," the duPont image was conjured up once again. The well-known columnist said that the magazine received more than $50,000 a year in advertising revenue from the duPont family.[85] Of course, the fact that there were no real members of the duPont family involved with the so-called Florida duPont interests other than Jessie Ball duPont, Alfred's widow and Ball's sister, was of little relevance in the charged hyperbole of the campaign. The duPont name fueled the image of Pepper doing battle on behalf of the masses against the evil capitalist-monopolists, and that was exactly as he intended. This promoted the growing national attention on the race and was the focus of the Soviet news coverage of the campaign. The *New York Times* reported that *Izvestia*, the official Soviet government newspaper, attributed Smathers's victory to the "duPont chemical kings," adding that those "kings" were the "complete bosses" in Florida.[86]

Pepper's use of the duPont name to smear Smathers was not without some effect. Those accusations seemed damaging to Smathers because he attempted to turn the charge on Pepper. While denying that he was a duPont lawyer, he added that when Pepper ran for office the first time, he received substantial help from the "duPont interests of which Ed Ball is the trustee," adding for good measure that Pepper's current campaign treasurer was also a duPont lawyer.[87] The charge had come full circle, and use of the duPont label had approached the realm of the absurd. It must have been faintly amusing to Ball's sardonic sense of humor. In a more serious context, the constant reference to the duPont name was an indication of Pepper's proclivity for not so thinly veiled appeals to class warfare in the time-honored custom of pitting rich against poor. The inherently divisive and misleading nature of that tactic has been largely overlooked in accounts of Pepper's political career.

Ed Ball was inextricably woven into the fabric of the campaign by several issues. First, and most important, Ball put himself in by choosing to defeat Pepper for reasons accruing since 1944. Second, Pepper brought him in by deliberately choosing, as his newspaper friend advised, to "tilt his lance" at him. The matter of Pepper's opposition to the duPont takeover of the Florida East Coast also aroused strong resentment along the east coast, and in Miami, where local support for Ball's effort to acquire the railroad was all but overwhelming. As already noted, the FEC rail unions, that is, the Florida membership as distinguished from the national leadership, were adamantly opposed to Pepper because of his effort to aid the Atlantic Coast Line. While all these linked Ball's presence to the bitter campaign in one sense or another, he was still but a collateral figure to the main players in the unfolding drama. Despite Pepper's determined effort to make Ball and the "Dupont interests" a focal issue, the campaign did not take that turn.

George Smathers had set the tone of the campaign with his especially strong and accusatory opening speech in Orlando, forcing Pepper to assume a defensive posture. The principal issue was Pepper's Cold War stance. It was not difficult to arouse voter emotions based purely on his pro-Soviet speeches, which were on the record for all to behold. The subsequent label of McCarthyism tagged on the entire campaign begs the question whether the attacks on Pepper were relevant or based on fact. It also ignores the other issues in the race, on most of which Smathers's position was diametrically opposed to Pepper's.

There were many episodes in the bitter fight that fell below the always nebulous standards of fair campaigning. The example most often cited was the publication of "The Red Record of Claude Pepper" in the waning days of the campaign. This booklet contained numerous excerpts of Pepper's speeches, all dwelling on his pro-Soviet stance, plus photographs of him in the presence of Paul Robeson, Henry A. Wallace, and other well-known far-left activists or communist sympathizers. Edited in such a way as to focus on the more extreme dimensions of Pepper's statements, the excerpts ignored any clarifying or cautionary parts of the speeches. The picture of Pepper and Paul Robeson was obviously intended to inject racial prejudice into the already inflamed context of Pepper's pro-Soviet position. There is some evidence that it was actually a "doctored" photograph. Taken literally, Pepper had said these things attributed to him. Yet the aggregate impact of the booklet was a distortion of his views without crossing the line of deliberately lying. In politics, the distinction between deliberate lying and presenting facts calculated to mislead is always blurred by ambiguity.

Pepper was infuriated by the appearance of the "Red Pepper" booklet in the last days of the campaign, but his denials and attempted explanation were lost in the backwash of the acrimonious struggle. He presumed the booklet was the work of Ed Ball.[88] There is no direct evidence to support this, but the general tenor of Jacob Belin's description of Ball's tactics discussed earlier is consistent with that conclusion. It was certainly within Crisp's capabilities as a professional political tactician to have arranged its publication and dissemination. Pepper's problem throughout the campaign was that

Smathers's charges had truth and inferences woven into a single fabric, and they could not be separated in the fury of campaign rhetoric. Underlying all that, however, is the inescapable conclusion that Pepper had couched his vision of the future in terms of an extreme liberalism under the mantle of a revered but deceased leader. His was a vision of leadership from a fading era, a vision from which, in the prevailing Cold War atmosphere, his constituents did not perceive a future to their liking.

When the voters spoke, Pepper lost the election by a margin of more than 60,000 votes, a substantial margin at the time. The Alabama country boy who had seen the halcyon days of the Roosevelt era and the New Deal from the hallowed chamber of the U.S. Senate was impaled on his interpretation of the post-war world and the Cold War that defined it.

Pepper and Ball were not finished with each other. Although Pepper's deep-seated optimism and good nature enabled him to discard the outward trappings of animosity in favor of a pleasant affability, Ball was not of the same disposition. Shortly after the election, while Pepper was still the senior senator from Florida, there was a dinner meeting in Washington of the Florida Industrial Council, forerunner of today's Florida's Council of One Hundred. Such affairs brought together the elite of the state's business and political communities. Because Pepper was still the state's senior elected official in Washington, it was natural that he would attend. He approached Ball at the head table and congratulated him on "his" victory. Ball mildly acknowledged the pleasure of winning "the last round." Pepper intimated that it might not have been the "last round," and Ball dropped the feigned civility of the encounter. In a tone said by Pepper to "have silenced the room," he yelled the warning: "Claude if you ever run for public office in Florida again we'll lick you so bad you'll think this time was a victory."[89]

Pepper set about rebuilding his private life after fourteen years at the pinnacle of public affairs. He returned to law practice, opening offices in Miami and Tallahassee. Ball concentrated on reversing the setbacks he had earlier suffered at the hands of his now-defeated adversary in the battle for the FEC railroad. Their paths were to cross again, but never with the same directness or intensity as in Florida's 1950 Senate race.

10

Beyond the Senate: Diminishing Conflict

After Pepper's departure from the Senate, he had to make the difficult transition from public to private life. Coping with defeat is an especially trying phase of a political career and the higher the position, the greater is the sense of loss. Dismissal from one of the nation's central bastions of power by the voting public is by its nature a traumatic jolt to the ego. For some, it is an emotional entanglement of outward-directed bitterness coupled with feelings of personal inadequacy—all stemming from the humiliation of rejection. Claude Pepper experienced to some degree almost all of these reactions to defeat. Still, he had a strong measure of self-assurance and was further blessed with a nearly indomitable optimism in outlook.

The immediate need to rebuild a livelihood had a therapeutic effect on him. It caused him to focus on a positive course of action rather than become mired in self-pity. Fortunately, he was a highly competent lawyer with a radiating self-assurance on that score. He may have contemplated the reinvigorating idea of rising Phoenix-like to defeat the victorious adversary in the next election. How gratifying it would be to be restored to the same position of public honor or even some other higher one.

Even though fresh from the halls of power, he did not have an established law firm awaiting his return. Whatever he was going to have in the way of a private law practice, he would have to generate on his own. The new ex-senator wasted no time. He set about reestablishing his law practice in Tallahassee and also opened an office in Miami. In addition, he had plans for a Washington office in the near future. He faced a daunting task. The general dislike for his politics in the business community foreclosed much of that potentially lucrative client base. Most large corporations that needed access to Washington influence already had lawyers and lobbyists. To his disappointment, he found the same true for his labor allies.[1]

There was a positive side to his situation. Notwithstanding the large margin of defeat, almost 320,000 Floridians had approved of Claude Pepper's stewardship of the public interest. That gave him the favorable name recognition essential to rebuilding a law practice. He went about his task with his characteristic enthusiasm. Always popular as a speaker, he exhibited his good-natured optimism laced with an affable sense of humor. Returning to old haunts in the state capital, he told a Kiwanis luncheon: "I have returned to Tallahassee to represent the Florida Medical Association. Since they worked so hard to get me out of Washington and back to Tallahassee, they must want me to represent them."[2] It was hard to dislike a person who could treat himself with a dose of self-deprecating good humor.

Pepper still had some friends and supporters in the business community. Such prominent figures as Lou Wolfson, a well-connected Jacksonville industrialist and owner of the Washington Metro Transit System, and James Sattile, a Miami financier and banker, did not desert him. He had made a number of lasting friendships within the legal profession, including Charlie Murchison of Jacksonville, his Harvard classmate. With their help and his own legal abilities, he began to reestablish himself professionally. It was neither a quick nor an easy process. On several occasions, S. A. Lynch, the Miami businessman who had been both with and against Ed Ball in the FEC battle, and Pepper discussed having the former senator represent his interests in the continuing battle for control of the railroad. Nothing came of these conversations, nor did Lynch play a major role in the railroad proceedings thereafter. Pepper explored business contacts in Cuba to utilize the background and experience gained from his service on the Foreign Relations Committee. He also attempted to develop a business interest in railroad safety devices. In the process of rebuilding, he was often severely pressed financially.[3] It was a humiliating position for a man who had traveled in the highest circles of power for fourteen years. Nevertheless, he persevered, gradually restoring his personal situation. His diary entries over this trying interlude show both an admirable determination and a remarkable absence of self-pity.

In the difficult years following his defeat, the idea of returning to public service was never far from Pepper's thoughts. Once again, the idea of moving to New York to run for one of that state's Senate seats occurred to him. Not long after leaving office, he discussed with New York City's Cardinal Francis J. Spellman the possibility of moving to that liberal metropolis, where his political philosophy would be better received. The Catholic high churchman advised against it, and Pepper wondered if this was an indication that the Irish Catholics would oppose him.[4] For all of his considerable political acumen, Pepper often could not seem to grasp the obvious about his pro-Soviet positions. The persecution of the Catholic Church in Eastern Europe, epitomized by the imprisonment of the Hungarian Catholic prelate Josef Cardinal Mindszenty, had set the Catholic hierarchy against Russian communism and anyone remotely perceived as its supporter. Pepper dropped the idea of leaving his adopted state, and his thoughts returned to the Florida political scene.

As the end of George Smathers's first Senate term approached, Pepper considered his prospects for running against either Smathers or Holland. He discussed the matter with Bobby Baker, the Machiavellian assistant to Senator Lyndon B. Johnson of Texas. Baker told him that Johnson would probably raise money for him if he ran against Holland but would support Smathers should Pepper oppose the junior senator.[5]

By mid-decade, Pepper displayed a more realistic judgment of the political climate. When noted political columnist Walter Lippman opined that the top-three possible presidential candidates were Adlai Stevenson (governor of Illinois), Earl Warren (governor of California), and General Dwight D. Eisenhower, Pepper saw this as an unfavorable portent for his own aspirations. Lippmann construed it as indicating that America was settling into a mood of political moderation. A Gallup poll at the time showed six out of ten Americans wanted a middle-of-the-road president. This gave Pepper more to ponder about his far-left image, He wrote in his diary: "This gives me pause for its bearing upon my making a race. I cannot make myself a middle-of-the-roader in the public's mind even if I tried. Yet, I am not as bad as many think and not really very radical."[6]

With the retrospection afforded by the passage of time, that self-assessment had a ring of truthful objectivity about it. He was "not really very radical," but in politics, truthful objectivity and retrospection are not often active ingredients of crucial public perceptions. Wisely, he opted not to run against Smathers. Perhaps he remembered the words of Ed Ball at the Florida Industrial Council meeting five years earlier. Ball had told him, "Claude if you ever run for public office in Florida again we'll lick you so bad you'll think this time was a victory."[7] Still, the desire to return to public office burned intensely in him. Holland would be up for reelection in two years, and who could tell where Ball would be then? Of course, when the time came, Ball was exactly where Pepper must have known he would be—squarely behind Holland.

During the years when Pepper was rebuilding a law practice, Ed Ball continued expanding and consolidating the economic power of the vast duPont holdings. The number of banks in the Florida National group grew from twenty-two in 1950 to twenty-nine at the end of the decade, and in 1963 totaled thirty-one. In 1955, the Florida National group advertised itself as the "largest banking organization south of Philadelphia and east of the Mississippi."[8] The St. Joe Paper Company had grown into a paper-manufacturing conglomerate in its own right, owning and operating fourteen divisions with plants in cities from Baltimore to Houston. Eventually, manufacturing plants were acquired in foreign countries as well. The paper company also owned more than 1 million acres of land, all starting from the purchases initiated by Ball and W. T. Edwards in the depths of the depression at prices as low as $1.50 an acre. It owned the St. Joseph Telephone and Telegraph, and the Apalachicola Northern Railroad. Although relatively small companies, they had a monopoly on telephone and rail service in the heartland of the duPont west Florida holdings.[9] The Apalachicola Northern Railroad was the main transportation from the pulpwood forests of St. Joe Paper to its mill. The two companies were highly profitable elements in the interlocking network of the St. Joe Paper Company within the overall duPont business enterprises.

The number of banks under Ball's control does not adequately convey the economic power he wielded. To get a better sense of this, let us compare the extent of concentration of banking power in the nation overall to the concentration in Florida. At the national level in 1962, the single largest bank, or bank group, in the nation held 4.4 percent of the country's total deposits. The ten largest banking organizations held a combined total of 21.8 percent of the total, an average of 2.18 percent each. In Florida, the largest banking group, the Florida National banks, held 11 percent of the statewide deposits, almost five times the concentration of the largest bank group on a nationwide basis. Another measure of concentration is the ratio of population to banks. For the year 1962, that ratio was 7,498 people per bank nationwide, and 15,160 in Florida—more than double the national figure. The Florida ratio was greatly influenced by Ball's Florida National group. Taking into consideration the investment potential of the trust accounts of the Florida National banks, one economist estimated the pyramided assets subject to Ed Ball's control at over $2 billion at the end of 1962.[10] Today, in an era of megabillion-dollar combinations, that estimate may not seem unduly large. But in light of the fact that the duPont enterprises were all centered in Florida, all capitalized from the original duPont legacy of less than $40 million, it is truly impressive.

The increasing concentration of power in bank holding companies across the nation had prompted Congress to complete an agenda of banking reform left unfinished from the early days of the New Deal. The Banking Act of 1933 had taken the important step of divorcing investment banking from commercial banking, removing the nation's banking system from the temptations of speculative investments. It was one of the New Deal's hallmark pieces of regulatory reform legislation, but for a variety of political reasons, it did not deal with the looming problem of bank holding companies.[11] Banking chains were permitted to remain in common ownership with nonbanking concerns. Twenty-three years and a world war later, Congress was determined to close that avenue to concentration of economic power, and in 1956 it enacted major amendments to the banking law.

The new legislation effectively disentangled banking from common ownership with nonbanking enterprises. Stated simply, no longer could more than one bank be owned in common with—to use two pertinent examples—railroads and paper-manufacturing companies. But, as the complex legislation made its way through the legislative process, an exemption was carved out of the prohibition. If the proscribed common ownership was in a testamentary trust operated exclusively for charitable purposes, and "no part of the earnings of such inures to the benefit . . . of any individual," the prohibition was inapplicable.[12] The duPont Trust qualified for exemption from the divestiture provisions of the new legislation. As a practical matter, it was the only entity in the nation that was so favored. There were other exemptions, including one for multiple-bank ownership by labor unions, but the duPont Trust was the only entity of economic significance that qualified under the charitable trust exemption. That provision of the act had a strange history, one which was used nine years later as the centerpiece of a new strategy to defeat Ball's ownership of the Florida East Coast Railway. Then, it would figure in the intense struggle of the FEC nonoperating unions to force a labor contract on an unwilling Ball. The exemption had a history reflective of Ed Ball's shrewd use of the political power inherent in concentrations of economic power. To understand the events leading ultimately to repeal of the charitable trust exemption so crucial to the structure of the duPont empire over which Ball ruled, it is helpful to review how it came to be included in the original holding company legislation.

The 1956 Bank Holding Company Act was a major congressional statement of national economic policy. It was aimed primarily at the concentration of economic power inherent in the mixed ownership of banking and other business enterprises, an area of economic policy left unspoken in the original 1933 Banking Act. The Federal Reserve Board was the federal body having principal jurisdiction over the broader implications of economic policy. In 1955, it prepared the proposed bank holding company legislation and submitted it to the House and Senate banking committees. The proposed measure contained an exemption for charitable trusts circumscribed by very narrow conditions. This was not the first effort to fill the void left in the nation's 1933 banking law. In 1952, similar proposed legislation had also contained a "charitable" exemption, which was then recognized as benefiting primarily, if not exclusively, the Alfred I. duPont Testamentary Trust and its Florida banks.[13] The main proposal did not pass in 1952, and the duPont Trust's combination of banking and nonbanking businesses continued to thrive in concert. When the bill was reintroduced three years later, the same "charitable" exemption reappeared in the new draft of the proposed legislation. The recurrence of this specially focused exemption in the staff drafts of the proposed bill clearly indicated to those versed in the ways of the legislative process that it had been lobbied in the earliest stages of that process with considerable skill and influence.

Business entities seek to avoid regulatory legislation—that is, except when they actively seek it to protect a competitive advantage. Under Ed Ball's control, the duPont Trust, while legally structured and classified as a charitable institution, was in all practical respects a business operation. It was natural for Ball to seek to avoid the spreading regulatory net of the proposed Bank Holding Company Act, especially the divestiture provision which would unravel the concentration of economic power over which he presided. The ultimate charitable purpose of the duPont enterprises afforded what, if handled adroitly, could distinguish his group of banks from others facing the proposed regulatory jurisdiction.

No stranger to Washington politics, Ball was a friend of Senator A. Willis Robertson of Virginia, a ranking member of the Senate Banking and Currency Committee and the primary senatorial manager of the bank holding company bill. As discussed earlier, he was one of the "hunting guests" of Ed Ball who showed up at Tyndall Air Force base with three members of the joint chiefs of staff in 1962.[14]

Ball's relationship with Robertson is very interesting because eight years later the head of the duPont Trust denied any knowledge of how the exemption originally got into the legislation. He told the committee that neither he "nor . . . anyone connected with the duPont Estate" had appeared before the

House Banking Committee or any other committees seeking the exemption.[15] That statement may have been true, but explicit exemptions exclusively benefiting a narrow class or, as in this case, single entity do not simply appear in original drafts of proposed legislation without someone wanting them there. Sometimes they are inserted at the specific request of a congressman or senator, particularly one who is instrumental in managing the issue in tandem with the agency sponsoring the legislation. Robertson was in such a position, and the Federal Reserve, which prepared the banking legislation, probably agreed to the inclusion of the provision to solidify his support for it. The Virginia senator was to undergo a reversal of position in 1966 when the matter of the exemption came once again before the Senate. Then it was to be under circumstances far less favorable to Ball's interests.

The nature of the duPont exemption did not remain obscure during the course of debate on the 1956 Bank Holding Company Act, even though Robertson clearly intended that it should. The bill originated in the House, and when it was debated on the floor of that chamber, James A. Haley, a south Florida congressman, tried to obtain a similar exemption for another Florida company. Consolidated Naval Stores was primarily a land, turpentine, and citrus concern but also owned stock in two small banks as investments, not as operating assets. That was a highly relevant point in distinguishing the benign impact of the Consolidated Naval Stores' passive interest in two banks from the active impact of the Florida National chain in the concerted business operations of the duPont Trust. In the context of the problem at which the overall legislation was directed, the concentration of economic power personified by the empire over which Ball presided was clearly the primary object of the divestiture provision in the first place. Not wishing to open the door to a flood of similar exemption provisions, the measure's floor managers opposed Haley's amendment, and it failed by three votes. In his view, the Consolidated Naval Stores amendment was at least as justified as the duPont exemption, and he irately demanded to know the justification for the duPont exemption.[16] Of course, there was no response to that question on the House floor, but the answer was obvious for those experienced in the ways of the legislative process: Ball had the power to get the votes, and Consolidated Naval Stores did not.

The exemption phase was part of a much larger, complex policy debate on banking regulation. When the House manager for the legislation summarized the features of the bill in closing, he explained that the duPont exemption was based on the "irrevocable nature" of the charitable trust. He added that the Federal Reserve had not recommended inclusion of the duPont Trust under the divestiture provisions of the bill, and to do so might invalidate the whole act on constitutional grounds.[17] Of course these reasons would not stand close scrutiny, but in the larger context of the major issue, they were adequate to carry the exemption. Wary members could take refuge in the fact that the entity that would benefit from the provision was a "charitable" institution.

When the House bill reached the Senate, the specific nature of the duPont exemption had become a much-talked-about feature of the measure. Senator Robertson, as floor manager for the legislation, was responsible for explaining the bill to his fellow senators. He tried to avoid detailed discussion of the charitable trust exemption. His explanation of the innocent, generic-appearing charitable exemption was brief: "Religious and charitable organizations are exempted because the very nature of these organizations precludes the possibility of violating the spirit of this bill."[18] In the atmosphere engendered by prolonged debate over the numerous and complex issues in the legislation, that explanation of the charitable trust provision was only marginally accepted, implying that there remained much skepticism as to policy reasons for including the exemption in the legislation.

The attempt to wrap the duPont exemption in the sacrosanct mantle of a charitable exclusion was sufficient to carry the amendment, but it failed to satisfy certain reform-oriented senators—mostly Democrats—who were deeply committed to the fundamental purposes of the banking legislation. They were concerned that concentration of economic power was undesirable in and of itself. Their focus was not on how the concentrated wealth was intended to be utilized, but rather on how the acquisition of assets and their use in the generation of more wealth and monopoly power impaired the self-governing mechanisms of the competitive marketplace. They were focused on the economic policy considerations that lay at the heart of the proposed legislation, considerations which transcended the alleged charitable nature of institutions seeking to be exempted from it. To that end, they focused clearly on Ball and his concentration of economic power.

Senators Wayne Morse of Oregon, Paul Douglas of Illinois, and Homer Capehart of Indiana all bitterly opposed the duPont exemption. Capehart, a conservative Republican, submitted for the record most of Senator Patrick McCarran's earlier report from the Crummer investigation on the power of the duPont interests in Florida, and how that power was wielded by one individual—Ed Ball. He showed how the income of the giant trust went to

Jessie Ball duPont for her life, and only on her death did it become irrevo-
cably committed to the charitable purposes specified in Alfred's Last Will
and Testament. Even though Jessie Ball duPont assigned 12 percent of her
income from the trust to its charitable purposes, Capehart pointed to her as
the principal beneficiary instead of the crippled children and elderly. He
stated for the record: "The attempt of Senator Robertson to justify the
exclusion of the duPont trust, on that [charitable] basis . . . is completely
fallacious."[19]

Although this scathing indictment of duPont-Ball power was included in
the record, it was not actually part of the floor debate. Hence, during the
actual floor debate on the initial passage of the bill, the senators were not
treated to the full flavor of Ed Ball's ruthless power in Florida as reported by
Senator McCarran to the full Senate eight years earlier under circumstances
unrelated to bank holding company legislation. Then, the Senate had been
interested in Ball's power to destroy Roy E. Crummer's Florida bond business by manipulating state and federal investigative agencies.

The original measure passed in 1956, and President Eisenhower signed it
into law, but not before noting specifically the incongruity of the duPont and
other exemptions with the purposes of the new law. He urged that in the
future, Congress revisit those provisions and remove them from the act.[20]
There the issue rested quietly for eight years despite Eisenhower's admoni-
tion. The Florida National Bank group, the "largest banking organization"
south of Philadelphia and east of the Mississippi River, was exempt from the
divestiture provisions of the Bank Holding Company Act. The concerted
power of the duPont empire continued to grow in its multiple dimensions.
As the matter receded from what, relatively speaking, little public attention
it had captured, Senators Morse and Douglas did not forget the exemption
that gave the duPont Trust and Ed Ball a unique status in federal banking
law.

There was no evidence on the record from which to glean the roles, if any,
Florida's two senators, Smathers and Holland, played in the duPont exemption. They appeared and testified before the Senate committee in favor of the
Consolidated Naval Stores amendment, but unlike their House colleague
James Haley, they did not attack the duPont exemption on the floor after the
Consolidated amendment failed. In all probability, they favored the exemption but did not need to take a high profile in its passage since the matter was
well in hand with Robertson's actions. Given Ball's longtime relationship
with Holland and his well-known role in Smathers's election, the better

course of action was for the senators to avoid outward involvement and let a powerful non-Floridian oversee the matter through the process. Robertson nicely suited Ball's needs in that regard.

As floor manager of the measure, Robertson was certainly better positioned to accomplish the Jacksonville banker's purpose than either of the two Florida senators. As a senior committee member, he was far more capable of getting the necessary language embedded in the bill as it came out of committee. Smathers and Holland, or either of them, had they been the moving force, would have had to seek the amendment on the Senate floor, where they would have run up against the same situation that Haley confronted in the House. As a matter of legislative tactics, a major role by them would have called unwanted attention to the parochial nature of the provision. Robertson was in a position to "persuade" the Federal Reserve draftsmen to include the charitable exemption in the working drafts. Once it was in the final Federal Reserve draft, he was in an excellent position to keep it there during the legislative process of enactment. Sponsoring executive agencies often view such provisions as small prices to pay for achieving the larger purposes of regulatory legislation. Later, in the debate over repeal of the exemption, Robertson tried to justify his position by alluding to the necessity of the duPont and other exemptions in order to pass the original act.[21] In light of what came out in that debate regarding the circumstances of its original enactment, his explanations to his fellow senators were disingenuous, at best.

In 1956, Pepper had observed events from afar as a private citizen, and even though his thoughts on the matter can only be surmised, he had real reason to be interested. His longtime friend and client James Sattile of Miami knew Ball and was engaged in preliminary talks regarding buying the Florida National Bank group. Sattile consulted with Pepper on the various phases of the talks, which continued over the same period that both houses of Congress were dealing with the Bank Holding Company Act and the duPont exemption.[22] Ball must have been hedging on the outcome of the debate, trying to generate potential purchasers should the exemption effort fail. Pepper's diary entries hint strongly at his anticipatory pleasure of involvement with the Florida National Bank if his friend and client assumed ownership. When the exemption survived with passage of the legislation, all prospects of Ball divesting the duPont Trust of the banks ended—that is, for the time being. They were, after all, the center of the economic kingdom over which he presided. Circumstances could and did change regarding the exemption, and, ironically, that change emanated from Ball's victory in the FEC battle a few years later.

As the 1956 primary season approached, there were more important things on Pepper's mind than the Bank Holding Company Act amendments. He was in close contact with his old labor allies assessing possible courses of action. He assumed that Eisenhower would run for reelection and win, and with him would be the "insufferable Nixon."[23] That did not bode well for a liberal Democrat in a state that the president had previously carried by almost 100,000 votes. He reflected in his diary, "I shall have to start early for '58, or abandon the idea of the senate again," then added laconically, "I guess it would not be the same as in the old days."[24]

Shortly afterward he asked a friendly labor official, William Grogan, to speak to Smathers to determine where the junior Florida senator's support would be if Pepper were to run against Holland. Direct conversations along similar lines between the two former adversaries two years earlier had ended in acrimonious exchanges reported in the newspapers, and their mutual distrust had continued unabated.[25] This time, Grogan's report was encouraging. As remembered by Pepper, Smathers was pleased with the overture and wanted to forget the past. More important, the first-term senator was weak with labor and considered the matter an opportunity to improve his standing in regard to the union vote. Pepper was still distrustful of Smathers but felt "labor is [his] weakest front, and my strongest. If he double-crosses me, labor will be embittered against him in the future." Pepper added a parting observation to his entry: "Smathers can be taken care of later if he does not show himself worthy of confidence."[26]

When Pepper ran against Holland in 1958, the race made little impression on the state's political landscape. Holland, with a solid base of support in the business community, had little trouble financing his campaign. Pepper had to rely heavily on loans from friends, most, if not all, of which he later repaid by going into personal debt.[27] The desegregation rulings of the Supreme Court starting four years earlier had stirred the state's not-so-latent racism. That turn of events played straight to Holland's strengths and Pepper's weaknesses. It was not the sole determinative factor, but it emphasized the conservative-liberal paradigm that became the controlling dimension of southern politics for the rest of the century. Even though Ball was a strong Holland supporter, this campaign did not involve him or the duPont interests as openly as did the 1950 Smathers-Pepper race. Holland won handily with 408,084 votes to 321,377 for Pepper.

Shortly after, and unrelated to, the campaign, the Jacksonville federal court awarded ownership of the Florida East Coast Railway to St. Joe Paper Company, ending Ball's long quest for control of the railroad. Pepper wrote a congratulatory letter, including an expression of hope that Ball would operate the railroad in the state's best interests. Ball responded with an unusual measure of grace, acknowledging Pepper's congratulations and assuring the former senator that he would operate the railroad "to best serve our great state." Ball later shared the letter with his friend Holland, who told him, "I could never understand why he would get into that fight [with you], and I think it will haunt him for the rest of his life."[28] In the same exchange, Holland also thanked Ball for his strong support in the primary race against Pepper and looked forward to his continued support in the general election campaign just beginning. By 1958, Florida was no longer firmly a one-party state in which the Democratic primaries were automatically decisive. After the 1956 presidential race in which General Eisenhower carried the state for the Republican Party, general elections began to assume some importance in the state's political process.

Defeat in the 1958 Senate campaign against Holland effectively fore-closed any prospects for a successful statewide race by Pepper, but he did not forsake further political ambition. There were other political possibilities yet to materialize that would offer opportunities to a man of his capabilities and determination. The 1960 decennial census and the congressional reapportionment that followed opened a new avenue for Claude Pepper to return to public life. The state's phenomenal growth in the 1950s produced a greatly expanded population in south Florida, requiring a new congressional seat in Dade County. Congressional district constituencies were more compact and homogenous in political philosophy than the unwieldy and heterogeneous statewide electorate. The new Dade County district was suitably configured for a candidate like Claude Pepper. There was another important feature of a House seat: it was not nearly as costly to campaign for as a Senate seat. The realities of his situation dictated that he forsake the Senate but not necessarily the House.

The Third Congressional District was created by the state legislature to include parts of the city of Miami and sections in northern Dade County. Besides having a representative mix of Dade County's overall population, it contained a large portion of Miami's Jewish constituency, many retired union members from the Northeast, and a substantial part of Miami's black vote. It was a constituency where his liberalism could stand alone on its merits without being unduly burdened by his past views on Soviet-American relations. The Korean War (which started shortly after his 1950 primary defeat by Smathers) and hardening patterns of a near-permanent state of Cold War had shaken many liberals, including Pepper, from their benign views on the Soviet Union. The naked aggression of the North Koreans with the thinly veiled connivance of the Soviet Union and China had disabused Pepper of any lingering doubts about Soviet intentions. Prior to leaving the Senate, he had made floor speeches to that effect.[29] He had subsequently worked to detach himself from his past "soft" positions on communism, but in the prevailing atmosphere of 1962, he could not be sure that he had adequately distanced himself from his past. That question would be answered in the affirmative by the voters of the newly formed Third Congressional District.

Pepper's campaign for the House seat was of little interest to Ed Ball, who now was busy integrating the newly acquired Florida East Coast Railway into the duPont business empire. Pepper later heard that Ball told his business allies that he would not oppose Pepper so long as he did not seek to return to the Senate.[30]

In 1962, the year in which Ball was completing his acquisition of the Florida East Coast, there were four candidates for the Democratic nomination to the seat in the new Third Congressional District. One of them, W. C. "Cliff" Herrell, was a long-standing member of the state senate and generally associated with the Pork Chop power bloc that controlled that body. He was the leading contender and received the *Miami Herald* endorsement.[31] Some of Pepper's past reemerged but did not seem to seriously damage him in the campaign. He had found a niche in Florida's political landscape where his liberalism was not only acceptable but appreciated as well. In an unsuccessful effort to dim Pepper's appeal to Jewish voters, Herrell brought up the latter's effort to obtain relief for the wartime confiscation of property belonging to a German émigré. The charge had been aired and refuted in the 1950 campaign and had little impact on the congressional race.[32]

During the campaign, Pepper pledged full support for President John F. Kennedy's programs. Kennedy was the son of his old supporter and friend Joseph Kennedy of Boston, who, as ambassador to Great Britain, had introduced Pepper into the circles of power in England before World War II. Pepper claimed the endorsement of the young president based on a letter written before the current campaign in which Kennedy, then just elected, had "hoped" for Pepper's return to office. Herrell tried to degrade Pepper's claimed endorsement by the popular president, questioning how this could have been intended as an endorsement for Pepper's campaign since the Third District had not even existed at the time the letter was written.[33] Pepper may have stretched the point somewhat, but it was not out of line with generally acceptable campaign "puffing." The Kennedy White House declined to contradict him, which was taken as an implicit affirmation of Pepper's claim.

Pepper continued to hearken back to the New Deal and ironically added Truman's Fair Deal to it in his litany of what best served the public welfare. He remained steadfastly an unabashed partisan of the old-style liberalism.[34] To the surprise of most, except Pepper himself, he won a first-primary victory, even if only by fifty-nine votes. He had little trouble in defeating the Republican nominee, and the Third Congressional District became the core of a rock-solid political bastion for Claude Pepper for the remainder of his life. He never detached himself from the deeply ingrained liberalism that was the hallmark of his life and career. His tenacity in pursuit of the public welfare through government action was every bit as remarkable as Ed Ball's pursuit of economic power through the duPont charitable trust.

In one respect, the former senator and newly elected House member did change dramatically. He hardened his position on communism, especially in the Western Hemisphere, and particularly after Miami was engulfed with Cuban expatriates seeking refuge from Fidel Castro's Communist regime. To support this seeming contradiction to his earlier positions, he paid homage to the Monroe Doctrine as the basis of excluding communism from the Western Hemisphere.[35] By 1963, Pepper's previous foreign policy views had all but receded from the public consciousness. They were no longer the political millstone around his neck they had once been. He had become a "cold-warrior."

While Pepper was successfully reentering public life after a dozen years in political limbo, Ball was pulled into the most controversial segment of his controversial career: the Florida East Coast Railway strike. It never required very much "pulling" to get the crusty financier into a fight, and he was always willing to battle for what he believed to be the prerogatives of property rights. Just as liberalism was the polestar that guided Pepper's course of conduct, property rights were at the core of Ball's philosophy of political action. When Ball took control of the bankrupt railroad, he extended his concept of property rights to embrace its operations.

The Florida East Coast was a member of the National Railroad Conference. The nation's rail lines had established that organization to present a united front to the different unions that represented the various categories of trades and skills necessary to operate a railroad. The FEC was a very small company compared to the larger systems, which dominated the railroad industry and its national association. In the throes of the long-running battle for control of the FEC, its management had not been deeply involved in the collective bargaining process at the national level. In the 1950s, there was a certain complacency in railroad management regarding the rail unions' demands for higher wages. It was a period when organized labor was in the ascendancy, and America's railroad industry showed little inclination to vigorously contest wage demands. But there was no room in Ed Ball's scheme of management for complacency or acquiescence in the matter of wages and operating efficiency. That someone should dictate the terms of operation of one of his businesses was contrary to the very essence of his concept of property rights.

In September 1961, eleven nonoperating unions served notice on the National Railroad Conference of demands for certain work rule changes and a wage increase amounting to twenty-five cents an hour. (Nonoperating personnel were the employees not directly involved with the actual operation of the trains, including such jobs as telegraphers, clerks, and right-of-way maintenance employees.) In March 1962, a special emergency board established by President Kennedy under the Railway Labor Act recommended a wage increase of 10.28 cents an hour. The unions and 192 railroads accepted the recommendation, and a nationwide rail strike was averted. All this was at the national level, where the FEC situation was virtually indiscernible as a part of the whole. Yet for Ed Ball, it *was* the whole. He saw the FEC financial situation as unable to sustain the increase, and refused to be bound by the proposed national settlement. The FEC unions demanded that he accept it and would not agree to anything less. They had the full support of national labor organizations, their power enhanced by that unity which was the historical basis of union strength. It was almost inconceivable that the small FEC, still struggling to recover from almost thirty years of insolvency, could stand up to the collective might of the national rail unions, organized labor in general, and their allies in the federal government.

On January 23, 1962, 1,200 nonoperating FEC personnel went on strike, initiating what is thought to be the longest labor dispute in American history.[36] To maximize the pressure for quick settlement, the strike was timed for the period when the FEC traditionally hauled the lucrative Florida citrus harvest to national markets. It also coincided with the 1962 primary campaign season. Labor was always stronger when its actions were seen by political officials in the context of elections.

The unions had two related streams of logic that bolstered the steadfastness of their demands. These were grounded more in moral and equitable considerations than legal grounds. In the battle for public support in a labor-management battle, these are often tactically much more important than legal grounds. First, they believed the wage increase and terms negotiated at the national level were fairly won in the proper process of collective bargaining and were binding on the Florida East Coast as a member of the conference. In addition, the increase was further sanctioned by the presidential emergency board recommendation, which had reduced their wage demands by more than half. They thought their position represented a compromise arrived at through good-faith collective bargaining. Second—and more important emotionally and morally—the Florida union members felt Ball's intransigence was a grievous betrayal in light of their valuable support for him in the takeover battle with the ACL and Claude Pepper. Regardless of their arguments' moral or equitable merits, the union's legal position was not so strong. Ball was not bound to the national settlement.

As in all labor disputes, the underlying issue was economic, and Ed Ball made business decisions primarily for economic reasons and then stood on legalities to uphold them. Moral and equitable grounds were collateral to his primary decisional parameters. Ball framed the morality of an issue differently than did the social collectivist reasoning that cast labor and management as equals in the process of production. For him, it was immoral for others to seek to compel him to do with his property what he did not want to do, and was not legally obligated to do. It was the age-old conflict between the rights of the individual versus the collective rights of society—the grist on which turned the millstone of politics in the American democracy.

When Ball assumed control of the Florida East Coast, its work rules reflected the national norms for the industry. In the forefront of contention was the issue of "featherbedding." That was the term applied to the practice of requiring more men to perform required tasks than deemed necessary by management. For unions, it meant preservation of jobs, a near-sacred objective of organized labor. To management, it meant the burden of highly inefficient operating conditions needlessly cutting into profit margins. In the early 1960s, most railroad work standards were relics of a bygone era. They had been fashioned long before such technological advances as the widespread use of diesel locomotives fired by mechanical injection of liquid fuel. Unlike the older steam engines, the new ones needed no fireman to shovel coal into the combustion chamber. In 1950, the unions, to increase the number of jobs for their members, had tried to get a third fireman added to the standard crew because of additional diesel units being added.[37] The issue remained unresolved, and by the end of the decade, the retention of the unnecessary fireman's position was a major irritant in national rail labor negotiations. Unions defended the extra personnel as a safety feature, but management condemned the practice as "featherbedding." There the lines were drawn, and for a person of Ed Ball's temperament, only one option existed: he would fight. Given little credence by rail unions increasingly used to having their own way, Ball and the little FEC railroad stood alone.

Another work standard tied to earlier days set 100 miles as a "day's work" for a train crew. It derived from the period when a train was normally expected to make good a distance of approximately 100 miles a day. Newer, more powerful engines could achieve greater speeds and hence better distances in the same time. Under the old standard, an FEC train from Jacksonville to Miami required the wage-equivalent of slightly more than three crews, each consisting of five men and each paid a full day's wages. The first crew operated the train a distance of 97 miles to New Smyrna. The next crew operated to Fort Pierce, a distance of 124 miles, and received 1¼ days' wages, and the third crew took the train into Miami, receiving another 1¼ days' pay.[38] Thus, for something like ten hours of operation, fifteen men each received 3½ days' wages. For the unions, that was the norm, and if other railroads could do it, so could the Florida East Coast. That dimension of the work rules had not been an issue in the national negotiations, but the inefficiency of it was repugnant to Ball and he made it a cardinal point in his position.

Ball knew that the FEC could not afford the pre-strike operating costs in competition with truckers (the beneficiaries of the new Interstate Highway system, one route of which paralleled the FEC track). Coastal seaborne transportation, which also paralleled the railroad's line of service, was another competitive factor that influenced Ball's insistence on reducing operating costs. His strategy was to refuse the wage increases and, with the reopening of the negotiations focused exclusively on the FEC, to attack the whole issue of featherbedding, going even beyond the issue of firemen's positions.[39] There was no mistaking his real purpose: Ed Ball was intent on breaking the union's control of operating conditions on his recently acquired railroad. For the unions, this was unheard of and totally unacceptable, a challenge to the fundamental rights of labor and the dignity of the working man. In their perspective, it was the height of arrogance and tyrannical power exercised through the medium of a billion-dollar "charitable" trust in defiance of the federal government's power and the rule of law.

The union view had some currency in the political arena, but as is inevitably the case, there were persuasive elements of truth on both sides. In the early 1960s, organized labor possessed substantial political power. Unions were strong, and with their national solidarity, wielded their power using sophisticated political techniques. Each union had skilled and well-funded lawyers and lobbyists in Washington, and they were major players in the political arena. In the era before corporate political action committees, labor was the biggest single source of political action committee contributions, mainly to the Democratic Party. Speaking for large and highly disciplined blocks of voters, the voices of labor representatives were listened to in the halls of power at both state and federal levels.

Ball was likewise not without the means to implement his intentions. After being closed down for less than a week, the FEC resumed operations with hastily assembled crews of office personnel and newly hired employees. Much to the surprise of everyone, the FEC resumption of operations went relatively smoothly, confounding the expectations of the unions. A week after the strike commenced, Ball was using one four-man crew for the eight-hour run from Jacksonville to Miami with time-and-a-half for overtime.[40] Reduction in workforce was not known then as downsizing or cost cutting; it was called union busting, and in the political climate of the period, it generated great controversy.

There were other political considerations that had an impact on the situation. The Florida East Coast served the newly established Space Center at Cape Canaveral, where vast national resources were being marshaled to launch the U.S. space program. Following the Soviet Union's initiation of the space age, President John F. Kennedy had vowed that the United States would be the first country to put a man on the moon. The race to the moon was on, and progress in building the Space Port at the cape was the visible embodiment of that commitment. The FEC was in the process of building a spur track to serve the huge construction projects then getting under way there. The possibility of the railroad's labor dispute spilling over to the thousands of construction workers inside the complex was a serious threat to the space program's timetable. That sharpened the Democratic adminis-tration's normal bias toward organized labor, energizing the various sources of extralegal pressure that could be brought to bear by the federal govern-ment.

A specially convened presidential board of inquiry found that Ball's rail-road should accept Secretary of Labor Willard Wirtz's recommendation of the national settlement. To add force to its conclusion, it said that all federal contracting agencies should cease using the FEC until it agreed to the settle-ment. It meant that Ball would have accepted the unions' full national pack-age. He refused. The Postal Service and the military then instituted an em-bargo on use of the FEC as part of the mounting pressure. Nevertheless, the National Aeronautics and Space Administration (NASA), acutely conscious of its timetable in the space race with the Soviets and the president's pledge to be first on the moon, continued to use the railroad. For the railroad, the additional business from the Space Center was essential to Ball's strategic plan to turn the FEC into a profitable component of the duPont enterprises.[41]

As the railroad progressed to normal operations with a reduced labor force, not only did the striking union members sense a deep-seated frustra-tion over denial of the wage increase, but they also faced the distinct possi-bility of losing their jobs. Ball had let it be known that he would not displace nonunion workers hired during the strike. To the strikers' rising level of irritation was now added a bitterness born of fear of becoming unemployed. For them, the threat was real and imminent. The railroad men were both proud of and dependent on the economic security embodied in their employ-ment. To them, their job was in the nature of a property right, much like what Ball cherished as his own property rights in the railroad, and all other assets of the duPont Trust under his control.

The strikers' self-concept was bound up by the twin sentiments of pride and self-respect, the fundamental legacy of the American labor movement to the working class. Their jobs were the key to their, and their families', health, happiness, and material well-being, and the union was the guarantor of all this. There was an intensely personal dimension about the strike, a dimen-sion not easily articulated, but nevertheless very real in the scheme of things. The threat posed by Ed Ball's management of the railroad evoked a grim determination in the union men and their allies. As the strike settled into what seemed a hopeless stalemate, fear and frustration began to cloud what-ever framework of logic governed such matters. The threat to their welfare was personified in Ed Ball, and he assumed demonic proportions for the striking workers.

In such an atmosphere, the individual's judgment and sense of fair play can be subsumed by the frustration and fear of the group. A sense of collective justification can be conjured up for actions not otherwise tolerated under perceptions of less threatening circumstances. Within this psychological framework, the strikers responded to their worsening position by resorting to violence in an effort to bring the railroad to submission.

But their action had the opposite effect. Ball now considered himself and his railroad to be the victims of mob violence, always the arch-demon to any notion of classical property rights. Moreover, he believed that he and his property were deprived of the protective agency of governmental enforcement of the laws because of union political power. This view contained elements of truth and was well received in the conservative atmosphere of Florida politics. Local police and federal agents did pursue the perpetrators of the violence, but with little effective consequences.

The violence started on February 26, 1963, when a fourteen-inch piece of rail and two pieces of "tie-plates" were jammed into a "frog," a part of a standard track switching mechanism. It was a deliberate act intended to cause a derailment. Fifteen months later, there had been 269 more incidents, including random shootings into trains, dynamiting of tracks and other facilities, and assaults on the railroad's working employees.[42] Ball later submitted these figures to a congressional committee conducting hearings on proposals to remove the duPont exemption from the Bank Holding Company Act as an offshoot of the strike. They were not refuted, and in the end, there were almost 300 such episodes. Six union members were implicated and charged in different episodes, and some convictions were obtained, but they were later reversed on appeal.[43] The union helped raise funds for the defense of those charged.[44] All in all, the number of individuals involved was small, but that the unions condoned the illegal acts was unmistakable.

The atmosphere at company facilities and on picket lines became extremely hostile, and the threat of violence along the company tracks was pervasive. Ball terminated daily passenger service between Jacksonville and Miami, a service mandated by a state statute that had originally granted incentives to Henry Flagler for building the railroad. This activated the jurisdiction of the Florida Railroad and Public Utilities Commission, the state agency charged with regulating railroads, and it ordered the FEC to resume the service. Ball initially refused but later bowed to the commission mandate and resumed operation of the passenger service after exhausting all appellate remedies. The order to operate the daily trains was more than a symbolic victory for the unions. It was an added expense without any reasonable expectation of increased revenues because there were virtually no passengers on the trains. They had been scared off by notices—posted in terminals by the FEC management—warning of possible violence due to the strike.[45] These notices were an attempt to gain public support by showing that government power was being used to compel the FEC to operate under unsafe conditions caused by the strikers. At the same time, airline travel was coming into its own, materially reducing passenger train profitability. The Jacksonville-to-Miami passenger route had not been profitable for some time, and Ball eagerly seized on the strike to facilitate a way out of the legal obligation to run the unprofitable daily passenger service along the state's east coast.

The union maintained, without any convincing proof, that Ball himself instigated the violence in an effort to discredit the striking unions.[46] Without question, the strike generated a highly charged atmosphere, even more so than most other labor disputes of the era. The strikers' anger over Ball's refusal to accept the national wage increase was further inflamed by what to them was clearly a betrayal by Ball after their strong effort on his behalf in the struggle for control of the railroad. This, coupled with the real prospect of losing their jobs to "scabs," created a situation fraught with prospects of violence.

Claude Pepper had watched the unfolding drama of the strike with great interest, but also with a reasoned detachment. When the dispute started, his chief concern was getting elected as a congressman from Miami's Third Congressional District, and he kept his distance from the politics of the strike.

As the strike continued, the unions cast about for a strategy that would weaken Ball's position. In their view, the entire duPont Trust business complex was their enemy. The whole thing was held together by the the charitable trust exemption. That provision of the Bank Holding Company Act had existed in relative obscurity since its enactment seven years earlier, but it did not take the labor strategists long to determine that the exemption was the weak link in the duPont empire.

Without the exemption, the duPont Trust would have to divest itself of either the Florida National Bank group or all the other enterprises, including of course the Florida East Coast Railway. The bank group was Ball's favorite part of the far-flung empire over which he presided. By nature and disposition, he was much more inclined to the world of financial dealings than to the less spectacular realms of manufacturing and transportation.[47] There was no question that the banks were the foundation of the economic power that he cherished. Union strategists assumed that Ball would opt to divest the trust of the nonbanking enterprises. Then the unions could deal with a new, more pliant FEC management. There was something of a gamble in such an assumption, but from the unions' perspective, a disappointing outcome could be no worse than the status quo of the strike.

The union strategists recalled that when the original 1956 law was passed, the exemption had attracted opposition from several members of the Senate and House, particularly Senators Wayne Morse of Oregon and Paul Douglas of Illinois, along with Representative Wright Patman of Texas. These men were liberal, pro-labor, and Democrats. Their political affinities lay naturally with organized labor, especially when pitted against the likes of Ed Ball. With some prodding by union officials, Morse and Douglas got involved in the effort to repeal the exemption.

All in all, it was a very well thought out strategy by the unions. To determined labor leaders, the implementation of such a strategy in the political arena was what representative government was really all about. Such an attitude was no different from the attitude that produced the charitable trust exemption in the first place. It all has to do with purpose, power, and politics.

That the unions initiated the movement to amend the act is indicated by the 1965 testimony of the vice chairman of the Federal Reserve Board before the House Committee on Banking and Currency. When asked by a House committee member if he knew what had prompted the proposed amendments, he answered, "I had understood that the strike on the railway controlled by the duPont Estate had stirred up some interest in the matter on the part of union officers," adding, "but there again, I am giving you second hand information."[48] There was little doubt as to the accuracy of what he told the committee. Just as the exemption did not appear in the first instance without someone in 1956 wanting it very badly, the effort to repeal it in 1965 required some special interest to energize congressional action in that direction.

Senator Wayne Morse did not need much prodding. A fiery liberal with strong ties to organized labor, he had a good memory of how the exemption had come about in the first place. He became the champion of repeal. Beginning in early February of 1964, he took the Senate floor several times to lecture his colleagues on the evils of the duPont power wielded by Ed Ball in Florida. Such monologues on the Senate floor are not generally well listened to, but Morse was persistent and in time held the attention of his fellow senators. He conjured up vivid images of Ball defying the government and running roughshod over the provisions of the Railway Labor Act. He castigated the head of NASA for refusing to prohibit the FEC from operating its trains in the Space Center, all the while ignoring the fact there was a valid contract calling for such operation.[49] A week after his first floor speech on the matter, the Oregon senator continued in the same vein. He reminded the Senate that Ball's great combination of power, by which he defied those who crossed him, was the result of the Congress not having grasped what it was told in 1956 about the duPont Trust and its master, Ed Ball.[50]

Pepper and Wayne Morse were close friends and kindred liberals in their political philosophies.[51] It would be tempting to assume that Morse was taking up Pepper's battle with Ball, and there may have been trappings of friendship involved. Still, the evidence points to Morse's acting more out of a conviction that the exemption should never have been enacted in the first place, a conviction strengthened by the railway unions lobbying for the repeal.

The only public figure in Florida publicly urging curtailment of the duPont-Ball power was Mayor Robert King High of Miami, then a candidate for governor. He worked closely with the unions in lobbying the question in Washington and repeatedly attacked the FEC and Ball for being disdainful of the public welfare and safety in operating the railroad.[52] Even though Pepper carefully refrained from playing a prominent role in the developing fight, it must have been gratifying to him to find his old Senate colleagues Wayne Morse and Paul Douglas in hot pursuit of Ball's special position under the Bank Holding Company Act.

Pepper entered the fray after his election to the House, but he played a relatively minor role compared to Morse and Representative Wright Patman, a Texan and old friend of his from New Deal days.[53] He met with representatives of the FEC unions in August of his first year in the House. They apologetically told him how wrong they had been to oppose him in 1950, and he offered to help on nationwide rail legislation but held back from volunteering his assistance on the duPont-specific legislation.[54] It was puzzling behavior for the man who was always outspoken in his views and so direct in his action to implement them. It may have been a newfound sense of discretion after a dozen years out of office. Or he may have relished the contrite attitude of the union men and wanted to maximize the political indebtedness it implied by prolonging their discomfort a little longer. In any event, Pepper was made a member of the House Banking and Currency

Committee, which was chaired by Patman, his old friend. He could not avoid the issue as that was the committee of jurisdiction over amendments to the Bank Holding Company Act. It is possible that he requested that assignment to be close to the repeal effort, but there is no explicit evidence to that effect. Certainly, he did not turn down the assignment so as to distance himself from the dispute. Pepper was a political warhorse. While naturally wary of Ball, and perhaps still chagrined with the unions for their role in the FEC takeover battle, he could not resist at least getting close to the smell of battle where Ed Ball was involved.

While Morse was prodding the Senate into awareness of the FEC labor dispute and Ball steadfastly refused to accede to government efforts to settle the strike, the situation was gaining national notoriety.[55] Ball's tough stand against the unions and their allies in government appealed to certain segments of the public. Many agreed with the general thrust of J. Richard Elliott's article about the controversy, "Road from Serfdom," with its Ayn Rand theme of defying big government's intrusion on individual rights. The featherbedding issue contributed to a growing negative image of unionism, not just in Florida but across the nation.[56] Ball and his associates missed no opportunities to emphasize the senseless use of three five-man crews to do what they now had a single crew of four doing in less time and far more efficiently.

While federal officials, including the assistant secretary of labor responsible for administering the Railway Labor Act, were trying to force Ball to accept the national settlement, state officials, mostly Ball supporters under normal circumstances, were viewed as reluctant to take action. (The Railroad and Public Utilities Commission was the only exception.) In fact, in almost all aspects of labor disputes, state authorities had been preempted by federal legislation from meaningful state action other than in the area of law enforcement. Even in that realm, federal law gave the Federal Bureau of Investigation the dominant position in investigation of the violence that had occurred in facilities involved in interstate commerce. Still, the state was taken to task in some liberal quarters for tolerating Ed Ball's unbridled political power. Robert Sherrill, the same author who took such a critical view of George Smathers's campaign against Pepper, thought state officials were either derelict in their duty or corrupt for not bringing Ball to heel.[57]

For Ball, the unions' tactic of congressional repeal of the exemption was no more than big government teaming with its own special interest supporters to destroy private initiative and individual rights. It was just another episode in his ongoing battle to protect the duPont legacy left to his care. He was not going to let his exemption from the Bank Holding Company Act's divestiture provisions be repealed without a fight, any more than he intended to let the unions impose their collective will on the operation of his railroad.

That quality of Ed Ball's character was seen by many in the context of the strike as strength of conviction that individual property rights were the bedrock of American democracy. The unions and their allies saw it as an arrogant display of tyrannical power fueled by the almost unlimited duPont resources at the disposal of a single arbitrary individual. To them, this concentration of power was made possible by a provision of law highly suspect

11. Ed Ball at the height of his battle with Claude Pepper and the Atlantic Coast Line Railroad for control of the Florida East Coast Railway.

12. Ed Ball, his sister, Jessie Ball duPont, and Roger Main, a longtime executive of the Florida National Bank and a principal lieutenant of Ed Ball, at the time of Ball's victory in the battle over the Florida East Coast Railway.

in its origins, and totally unjustifiable given the underlying rationale of the Bank Holding Company Act.[58] The concentration of economic power in the duPont empire was a clear example of the myriad evils that the Bank Holding Company Act was passed to prevent. That was the linchpin of the unions' ironically successful strategy.

Two fundamental facts about the repeal of the duPont exemption emerge from the congressional debate on the matter. First, in terms of economic policy considerations, there was no logical basis in the first place for the exemption in the 1956 act. It was clearly a special interest exemption that, for one favored entity, short-circuited the clear purpose of the act. Second, after seven years of operation, there had been no effort to repeal it until the unions made it the centerpiece of their strategy to fight Ball in the FEC strike. Without union involvement, the exemption would most likely have remained unobtrusively on the books. It was a vivid illustration of the dynamics of special interests driving the legislative process, very much the same as when the duPont exemption was placed in the original Bank Holding Company Act. The matter evolved into single-purpose legislation focused on an economic dispute between two powerful parties, Ed Ball and the unions. The unions, in the name of curtailing Ball's alleged despotism, used their own considerable political power to enlist the might of the U.S. Congress in their support. In the partisan nature of congressional proceedings, Democrats aligned mostly with the unions, and Republicans supported Ball. Still, there was considerable crossing of party lines as the dispute made its way through the legislative process.

The repeal was initially taken up by the House Committee on Banking and Currency in April 1964 under the chairmanship of Representative Wright Patman of Texas. He was the main House proponent of eliminating the exemption. Mayor Robert King High of Miami, embroiled at the time in a bitter primary battle for the Democratic gubernatorial nomination with Mayor Haydon Burns of Jacksonville, was the first witness. Appearing at his own request and expense, the mayor testified to the effect that Ball—a known Burns supporter—was a malignant political force in Florida. He accused the duPont Trust of thwarting his city's efforts to build two main traffic arteries by refusing to accept a ground elevation route through the FEC switching yards. High ignored the fact that the city or state Road Department could have condemned as much of the property as needed upon payment of proper compensation for the taking. The essence of his complaint was that Ball was thwarting the public interest because he would not agree to the city's proposal. He also indicted the FEC for not installing signals at many of its crossings. He accused the duPont Trust of not paying proper state intangible taxes and of impeding the collection of other local tax levies. The intangible tax charge was subsequently validated when St. Joe Paper Company delivered over $153,000 in back taxes due on undervalued intangible properties (the securities alluded to by High).[59] Still, High's main concern was the fifteen-month-old strike and its negative effects on Miami's tourist business and overall economy. All of these, he pointedly advised the committee, were the result of the pervasive power and economic might of Ed Ball, which could be brought under control only if the exemption were repealed.[60]

While the unions were the immediate beneficiaries of his testimony, High's real intention was to create the impression that his opponent for the gubernatorial nomination, Haydon Burns of Jacksonville, was tarnished by association with Ed Ball. It was part of the inter-regional political competition that has always been part of the Florida political scene.

Legendary labor leader George Meany, whose name garnered far more attention from Congress than Ed Ball ever could, submitted a lengthy state-ment urging the breakup of the duPont Trust.[61]

Leon Keyserling, a noted economist and former economic adviser to President Harry Truman, appeared as a paid expert witness for the Railway Labor Executives Association. His testimony made a convincing case on policy grounds for including the Florida National Bank group under the full range of the Bank Holding Company Act's provisions. He testified that the concentrated power of the bank group in conjunction with the other duPont enterprises was precisely what the original framers of the act intended to curtail. The fact that proceeds from the trust's assets ultimately went to charity did not obviate the inherent dangers of the concentrated economic power utilized in the acquisition of those assets.[62] In effect, he was elaborat-ing the fallacy in Senator Robertson's 1956 explanation to the Senate that "the very nature of [charitable] organizations precludes the possibility of violating the spirit of the act." More telling than his policy reasoning was Keyserling's reference to "misrepresentations of fact" regarding the chari-table nature of the trust made at the time of its enactment.[63] Here, the thrust of his testimony shifted from economic policy to Ball as a person, which was what it was all about in the first place. Misrepresentation in explaining legislation is taken as a grievous offense—when exposed. That revelation, more than any other feature of the prolonged debate, played into the unions' hands, eventually dooming the exemption.[64]

To counter what the unions produced, Ball appeared before the commit-tee the following month. He was combative from the outset, even question-ing the bona fides and methods by which the chairman had requested him to testify. The crusty financier was especially irate over Senator William Proxmire's allegations that the duPont Trust had avoided payment of income taxes, inferring that the whole gamut of duPont enterprises as well as Jessie Ball duPont, as beneficiary of the trust, had escaped payment of legitimate taxes. Those charges were grounded in clever half-truths. Ball produced canceled checks and other irrefutable evidence to show that the trust-owned businesses had paid taxes the same as any others, and that Jessie Ball duPont had paid income tax on the full measure of taxable income she received from the trust. Proxmire had tried to convey the impression that all income related to the duPont interests escaped taxation. Ball's testimony exposed the fallacy in that by showing income taxes were paid on money that went into the trust, as well as the money that went to his sister from it.[65] Still, the trust itself was not a taxable entity because of its ultimate status as a charitable body under the Internal Revenue Code, a body of law not under consideration in the debate. Proxmire knew that but chose to intimate to the contrary to cast Ball in the worst light possible.

In the House Banking and Currency Committee, Chairman Patman focused on the idea that the whole duPont empire escaped taxes because the Nemours Foundation was tax exempt as a charitable institution. Patman distorted the real facts, as Ball had already shown. Undaunted by the power of the chairman, Ball referred to his allegations as "amazing" but "not true or correct." It was strong language with which to address a committee chairman to his face, particularly one of the caliber of Patman. Republican member Burt L. Talcott of California joined with Ball in challenging the veracity of the chairman's insinuations.[66] When the question of removing the exemption for all trusts with assets over $100 million was discussed, Republican William E. Brock of Tennessee noted that such a provision would leave a similar, but smaller, trust established by Lyndon B. Johnson exempt. He pointedly inquired of a friendly interlocutor if there was a basis for such distinction, and the negative reply was quick and strictly along partisan lines.[67]

In spite of his heated defense of the exemption, Ball could not present a rational policy basis for it when asked if he could justify the existing provision. He lamely maintained that it had been the will of Congress in 1956, and he only complied with its terms. He insisted that neither he nor any other duPont representative had testified for the exemption.[68] That was clearly disingenuous even if literally true.

Ball's main line of defense, however, was to discredit his enemies. He set out to show that the repeal of the exemption was nothing more than special interest legislation fostered by organized labor with the aid of its liberal, mostly Democratic congressional allies. Since the unions made no effort to conceal their role, his point was easily made. Still, that revelation did not impede the growing momentum for repeal. To counter the union charges that the combined power and might of the duPont empire should be broken up, he showed that numerous unions had assets and receipts in the millions of dollars on which no taxes were paid. In Ball's line of reasoning, these represented privileged concentrations of power similar to that charge against him.[69]

His arguments had little or no impact on the unions' supporters in the Democratic majority. Ball could not obfuscate the growing realization that the duPont Trust charitable exemption was glaringly inconsistent with the manifest purposes of the Bank Holding Company Act. Such a realization followed easily from the unions' portrayal of Ball as an arrogant despot using an economic empire, held together by specially favored status under federal law, to dominate the business and political life of nearly an entire state.

In the course of the long hearings, Pepper questioned Ball only briefly, and without apparent rancor. He prefaced that questioning by disclaiming any role in introducing the bill, and said he had only heard of it for the first time when it was filed. Pepper's line of questioning was vaguely directed at the wording of the exemption and the fact that the trustees could exercise virtually total discretion in how they utilized the income and assets of the trust. His point was that they could keep building the trust corpus without ever putting appreciable amounts into projects designed to fulfill the broadly described charitable purposes.[70] His questioning, though brief and free of any apparent rancor, reaffirmed a telling point: Ball, with the other trustees, had almost unbridled discretion in utilizing the vast income from the various duPont enterprises. They were free to keep building the economic power of the duPont Trust without any material vesting of the proceeds in its charitable purpose. The unions made clear that economic power of the trust was being used to destroy the jobs and rights of their members. Even though Pepper had not overtly attacked Ball, his view of him continued to be highly negative. He wrote in his diary that "Ed Ball the witness . . . [was] cocky, testy, persistent and able in his presentations, though he showed he belonged to a by-gone age in his attitude and point of view."[71] There was a subtle irony to Pepper's observation that Ball "belonged to a by-gone age" in view of his own transition to a new set of political realities.

When the matter reached the house floor, the issue was confused when the question was raised of repealing all the exemptions in the Bank Holding Company Act, not just the duPont provision. This was seen as an effort to defeat the narrower repealer favored by the unions by aggregating other special interests in opposition to the wider measure.[72]

The sponsor of the broadening amendment was Representative Charles E. Bennett of Jacksonville, home of Ed Ball and the duPont empire. He had talked with Ball about the matter over breakfast on the financier's seventy-fifth birthday two years earlier, and Ball had told him that his primary objection was the legislation's single-purpose thrust. If all exemptions were removed, and the duPont Trust not singled out, Ball said he would have no objection to the bill.[73] Bennett acknowledged that some people assumed he was trying to defeat the provision by adding the controversial amendment, but added that he would vote for the bill even if his proposal failed. Although Pepper voted for Bennett's amendment, he thought it was a victory for Ball. He noted in his diary after the vote, "Another Ed Ball victory as he observed it from the gallery because he favored all exemptions being removed thinking that would defeat the bill to eliminate his [exemption]."[74]

The entire Florida House delegation present voted with Bennett, and the broadened version passed by a twenty-one-vote margin.[75] There was a superficial element of fairness that was persuasive in Ball's contention that all exemptions should be removed, and that is how the House sent the bill to the Senate. As Pepper well understood, the Jacksonville financier's purpose was not to add symmetrical consistency to the act. It was to widen the scope of opposition by expanding the range of exemptions to be foreclosed, including one that benefited a union-owned banking concern. Even if he lost, his contentious disposition would be placated somewhat by taking his enemies down with him. In the final analysis, that is not what happened.

Senator Morse opened the Senate committee hearing with a frank reference to the FEC strike as his motivating purpose in proposing repeal of the exemption. For him, Ball's ability to withstand the strike was due to the unreasonable concentration of economic resources he was permitted under the exemption. He also stated that the Senate committee had previously been misled as to the true nature of the duPont Trust: since the income went to Jessie Ball duPont during her life, it was not the charitable trust portrayed to the committee when the bill was originally enacted ten years earlier.[76] The unmistakable tenor of his testimony was that Ball had lied when the original bill was being considered. He left unclear to whom Ball had lied, affording some room for Senator Robertson to explain away his earlier support for the provision.

The attacks on Ball and the economic power of the duPont interests continued when the House bill reached the upper chamber. Robert King High appeared before the Senate committee and once again portrayed Ball as wielding controlling and evil power over Florida's political and economic fortunes. Spessard Holland, openly defending his friend, countered that Ball and the duPont influence in Florida had a positive impact on the well-being of the state. He presented a statement from former governor Millard Caldwell to the same effect and introduced former Florida banking commissioner Clarence M. Gay, who gave testimony in support of Ball.

Still, the details of the duPont Trust, with Jessie Ball duPont as the primary beneficiary during her life, were well known in 1956 to both House and Senate. In light of this, it is doubtful that the House and Senate were materially deceived at the time of the bill's original passage. The better explanation is that a majority in both houses knew what they were doing and decided that the exemption was simply part of the overall price of getting the legislation passed. The future charitable dimension of the trust afforded a facade of justification. Senators Morse and Douglas never accepted that line of thought, and now they had a second opportunity to convince their colleagues of the correctness of their view.

When the repealer measure reached the full Senate for consideration, Senator Robertson of Virginia was the floor manager for the proposed amendment. His new position on the duPont Trust was diametrically opposed to his stand in 1956, when he had assured the Senate that the charitable nature of the duPont Trust was ample safeguard for the public interest. Ten years later, he was in an awkward position. His role in passing the original exemption and his defense of the duPont Trust as a charitable entity implied complicity in deceiving his Senate colleagues. In the clublike atmosphere of the Senate, such a transgression was never directly discussed, but a veiled inference of it pervaded the Senate proceedings. Under the circumstances, Robertson's ardor for closing the duPont exemption was perhaps intended as a measure of self-expiation from such inferences. Robertson was also engaged in a heated primary battle in which he received the assistance of the rail unions as a result of his efforts in closing the duPont exemption.[77] (He later lost the nomination, but not because of the holding company issue over the duPont Trust.) When Holland stated the proposal was clearly discriminatory against the duPont Trust, Robertson candidly replied, "I do not challenge that statement at all."[78]

After confusing debate on the range of possible exemptions, the Senate voted to amend the repealer regarding testamentary trusts to embrace only the duPont Trust. Even so, it was not truly a "single-purpose" piece of legislation as contended by Ball and its opponents. A large investment company, Financial General Corporation, also lost its exemption as a registered investment company. It is unlikely that its status would have come under scrutiny if Ball had not energized the unions to action on the duPont exemption as a result of the strike. The company was—if such a thing is possible—an innocent victim of political warfare. Such are the vicissitudes of democracy. The House concurred in the Senate amendment. Under the new law, the duPont Trust was given five years to divest itself of either the Florida National Bank group or its nonbanking holdings. Conspicuously, the exemption for multiple-bank ownerships by labor unions was left intact.

It appeared to be a clear victory for the unions on the assumption that Ball would opt to retain the banks and sell the other enterprises, including the Florida East Coast Railway. Such a conclusion, while logical, did not accurately gauge Ball's tenacious sense of principle or, it might be said, his orneriness. His first recourse was to seek an amendment to state law to permit branch banking. Under such an arrangement, it was supposed that he could convert the Florida National banks into a single entity with numerous branches not subject to the Bank Holding Company Act. Failing in that effort, he opted to keep the railroad and other nonbanking holdings, divesting the trust instead of the Florida National Bank holdings. The unions had won the battle and lost the war. But Ball had not won either.

The core of the economic power at the command of the Jacksonville financier had been cut out of the combined might of the duPont empire. Even so, the divestiture of bank control was not quickly accomplished. Not until eleven years after the repeal of the exemption did the Federal Reserve order the final disposition of Florida National stock then remaining under control of Ball and the trust. By then, Ball was faced with complex and strong challenges to his unilateral control from within the small inner circle of the trustees. Still, he retained personal ownership of 10.34 percent of the bank stock and controlled another 5.6 percent reposing in the estate of Jessie Ball duPont, his deceased sister. There was widespread speculation within circles close to the internal affairs of the trust that Ball still exercised persuasive power over the affairs of the giant banking combine.[79] While he could not control the myriad resources of the duPont empire in concert as he once did, Ball was still a formidable force in economic and political affairs in the state. Only when he died in 1981 at ninety-three years of age were the reins of power over the vast duPont business empire completely wrested from his solitary grip.

Claude Pepper continued to serve as congressman from Miami until his death, achieving national prominence as the unofficial custodian of the Social Security program, the primary social welfare legacy from Franklin Roosevelt's New Deal. His became the voice of a new and growing force in politics: the aging sector of the population. After Pepper returned to Washington in 1964, six more presidents would pay attention to his views regarding the welfare of older Americans. The seeming permanency of the Cold

War and the staunch anticommunism of a growing Cuban expatriate population continued to moderate his views on the Soviet Union, and little of his image as the post-war radical remained, though he never abandoned his basic liberalism.

Through the process of seniority, Pepper ascended to the chairmanship of the House Rules Committee. Ironically, he had to be prevailed upon by members of the Florida business community to accept that position. His reluctance stemmed from the fact that it entailed giving up his place as chairman of the House Select Committee on Aging, a position he greatly cherished. The Rules Committee chairmanship was a position of immense power in the nation's legislative process, one from which Florida business interests could and did receive powerful backing from him in the never-ending political battle for competitive advantage in the marketplace.

The juxtaposition of the careers and characters of Ed Ball and Claude Pepper in this account of Florida politics is not intended to provide a moral or philosophical judgment of their roles in Florida political history. Rather, it is to illustrate through them the pursuit of individual interests and ambitions as a central dynamic in the energizing force of American politics. The focus has been on the combined input of individual purpose and ambition that fuels the process rather than a philosophical evaluation of its output. Too often, such input is relegated to nothing more than pejorative consideration as "special interests," inferring that it should somehow be purged from the process in pursuit of a higher good. This fails to recognize the blending of competing interests, mostly economic, through the process into an abstract unity termed the "public interest."

Ed Ball and Claude Pepper had different expectations of the process, but they shared the essential commonality of it: the pursuit and exercise of power. For each, power was the goal. Ball pursued economic power, and Pepper sought political power. In the final analysis, both forms of power are one and the same. One may arguably be for self, and the other selfless, but the essence of each is the ability to wield control over others. Therein lies both the contrast and commonality between these two formidable adversaries. The political process in which they played out their roles accommodated and reconciled the tension between their respective purposes. Implicit in the process is the fact that the public interest is, at any given point, nothing more than a mosaic of currently prevailing special interests.

NOTES

1. Florida in the Twenties

1. Robert Sobel, *The Big Board: A History of the New York Stock Market*, 232.

2. U.S. Department of Commerce, Bureau of the Census, *Historical Statistics of the United States: Colonial Times to 1970*, "Average Annual Earnings of Employees: 1900–1970," pt. 1, 164; see John J. McCusker, "How Much Is That in Real Money? A Historical Price Index for Use as a Deflator of Money Values in the Economy of the United States," 347.

3. *Wall Street Journal*, February 23, 1925.

4. Sobel, *The Big Board*, 221–27.

5. Robert Sobel, *The Great Bull Market: Wall Street in the 1920's*, 104–6.

6. John Kenneth Galbraith, *The Great Crash: 1929*, 83.

7. Sobel, *The Big Board*, 252–53.

8. Sobel, *The Great Bull Market*, 12.

9. Galbraith, *The Great Crash*, 16.

10. Bureau of the Census, *Historical Statistics of the United States*, pt. 2, "Bond and Stock Prices: 1871 to 1970," ser. 10, 492–98, 1004.

11. U.S. Congress, Senate Committee on Banking and Currency, *Stock Exchange Practices*, 73d Cong., 2d sess., 1936, 1–395; hereafter cited as *Stock Exchange Practices*.

12. Ibid., 11–17.

13. *Electrical World*, August 25, 1925, 329.

14. *Stock Exchange Practices*, 33–45.

15. Ibid.

16. H. L. Mencken. "On Being an American," 354; editorial, *American Mercury* 6, no. 23 (1925), 286–88.

17. Galbraith, *The Great Crash*, 11.

18. Ibid.

19. Sobel, *The Great Bull Market*, 17–19.

20. *Jacksonville Journal*, November 7, 1925, including complete text of Ponzi's statement.

21. *Jacksonville Journal*, April 3, 1926; *New York Times*, April 3, 1926.

22. *New York Times*, September 2, 1926.

23. John Gifford, "From Miami Southward," *Miami Metropolis*, January 10, 1919; C. W. Barron, "Florida by the Air Line," *Wall Street Journal*, February 26, 1925; Frank Parker Stockbridge, "Florida—the Pioneer State," 491; Frederick Lewis Allen, *Only Yesterday: An Informal History of the Nineteen-Twenties*, 272–73.

24. *Wall Street Journal*, January 7, 1925.

25. Ed Ball to Alfred I. duPont, May 14, 1927, Alfred I. duPont Collection, Washington and Lee University Library, ser. 9, box 62, folder 1; hereafter cited as AID Collection.

26. Raymond B. Vickers. *Panic in Paradise: Florida's Banking Crisis of 1926*, 33–34.

27. *New York Times*, January 10, 24, 1926.

28. *Daily Metropolis* (Miami), July 2, 1904.

29. Editorial, *Miami Metropolis*, January 10, 1919.

30. Homer B. Vanderblue, "The Florida Land Boom II."

31. *New York Times*, December 31, 1922.

32. Kenneth L. Roberts, *Florida Loafing: An Investigation into the Peculiar State of Affairs Which Leads Residents of 47 States to Encourage Spanish Architecture in the 48th*, 5.

33. "Florida Invites the Rich," *Literary Digest*, November 29, 1924, 15; *Wall Street Journal*, February 6, 1925; editorial, *New York Times*, November 10, 1924; editorial, Boston News Service, reproduced in *Wall Street Journal*, March 4, 1925.

34. Allen, *Only Yesterday*, 277–78.

35. T. H. Weigall, *Boom in Paradise*, 224.

36. *New York Times*, September 2, 13, 1925.

37. Homer B. Vanderblue, "The Florida Land Boom," 118.

38. *New York Times*, January 3, 1927.

39. Allen, *Only Yesterday*, 278; see also Clarence W. Barron, *What They Told Barron: The Notes of Clarence W. Barron*, 264–65; Barron, "Florida by the Air Line," *Wall Street Journal*, February 26, 1925; Stockbridge, "Florida—the Pioneer State," 481, describing the Florida holdings of Otto H. Kahn, John D. Rockefeller, Jr., Henry Ford, and Barron G. Collier.

40. Galbraith, *The Great Crash*, 23–24.

41. Marquis James, *Alfred I. DuPont: The Family Rebel*, 392, 396.

42. *New York Times*, July 3, November 8, 1925.

43. Galbraith, *The Great Crash*, 48–49.

44. Lloyd Wendt, *The Wall Street Journal: The Story of Dow Jones and the Nation's Business Newspaper*, 165.

45. *New York Times*, February 28, 1926.

46. Ibid., March 11, 1926; Allen, *Only Yesterday*, 286–89; Robert A. Caro, *The Power Broker; Robert Moses and the Fall of New York* (New York: Random House, Vintage Books, 1974), 204–5.

47. Vickers, *Panic in Paradise*, 71–74.

48. Ibid., xi–xiv.

49. Allen, *Only Yesterday*, 280.

50. *New York Times*, January 3, 1927.

51. Allen, *Only Yesterday*, 286–88.

52. Florida Institute of Government, *Florida City and County Government: A Condensed Reference Version*, 24.

53. William H. Jourbert, "Local Public Debt Policy in Florida, Part 1," *Economic Leaflets* 3, no. 9 (1944).

54. Vickers, *Panic in Paradise*, 33–34.

55. Florida House of Representatives, *Bond Refund Investigation Committee Report to the 1943 House of Representatives, as Authorized by That Body in the 1941 Legislature*, pt. 1, 1–4; *New York Times*, May 15, 1927.

56. Tracy E. Danese, "The Florida Political System to Mid–Twentieth Century: Motion without Movement," master's thesis, Florida State University, 1994, 107–8.

57. *1927 Florida House Journal*, 27–43, 28.

58. See *1927 Florida Comptroller's Report*, 115; *1929 Florida Comptroller's Report*, 141; *1932 Florida Comptroller's Report*, 113.

59. Jourbert, "Local Public Debt Policy in Florida, Part 1."

60. *Wall Street Journal*, May 29, 1931; Florida Special Committee on Taxation and Public Debt, *Report of Special Committee on Taxation and Public Debt*, 117.

2. Alfred I. duPont and Ed Ball

1. Alfred I. duPont to Ed Ball, June 5, 1930; Ed Ball to Alfred I. duPont, June 10, 1930; AID Collection, ser. 11, box 363, folder 4.

2. James, *The Family Rebel*, 47–49.

3. Joseph Frazier Wall, *Alfred I. DuPont: The Man and His Family*, 122–26.

4. Gerard Colby Zilg, *DuPont: Behind the Nylon Curtain* (Englewood Cliffs, N.J.: Prentice-Hall, 1974), 78–82; Wall, *Alfred I. DuPont*, 133–44; James, *The Family Rebel*, 61–68.

5. Wall, *Alfred I. DuPont*, 343–55; Gerard Colby, *DuPont Dynasty*, 172–77;

Leonard Mosley, *Blood Relations: The Rise and Fall of the DuPonts of Delaware* (New York: Atheneum, 1980), 242–49.

6. Jessie Ball duPont to Ed Ball, September 20, 1956, Jessie Ball duPont Papers, Washington and Lee University Library, box 7, folder 1, hereafter cited as JBD Papers; see also Wall, *Alfred I. DuPont*, 297.

7. James, *The Family Rebel*, 327.

8. Wall, *Alfred I. DuPont*, 422.

9. Ibid., 424–26.

10. Richard Greening Hewlett, *Jessie Ball duPont*, 11–12, 17–19; James, *The Family Rebel*, 186–87.

11. Hewlett, *Jessie Ball duPont*, 21; Wall, *Alfred I. DuPont*, 415.

12. Hewlett, *Jessie Ball duPont*, 413–18; Wall, *Alfred I. DuPont*, 443–44.

13. Freeman Lincoln, "The Terrible-Tempered Mr. Ball."

14. James, *The Family Rebel*, 331–32.

15. Ibid., 335.

16. Ibid.

17. Raymond K. Mason and Virginia Harrison, *Confusion to the Enemy: A Biography of Edward Ball*, 31–32; Wall, *Alfred I. DuPont*, 473–75.

18. James, *The Family Rebel*, 357; Wall, *Alfred I. DuPont*, 472–75.

19. Ibid.

20. Hewlett, *Jessie Ball duPont*, 65.

21. Colby, *DuPont Dynasty*, 521.

22. Ibid., 257, 288; Vickers, *Panic in Paradise*, 23, 29–30; *Florida Times-Union*, August 21, 1925.

23. *Wall Street Journal*, April 4, 1925

24. Colby, *DuPont Dynasty*, 484.

25. See Wall, *Alfred I. DuPont*, 484; James, *The Family Rebel*, 396–98.

26. James, *The Family Rebel*, 397; Wall, *Alfred I. DuPont*, 484–85.

27. Ed Ball to Alfred I. duPont, April 17, 1935, AID Collection, ser. 9, box 65, folder 1.

3. Claude Pepper

1. William Warren Rogers, *The One-Gallused Rebellion*, 329–31.

2. Claude Pepper to George H. Cooper, March 5, 1963, Claude Pepper Collection, Florida State University Library, record group 200, vertical file—biography folder; hereafter cited as Pepper Collection.

3. Claude Denson Pepper, *Pepper: Eyewitness to a Century*, 4.

4. Joseph Guttman, "Early Career of Senator Claude Pepper," 14.

5. Ibid.

6. Claude Pepper to J. Robert Olin, February 25, 1954, Pepper Collection, vertical file—biography folder.

7. Ellis Hollums, "Claude Pepper Learned Bitterness of Hard Work, Long Hours, Disappointments and Glory of Winning," *Miami Herald*, October 17, 1936.

8. Kenneth Stewart, "Serious Senator Pepper," *PM*, June 1, 1947.

9. Pepper, *Eyewitness*, 12; Hollums, "Claude Pepper Learned Bitterness of Hard Work," 1936.

10. See Stewart, "Serious Senator Pepper."

11. Claude Pepper Diary, January 15, June 4, 1946, Claude and Mildred Pepper Foundation, Tallahassee, Florida.

12. Claude D. Pepper, "When I Was a Teener," unpublished manuscript, Pepper Collection, vertical file—biography folder.

13. Pepper, prologue to *Eyewitness*, xii; Stewart, "Serious Senator Pepper."

14. Ric A. Kabat, "From New Deal to Red Scare: The Political Odyssey of Senator Claude D. Pepper," 31–33; Guttman, "Early Career," 41–43.

15. Pepper, *Eyewitness*, 10.

16. Ibid., 14; Hollums, "Claude Pepper Learned Bitterness of Hard Work."

17. Claude Pepper to J. Robert Olin, February 25, 1954, Pepper Collection, vertical file—biography folder.

18. Pepper, *Eyewitness*, 16–24, 19.

19. Ibid.; Claude Pepper to George H. Cooper, March 5, 1963, Pepper Collection, vertical file—biography folder.

20. Claude Pepper to J. Robert Olin, February 25, 1954, ibid.

21. Guttman, "Early Career," 24–27; Pepper, *Eyewitness*, 23–25.

22. Pepper, *Eyewitness*, 26.

23. Guttman, "Early Career," 55–57.

24. Claude Pepper to George H. Cooper, March 5, 1963, Pepper Collection, vertical file—biography folder.

25. Guttman, "Early Career," 70–71.

26. Pepper, *Eyewitness*, 31.

27. Ibid., 27–28.

28. Pepper Diary, March 20, April 24, 1943.

29. Ibid., February 16, 1937; Jordon A. Schwarz, *The New Dealers: Power Politics in the Age of Roosevelt*, 152.

30. Claude Pepper to Thomas G. Corcoran, May 13, 1949, Pepper Collection, record group 200, ser. 201, box 31, folder 7.

31. Guttman, "Early Career," 27.

32. Pepper Diary, December 1, 1946.

33. Robert W. Fokes, administrative assistant to Senator Claude Pepper, interview by author, Tallahassee, Florida, tape recording, July 27, 1995.

34. Pepper Diary, January 5, 1946.

35. James C. Clark, "Claude Pepper and the Seeds of His 1950 Defeat, 1944–1948."

36. Pepper's memoirs, cited herein as *Eyewitness*, and particularly his assessment of Harvard's impact on him, support this interpretation; see also Kabat, "From New Deal to Red Scare," 31–34.

37. Kabat, "From New Deal to Red Scare," 46–47.

38. Florida Commissioner of Agriculture, *The Fifth Census of the State of Florida (1925)*, 51, 75, 82.

39. *Florida Times-Union*, October 29, 1925.

40. "Edwards Tells of Highway Progress." *Panama City Pilot*, October 25, 1928; "DuPont Sees Wonderful Prosperity in Prospect," ibid., December 13, 1928.

41. Robinson and Steinman, consulting engineers, to Alfred I. duPont, June 11, 1927, AID Collection, ser. 11, box 62, folder 1.

42. George A. Smathers, interview by author, Jacksonville, Florida, tape recording, June 4, 1996.

43. Pepper, *Eyewitness*, 36–37.

44. Ibid., 39–40; Kabat, "From New Deal to Red Scare," 47–48.

45. Pepper, *Eyewitness*, 41.

46. *Lakeland Polk County Record*, January 26, 1938; Pepper Diary, March 26, 1944; Jim Clements to Claude Pepper, July 29, 1944, Pepper Collection, ser. 431 A, box 27, folder 12; Fred Rodell, "Senator Claude Pepper," *American Mercury*, October 1946, 389–96; Howard Jay Friedman, "Pepper Ahead of His Time," *Tallahassee Democrat*, August 1981; Kabat, "From New Deal to Red Scare," 191–93.

47. *Tallahassee Daily Democrat*, April 23, 1929.

48. B. K. Roberts, interview by author, Tallahassee, Florida, tape recording, March 5, 1996; address of Claude Pepper, "A Practitioner from the Past Returns to the Court," *Florida Supreme Court Historical Society* 1 (Spring 1985), 6–8.

49. Drew Pearson, "The Washington Merry-Go-Round," *Miami Herald*, June 28, 1937; Charles Dexter, "Claude Pepper," *Readers Scope*, September 1946, 106–8.

50. Editorial, "Brown-Crummer Plan a Menace to Bay County," *Panama City Pilot*, April 25, 1929.

51. *Tallahassee Daily Democrat*, April 3, 1929.

52. This litigation generated more than 27,000 pages of depositions in its

first four years and 13,000 pages of exhibits. These figures do not include trial testimony from either of the two jury trials that transpired before culmination of the litigation. This illustrated Ball's tenacity in pursuing litigation without compromise.

53. Editorial, *Panama City Pilot*, April 25, 1929.

54. *Tallahassee Daily Democrat*, May 16, 1929.

55. Ibid., May 15, 1929.

56. Original complaint, 4–6, 12–13, *The Crummer Company v Jessie Ball DuPont, Edward Ball, Florida National Bank of Jacksonville, et al.*, case no. 470, Orlando, District Court of the United States in the Southern District of Florida. This case was transferred to Tallahassee in the Northern District of Florida and assigned case no. 313-T-Civil; references hereafter will be to case no. 313-T-Civil, Northern Division of Florida, Tallahassee Division. All the trial court records of that case are in permanent storage at National Archives, Southeast Region, Atlanta, Georgia, record group 21, U.S. District Courts. Hereafter, citations will be to *Crummer v DuPont* and provide caption of document or exhibit with archival box and folder numbers.

57. Original complaint, 5.

58. Ed Ball to Alfred I. duPont, May 2, 1927; Alfred I. duPont to Ed Ball, May 12, 1927; Ed Ball to Alfred I. duPont, May 14, 1927; Ed Ball to Alfred I. duPont, May 16, 1927, AID Collection, ser. 11, box 62, folder 1.

59. *Tallahassee Daily Democrat*, April 18, 1929.

60. Ibid.

61. See Brown-Crummer Company letterhead reflecting move from Orlando to Exchange Building in Tallahassee and telegram from Guarantee Title & Trust Co. to Roy E. Crummer, April 29, 1929, Governor Doyle E. Carlton Correspondence, Florida State Archives, record group 201, ser. 204, box 1, folder 4; hereafter cited as Carlton Correspondence.

62. *Tallahassee Daily Democrat*, May 15, 16, 1929.

63. U.S. Congress, Senate Subcommittee of the Committee on the Judiciary (hereafter cited as McCarran Subcommittee), *Activities of the Securities and Exchange Commission and the Post Office in Florida*, 79th Cong., 2d sess., 1946, 7–8.

64. *Crummer v DuPont*, "Record on Appeal," 1192–1209, box 82, vol. 3.

65. *Tallahassee Daily Democrat*, May 16, 1929.

66. Ibid., May 17, 1929.

67. Ibid.

68. Ibid.

69. *1929 Florida House Journal*, 503, 531–33, 753–57; *Florida Times-Union*, May 17, 1929.

70. *Tallahassee Daily Democrat*, June 7, 1929.

71. Ibid., May 19, 1929.

72. *Florida Times-Union*, April 18, 1929.

73. Florida National Bank, *Celebrating 100 Years: A History of the Florida National Bank* (Jacksonville: History Associates, n.d.), 9–10.

74. Samuel Gilbert Register, interview by author, Perry, Florida, tape recording, October 21, 1996.

4. DuPont-Ball

1. James, *The Family Rebel*, 392.

2. Wall, *Alfred I. DuPont*, 493.

3. Florida State Chamber of Commerce, *Florida Takes Inventory Proceedings, April 16, 1926, West Palm Beach*, report of Herman Dann, "Florida's Liabilities," 57; hereafter cited as *Florida Takes Inventory, 1926*.

4. Ibid., report of J. C. Penney, "Population and Farming," 24–28.

5. Danese, "The Florida Political System to Mid–Twentieth Century," 109–10.

6. John H. Perry, "Florida and the Gulf Coast," *American Review of Reviews*, May 1931, 62–65.

7. James, *The Family Rebel*, 396.

8. *Florida Times-Union*, January 20, 1925.

9. Alfred I. duPont to Ed Ball, October 11, 1925, AID Collection, ser. 11, box 65, folder 2.

10. James, *The Family Rebel*, 397; Wall, *Alfred I. DuPont*, 484–85.

11. "Answer of Defendants Ed Ball, et al.," in *Crummer v DuPont*, case no. 313-T-Civil, Northern District of Florida, Tallahassee Division.

12. Hewlett, *Jessie Ball duPont*, 68.

13. John Zimmerman, CPA, "Alfred I. DuPont Report for the Year Ended December 31, 1926," 1, AID Collection, ser. 9, box 63, folder 2.

14. James, *The Family Rebel*, 421.

15. Bureau of the Census, *Historical Statistics of the United States: Colonial Times to 1970*, ser. Y, 402–11, "Individual Income Tax Returns, 1913 to 1943," pt. 2, 1110, and ser. G, 269–82, "Percent Distribution of Families and Unattached Individuals, by Income Levels, 1929 to 1964," pt. 1, 299.

16. James, *The Family Rebel*, 372.

17. Wall, *Alfred I. DuPont*, 456.

18. Ed Ball to Alfred I. duPont, March 14, 1930, AID Collection, ser. 9, box 65, folder 7.

19. *Florida Takes Inventory, 1926*, report of Harry B. Hoyt, "Report of the City of Jacksonville," 81–83.

20. Wall, *Alfred I. DuPont*, 483.

21. U.S. Congress, Senate Subcommittee of the Committee on Banking and Currency, *Amend the Bank Holding Company Act of 1956*, pt. 1, 89th Cong., 2d sess., 1966, 23–24, 29–33, 291.

22. Alfred I. duPont to E. H. Batson, June 8, 1931, AID Collection, ser. 11, box 65, folder 9.

23. James, *The Family Rebel*, 399–401; Wall, *Alfred I. DuPont*, 486; Hewlett, *Jessie Ball duPont*, 73.

24. Alfred I. duPont to Ed Ball, March 22, 1935, AID Collection, ser. 11, box 65, folder 5.

25. For example, Colby, *DuPont Dynasty*, 520–61; Mosley, *Blood Relations*, 337–46.

26. *Crummer v DuPont*, complaint, 10, record group 21, box 66, folder 2.

27. Ibid., "Answer of Ed Ball," record group 21, box 66, folder 3.

28. Alfred I. duPont to Edward Ball, March 22, 1935, AID Collection, ser. 11, box 65, folder 5.

29. Pepper Diary, January 23, 1946; see also "Memorandum of Claude Pepper, Senator from the State of Florida," filed with the Interstate Commerce Commission, finance docket no. 13170, 15–23, Pepper Collection, ser. 201, box 45, folder 2.

30. Wall, *Alfred I. DuPont*, 496–504.

31. Ibid.

32. Florida Department of Agriculture, *Florida—an Advancing State: 1907–1917–1927*, 67.

33. Ibid., 55.

34. Florida Department of Agriculture, *All Florida, 1926* (Tallahassee: Florida Department of Agriculture, 1926), 179.

35. *Florida Takes Inventory, 1926*, report of J. C. Penney, "Population and Farming," 25–26.

36. Hewlett, *Jessie Ball duPont*, 68.

37. James, *The Family Rebel*, 400.

38. Ibid., 525–57.

39. Axel H. Oxholm, "Florida's Future Forest Industries Must Depend upon Second Growth Timber," in Florida Department of Agriculture, *Florida—an Advancing State*, 69–76.

40. Charles H. Herty, "Southern Pine for White Paper."

41. Ed Ball to Alfred I. duPont, March 12, 1935, AID Collection, ser. 11, box 65, folder 5.

42. *Panama City Pilot*, March 5, April 30, 1931.

43. Florida Department of Agriculture, *Florida—an Advancing State*, 81; Perry, "Florida and the Gulf Coast," 64.

44. Memorandum, W. T. Edwards to Mr. duPont and Mr. Ball, September 14, 1931; W. T. Edwards to Alfred I. duPont, November 10, 1931, AID Collection, ser. 11, box 64, folder 3.

45. Perry, "Florida and the Gulf Coast," 64.

46. Memorandum, W. T. Edwards to Mr. duPont, September 14, 1931, 2.

47. Memorandum, G. P. Wood to W. T. Edwards, July 24, 1936, JBD Papers, box 57, folder 11.

48. B. K. Roberts interview, Tallahassee, February 5, 1996.

49. Pepper Diary, March 19, 1944.

50. Memorandum, Wood to Edwards, July 24, 1936.

51. W. T. Edwards to Alfred I. duPont, September 16, 1931, AID Collection, ser. 11, box 64, folder 3.

52. *New York Times*, March 11, 1926.

53. *Florida Takes Inventory, 1926*, report of J. A. Griffin, "Florida's Financial Assets," 9–13, 10.

54. Vickers, *Panic in Paradise*, 43–47, 73–74, 77.

55. Ibid., 64–65, 83.

56. Alfred I. duPont to Edward Ball, June 16, 1930, AID Collection, ser. 11, box 63, folder 4.

57. Florida National Bank, *Celebrating 100 Years*, 8.

58. Edward Ball to Alfred I. duPont, April 1, 1935, AID Collection, ser. 11, box 65, folder 1.

59. *Florida Times-Union*, April 28, 1929.

60. Wall, *Alfred I. DuPont*, 487–88, citing an interview given by Ed Ball to Marquis James in preparing *The Family Rebel*.

61. *Tampa Morning Tribune*, July 18, 1929.

62. Wall, *Alfred I. DuPont*, 489.

63. Gene Burnett, "Cool Leadership during Florida's Banking Crisis," *Florida Trend*, June 1980, 103–5; James, *The Family Rebel*, 435.

64. Alfred I. duPont to Edward Ball, June 18, 1930, AID Collection, ser. 11, box 63, folder 4.

5. Banks, Pulpwood, and Depression

1. Florida National Bank, *Celebrating 100 Years*, 10–11.

2. James, *The Family Rebel*, 443.

3. Arthur M. Schlesinger, Jr., *The Crisis of the Old Order: 1919–1933*, 474–75.

4. James, *The Family Rebel*, 437–57; Florida National Bank, *Celebrating 100 Years*, 12–13.

5. Vickers, *Panic in Paradise*, 196–98.

6. Wayne Flynt, *Duncan Upshaw Fletcher: Dixie's Reluctant Progressive*, 44.

7. Peter O. Knight to J. W. Pole, November 18, 1929, Carlton Correspondence, record group 102, ser. 204, box 48, folder 11.

8. Peter O. Knight to Doyle E. Carlton, April 30, 1930, cited in Vickers, *Panic in Paradise*, n. 20.

9. Peter O. Knight to Doyle E. Carlton, June 25, 1930, Carlton Correspondence, record group 102, ser. 204, box 48, folder 11.

10. Doyle E. Carlton to Peter O. Knight, July 3, 1930, ibid.

11. Allen Morris, "Cracker Politics," *Jacksonville Journal*, January 21, 1956.

12. James, *The Family Rebel*, 445.

13. Peter O. Knight to Claude Pepper, July 29, 1934, Pepper Collection, ser. 201A, box 32, folder 19; Pepper Diary, December 30, 1940.

14. Edward Ball to Alfred I. duPont, May 20, 1930, AID Collection, ser. 11, box 63, folder 4.

15. Edward Ball to Alfred I. duPont, June 6, 1930, ibid.

16. Ibid.; Alfred I. duPont to Edward Ball, June 9, 1930, AID Collection, ser. 11, box 63, folder 4.

17. Edward Ball to Alfred I. duPont, June 11, 1930, in ibid.

18. Edward Ball to Alfred I. duPont, June 16, 1930, in ibid.

19. James, *The Family Rebel*, 443.

20. Edward Ball to Alfred I. duPont, May 23, 1930, AID Collection, ser. 11, box 63, folder 4; Edward Ball to Frank C. Schwable, May 27, 1930, ibid., box 62, folder 5.

21. Ball to Schwable, May 27, 1930, ibid.

22. Edward Ball to A. A. Payne, January 13, 1930, ibid., folder 6.

23. Alfred I. duPont to Edward Ball, June 23, 1930; Edward Ball to Alfred I. duPont, June 27, 1930; ibid., box 63, folder 3.

24. Edward Ball to Alfred I. duPont, June 20, 1930, ibid., box 63, folder 4.

25. Jacob C. "Jake" Belin, interviews by author, March 11, May 29, 1996, tape recordings, Port St. Joe, Florida; Florida National Bank, *Celebrating 100 Years*, 11.

26. Florida Department of Agriculture, *Florida State Census, 1925*, 9.

27. *Tampa Tribune*, December 28, 1958.

28. Edward Ball to Alfred I. duPont, April 17, 1935, AID Collection, ser. 11, box 65, folder 1.

29. Wall, *Alfred I. DuPont*, 279–81.

30. Allen Morris, "Cracker Politics," *Jacksonville Journal*, April 23, 1955; Belin interview, May 29, 1996.

31. *Tallahassee Daily Democrat*, June 13, 1929.

32. *Florida Times-Union*, October 29, 1925.

33. Wall, *Alfred I. DuPont*, 487–88.

34. *New York Times*, January 3, 1927.

35. *1927 Florida House Journal*, 27–43, 28.

36. Edward Ball to Alfred I. duPont, May 2, 1927, AID Collection, ser. 11, box 62, folder 1.

37. Alfred I. duPont to Ed Ball, May 12, 1927, ibid.

38. Edward Ball to Alfred I. duPont, May 14, 1927, ibid.

39. Ibid.

40. Belin interview, March 11, 1996.

41. U.S. Congress, House Committee on Banking and Currency, *To Amend the Bank Holding Company Act*, 89th Cong., 1st sess., 1965, 64–68; Leon Odell Griffith, *Ed Ball: Confusion to the Enemy*, 61–65.

42. Ibid.

43. Belin interview, March 11, 1996.

44. Allen Morris, "Cracker Politics," *Jacksonville Journal*, April 23, 1955.

45. Pepper Diary, November 15, 1938.

46. F. T. Forrester to T. W. Weathers, April 1, 1930, AID Collection, ser. 11, box 62, folder 5.

47. Edward Ball to Alfred I. duPont, June 17, 1930, ibid., box 63, folder 4.

48. Ibid.

49. Allen Morris, "Cracker Politics," *Jacksonville Journal*, April 23, 1955.

50. James, *The Family Rebel*, 408.

51. *New York Times*, September 22, 1928.

52. Wall, *Alfred I. DuPont*, 522–23.

53. Colby, *DuPont Dynasty*, 277.

54. Edward Ball to Marsh and Saxelbye, November 19, 1930, AID Collection, ser. 11, box 62, folder 5.

55. James, *The Family Rebel*, 464.

56. Edward Ball to Alfred I. duPont, December 4, 1930, AID Collection, ser. 11, box 62, folder 7.

57. Memorandum, Ed Ball to Alfred I. duPont, November 29, 1930, ibid., box 65, folder 7.

58. Alfred I. duPont to Edward Ball, November 17, 1930; Edward Ball to Alfred I. duPont, November 19, 1930; ibid., box 62, folder 7.

59. Alfred I. duPont to Edward Ball, May 25, 1931, ibid., box 65, folder 9.

60. Alfred I. duPont to Edward Ball, May 27, 1931, ibid.

61. Vickers, *Panic in Paradise*, 6–7.

62. Florida National Bank, *A Century of Banking*, 11.

63. *Florida Times-Union*, July 2, 1941; Pepper Diary, December 27, 1941.

64. Pepper Diary, October 31, 1940.

65. Herty, "Southern Pine for White Paper"; Wall, *Alfred I. DuPont*, 499–504.

66. Wall, *Alfred I. DuPont*, 505–7.

67. Hewlett, *Jessie Ball duPont*, 196–97.

6. A Florida Senator and the New Deal

1. Pepper, *Eyewitness*, 44–45.

2. Frank Freidel, *Franklin D. Roosevelt: A Rendezvous with Destiny*, 54–56.

3. Pepper, *Eyewitness*, 45.

4. Claude Pepper to Franklin Delano Roosevelt, December 22, 1928, Papers of the New York Democratic Committee (1928–32), Franklin Delano Roosevelt Library, box 118, also quoted in *Congressional Record* (February 25, 1944), 2049.

5. *Tallahassee Democrat*, June 2, 1930.

6. Pepper, *Eyewitness*, 46.

7. Wesley Price, "Pink Pepper," *Saturday Evening Post*, August 31, 1946, 117.

8. Spessard L. Holland to J. A. Allen, August 16, 1950, Spessard Holland Collection, Florida State University Library, box 812, MSS 76–5, c-76; Smathers interview.

9. *Tallahassee Democrat*, February 15, 1934.

10. *Tallahassee Daily Democrat*, December 6, 9, 1931.

11. Ibid.

12. Ibid.

13. *Florida Times-Union*, April 14, 1932.

14. Ibid., December 2, 1931.

15. Schlesinger, *The Crisis of the Old Order*, 266–69; Robert S. McElvaine, *The Great Depression: America, 1929–1941*, 35–37, 134–35, 147.

16. Schlesinger, 168–73.

17. Pepper, *Eyewitness*, 46.

18. For example, Walter S. Hardin (Manatee County) to Claude Pepper, January 8, 1934; C. C. Bailey (Jacksonville) to Fred M. Ivey, January 11, 1934; Fred Hartnett (Miami) to Claude Pepper, January 11, 1934; Harry E. King (Winter Haven) to Fred M. Ivey, January 17, 1934; Pepper Collection, ser. 204A, box 47, folder 11.

19. Alexander R. Stoesen, "The Senatorial Career of Claude D. Pepper," 33, citing *Time*, November 11, 1929, and *Washington Herald*, August 2, 1934.

20. Hart McKillop to Fred M. Ivey, January 10, 1934, Pepper Collection, ser. 204A, box 47, folder 11.

21. John H. Perry to Claude Pepper, January 11, 1934, ibid.

22. Fokes interviews, July 27, 1995, May 30, 1996.

23. Belin interviews, March 11, May 29, 1996.

24. Lincoln, "The Terrible Tempered Mr. Ball," 156.

25. William J. Ray to Claude Pepper, November 6, 1933, Pepper Collection, ser. 204A, box 447, folder 11A; Stoesen, "Senatorial Career of Claude Pepper," 30.

26. Belin interviews, March 11, May 29, 1996.

27. *Miami Herald*, May 31, 1934.

28. Park Trammell speech delivered in Ocala, Florida, May 17, 1934, Pepper Collection, ser. 204G, box 2, folder 8.

29. *Tampa Morning Tribune*, June 13, 1934.

30. *Miami Herald*, June 3, 1934.

31. *Tampa Morning Tribune*, June 6, 1934; *Miami Herald*, June 6, 1934.

32. W. J. Bivens to Oscar Johnson, June 7, 1934, Pepper Collection, ser. 204, box 42, folder 11; Tom Walden to Oscar Johnson, June 13, 1934, ibid., ser. 204A, box 42, folder 11.

33. *Miami Herald*, June 13, 1934.

34. Ibid., June 16, 1934.

35. *Tampa Morning Tribune*, June 6, 1934.

36. Pepper Diary, February 12, 1937.

37. See letters and telegrams to this effect in Pepper Collection, ser. 204A, box 64, folder 3.

38. *Miami Herald*, June 26, 1934.

39. *Tampa Morning Tribune*, June 21, 1934.

40. Allen Morris, "Cracker Politics," *Miami Herald*, March 24, 1940.

41. Stoesen, "Senatorial Career of Claude D. Pepper," 41–42.

42. *Tampa Morning Tribune*, June 28, 1934.

43. Claude Pepper, "Not for Publication," Pepper Collection, ser. 204A, box 32, folder 19, also cited in Stoesen, "Senatorial Career," 41.

44. Ibid.

45. Affidavit of Mrs. W. W. Goins, dated May 18, 1936, Pepper Collection, ser. 204A, box 54, folder 11.

46. Campaign Committee, Hillsborough County Democratic Executive Committee, "Report of the Campaign Committee of the Hillsborough County Democratic Executive Committee of VOTE FRAUD," n.d., ibid., box 32, folder 9.

47. Peter O. Knight to Claude Pepper, July 29, 1934, ibid.

48. *Florida Times-Union*, May 3, 1930.

49. Associated Press "Morgue File" sketch of Peter O. Knight, sent to W. T.

Cash, historian of Florida Democratic Party; Peter O. Knight to W. T. Cash, July 2, 1932; Florida State Library, Special Collection, biographical file Kn–Kz.

50. Stoesen, "Senatorial Career of Claude D. Pepper," 47.

51. Knight to Pepper, July 29, 1934.

52. Ibid.

53. Pepper Diary, May 10, 1939.

54. Bivens to Johnson, June 7, 1934.

55. Stoesen, "Senatorial Career of Claude D. Pepper," 446, citing numerous newspaper articles from throughout the state to that effect.

56. *Tallahassee Florida State News* (*Tallahassee Democrat*), May 12, 1936.

57. *Orlando Sentinel*, August 7, 1934.

58. Pepper Diary, December 27, 28, 1941, January 11, 1942.

59. Arthur M. Schlesinger, Jr., *The Age of Roosevelt*, vol. 3, *The Politics of Upheaval*, 20–68; Michael Barone, *Our Country: The Shaping of America from Roosevelt to Reagan*, 81–83.

60. *New York Times*, February 6, 1937; *Business Week*, February 20, 1937, 25; *Time*, February 15, 1937, 18.

61. Pepper, *Eyewitness*, 56–57.

62. Pepper Diary, February 16, 1937.

63. Pepper, *Eyewitness*, 56–59; *New York Times*, February 6, 1937.

64. *New York Times*, June 18, 1937; Pepper, *Eyewitness*, 60–62.

65. Pepper, *Eyewitness*, 61.

66. Pearson, "The Washington Merry-Go-Round."

67. For example, Pepper Diary, November 13, 1937, June 19, 1945, March 31, 1946.

68. Harold Ickes, *The Secret Diary of Harold L. Ickes*, vol. 2, *The Inside Struggle, 1936–1939*, 342.

69. Pepper, *Eyewitness*, 72.

70. Pepper Diary, November 15, 1938.

71. *Tampa Tribune*, June 25, 1981.

72. Pepper Diary, February 13, 1938.

73. Ibid., December 23, 1955.

74. *Tampa Tribune*, April 16, 1988

75. Pepper Diary, March 2, 1938.

76. Friedel, *Franklin D. Roosevelt*, 280–81.

77. *Time*, May 16, 1938; Ickes, *The Secret Diary of Harold L. Ickes*, vol. 2, 386, 390; Pepper, *Eyewitness*, 68–74; Barone, *Our Country*, 117.

78. Pepper, *Eyewitness*, 75–77.

79. Pepper Diary, May 16, 1940.

80. Ibid., October 31, 1940.

81. Ibid., March 2, 1940.

82. Ibid., July 20, 28, 1942.

83. Ibid., September 1, 1942.

84. Ibid., August 22, 1940.

85. Ibid., May 17, 1941.

86. Ibid., May 8, 1940.

87. *Crummer v Ball*, "Testimony of Roger L. Main," vol. 9, 4130–38, record group 21, box 78.

88. Ed Ball to Claude Pepper, January 5, 1944, Pepper Collection, ser. 302B, box 3, folder 5.

7. Patterns of Conflict

1. Clark, "Claude Pepper and the Seeds of His 1950 Defeat"; James C. Clark, "The 1944 Florida Democratic Senate Primary."

2. See Pepper campaign speech in Bartow, Florida, quoted in *Florida Times-Union*, April 9, 1944; see also the May 3, 1943, issue of the same newspaper.

3. Editorial, *Business Week*, February 12, 1944, 116.

4. Ibid., March 4, 1944; Freidel, *Franklin D. Roosevelt*, 501–2.

5. *Time*, March 6, 1944, 79.

6. Ibid., March 13, 1944, 88.

7. *Business Week*, January 1, 1944, 17–18.

8. U.S. Congress, Senate Committee on Finance, *Revenue Act of 1943*, 78th Cong., 1st sess., December 29 ff., 1943, 925.

9. U.S. Congress, Senate, "Statement of Senator Claude Pepper," 78th Cong., 2d sess., *Congressional Record* (1944), vol. 90, pt. 2, 2059.

10. *New York Times*, August 5, 1942, quoting offer letter from Florida National Building Corporation (a duPont company) to Bondholders Committee for defaulted FEC bonds.

11. *U.S. Statutes at Large*, 78th Cong., 2d sess., sec. 121 (1944), vol. 58, pt. 1, 40.

12. *Business Week*, January 1, 1944, 17.

13. *Time*, March 6, 1944, 17–21; Allen Drury, *A Senate Journal, 1943–1945*, 88–97.

14. Drury, *A Senate Journal*, 88–97.

15. "Statement of Senator Claude Pepper" (see n. 9).

16. Ibid.

17. Drury, *A Senate Journal*, 86.

18. Pepper, *Eyewitness*, 117.

19. Pepper Diary, February 23, 1944.

20. Ibid., February 24, 1944.

21. Ibid., February 25, 1944.

22. Pepper, *Eyewitness*, 117–18.

23. Fokes interview, June 4, 1996.

24. Smathers interview, June 4, 1996.

25. "Statement of Senator Claude Pepper" (see n. 9).

26. Ibid.

27. Drury, *A Senate Journal*, 95.

28. The twelve Democrats were the last of the ardent New Dealers. They were James M. Tunnell (Del.), J. Lister Hill (Ala.), Pepper, James E. Murray (Mont.), Homer T. Bone and Monrad C. Wallgren (Wash.), James M. Meade and Robert "Bob" Wagner (N.Y.), Elbert D. Thomas (Utah), Theodore F. Green (R.I.), Joseph F. Guffey (Penn.), and Harley M. Kilgore (W. Va.).

29. Allen Morris, "Cracker Politics," *Miami Herald*, April 18, 1943.

30. Pepper Diary, March 13, 19, 1944.

31. Ibid., January 7, 1944.

32. Fokes interviews, July 27, 1995, May 30, 1996.

33. *New York Times*, April 8, 1944.

34. Ibid.

35. *New York Times*, April 14, 19, 1944; *New York PM*, January 23, 1944; *New Republic*, May 1, 1944, 592.

36. Mason and Harrison, *Confusion to the Enemy*, 144.

37. In re: FEC Railway Company Reorganization (January 8, 1945), 261 ICC 151.

38. Fokes interview, May 30, 1996.

39. Clark, "The 1944 Democratic Senate Primary," 369.

40. Pepper Diary, June 6, 1955.

41. Ibid.

42. Ibid.

43. Ibid., March 13, 22, 1944.

44. Clark, "The 1944 Democratic Senate Primary," 372.

45. Lincoln, "The Terrible Tempered Mr. Ball," 156. This anecdote has appeared in several articles based on interviews with Ball by various authors.

46. *Florida Times-Union*, April 5, 1944.

47. *New York Times*, October 7, 1944.

48. Pepper Diary, February 27, April 2, 1944.

49. Ibid., June 22, 26, 1945.

50. Ibid., April 4, 1944; *Florida Times-Union*, April 5, 1944.

51. Pepper Diary, March 26, April 4, 1944.

52. In re: Florida East Coast Railway Company Reorganization (January 8, 1945), 261 ICC 151, at 155.

53. Claude Pepper to McD. C. Davis, January 23, 1945, Pepper Collection, ser. 201, box 39, folder 3.

54. Alexander R. Stoesen, "Road from Receivership: Claude Pepper, the DuPont Trust, and the Florida East Coast Railway," 140, citing Pepper "Memorandum."

55. Pepper Diary, July 4, 1945.

56. Ibid., July 26, 1945.

57. Ibid., August 2, 1945.

58. Ibid., August 4, 5, 13, 1945.

59. Ibid., August 22, 1945.

8. A Railroad War and Its Aftermath

1. *New York Times*, August 28, 1924.

2. *Wall Street Journal*, February 3, 1925.

3. Florida East Coast Railway, "Statement of Giles Patterson," September 10, 1948, testimony vol. 1, 100–101, record group 21, box 167. See also FECR, "Judge Louie W. Strum's Opinion," Circuit Judge for the Fifth Circuit Court of Appeals, sitting as District Judge, filed March 11, 1952, record group 21, box 170, folder 49-A, for a history of the proceedings up to that time; hereafter cited as "Strum Opinion."

4. *New York Times*, August 28, 1924; FECR, "Memorandum" prepared by Robert K. Frey, dated September 14, 1945, Exhibit 6, Champion Deposition, record group 21, box 163.

5. FECR, "Exhibit A, Bill of Complaint," *Standard Oil Company v Florida East Coast Railway*, case no. 737-J-Eq., record group 21, box 163.

6. "Strum Opinion," 17.

7. *Florida Times-Union*, July 20, 1943.

8. Florida East Coast Railway Company Reorganization (April 6, 1942), 252 ICC 423, at 463.

9. FECR, "Bill of Complaint of Bankers Trust Company," record group 21, box 175.

10. *New York Times*, October 21, November 7, 1939.

11. *Miami Friday Night*, June 1, 1945.

12. FECR, "Ed Ball Testimony," ICC Hearing, fin. docket no. 13170, May

31, 1944, 1152–61, record group 21, box 180; "Ed Ball Testimony," ICC Hearing, West Palm Beach, November 29, 1945, 4180, 4190–92; Pepper Collection, ser. 201, box 48, folder 2.

13. FECR, "Charles B. Quarles Testimony," ICC Hearing, West Palm Beach, November 27, 1945, 3699–3719, record group 21, box 180.

14. Congress, Senate, 78th Cong., 2d sess., *Congressional Record* (1944), vol. 90, pt. 1., 1301.

15. See "Charles B. Quarles Testimony," cited in n. 13 above, and "Testimony of Fred K. Conn," ICC Hearing, West Palm Beach, November 27, 1945, 3725–36.

16. *New York Times*, August 1, 1942.

17. "Testimony of Ed Ball," ICC Hearing, West Palm Beach, November 29, 1945, 4193, Pepper Collection, ser. 201, box 48, folder 2.

18. Ibid., 4183–90.

19. FECR, "Florida Bonds: Quotations and Information," published by Clyde C. Pierce Corporation, January 1, 1941, record group 21, box 78.

20. McCarran Subcommittee, *Activities of the Securities and Exchange Commission and the Post Office Department in Florida*, 79th Cong., 2d sess., 1946, 17.

21. Congress, House Special Subcommittee of the Committee on the Judiciary, *To Investigate the Department of Justice*, 83d Cong., 1st sess., 1953, passim; *Congressional Quarterly* 11 (May 1, 1953), 582, 588; *New York Times*, November 17, 1951. See also Congress, Senate stenographic transcript (unpublished) of *Hearings before the Subcommittee of the Committee on the Judiciary on Activities of the Securities and Exchange Commission and the Post Office Department in Florida*, July 17, 1947, access number (80) sj-T-157, Congressional Information Service, 1–20.

22. 267 ICC 295, at 346 (April 8, 1947).

23. *Crummer v Ball*, "Testimony of Roger O. Main," 4149–4200, vol. 10, record group 21, box 81.

24. *New York Times*, November 17, 1951; U.S. Congress, House Special Subcommittee of the Committee on the Judiciary, *To Investigate the Department of Justice*, 769–77, 857.

25. "Strum Opinion," 8.

26. 252 ICC 423 (April 6, 1942), 425–39.

27. Ibid., 478–79. See also Stoesen, "Road from Receivership," 132–56.

28. 252 ICC 424, 463–64 (April 6, 1942).

29. Pepper Diary, December 19, 1941.

30. Ibid., June 22, 26, 1945.

31. Ibid., September 27, 1941.

32. *Crummer v DuPont*, "Testimony of Roger Main," vol. 9, 4108–12, record group 21, box 78. See also Pepper Diary, October 1, 1941.

33. *New York Times*, July 31, 1942; FECR, "Ball Testimony, "ICC Hearing, West Palm Beach, November 26, 1945, 3511–16.

34. FECR, "Deposition of Thomas B. Butler," 56–61, record group 21, box 66.

35. FECR, "Ball Testimony," ICC Hearing, West Palm Beach, November 26, 1945, 3518–24; 267 ICC 295 (April 8, 1947), 313.

36. *Florida Times-Union*, September 5, 1943.

37. FECR, "Ball Testimony," 3459–61.

38. *Florida Times-Union*, October 20, 1943; *New York Times*, October 20, 1943.

39. *Business Week*, January 15, 1944, 21–22.

40. FECR, "Deposition of McD. Champion Davis," September 28, 1948, 10–27, record group 21, box 66; hereafter cited as "Davis Deposition."

41. *Florida Times-Union*, April 5, 1944; Royal W. France, "Five against Pepper," *The Nation*, April 29, 1944, 507–8; Pepper Diary, March 13, 22, 1944.

42. "Davis Deposition," 39–40.

43. 261 ICC 15, 192 (January 8, 1945).

44. FECR, "Testimony of Edward Ball," West Palm Beach Hearing, November 26, 1945, 3524–26; Mason, *Confusion to the Enemy*, 76–77.

45. 261 ICC 151, 173 (January 8, 1945).

46. FECR, "Deposition of Edward Ball" (November 9, 1948), 22–35, record group 21, box 166.

47. Ibid.

48. Edward Ball to Fred K. Conn, January 15, 1946, Pepper Collection, ser. 201, box 39, folder 1.

49. "Testimony of J. Hardin Peterson," 37–49, in *FEC Receivership Proceedings, Washington Hearing*, November 7, 1945, ibid., box 46, folder 1.

50. See, for example, Pepper Diary, January 23, 1946, where Pepper writes, "The sinister and dangerous character of Ball's domination of the state of Florida becomes more distinct as one sees it more closely."

51. J. A. Cawthon to Claude Pepper, February 24, 1946, Pepper Collection, ser. 201, box 40, folder 4.

52. McD. C. Davis to Claude Pepper, January 27, 1945, ibid., box 39, folder 2.

53. McD. C. Davis to Claude Pepper, February 22, May 16, 1945 (both marked "personal"), ibid., box 39, folder 3; Pepper Diary, May 17, 28, 29, 1945.

54. Claude Pepper to "Champ" Davis, January 23, 1945, Pepper Collection, ser. 201, box 39, folder 1.

55. *Orlando Sentinel,* February 1, 1945.

56. Pepper Diary, February 27, 1944, August 5, 1945.

57. Telegram, Claude Pepper to Davis, May 24, 1945, Pepper Collection, ser. 201, box 39, folder 3.

58. W. F. Howard to Claude Pepper, May 28, 1946; Claude Pepper to W. F. Howard, July 18, 1946; ibid., box 40, folder 2.

59. "Champ" Davis to Claude Pepper, January 27, March 8, 1945, ibid., box 39, folder 2.

60. Claude Pepper to Commissioner J. Monroe Johnson, May 22, 1945, ibid., folder 3.

61. Pepper Diary, January 24, February 25, 26, March 1, 1945.

62. Stoesen, "Road from Receivership," 138–39.

63. *Orlando Sentinel,* February 1, 1945.

64. *Florida Times-Union,* June 16, 1945.

65. Editorial, *Miami Herald,* April 5, 1950; *Miami Friday Night,* May 4, 1945.

66. Witnesses testified before the ICC of community pride in the FEC as a local institution. See 267 ICC 295, 328 (April 8, 1947) and 282 ICC 81, 125 (July 12, 1951).

67. FECR, "Testimony of Thomas B. Butler," 62–65, September 10, 1948, record group 21, box 66.

68. *New York Times,* August 15, September 12, 1945.

69. Ed Ball to Claude Pepper, June 30, 1958, Spessard Holland Collection, MSS 76–5, box 812, file C-77.

70. W. F. Howard, *The Cat Is Out of the Bag* (Jacksonville, n.d.), 3–4, Pepper Collection, ser. 201, box 39, folder 5. Howard was the leading union spokesman against the ACL and ultimately opposed Pepper's 1950 reelection bid, breaking with the national union leadership over the issue.

71. *Florida Times-Union,* August 10, 1945, February 20, 1946.

72. J. A. Cawthon to Claude Pepper, February 24, 1946, Pepper Collection, ser. 201, box 40, folder 4.

73. *Miami Herald,* April 5, 1950.

74. Edward W. Bourne to James C. Clements, December 8, 1945, Pepper Collection, ser. 201, box 50, folder 4.

75. In re: Florida East Coast Railway Company Reorganization, "Memorandum by Claude Pepper, Senator from the State of Florida," 5 (February 14, 1946), ibid., box 45, folder 2.

76. Ibid., 18.

77. 267 ICC 295, 316 (April 8, 1947).

78. Ibid.

79. Ibid., 372.

80. Pepper Diary, May 20, 1947.

81. Ibid., May 31, 1947.

82. Ibid., January 29, February 16, 1948.

83. Ibid., March 15, 1948.

84. In re: Florida East Coast Ry. Co., 81 Fed. Supp. 927 (1949); *Atlantic Coast Line R. Co. v St. Joe Paper Co.*, 179 Fed. (2d) 538 (1950); *Atlantic Coast Line R. Co. v St. Joe Paper Co.*, 339 U.S. 929 (1950).

85. *Atlantic Coast Line R. Co. v St. Joe Paper Co.*, 179 Fed. (2d) 538 (1950).

86. W. F. Howard (Brotherhood of Railway and Steamship Clerks) to Claude Pepper, May 26, 1946, Pepper Collection, ser. 201, box 40, folder 2; W. F. Howard to George M. Harrison (chairman, Railway Labor Political League), February 5, 1950, ibid., box 45, folder 1.

87. 282 ICC 81 (July 12, 1951), 282 ICC 195 (October 25, 1951).

88. 307 ICC 5 (November 3, 1958).

9. The Election of 1950

1. Pepper, *Eyewitness*, 193, 203.

2. Robert Sherrill, *Gothic Politics in the Deep South: Stars of the New Confederacy*, 152–60.

3. *New York Times*, April 2, 1944; John Lewis Gaddis, *The United States and the Origins of the Cold War: 1941–1947*, 257–58, 283–84; Martin Walker, *The Cold War: A History* (New York: Henry Holt, 1993), 36–52.

4. Harvey Klehr, John Earl Haynes, and Fridrikh Igorevich Firsov, with Russian documents translated by Timothy D. Sergay, *The Secret World of American Communism*, 322–33.

5. "What Is Pepper About?" (editorial), *Orlando Sentinel*, September 25, 1945; Richard L. Strout, "Mr. Pepper Presents the Russian View," reprint from the *Christian Science Monitor* in *Deland Volusia Mirror*, April 5, 1946; editorial, *Evening Independent* (St. Petersburg), March 23, 1946.

6. For example, editorial, *Daily Worker*, September 14, 1945; Clark, "Claude Pepper and the Seeds of His 1950 Defeat," 1–22.

7. Pepper Diary, August 2, 1945; *Miami Herald*, June 26, 1947.

8. Robert J. Donovan, *Conflict and Crisis: The Presidency of Harry S. Truman, 1945–1948*, 186–87; Gaddis, *Origins of the Cold War*, 284.

9. U.S. Congress, House, "What about Russia?" extension of remarks by William M. Colmer, 79th Cong., 2d sess., *Congressional Record* (1946), vol. 92, pt. 2, A4895–98.

10. Chargé in the Soviet Union (Kennan) to the secretary of state, September

30, 1945, Moscow, *Foreign Relations of the United States*, vol. 5 (Washington: U.S. Department of State, 1945), Europe, 884–86.

11. Donovan, *Conflict and Crisis*, 187–88; Gaddis, *Origins of the Cold War*, 302–3.

12. W. Averell Harriman and Elie Abel, *Special Envoy to Churchill and Stalin 1941–1946*, 456–57.

13. Chargé in the Soviet Union (Kennan) to the secretary of state, Moscow, September 15, 1945, *Foreign Relations of the United States*, vol. 5, 881–84.

14. Radio address of Senator Claude Pepper from Moscow, September 18, 1945, Pepper Collection, record group 200, ser. 201, box 161, folder 15.

15. *New York Times*, October 1, 1945.

16. Ibid.

17. Pepper Diary, January 2, 5, 1946.

18. David McCullough, *Truman*, 282.

19. Pepper Diary, July 4, 1945; see also May 27, 1945, diary entry lamenting Truman's petty vindictiveness.

20. Ibid., March 31, 1946.

21. Senate, "Statement of Senator Claude Pepper on President's Veto Message," *Congressional Record*, 78th Cong., 2d sess. (February 25, 1944), 2049.

22. Pepper, *Eyewitness*, 196.

23. Brian L. Crispell, "George Smathers and the Politics of Cold War America, 1946–1968," 81.

24. Pepper Diary, December 1, 1946; Pepper, *Eyewitness*, 234–35.

25. *Miami Herald*, June 26, 1947.

26. Pepper Diary, January 15, 1946.

27. Ibid., November 27, 1946.

28. Claude Pepper to Lovick P. Williams, attorney-at-law, February 11, 1944, Pepper Collection, ser. 431A, box 14, folder 16.

29. Pepper Diary, January 15, 1946.

30. Ibid., January 11, 1946.

31. U.S. Congress, Senate, "Extension of Remarks of Hon. Claude Pepper," 79th Cong., 2d sess., *Congressional Record* (1946), vol. 92, pt. 9, A517–18.

32. Arthur H. Vandenberg, *The Private Papers of Senator Vandenberg*, 266–67, 311.

33. Pepper Diary, April 1, 1946; Clark, "Claude Pepper and the Seeds of His 1950 Defeat," 7.

34. U.S. Congress, Senate, 79th Cong., 2d sess., *Congressional Record* (1946), vol. 92, pt. 2, 2463–69.

35. Price, "Pink Pepper," 19, 116–17.

36. Pepper Diary, May 27, 1946.

37. Pepper, *Eyewitness*, 153–55; Pepper Diary, May 27, 1946, April 14, 19, 1947.

38. Crispell, "George Smathers and the Politics of Cold War America," 64–66.

39. For example, Allen Morris, "Cracker Politics," *Jacksonville Journal*, January 10, September 11, 1948, July 23, 1949.

40. Edward Ball to Fred K. Conn, January 15, 1946, Pepper Collection, ser. 201, box 39, folder 1.

41. Allen Morris, "Cracker Politics," *Jacksonville Journal*, February 22, 1947.

42. Belin interview, May 29, 1996.

43. For example, *American Mutual Life Ins. Co. v City of Avon Park*, 311 U.S. 138 (U.S. Sup. Ct., November 25, 1944), citing Florida Supreme Court opinion holding certain Crummer actions illegal. See also cases to the contrary, such as *Meredith v City of Winter Haven*, 320 U.S. 228 (U.S. Sup. Ct., November 8, 1943).

44. David R. Colburn and Richard K. Scher, *Florida's Gubernatorial Politics in the Twentieth Century*, 72.

45. McCarran Subcommittee, *Investigation of the Activities of the Securities and Exchange Commission and the Post Office in Florida*, 79th Cong., 2d sess. (1946), 17; see also *Crummer v Ball*, "Deposition of Roy E. Crummer," vol. 2, 327–28, record group 21, box 60.

46. Ed Ball to Ed Larsen (comptroller of Florida), January 14, 1943, and Ed Larsen to Ed Ball, February 1, 1943, *Crummer v Ball*, Plaintiff's Exhibit 58, record group 21, box 70, folder 2, and Defendant's Exhibit 170, ibid., box 67, folder 89. In the second letter, Larsen addressed Ball as "MY dear Friend" and asked him to set a time and date "that will best suit you [Ball]" for a hearing on Crummer's license. See also Spessard Holland to R. E. Crummer, October 9, 1941, *Crummer v Ball*, Defendant's Exhibit 106, record group 21, box 67, folders 89–106, in which Holland outlines his displeasure with Crummer's Sarasota County bond refunding contract.

47. U.S. Congress, Senate, "Statement of Senator Patrick McCarran on Study of Activities of SEC and Post Office Department," 80th Cong., 1st sess., *Congressional Record* (1947), vol. 93, pt. 8, 9952–9971, at 9953.

48. Ibid., 9953.

49. McCarran Subcommittee, *passim*; House Special Subcommittee of the Committee on the Judiciary, *To Investigate the Department of Justice*, 659–82, 691–780, passim.

50. Senate, "Statement of Senator McCarran," 9964–65.

77. *Tampa Morning Tribune,* January 12, 1950.

78. *Florida Times-Union,* January 5, 1950; *Miami Herald,* January 14, 1950.

79. *Miami Herald,* January 13, 1950.

80. J. A. Cawthon to Claude Pepper, February 24, 1946, Pepper Collection, ser. 201, box 40, folder 40.

81. *Miami Herald,* March 24, 1950; *St. Petersburg Times,* March 24, 1950.

82. Ibid., March 26, 1950.

83. Ibid., April 5, 1950.

84. Ibid., April 7, 1950.

85. Drew Pearson, "The Washington Merry-Go-Round," *Tallahassee Democrat,* April 27, 1950.

86. *New York Times,* October 30, 1950.

87. Ibid., March 30, 1950.

88. Pepper, *Eyewitness,* 206.

89. Lincoln, "The Terrible Tempered Mr. Ball," 158. See also Pepper, *Eyewitness,* 212. Pepper gives a similar account of the episode, adding that Ball would not allow him a seat at the head table as befitting the status of senior senator, even if a defeated one.

Beyond the Senate

Pepper, *Eyewitness,* 218–19.

Allen Morris, "Cracker Politics," *Jacksonville Journal,* December 30, 1950.

Pepper, *Eyewitness,* 218–21; Pepper Diary, December 19, 1951, January 5, November 14, 25, December 19, 1952.

Pepper Diary, October 11, 1951; Pepper, *Eyewitness,* 234–35.

Ibid., June 9, 1955.

Ibid., November 17, 20, 1955.

Lincoln, "The Terrible Tempered Mr. Ball," 158; Pepper, *Eyewitness,* 212.

U.S. Congress, House Committee on Banking and Currency, *Bank Holding Company Legislation,* 88th Cong., 2d sess. (1964), 68–73.

Ibid.

Ibid.

Ellis W. Hawley, *The New Deal and the Problem of Monopoly,* 308–10.

Bank Holding Company Act of 1956, 12 U.S.C., sec. 1841(b).

U.S. Congress, House Committee on Banking and Currency, *Control and Regulation of Bank Holding Companies,* 82d Cong., 2d sess., 1952, 11.

Washington Labor, June 15, 1963; Belin interview, May 29, 1996.

51. Senate, stenographic transcript (unpublished) of *Hearings befor* committee of the Committee on the Judiciary on Activities of the Securiti change Commission and Post Office in Florida.

52. Belin interview, March 11, 1996.

53. Associated Industries of Florida, "Communist Party Unit America," September 19, 1946, Spessard Holland Collection, bc 76–75; Associated Industries of Florida, "The Growing Menace c State'," July 13, 1946, Pepper Collection, ser. 204A, box 4, fold

54. William A. McRae, Jr., to Ralph Davis, September 7, Holland Collection, box 812, folder 76–5.

55. Pepper, *Eyewitness*, 190.

56. *Miami Herald*, January 12, 1950.

57. Smathers interview, June 4, 1996.

58. See series of letters from George Smathers to Claude ! Fokes, Pepper Collection, ser. 201, box 161, folder 16.

59. Allen Morris, "Cracker Politics," *Jacksonville Journe* 29, 1949.

60. Smathers interview, June 4, 1996.

61. Ibid.

62. Pepper, *Eyewitness*, 196–97.

63. Crispell, "George Smathers and the Politics of C 73.

64. Smathers interview, June 4, 1996.

65. Ibid.

66. Ibid.

67. Ibid.

68. Lincoln, "The Terrible Tempered Mr. Ball,' terview with Ed Ball, *Florida Trend*, December Smiley, "The Unofficial Prime Minister of Flori May 5, 1968, 12–16, 13; Hand Drane, "A Vengef Career," *Florida Times-Union*, June 25, 1981.

69. Sherrill, *Gothic Politics*, 154–55.

70. Belin interview, May 29, 1996.

71. Ibid.

72. Smathers interview, June 4, 1996.

73. Pepper, *Eyewitness*, 199.

74. *Jewish Floridian*, November 4, 1949.

75. Pepper, *Eyewitness*, 195.

76. *Miami Herald*, January 12, 1950.

15. House Committee on Banking and Currency, *Bank Holding Company Legislation*, 841.

16. U.S. Congress, House, "Control of Bank Holding Companies," 84th Cong., 1st sess., *Congressional Record* (1955), vol. 101, pt. 6, 8021.

17. Ibid., 8183.

18. U.S. Congress, Senate, "Definition and Control of Bank Holding Companies," 84th Cong., 2d sess., *Congressional Record* (1956), vol. 102, pt. 5, 6751.

19. Ibid., 6960–63.

20. *Washington Labor,* June 15, 1963.

21. U.S. Congress, Senate, 89th Cong., 2d sess., *Congressional Record* (1966), vol. 112, pt. 9, 12381.

22. Pepper Diary, July 26, 31, October 3, December 23, 1955.

23. Ibid., February 29, 1956.

24. Ibid.

25. Pepper, *Eyewitness*, 238.

26. Ibid., March 1, 1956.

27. Pepper Diary, December 22, 23, 1958.

28. Ed Ball to Claude Pepper, June 30, 1958, and Spessard Holland to Ed Ball, July 3, 1958, Spessard Holland Collection, MSS 76-5, box 812, folder C-77.

29. U.S. Congress, Senate, "Speech of Claude Pepper to U.S. Senate," 81st Cong., 2d sess., *Congressional Record* (1950), vol. 96, pt. 10, 13952–57; U.S. Congress, Senate, "Report on World Conditions," 81st Cong., 2d sess., *Congressional Record* (1950), vol. 96, pt. 12, 16990–17005; see also William L. O'Neill, *A Better World—the Great Schism: Stalinism and the American Intellectuals*, 202–3.

30. Pepper, *Eyewitness*, 250.

31. *Miami Herald*, May 1, 1962.

32. Ibid.

33. *Miami News*, May 6, 1962.

34. Ibid., May 1, 1962.

35. Ibid., 226.

36. Burton Altman, "'In the Public Interest?' Ed Ball and the FEC Railway War."

37. *Miami Herald*, April 15, 1950.

38. R. W. Wyckoff (FEC vice president for personnel during strike), interview by author, telephone, July 19, 1995; J. Richard Elliott, Jr., "Road from Serfdom," pt. 2, *Barron's*, May 18, 1964, 3.

39. R. W. Wyckoff to H. O. Van Arsdall, Sr. (general chairman, Brotherhood

of Railway Trainmen), December 29, 1965, Pepper Collection, ser. 301, box 58, folder 1.

40. Address by W. L.Thornton (vice president and chief operating officer, FEC) to Miami Kiwanis Club, February 21, 1964, Florida State Archives, Governor Farris Bryant Correspondence, record group 102, ser. 756, box 77, folder 2.

41. "Rail Strike That Reaches into Space," *Business Week*, October 26, 1963, 46.

42. House Committee on Banking and Currency, *Bank Holding Company Legislation*, 808–20.

43. Altman, "In the Public Interest?" 38.

44. G. E. Leighty, *Report of the President to the Thirty-seventh Regular Session of the Grand Division of the Transportation-Communication Employees Union*, July 1968, 93–96, 94, Cornell University Library, Labor Management Documentation Center, Collection 5488-A, box 2.

45. Ibid.

46. H. C. Crotty, "Appendix" to *Report of the Grand Lodge President to the Thirty-Fifth Regular Convention of Brotherhood of Maintenance of Way Employees*, July 11, 1966, A-233, Collection 5488-A, box 2.

47. Belin interview, May 29, 1996.

48. House Committee on Banking and Currency, *To Amend the Bank Holding Company Act*, 16.

49. U.S. Congress, Senate, "Florida East Coast Railway Strike," 88th Cong., 2d sess., *Congressional Record* (1964), vol. 110, pt. 2, 2118–23, pt. 3, 3294–95.

50. Ibid., pt. 3, 3763–71.

51. See Pepper, *Eyewitness*, 297, where Pepper adopts Morse's definition of "liberal" as his own, while misguidedly using the poetry of Ovid to illustrate its meaning. Pepper was well educated, but aligning his liberal philosophy with a humanist education is a misunderstanding of the classical meaning of "liberal" as applied to the humanist curriculum.

52. *Miami Herald*, September 30, October 9, 17, 1963; G. E. Leighty (chairman, Railway Labor Executives' Association [RLEA]) to all chief executives, RLEA, May 13, 1966, G. F. Harris (president of Order of Railway Conductors and Brakemen [OrC&B]) to all OrC&B members, State of Florida, May 17, 1966, Cornell University Library, Labor Management Documentation Center, Collection 5488-A, box 21, folder 20.

53. Pepper Diary, September 23, 1963.

54. Ibid., August 31, 1963.

55. *Washington Sunday Star*, February 23, 1964; *Miami Herald*, October 9, 1963; *New York Times*, February 19, 20, 1964; *Business Week*, October 26, 1963.

56. *Wall Street Journal*, June 12, 1964.

57. For example, Robert Sherrill, "A Few Sticks of Dynamite," *The Nation*, March 9, 1964, 227–30. This is the same author who interviewed Dan Crisp about his connection with Ed Ball in Florida's 1950 Senate campaign.

58. *Washington Labor*, June 15, 1963.

59. *St. Petersburg Times*, June 22, 1965.

60. House Committee on Banking and Currency, *Bank Holding Company Legislation*, 5–15.

61. Ibid., 789–91.

62. Ibid., 74–112.

63. Ibid., 109.

64. Paul H. Douglas, *In the Fullness of Time: The Memoirs of Paul H. Douglas*, 360.

65. House Committee on Banking and Currency, *Bank Holding Company Legislation*, 152–65.

66. Ibid., 801–3.

67. Ibid.

68. Ibid., 826.

69. Ibid., 166–86.

70. Ibid., 838.

71. Pepper Diary, June 24, 1964.

72. G. E. Leighty to W. M. Harman, July 1966, Cornell University Library, Labor Management Documentation Center, Collection 5149, Brotherhood of Railroad Trainmen, box 14, folder: Florida Political, 1966–67.

73. Charles E. Bennett, *Twelve on the River St. Johns*, 132–34.

74. Pepper Diary, September 23, 1965.

75. U.S. Congress, House, "To Amend the Bank Holding Company Act," 89th Cong., 1st sess., *Congressional Record* (1965), vol. 111, pt. 18, 24929–40.

76. Senate Subcommittee of the Committee on Banking and Currency, *Amend the Bank Holding Company Act*, 27–33, 28.

77. W. M. Harman to G. E. Leighty, June 25, 1966, Cornell University Library, Labor Management Documentation Center, Collection 5149, box 14, folder: Florida Political, 1965–66.

78. U.S. Congress, Senate, *Bank Holding Company Amendments of 1966*, 89th Cong., 2d sess. *Congressional Record* (June 6, 1966), vol. 112, pt. 9, 12382.

79. Robert D. Shaw, Jr., "Ed Ball Has a Big Battle on His Hands," *Tallahassee Democrat*, October 2, 1977; Jon Nordheimer, "Ed Ball," *Tampa Tribune*, March 15, 1979; *Florida Times-Union*, June 25, 1981.

BIBLIOGRAPHY

Secondary Sources

Allen, Frederick Lewis. *Only Yesterday: An Informal History of the Nineteen-Twenties.* New York: Harper and Row, 1937; reprint 1957.

Altman, Burton. "'In the Public Interest'? Ed Ball and the FEC Railway War." *Florida Historical Quarterly* 64 (July 1985), 32–47.

Barone, Michael. *Our Country: The Shaping of America from Roosevelt to Reagan.* New York: Macmillan, Free Press, 1990.

Barron, Clarence W. *What They Told Barron: The Notes of Clarence W. Barron.* Ed. Arthur Pound and Samuel Taylor Moore. New York: Harper and Brothers, 1930.

Bennett, Charles E. *Twelve on the River St. Johns.* Jacksonville: University of North Florida Press, 1989.

Brinkley, Alan. *The End of Reform: New Deal Liberalism in Recession and War.* New York: Alfred A. Knopf, 1995.

Clark, James C. "Claude Pepper and the Seeds of His 1950 Defeat, 1944–1948." *Florida Historical Quarterly* (Summer 1995), 1–22.

———. "The 1944 Democratic Senate Primary." *Florida Historical Quarterly* 66 (April 1988), 365–85.

Colburn, David R., and Richard K. Scher. *Florida's Gubernatorial Politics in the Twentieth Century.* Tallahassee: University Presses of Florida, 1980.

Colby, Gerard. *Dupont Dynasty.* Secaucus, N.J.: Lyle Stuart, 1984.

Crispell, Brian L. "George Smathers and the Politics of Cold War America, 1946–1968." Ph.D. diss., Florida State University, 1996.

———. "The Senator from Latin America." Master's thesis, Florida State University, 1993.

Donovan, Robert J. *Conflict and Crisis: The Presidency of Harry S. Truman, 1945–1948.* New York: W. W. Norton, 1977.

Douglas, Paul H. *In The Fullness of Time: The Memoirs of Paul H. Douglas.* New York: Harcourt Brace Jovanovich, 1971.

Drury, Allen. *A Senate Journal: 1943–1945*. New York: McGraw-Hill, 1963.

Duke, Marc. *The DuPonts: Portrait of a Dynasty*. New York: E. P. Dutton, 1976.

Florida National Bank. *Celebrating 100 Years: A History of the Florida National Bank*. Jacksonville: History Associates, n.d.

Florida State Chamber of Commerce. *Florida Takes Inventory Proceedings, April 16, 1926, West Palm Beach*. 1926.

Flynt, Wayne. *Duncan Upshaw Fletcher: Dixie's Reluctant Progressive*. Tallahassee: Florida State University Press, 1971.

Freidel, Frank. *Franklin D. Roosevelt: A Rendezvous with Destiny*. Boston: Little, Brown, 1990.

Gaddis, John Lewis. *The United States and the Origins of the Cold War, 1941–1947*. New York: Columbia University Press, 1972.

Galbraith, John Kenneth. *The Great Crash: 1929*. 3d ed. Boston: Houghton Mifflin, 1972.

Griffith, Leon Odell. *Ed Ball: Confusion to the Enemy*. Tampa, Fla.: Trend House, 1975.

Guttman, Joseph. "Early Career of Senator Claude Pepper." Ph.D. diss., University of Virginia, 1996.

Harriman, W. Averell, and Elie Abel. *Special Envoy to Churchill and Stalin 1941–1946*. New York: Random House, 1975.

Hawley, Ellis W. *The New Deal and the Problem of Monopoly*. New York: Fordham University Press, 1995.

Herty, Charles H. "Southern Pine for White Paper." *Scientific American* (May 1934), 499–504.

Hewlett, Richard Greening. *Jessie Ball duPont*. Gainesville: University Press of Florida, 1992.

Ickes, Harold L. *The Secret Diary of Harold L. Ickes*. Vol. 1, *The First Thousand Days, 1933–1936*. New York: Simon and Schuster, 1953.

———. *The Secret Diary of Harold L. Ickes*. Vol. 2, *The Inside Struggle, 1936–1939*. New York: Simon and Schuster, 1953.

———. *The Secret Diary of Harold L. Ickes*. Vol. 3, *The Lowering Clouds*. New York: Simon and Schuster, 1955.

James, Marquis. *Alfred I. DuPont: The Family Rebel*. New York: Bobbs-Merrill, 1941.

Kabat, Ric A. "From New Deal to Red Scare: The Political Odyssey of Senator Claude D. Pepper." Ph.D. diss., Florida State University, 1995.

Kelley, Anne E. *Modern Florida Government*. Temple Terrace, Fla.: MDA Publications, 1981.

Klehr, Harvey, John Earl Haynes, and Fridrikh Igorevich Firsov. *The Secret World of American Communism*. New Haven: Yale University Press, 1995.

Lincoln, Freeman. "The Terrible Tempered Mr. Ball." *Fortune* (November 1952), 143–62.

Locke, Francis. "Claude D. Pepper." In *Public Men: In and Out of Office.* Chapel Hill: University of North Carolina Press, 1946.

Mason, Raymond K., and Virginia Harrison. *Confusion to the Enemy: A Biography of Edward Ball.* New York: Dodd, Mead, 1976.

McCullough, David. *Truman.* New York: Simon and Schuster, 1992.

McCusker, John J. "How Much Is That in Real Money? A Historical Price Index for Use as a Deflator of Money Values in the Economy of the United States." *Proceedings of the American Antiquarian Society* 101, pt. 2 (1992), 297–373.

McElvaine, Robert S. *The Great Depression: America 1929–1941,* New York: Random House, Times Books, 1993.

Mencken, H. L. "On Being an American." In *Prejudices,* 3d ser. Reproduced in *The Annals of America,* vol. 14. Chicago: William Benton, 1968.

Mosley, Leonard. *Blood Relations: The Rise and Fall of the DuPonts of Delaware.* New York: Atheneum, 1980.

O'Neill, William L. *A Better World—the Great Schism: Stalinism and the American Intellectuals.* New York: Simon and Schuster, 1982.

Pepper, Claude Denson. *Pepper: Eyewitness to a Century.* New York: Harcourt Brace Jovanovich, 1987.

Pontecorvo, Giulio. "Investment Banking and Security Speculation in the Late 1920's." *Business History Review* 32 (Summer 1958), 166–91.

Price, Wesley. "Pink Pepper." *Saturday Evening Post,* August 31, 1946, 19.

Roberts, Kenneth L. *Florida Loafing: An Investigation into the Peculiar State of Affairs Which Leads Residents of 47 States to Encourage Spanish Architecture in the 48th.* Indianapolis: Bobbs-Merrill, 1924.

Rogers, William W., Jr. *The One-Gallused Rebellion.* Baton Rouge: Louisiana State University Press, 1970.

Schlesinger, Arthur M., Jr. *The Age of Roosevelt.* Vol. 1, *The Crisis of the Old Order, 1919–1933.* Boston: Houghton Mifflin, 1957.

———. *The Age of Roosevelt.* Vol. 2, *The Coming of the New Deal.* Boston: Houghton Mifflin, 1959.

———. *The Age of Roosevelt.* Vol. 3, *The Politics of Upheaval.* Boston: Houghton Mifflin, 1960.

Schwarz, Jordan A. *The New Dealers: Power Politics in the Age of Roosevelt.* New York: Random House, Vintage Books, 1994.

Shalzman, Neil V. *Reform and Revolution: The Life and Times of Raymond Robins.* Kent, Ohio: Kent State University Press, 1991.

Sherrill, Robert. *Gothic Politics in the Deep South: Stars of the New Confederacy.* New York: Ballantine Books, 1968.

Sobel, Robert. *The Big Board: A History of the New York Stock Market.* New York: Free Press, 1965.

———. *The Great Bull Market: Wall Street in the 1920's.* New York: W. W. Norton, 1968.

Stockbridge, Frank Parker. "Florida—the Pioneer State." *American Review of Reviews* (May 1925), 486–93.

Stoesen, Alexander R. "Road from Receivership: Claude Pepper, the DuPont Trust, and the Florida East Coast Railway." *Florida Historical Quarterly* 52 (October 1973), 132–56.

———. "The Senatorial Career of Claude D. Pepper." Ph.D. diss., University of North Carolina, 1964.

Trippett, Frank. *The States: United They Fell.* Cleveland and New York: World Publishing, 1967.

Vandenberg, Arthur H., Jr., ed. *The Private Papers of Senator Vandenberg.* Boston: Houghton Mifflin, 1952.

Vanderblue, Homer B. "The Florida Land Boom." *Journal of Land and Public Utility Economics* (May 1927), 113–31.

———. "The Florida Land Boom II." *Journal of Land and Public Utility Economics* (August 1927), 252–69.

Vickers, Raymond B. *Panic in Paradise: Florida's Banking Crisis of 1926.* Tuscaloosa: University of Alabama Press, 1994.

Wall, Joseph Frazier. *Alfred I. DuPont: The Man and His Family.* New York: Oxford University Press, 1990.

Weigall, T. H. *Boom in Paradise.* New York: Alfred H. King, 1932.

Wendt, Lloyd. *The Wall Street Journal: The Story of Dow Jones and the Nation's Business Newspaper.* Chicago: Rand McNally, 1982.

Archival Sources

Brotherhood of Railroad Trainmen. Collection 5149, Cornell University, M. P. Catherwood Library, Labor Management Documentation Center. Ithaca, N.Y.

Carlton, Governor Doyle E. Correspondence. Florida State Archives, record group 102, series 204. Tallahassee.

duPont, Alfred I. Papers. Alfred I. DuPont Collection, Special Collections, Washington and Lee University Library. Lexington, Va.

duPont, Jessie Ball. Papers. Special Collections, Washington and Lee University Library. Lexington, Va.

Holland, Spessard. Papers. Spessard Holland Collection, Special Collections, Florida State University Library. Tallahassee.

Pepper, Claude. Papers. Claude Pepper Collection, Florida State University Library. Tallahassee.

Government Documents: State

Florida Commissioner of Agriculture. *The Fifth State Census of the State of Florida, 1925.* Tallahassee: Florida Department of Agriculture, 1925.

Florida Comptroller. *Florida Comptrollers Report(s),* 1927, 1929, 1932.

Florida Department of Agriculture. *Florida—an Advancing State: 1907–1917–1927.* Tallahassee: Department of Agriculture, 1927.

Florida House of Representatives. *Bond Refund Investigation Committee Report to the 1943 House of Representatives, as Authorized by That Body in the 1941 Legislature.* Pt. 1. Tallahassee, 1943.

Florida Institute of Government. *Florida City and County Government: A Condensed Reference Version.* Tallahassee: Florida Department of Education, 1991; rev. 1993.

Florida Special Committee on Taxation and Public Debt. *Report of Special Committee on Taxation and Public Debt.* Tallahassee, [1935].

Government Documents: Federal

U.S. Department of Commerce, Bureau of the Census. *Historical Statistics of the United States: Colonial Times to 1970.* Pts. 1, 2. Washington: U.S. Department of Commerce, 1975.

U.S. Department of State. *Foreign Relations of the United States.* Vol. 5. Washington: U.S. Department of State, 1945.

INDEX

Note: Page numbers in italics indicate illustrations.

Tracy E. Danese is a native of Jacksonville and has lived in Florida all his adult life. He is a graduate of the U.S. Merchant Marine Academy and holds a law degree from the University of Florida and a Ph.D. in modern American history from Florida State University (1997). He completed the Harvard Advanced Management Program of 1976 and has practiced law and worked as a utility executive and lobbyist for over thirty-five years.